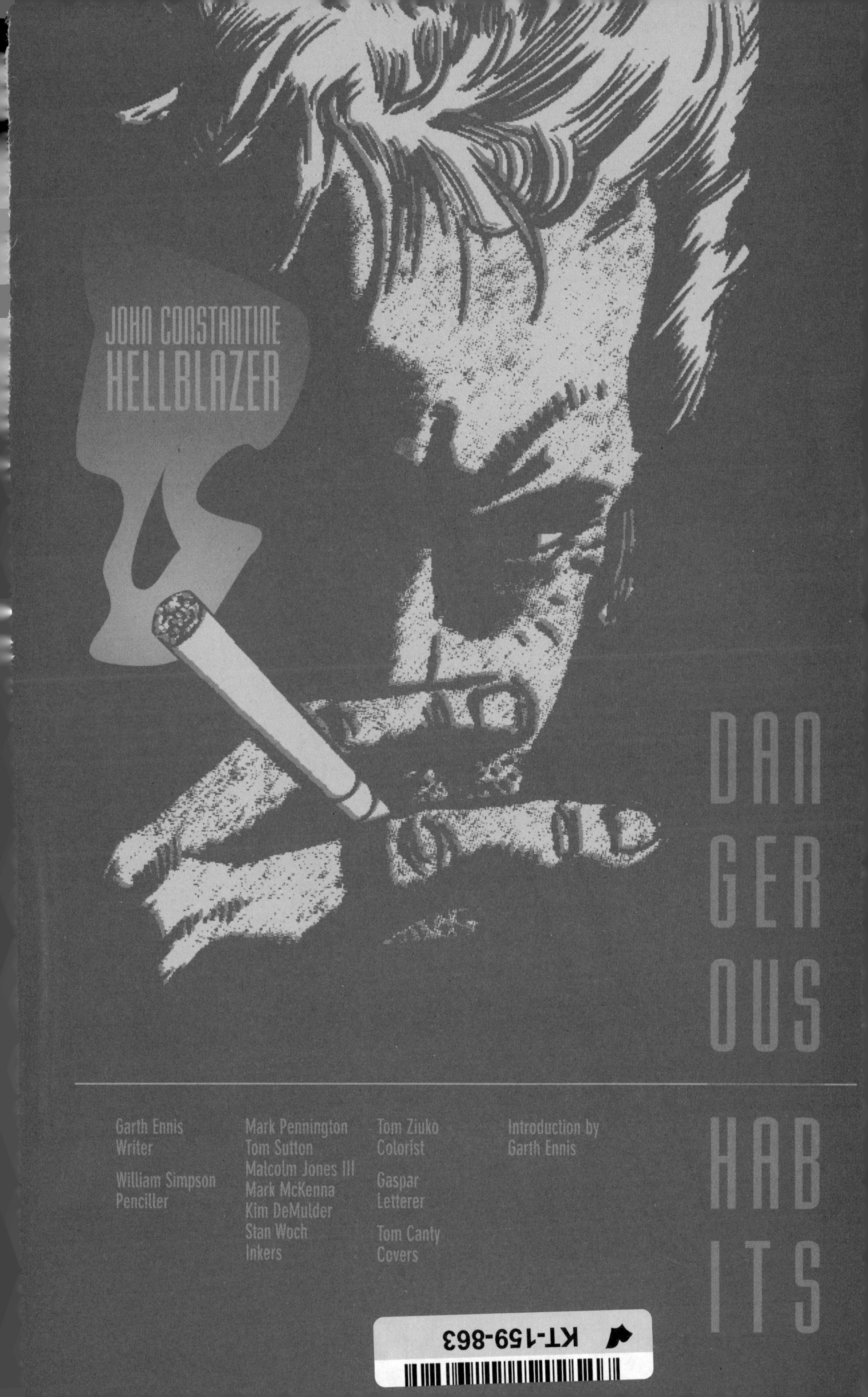

JOHN CONSTANTINE HELLBLAZER

DANGEROUS HABITS

Garth Ennis
Writer

William Simpson
Penciller

Mark Pennington
Tom Sutton
Malcolm Jones III
Mark McKenna
Kim DeMulder
Stan Woch
Inkers

Tom Ziuko
Colorist

Gaspar
Letterer

Tom Canty
Covers

Introduction by
Garth Ennis

JOHN CONSTANTINE, HELLBLAZER:
DANGEROUS HABITS

Published by DC Comics.
Cover, introduction and compilation
copyright © 1994 DC Comics.
All Rights Reserved.

Originally published in single magazine
form as HELLBLAZER 41–46. Copyright
© 1991 DC Comics. All Rights Reserved.
VERTIGO and all characters, their
distinctive likenesses and related
indicia featured in this publication
are trademarks of DC Comics.

The stories, characters, and incidents
featured in this publication are entirely
fictional. DC Comics does not read or
accept unsolicited submissions of ideas,
stories or artwork.

DC Comics, 1700 Broadway,
New York, NY 10019
A division of Warner Bros. –
An AOL Time Warner Company
Printed in Canada. Fourth Printing.
ISBN: 1-56389-150-6
Cover painting by Glenn Fabry.
Publication design by Richard Bruning.

"DYIN' AIN'T MUCH OF A LIVIN', BOY."

Clint Eastwood in "The Outlaw Josey Wales"

How very true that is. And yet, in a strange kind of way, it's possible to make quite a decent living off dying – as long as you can persuade someone else to do the dying so that you can make the living by exploiting it, if you see what I mean. Just ask the bloke who invented napalm. Or Quentin Tarantino, who had quite a few people copping it in the brilliant Reservoir Dogs. Or even me.

About three years ago I was given the job of writing DC Comics' premier horror title, HELLBLAZER. This was a real bit of luck, I can tell you. The success of this book had always been grounded in its adherence to real-life characters and situations, most of all in its protagonist, the one and only John Constantine. Respect is due to Alan Moore, Steve Bissette, and John Totleben for creating such a character, and to Jamie Delano and the many artists he worked with for maintaining the book's integrity.

The canvas before me was vast: I could tell stories about ordinary people and the lives they lead, their feelings for their friends and their reactions to the events that overtook them. Here was a comic without an agenda, without some loathsome morality at its core, but instead with a central character who made and broke his own rules as he staggered through life, and could only face the consequences of his actions with the same frail, human defenses that are available to you or me. And not only that, but I'd be able to use horror fiction to plumb the depths of evil and explore the dark underbelly of human life, which is always a bit of a laugh.

So there I was with this marvelous book to write. I fact, my arrival was just part of a changing of the guard on HELLBLAZER. Stuart Moore was the incoming editor, and he had planned a general overhaul: a new cover artist and logo for the outside, and my good mate Will Simpson providing the pencilled art on the inside. Poor Will...all he really wanted was to draw mightily thewed barbarians, ray guns ripping into spaceships, beautiful women wearing next to nothing and people who would usually say things like, "You're coming with me one way or the other, Voltar. If it has to be dead...then so be it." And I gave him inner-city London, cups of tea, people having nervous breakdowns and "Mine's a gin and tonic, squire." I think he coped admirably, but then Will has never been anything else than a consummate professional.

Anyway, we were all ready to go, and all that was required was the first script, from yours truly, of course. And I was hard at it, believe me. I was straining my brain trying to come up with a real winner – this was my big break, after all. I had to hit the ground running, come up trumps, get 'em right between the eyes, kick 'em in the balls! And I couldn't think of a bloody thing. What could I write about that seemed new and fresh (and attention-grabbing, let's not deny it)? What could I possibly do to John Constantine that hadn't been done before? And then I began to think about all the stuff I mentioned back at the start of this mess — you know, living... dying...heh, heh, heh...and one course of action suddenly stood out above all others: Kill him.

Turned out it worked quite nicely. I enjoyed myself immensely writing the story you're about to read, and working with an editor as thoughtful as Stuart was a real joy. And it was always nice to get a phone call from Will now and again, cursing me up and down for putting too many panels on the page and agonizing over the "horrible, sick" story he was having to draw. "Dangerous Habits" went down pretty well with the readers, especially the rude bit at the end of part five, and here we are: a trade paperback. Thanks for buying it and helping me get one step nearer that Ferrari I've always wanted, by the way. If you're reading this in the shop — go on, shell out the cash, eh? Your mortgage payments aren't that important, and your kid can wait 'til next birthday for his puppy. He'll only get bored with it after a month anyway, and then you'll have to take the poor critter down to the lake with a sack and a heavy rock...

Yessir, all things considered I'd say this sucker did what it was supposed to do. None of the folks concerned with it ended up on the street, at any rate. In all seriousness, though, it's a bit odd having this story — the one that started me off — reappear like this after so much time's gone by, especially as it's miles away from the way I write HELLBLAZER today. I'd be interested in reading any comments you might have on it, but please remember to type your letters double-spaced, and that it's not big or clever to swear.

Guess that's about it. I would just like to take the opportunity to clarify my position on something vis-`a-vis that little quote at the start, there: I have no intention whatsoever of denigrating Clint Eastwood or his works. See, at the time he said it, Clint (as Josey Wales) was trying to persuade some no-good pistolero not to pull a gun on him — and damned if the stupid s.o.b. didn't go ahead and do it. And ol' Clint had to blow him away.

I think we can all learn something from that.

Garth Ennis

Belfast, October 1993

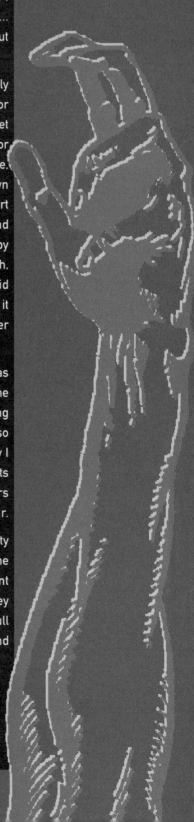

the beginning of the end

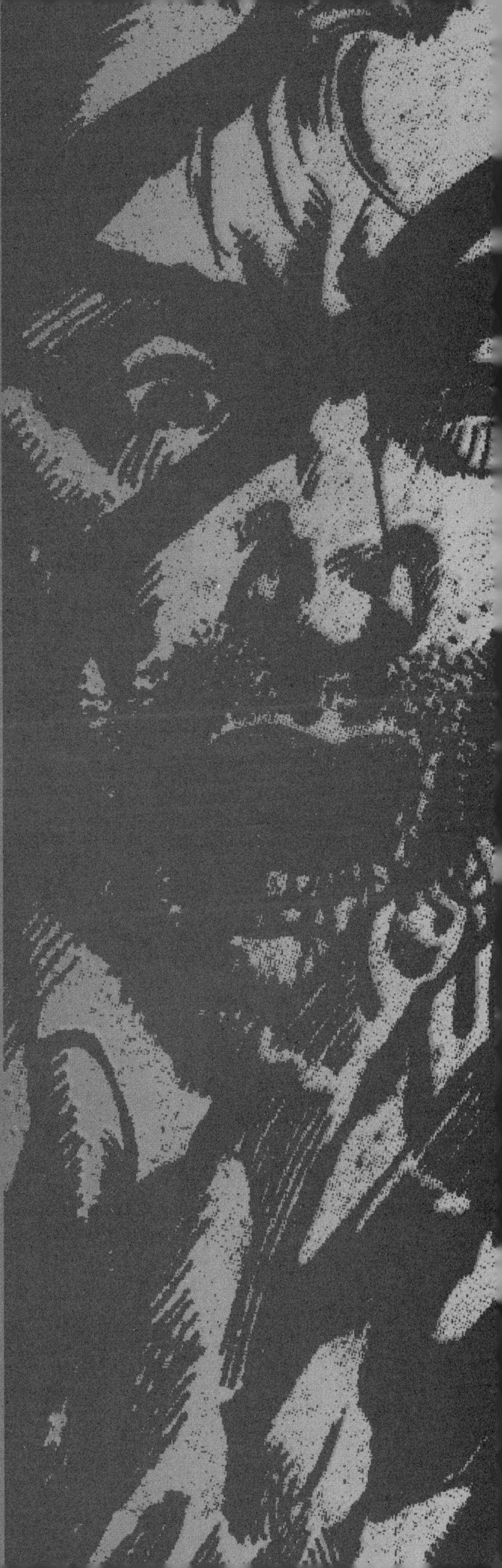

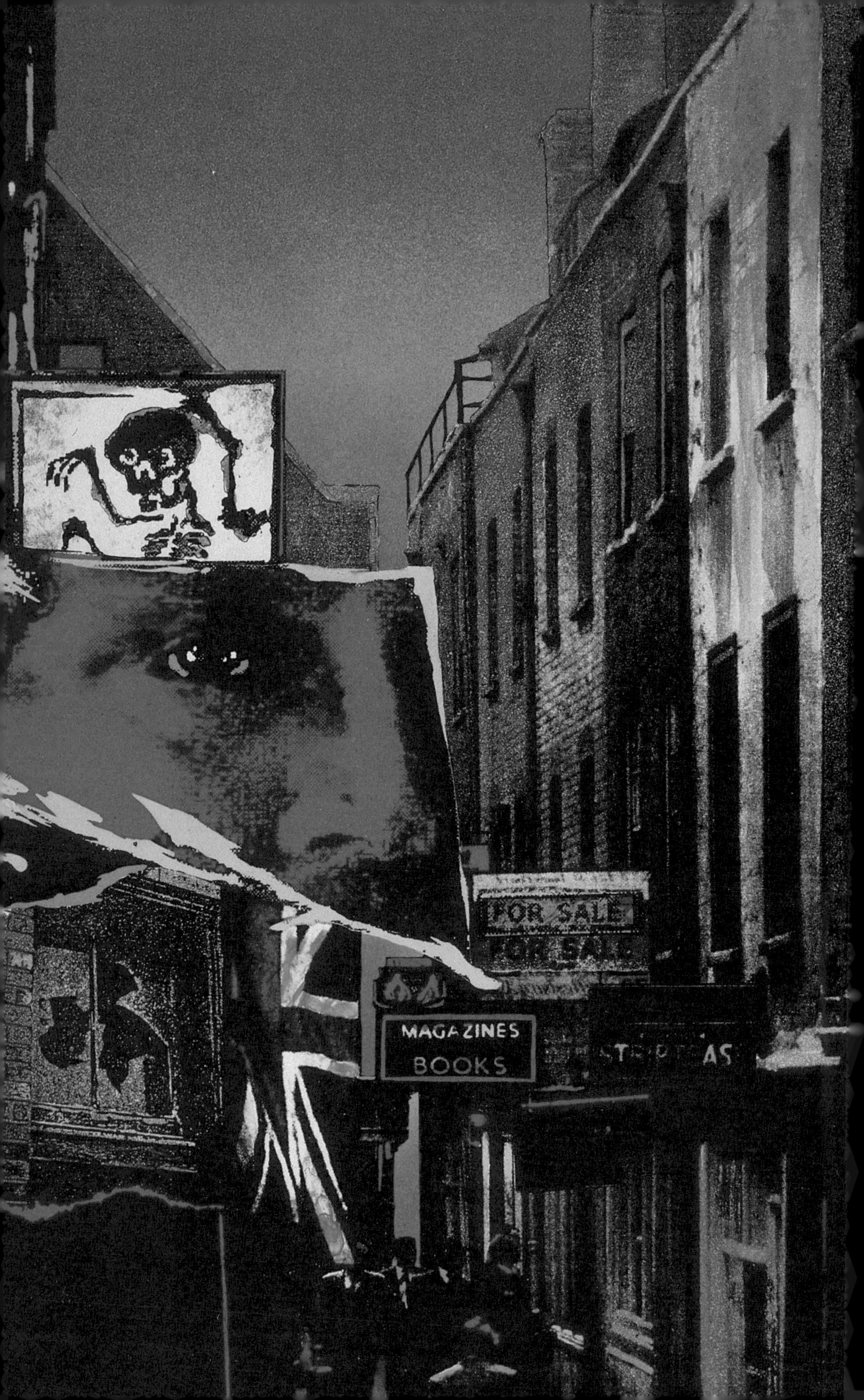
FOR SALE
MAGAZINES
BOOKS

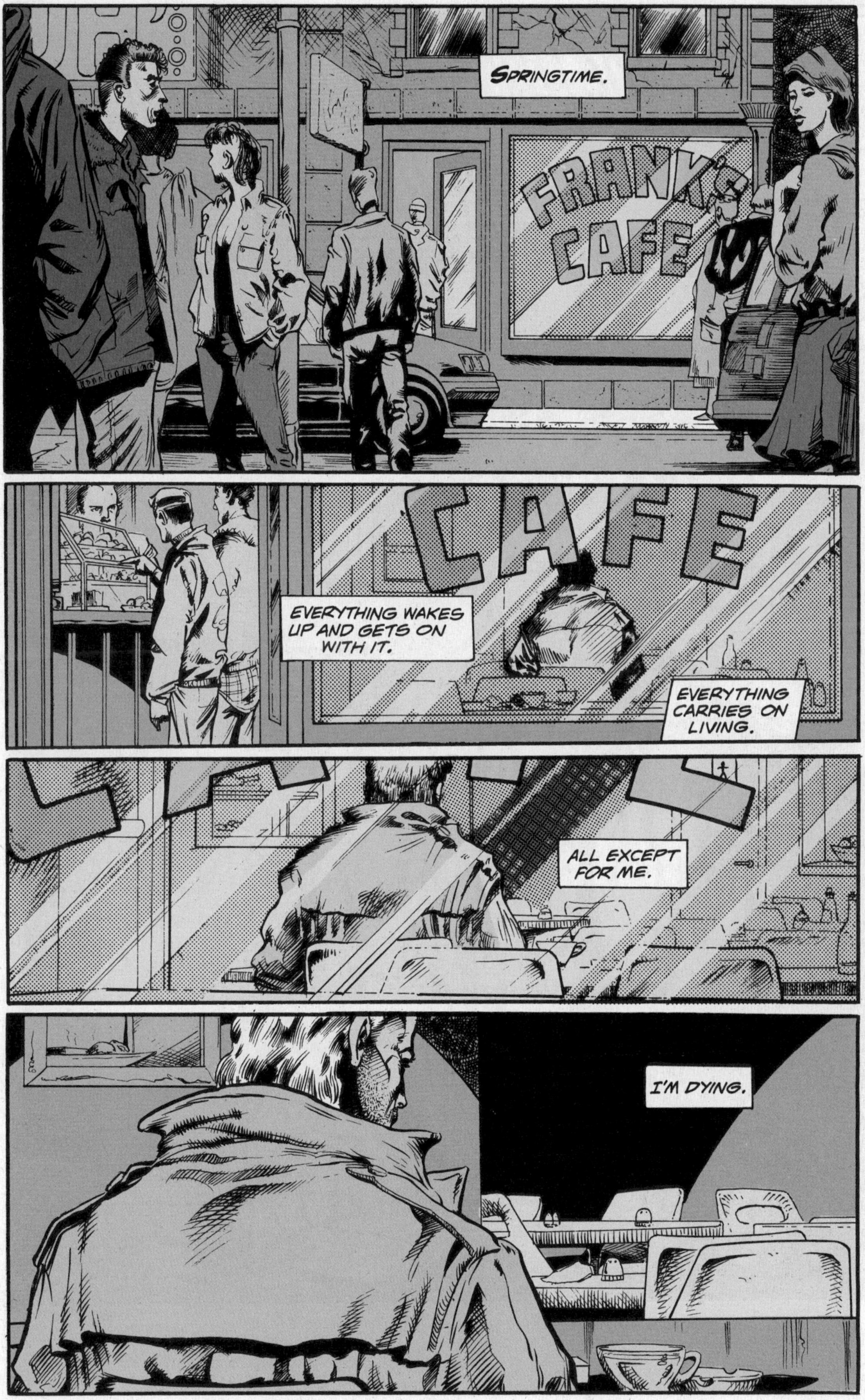
SPRINGTIME.
FRANK'S CAFE
CAFE
EVERYTHING WAKES UP AND GETS ON WITH IT.
EVERYTHING CARRIES ON LIVING.
ALL EXCEPT FOR ME.
I'M DYING.

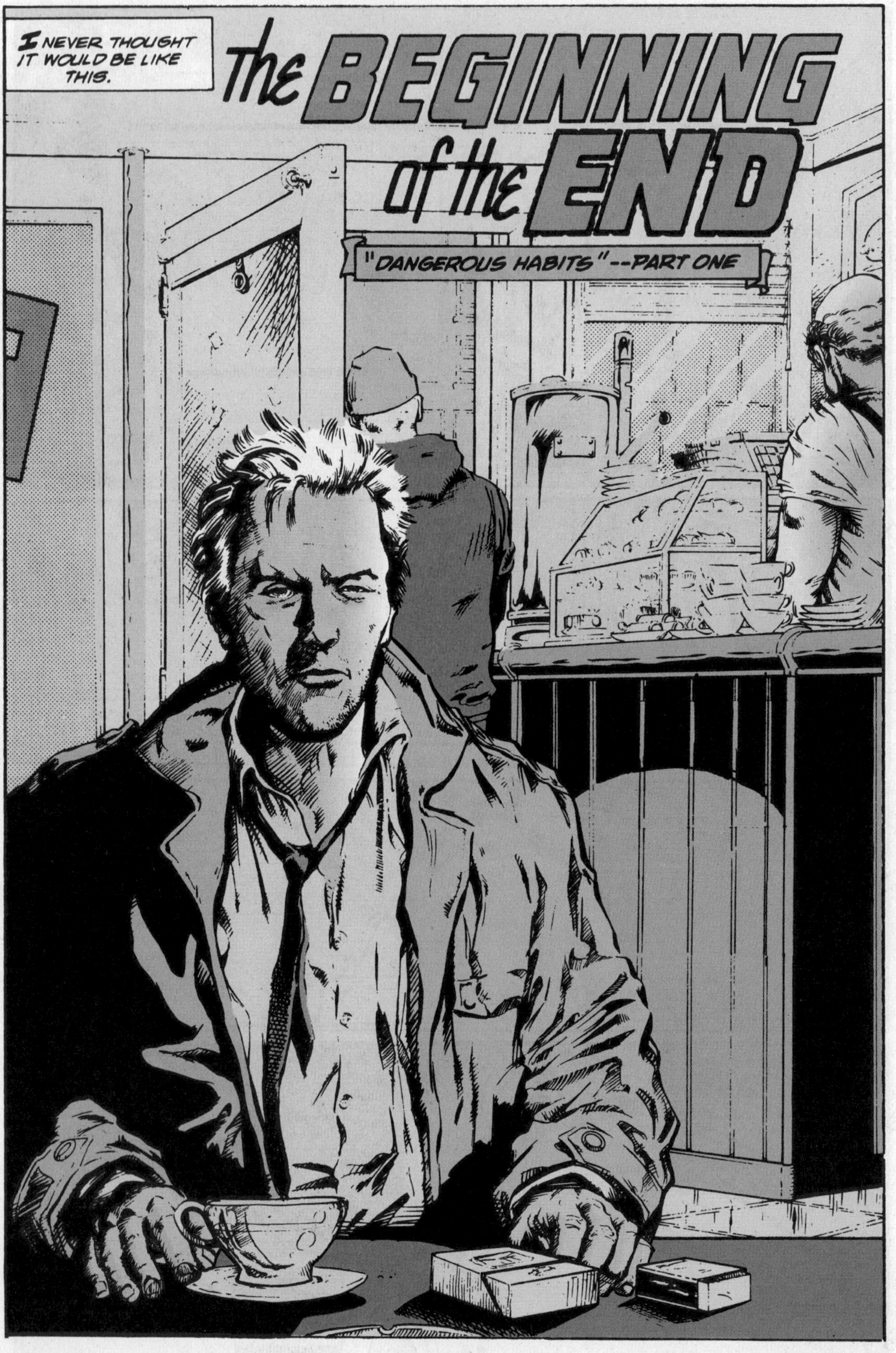
I NEVER THOUGHT IT WOULD BE LIKE THIS.
the BEGINNING of the END
"DANGEROUS HABITS"--PART ONE

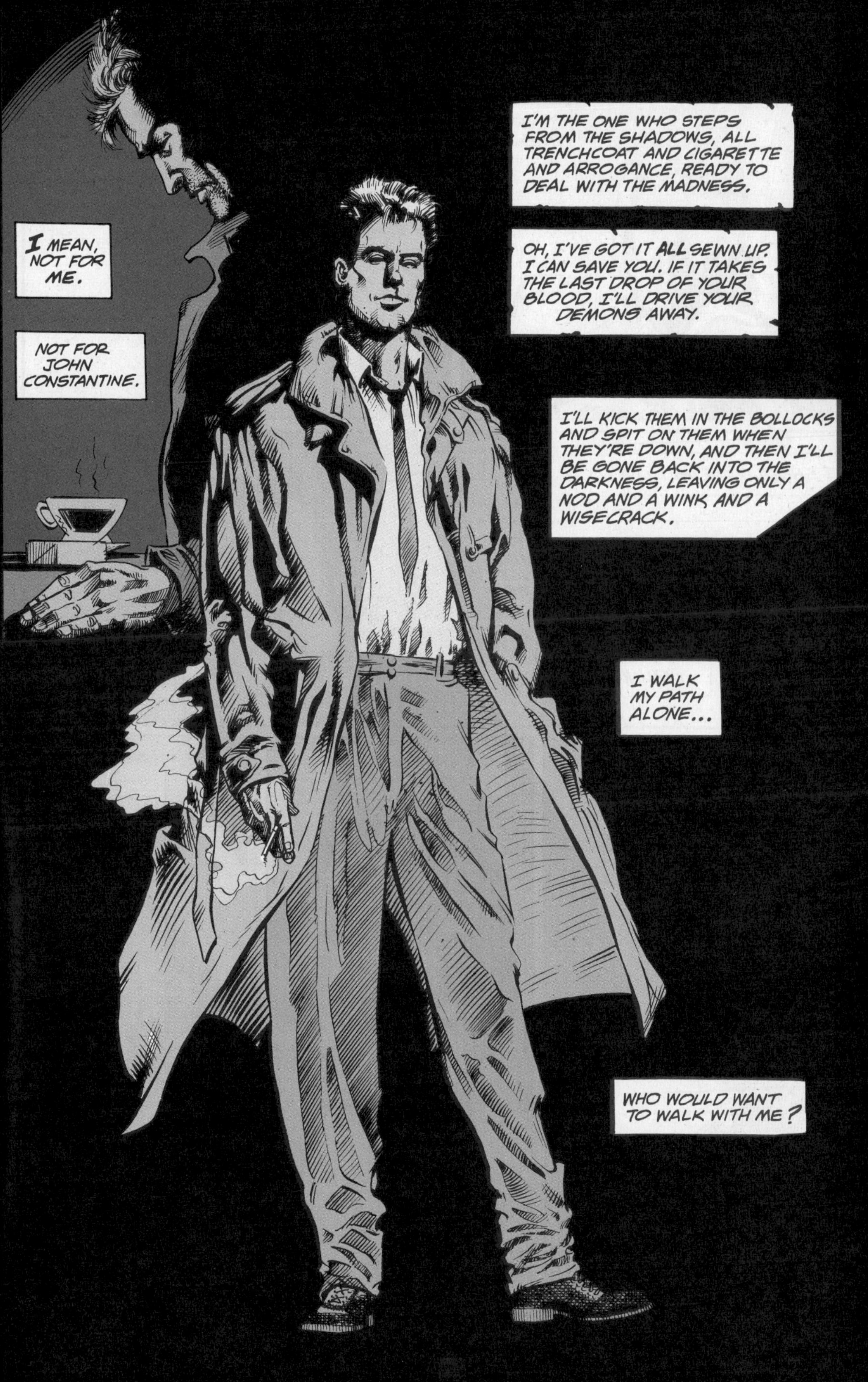
I MEAN, NOT FOR ME.
NOT FOR JOHN CONSTANTINE.
I'M THE ONE WHO STEPS FROM THE SHADOWS, ALL TRENCHCOAT AND CIGARETTE AND ARROGANCE, READY TO DEAL WITH THE MADNESS.
OH, I'VE GOT IT ALL SEWN UP. I CAN SAVE YOU. IF IT TAKES THE LAST DROP OF YOUR BLOOD, I'LL DRIVE YOUR DEMONS AWAY.
I'LL KICK THEM IN THE BOLLOCKS AND SPIT ON THEM WHEN THEY'RE DOWN, AND THEN I'LL BE GONE BACK INTO THE DARKNESS, LEAVING ONLY A NOD AND A WINK AND A WISECRACK.
I WALK MY PATH ALONE...
WHO WOULD WANT TO WALK WITH ME?

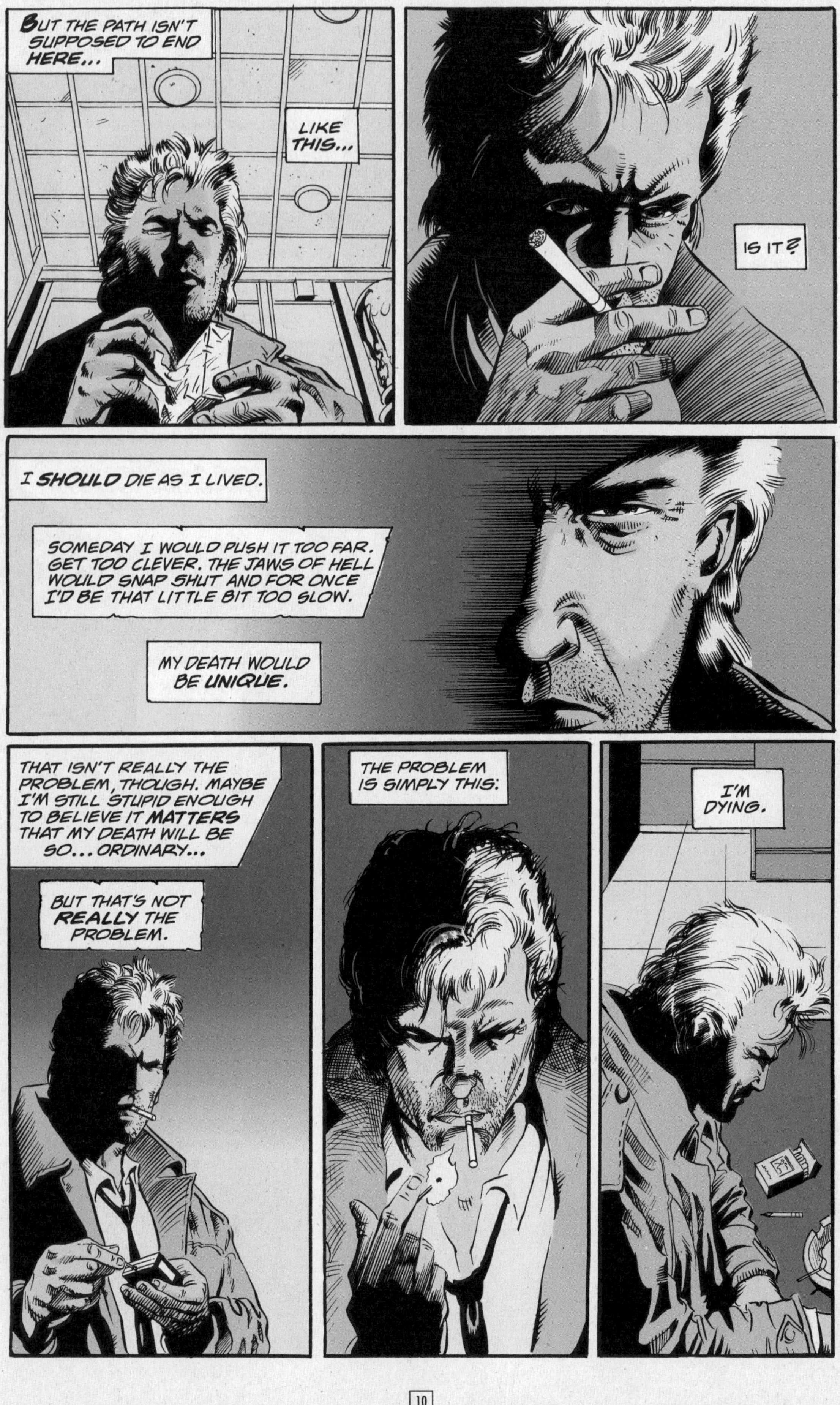
BUT THE PATH ISN'T SUPPOSED TO END HERE...
LIKE THIS...
IS IT?
I SHOULD DIE AS I LIVED.
SOMEDAY I WOULD PUSH IT TOO FAR. GET TOO CLEVER. THE JAWS OF HELL WOULD SNAP SHUT AND FOR ONCE I'D BE THAT LITTLE BIT TOO SLOW.
MY DEATH WOULD BE UNIQUE.
THAT ISN'T REALLY THE PROBLEM, THOUGH. MAYBE I'M STILL STUPID ENOUGH TO BELIEVE IT MATTERS THAT MY DEATH WILL BE SO... ORDINARY...
BUT THAT'S NOT REALLY THE PROBLEM.
THE PROBLEM IS SIMPLY THIS:
I'M DYING.

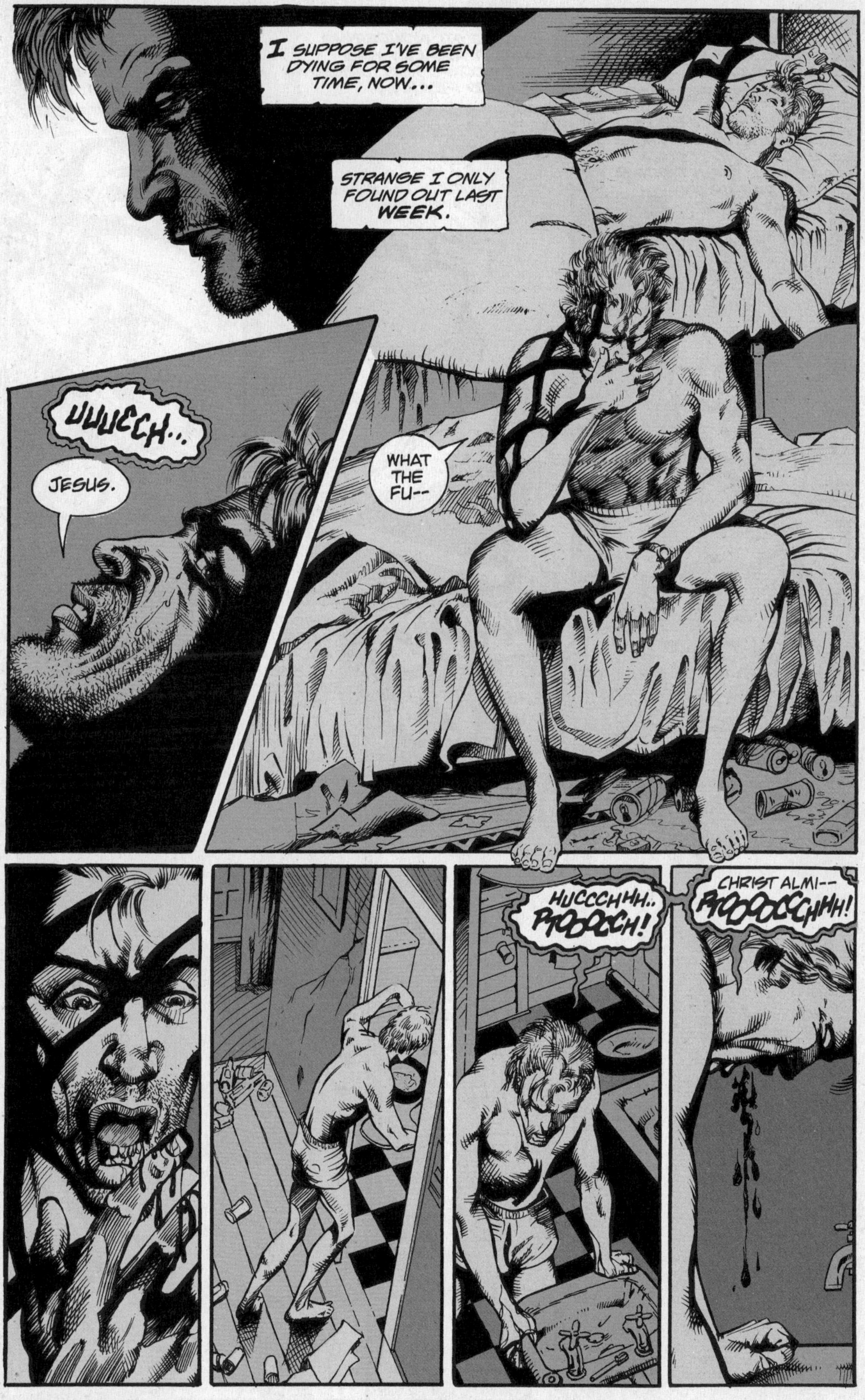
I SUPPOSE I'VE BEEN DYING FOR SOME TIME, NOW...
STRANGE I ONLY FOUND OUT LAST WEEK.
UUUCCH...
JESUS.
WHAT THE FU--
HUCCCHHH.. PTOOOCCH!
CHRIST ALMI-- PTOOOOCCCHHH!

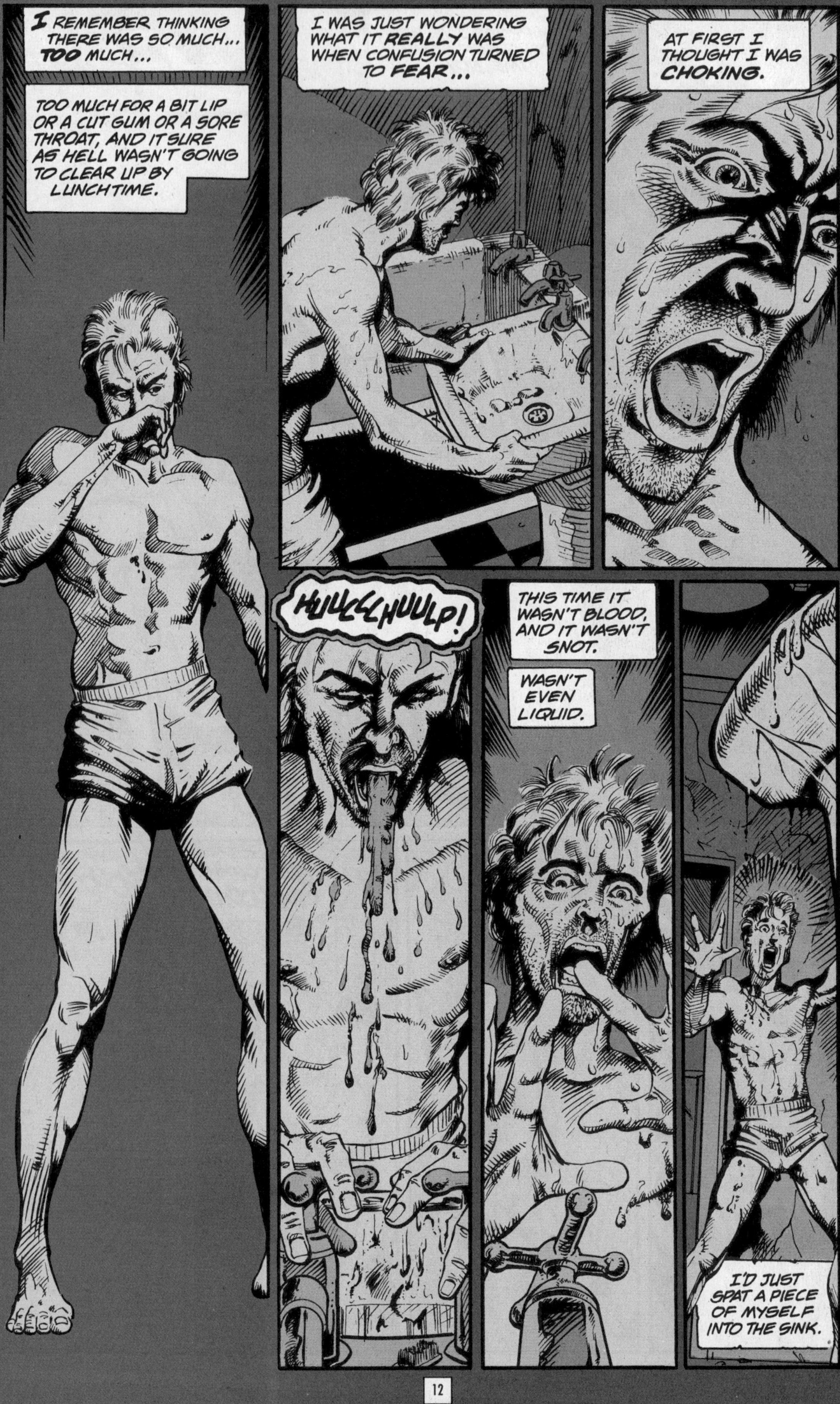
I REMEMBER THINKING THERE WAS SO MUCH... TOO MUCH...
TOO MUCH FOR A BIT LIP OR A CUT GUM OR A SORE THROAT, AND IT SURE AS HELL WASN'T GOING TO CLEAR UP BY LUNCHTIME.
I WAS JUST WONDERING WHAT IT REALLY WAS WHEN CONFUSION TURNED TO FEAR...
AT FIRST I THOUGHT I WAS CHOKING.
HUULGHUULP!
THIS TIME IT WASN'T BLOOD, AND IT WASN'T SNOT.
WASN'T EVEN LIQUID.
I'D JUST SPAT A PIECE OF MYSELF INTO THE SINK.

I STARTED THINKING FAST, RUNNING THROUGH THE POSSIBILITIES...

THE DEMON BLOOD? NERGAL WORKING SOME KIND OF REVENGE, ROBBING ME OF VICTORY TWO YEARS ON?

THAT WAS OBVIOUS, WASN'T IT?

OR MAYBE SOMETHING ELSE, ALMOST TOO STRANGE TO THINK ABOUT--

MY *TWIN.*

MY MEMORIES OF LAST AUTUMN IN THE WOMB-CAVE ARE HAZY... DID MY PERFECT BROTHER MERGE WITH ME, TURNING US INTO SOME-THING BETTER?

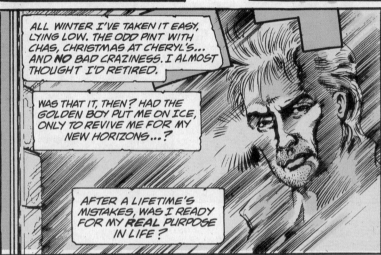

ALL WINTER I'VE TAKEN IT EASY, LYING LOW. THE ODD PINT WITH CHAS, CHRISTMAS AT CHERYL'S... AND *NO* BAD CRAZINESS. I ALMOST THOUGHT I'D RETIRED.

WAS THAT IT, THEN? HAD THE GOLDEN BOY PUT ME ON ICE, ONLY TO REVIVE ME FOR MY NEW HORIZONS...?

AFTER A LIFETIME'S MISTAKES, WAS I READY FOR MY *REAL* PURPOSE IN LIFE?

TO *DIE?*

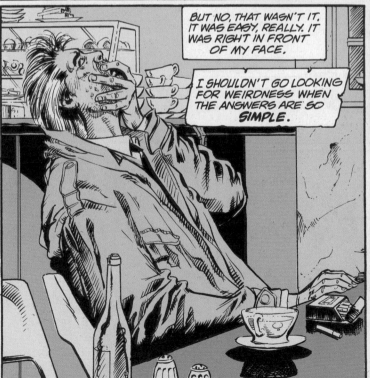

BUT NO, THAT WASN'T IT. IT WAS EASY, REALLY. IT WAS RIGHT IN FRONT OF MY FACE.

I SHOULDN'T GO LOOKING FOR WEIRDNESS WHEN THE ANSWERS ARE SO *SIMPLE.*

BUT EVEN NOW I KNOW THE TRUTH, IT SEEMS INCREDIBLE.

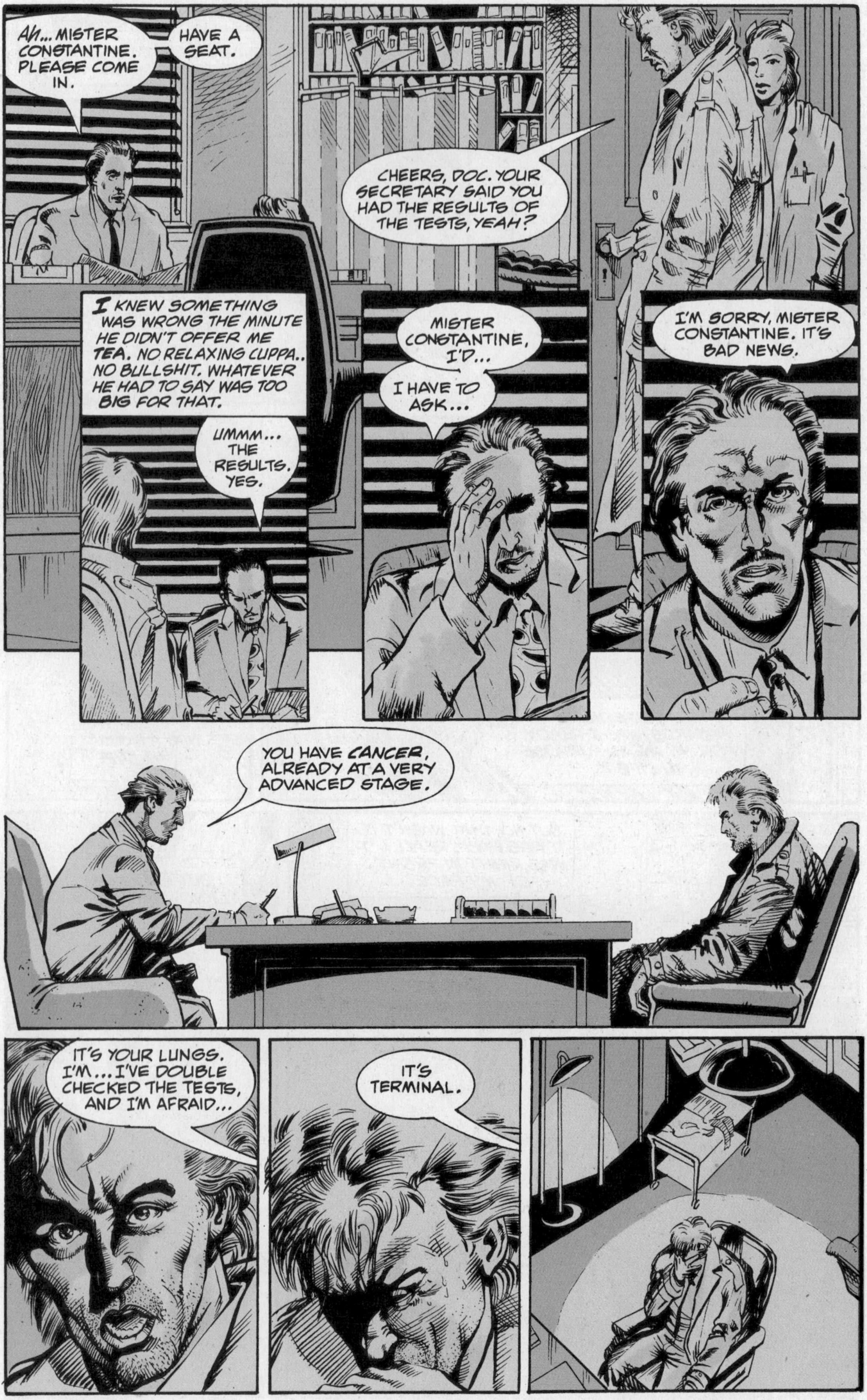
AH... MISTER CONSTANTINE. PLEASE COME IN.
HAVE A SEAT.
CHEERS, DOC. YOUR SECRETARY SAID YOU HAD THE RESULTS OF THE TESTS, YEAH?
I KNEW SOMETHING WAS WRONG THE MINUTE HE DIDN'T OFFER ME TEA. NO RELAXING CUPPA.. NO BULLSHIT. WHATEVER HE HAD TO SAY WAS TOO BIG FOR THAT.
UMMM... THE RESULTS. YES.
MISTER CONSTANTINE, I'D...
I HAVE TO ASK...
I'M SORRY, MISTER CONSTANTINE. IT'S BAD NEWS.
YOU HAVE CANCER, ALREADY AT A VERY ADVANCED STAGE.
IT'S YOUR LUNGS. I'M... I'VE DOUBLE CHECKED THE TESTS, AND I'M AFRAID...
IT'S TERMINAL.

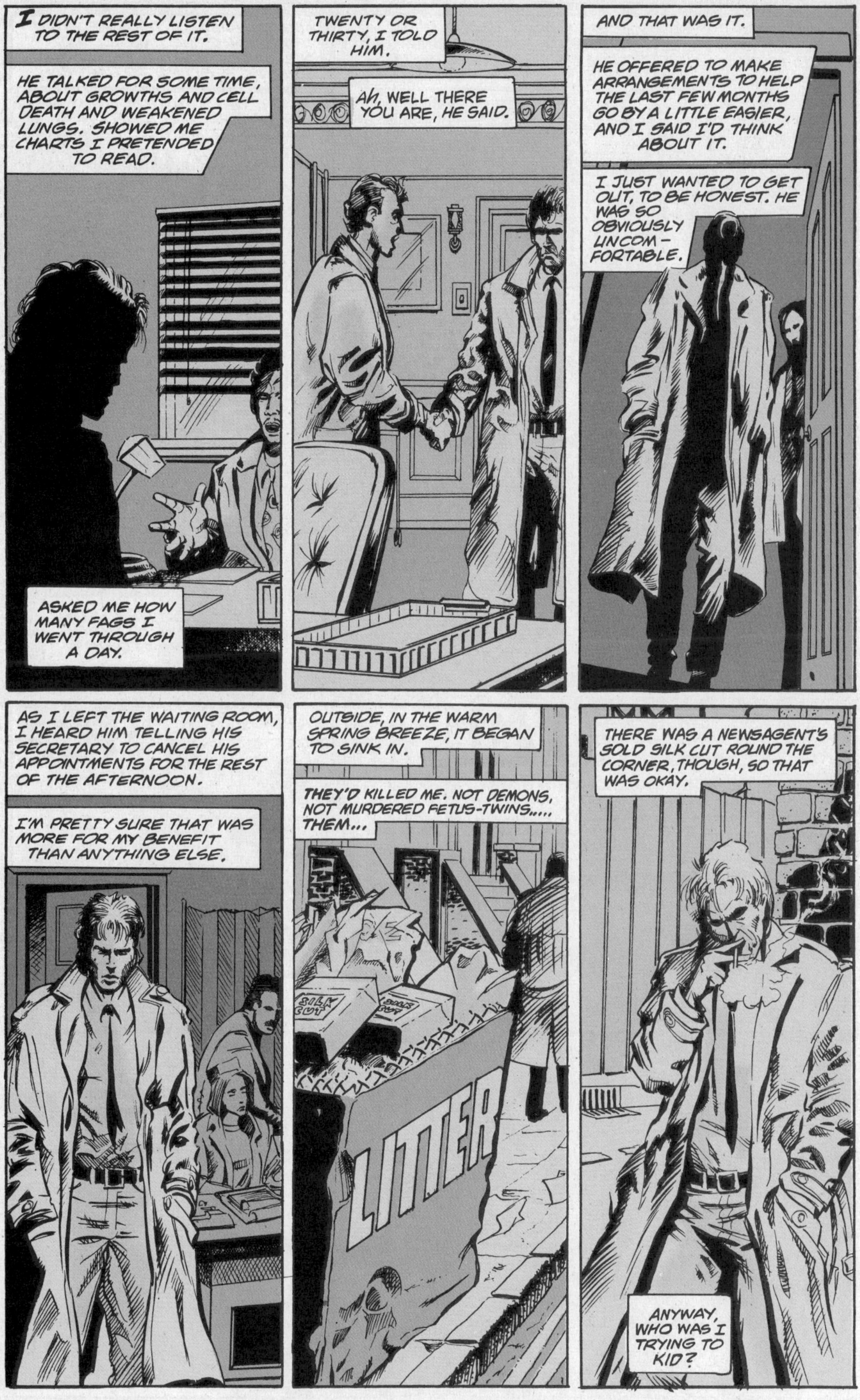
I DIDN'T REALLY LISTEN TO THE REST OF IT.
HE TALKED FOR SOME TIME, ABOUT GROWTHS AND CELL DEATH AND WEAKENED LUNGS. SHOWED ME CHARTS I PRETENDED TO READ.
ASKED ME HOW MANY FAGS I WENT THROUGH A DAY.
TWENTY OR THIRTY, I TOLD HIM.
AH, WELL THERE YOU ARE, HE SAID.
AND THAT WAS IT.
HE OFFERED TO MAKE ARRANGEMENTS TO HELP THE LAST FEW MONTHS GO BY A LITTLE EASIER, AND I SAID I'D THINK ABOUT IT.
I JUST WANTED TO GET OUT, TO BE HONEST. HE WAS SO OBVIOUSLY UNCOM-FORTABLE.
AS I LEFT THE WAITING ROOM, I HEARD HIM TELLING HIS SECRETARY TO CANCEL HIS APPOINTMENTS FOR THE REST OF THE AFTERNOON.
I'M PRETTY SURE THAT WAS MORE FOR MY BENEFIT THAN ANYTHING ELSE.
OUTSIDE, IN THE WARM SPRING BREEZE, IT BEGAN TO SINK IN.
THEY'D KILLED ME. NOT DEMONS, NOT MURDERED FETUS-TWINS..... THEM...
SILK CUT
LITTER
THERE WAS A NEWSAGENT'S SOLD SILK CUT ROUND THE CORNER, THOUGH, SO THAT WAS OKAY.
ANYWAY, WHO WAS I TRYING TO KID?

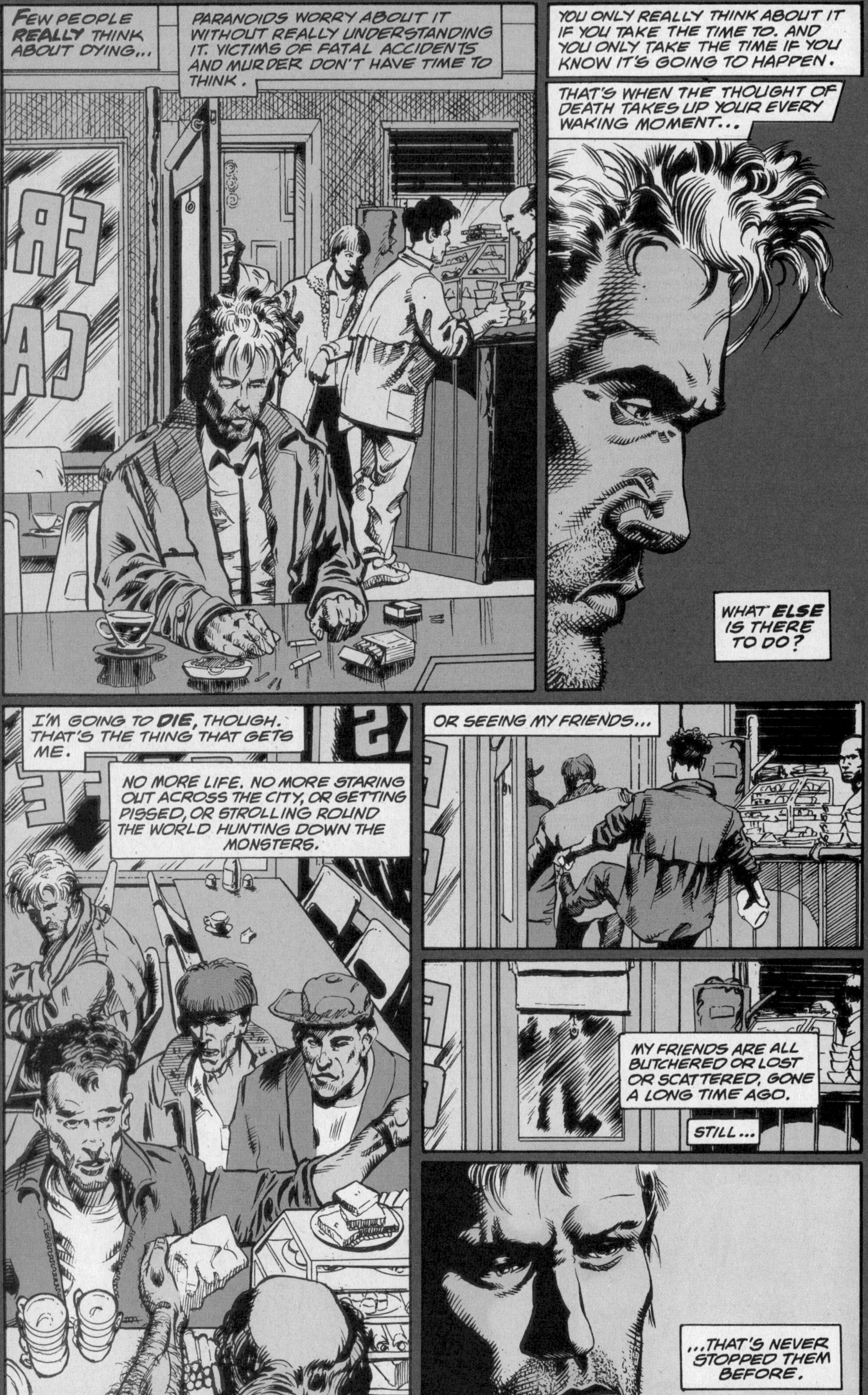

FEW PEOPLE REALLY THINK ABOUT DYING...
PARANOIDS WORRY ABOUT IT WITHOUT REALLY UNDERSTANDING IT. VICTIMS OF FATAL ACCIDENTS AND MURDER DON'T HAVE TIME TO THINK.
YOU ONLY REALLY THINK ABOUT IT IF YOU TAKE THE TIME TO. AND YOU ONLY TAKE THE TIME IF YOU KNOW IT'S GOING TO HAPPEN.
THAT'S WHEN THE THOUGHT OF DEATH TAKES UP YOUR EVERY WAKING MOMENT...
WHAT ELSE IS THERE TO DO?
I'M GOING TO DIE, THOUGH. THAT'S THE THING THAT GETS ME.
NO MORE LIFE. NO MORE STARING OUT ACROSS THE CITY, OR GETTING PISSED, OR STROLLING ROUND THE WORLD HUNTING DOWN THE MONSTERS.
OR SEEING MY FRIENDS...
MY FRIENDS ARE ALL BUTCHERED OR LOST OR SCATTERED, GONE A LONG TIME AGO.
STILL...
...THAT'S NEVER STOPPED THEM BEFORE.

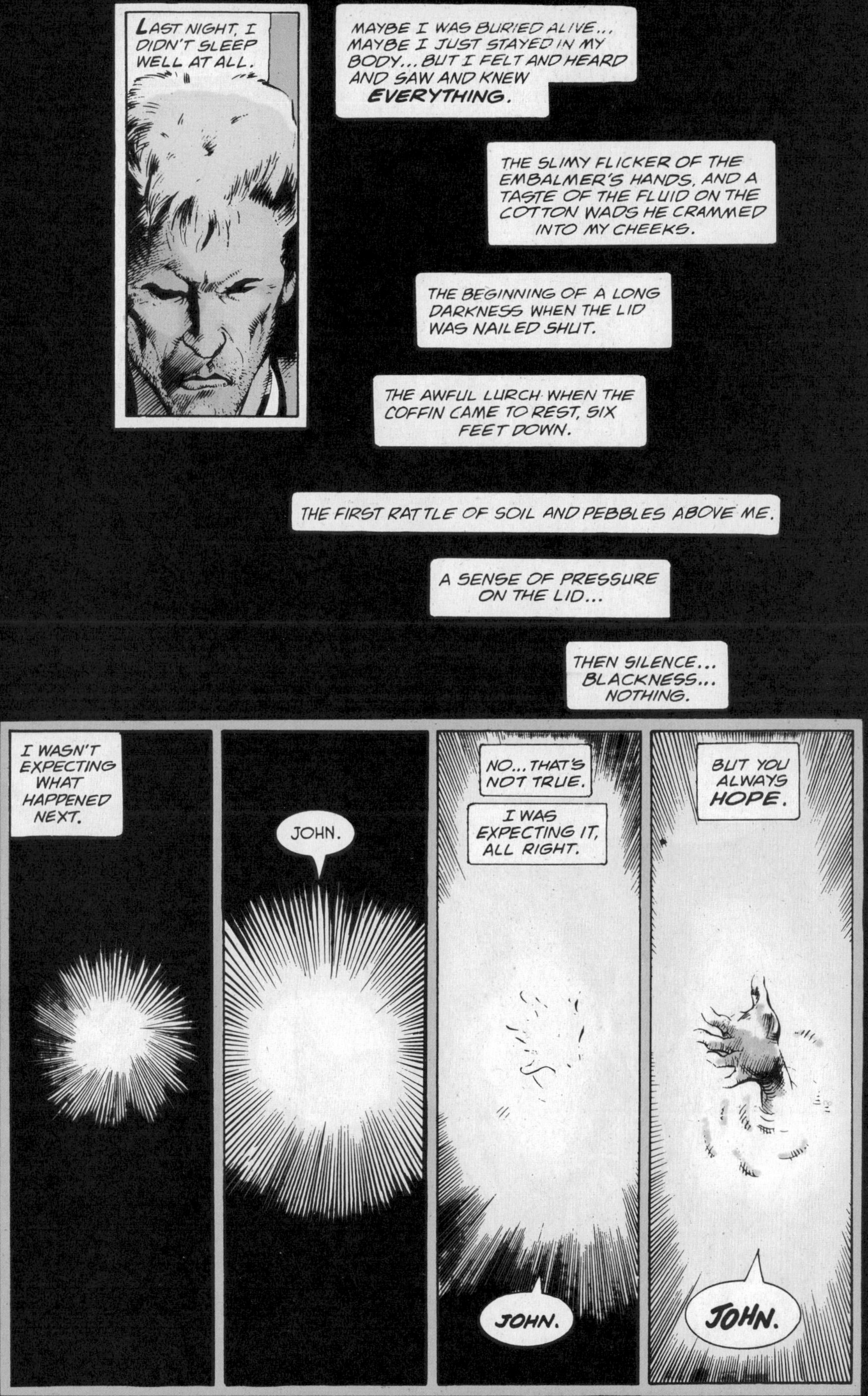
LAST NIGHT, I DIDN'T SLEEP WELL AT ALL.
MAYBE I WAS BURIED ALIVE... MAYBE I JUST STAYED IN MY BODY... BUT I FELT AND HEARD AND SAW AND KNEW EVERYTHING.
THE SLIMY FLICKER OF THE EMBALMER'S HANDS, AND A TASTE OF THE FLUID ON THE COTTON WADS HE CRAMMED INTO MY CHEEKS.
THE BEGINNING OF A LONG DARKNESS WHEN THE LID WAS NAILED SHUT.
THE AWFUL LURCH WHEN THE COFFIN CAME TO REST, SIX FEET DOWN.
THE FIRST RATTLE OF SOIL AND PEBBLES ABOVE ME.
A SENSE OF PRESSURE ON THE LID...
THEN SILENCE... BLACKNESS... NOTHING.
I WASN'T EXPECTING WHAT HAPPENED NEXT.
JOHN.
NO... THAT'S NOT TRUE.
I WAS EXPECTING IT, ALL RIGHT.
JOHN.
BUT YOU ALWAYS HOPE.
JOHN.

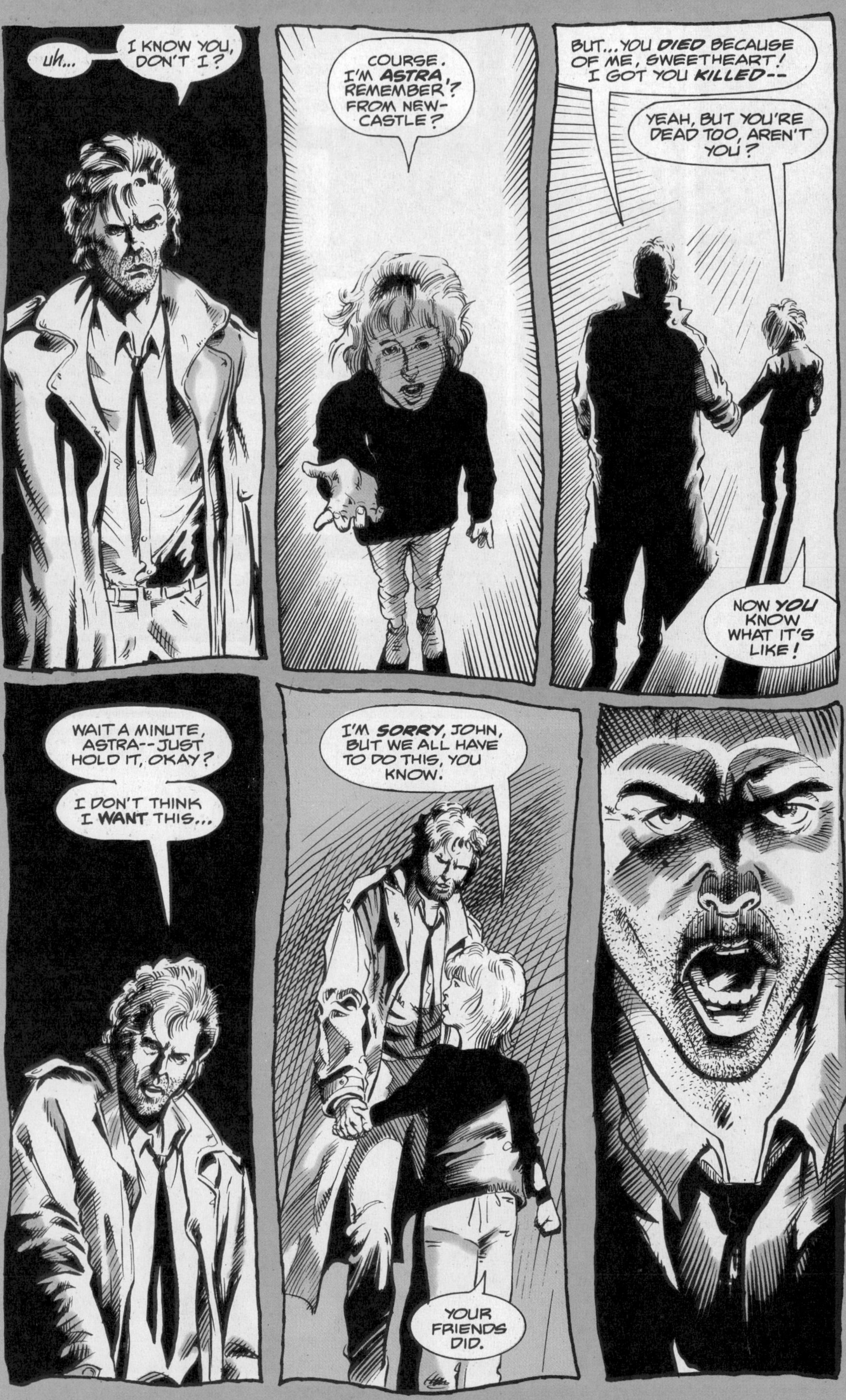
uh...
I KNOW YOU, DON'T I?
COURSE. I'M ASTRA, REMEMBER? FROM NEW-CASTLE?
BUT... YOU DIED BECAUSE OF ME, SWEETHEART! I GOT YOU KILLED--
YEAH, BUT YOU'RE DEAD TOO, AREN'T YOU?
NOW YOU KNOW WHAT IT'S LIKE!
WAIT A MINUTE, ASTRA--JUST HOLD IT, OKAY?
I DON'T THINK I WANT THIS...
I'M SORRY, JOHN, BUT WE ALL HAVE TO DO THIS, YOU KNOW.
YOUR FRIENDS DID.

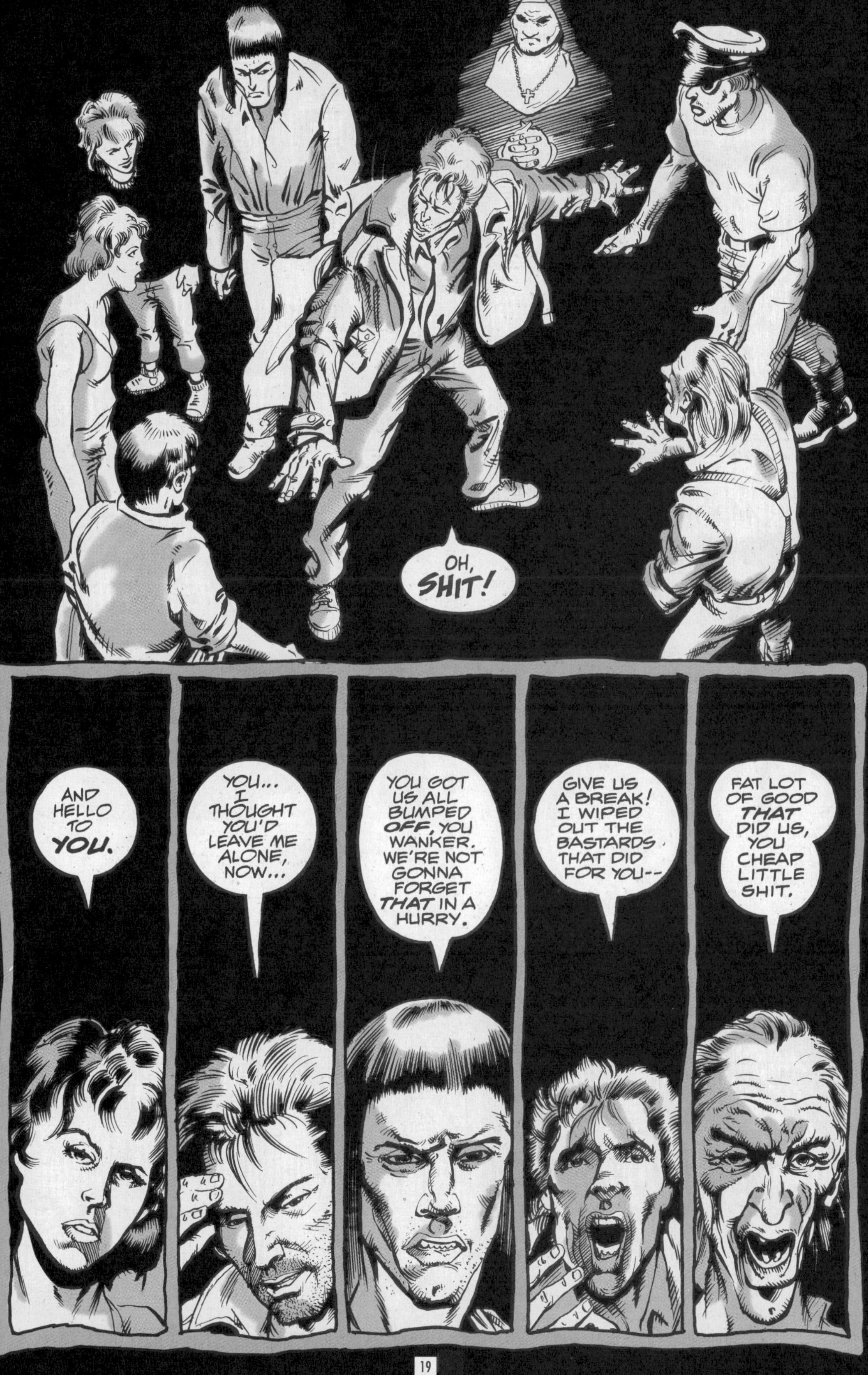
OH, SHIT!
AND HELLO TO YOU.
YOU... I THOUGHT YOU'D LEAVE ME ALONE, NOW...
YOU GOT US ALL BUMPED OFF, YOU WANKER. WE'RE NOT GONNA FORGET THAT IN A HURRY.
GIVE US A BREAK! I WIPED OUT THE BASTARDS THAT DID FOR YOU--
FAT LOT OF GOOD THAT DID US, YOU CHEAP LITTLE SHIT.

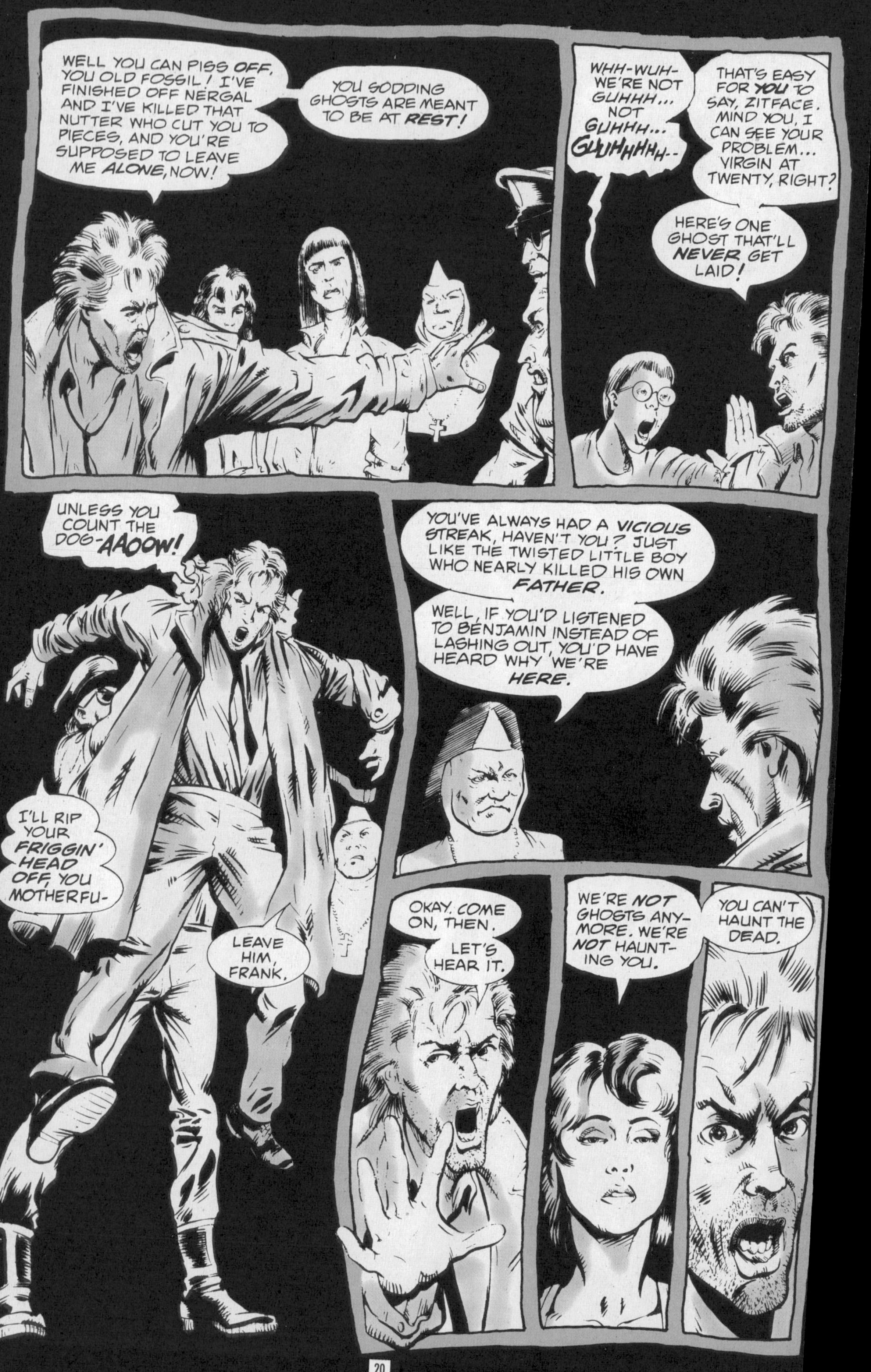
WELL YOU CAN PISS OFF, YOU OLD FOSSIL! I'VE FINISHED OFF NERGAL AND I'VE KILLED THAT NUTTER WHO CUT YOU TO PIECES, AND YOU'RE SUPPOSED TO LEAVE ME ALONE, NOW!
YOU SODDING GHOSTS ARE MEANT TO BE AT REST!
WHH-WUH- WE'RE NOT GUHHH... NOT GUHHH... GUUHHHH--
THAT'S EASY FOR YOU TO SAY, ZITFACE. MIND YOU, I CAN SEE YOUR PROBLEM... VIRGIN AT TWENTY, RIGHT?
HERE'S ONE GHOST THAT'LL NEVER GET LAID!
UNLESS YOU COUNT THE DOG-AAOOW!
I'LL RIP YOUR FRIGGIN' HEAD OFF, YOU MOTHERFU-
LEAVE HIM, FRANK.
YOU'VE ALWAYS HAD A VICIOUS STREAK, HAVEN'T YOU? JUST LIKE THE TWISTED LITTLE BOY WHO NEARLY KILLED HIS OWN FATHER.
WELL, IF YOU'D LISTENED TO BENJAMIN INSTEAD OF LASHING OUT, YOU'D HAVE HEARD WHY WE'RE HERE.
OKAY. COME ON, THEN.
LET'S HEAR IT.
WE'RE NOT GHOSTS ANY-MORE. WE'RE NOT HAUNT-ING YOU.
YOU CAN'T HAUNT THE DEAD.

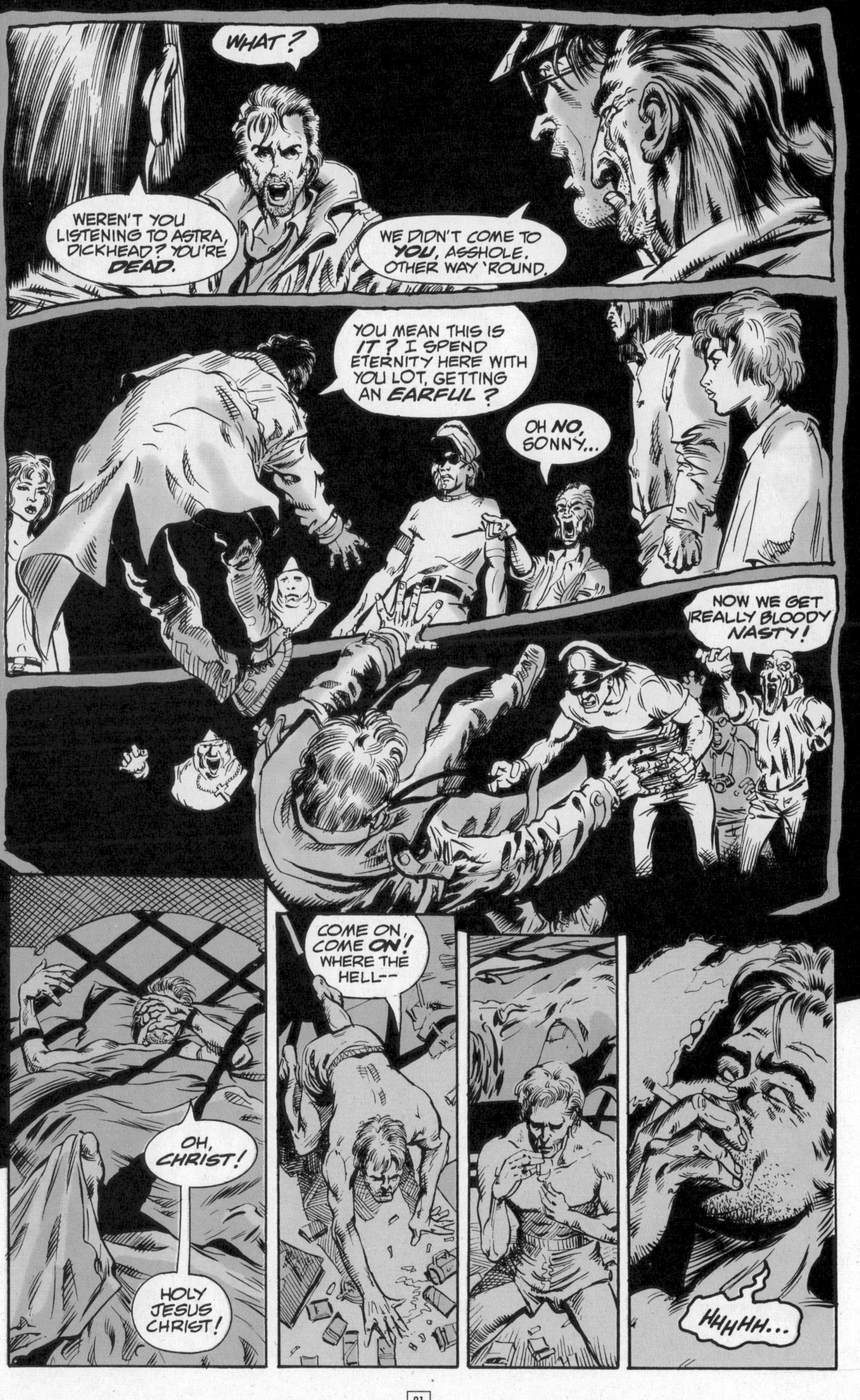
WHAT?
WEREN'T YOU LISTENING TO ASTRA, DICKHEAD? YOU'RE DEAD.
WE DIDN'T COME TO YOU, ASSHOLE. OTHER WAY 'ROUND.
YOU MEAN THIS IS IT? I SPEND ETERNITY HERE WITH YOU LOT, GETTING AN EARFUL?
OH NO, SONNY...
NOW WE GET REALLY BLOODY NASTY!
OH, CHRIST!
HOLY JESUS CHRIST!
COME ON, COME ON! WHERE THE HELL--
HHHHH...

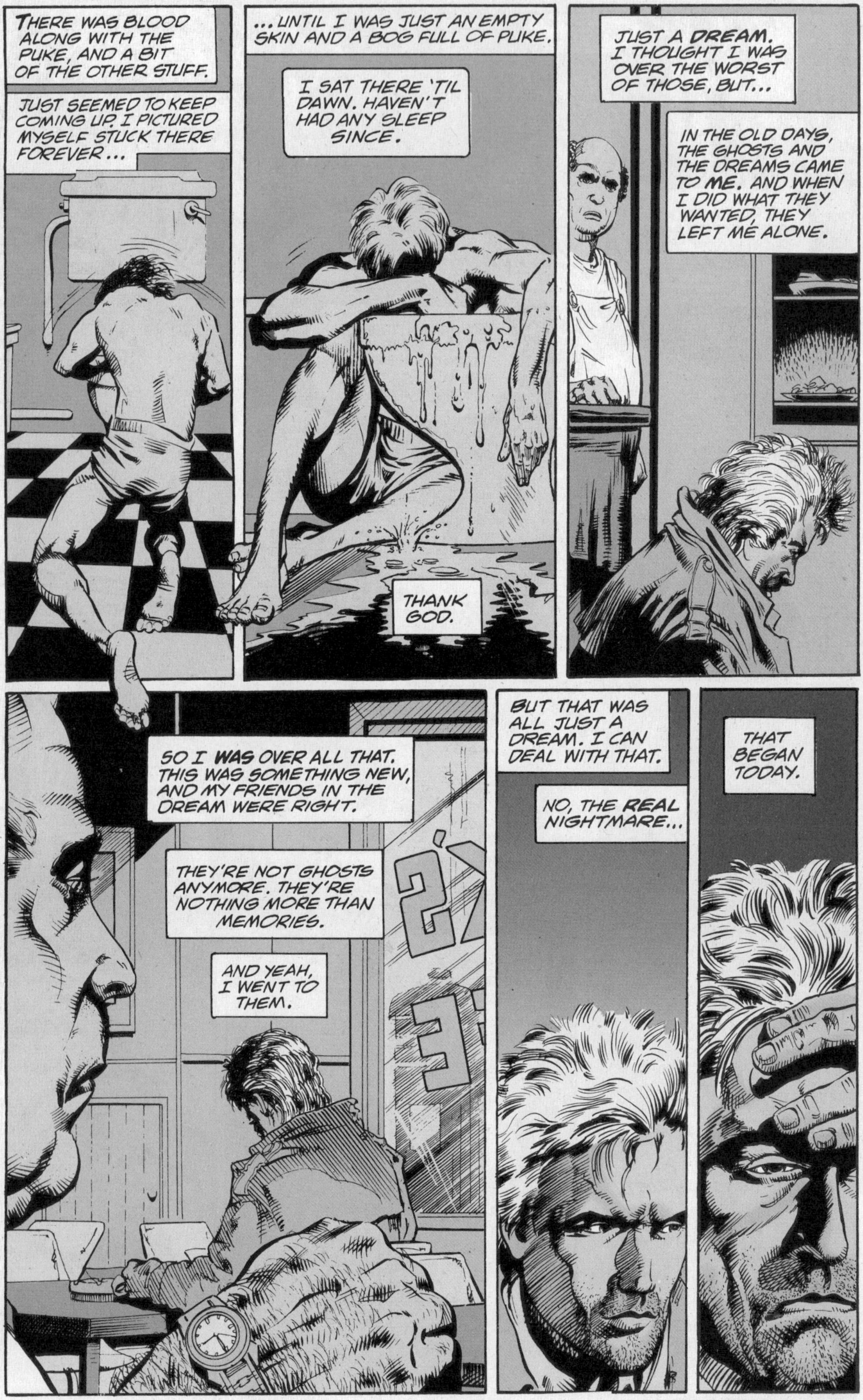
THERE WAS BLOOD ALONG WITH THE PUKE, AND A BIT OF THE OTHER STUFF.
JUST SEEMED TO KEEP COMING UP. I PICTURED MYSELF STUCK THERE FOREVER...
...UNTIL I WAS JUST AN EMPTY SKIN AND A BOG FULL OF PUKE.
I SAT THERE 'TIL DAWN. HAVEN'T HAD ANY SLEEP SINCE.
THANK GOD.
JUST A DREAM. I THOUGHT I WAS OVER THE WORST OF THOSE, BUT...
IN THE OLD DAYS, THE GHOSTS AND THE DREAMS CAME TO ME. AND WHEN I DID WHAT THEY WANTED, THEY LEFT ME ALONE.
SO I WAS OVER ALL THAT. THIS WAS SOMETHING NEW, AND MY FRIENDS IN THE DREAM WERE RIGHT.
THEY'RE NOT GHOSTS ANYMORE. THEY'RE NOTHING MORE THAN MEMORIES.
AND YEAH, I WENT TO THEM.
BUT THAT WAS ALL JUST A DREAM. I CAN DEAL WITH THAT.
NO, THE REAL NIGHTMARE...
THAT BEGAN TODAY.

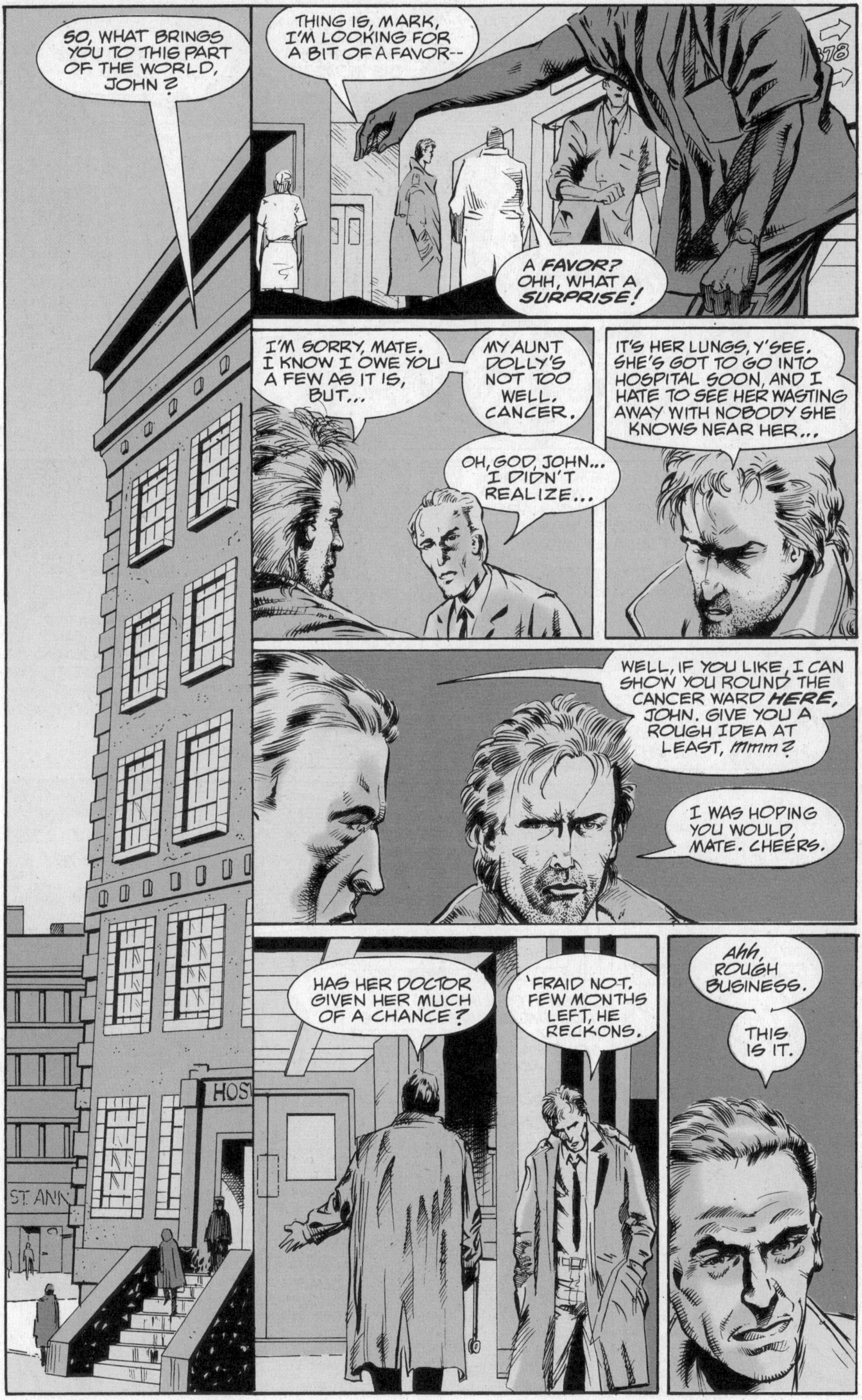
SO, WHAT BRINGS YOU TO THIS PART OF THE WORLD, JOHN?
THING IS, MARK, I'M LOOKING FOR A BIT OF A FAVOR--
A FAVOR? OHH, WHAT A SURPRISE!
I'M SORRY, MATE. I KNOW I OWE YOU A FEW AS IT IS, BUT...
MY AUNT DOLLY'S NOT TOO WELL. CANCER.
OH, GOD, JOHN... I DIDN'T REALIZE...
IT'S HER LUNGS, Y'SEE. SHE'S GOT TO GO INTO HOSPITAL SOON, AND I HATE TO SEE HER WASTING AWAY WITH NOBODY SHE KNOWS NEAR HER...
WELL, IF YOU LIKE, I CAN SHOW YOU ROUND THE CANCER WARD HERE, JOHN. GIVE YOU A ROUGH IDEA AT LEAST, MMM?
I WAS HOPING YOU WOULD, MATE. CHEERS.
HAS HER DOCTOR GIVEN HER MUCH OF A CHANCE?
'FRAID NOT. FEW MONTHS LEFT, HE RECKONS.
AHH, ROUGH BUSINESS.
THIS IS IT.
ST. ANN
HOS

IF IT'S TERMINAL, ALL WE CAN DO, REALLY, IS PUMP THEM FULL OF DRUGS. NEVER QUITE *STOPS* THE PAIN, BUT... WELL, IT EASES IT A LITTLE.

THESE PATIENTS ARE ALL ON MEDICATION AT THE MOMENT.

YOU MEAN THEY'RE ALL GOING TO--

NO, NO. CHEMOTHERAPY TREATMENT WILL SAVE A LOT OF THESE CHAPS. IT'S VERY PAINFUL, BUT IT USUALLY WORKS.

SO AUNT DOLLY WOULD BE SOMEWHERE LIKE THIS, RIGHT?

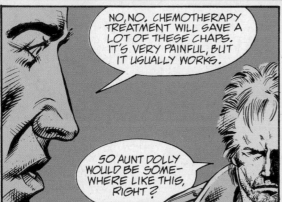

mmm... BUGGER!

LOOK, I HAVE TO *GO,* JOHN. CAN YOU SEE YOURSELF OUT?

eh? OH, SURE.

CHEERS.

I WAS LEFT ALONE THEN, IN THE SUDDEN SILENCE OF OLD MEN DYING BEFORE THEIR TIME.

OR DYING MEN OLD BEFORE THEIR TIME. WHATEVER.

I *WON'T* DIE LIKE THIS, I THOUGHT. COMING HERE WAS A MISTAKE, AS IF I EXPECTED SOME EASY WAY OUT. SOME CALM AND QUIET DEATH. I'D BE BETTER OFF CUTTING MY *THROAT.*

I HAD TO GET OUT OF THERE.

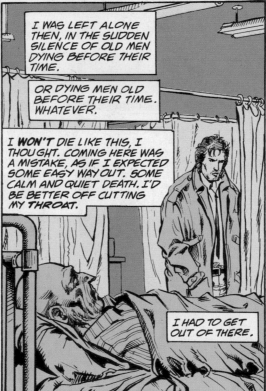

OI! BLONDIE!

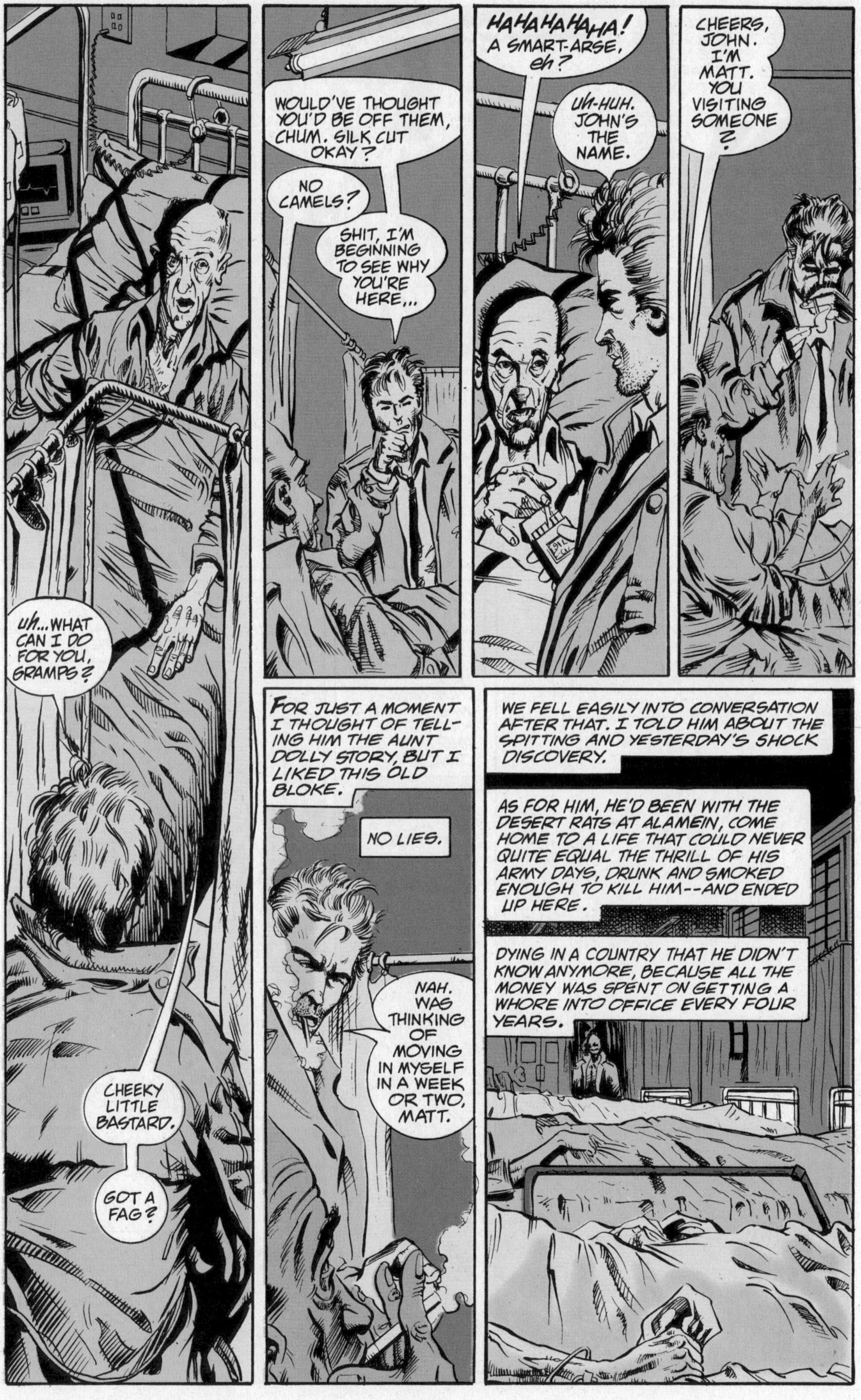
uh... WHAT CAN I DO FOR YOU, GRAMPS?
CHEEKY LITTLE BASTARD.
GOT A FAG?
WOULD'VE THOUGHT YOU'D BE OFF THEM, CHUM. SILK CUT OKAY?
NO CAMELS?
SHIT, I'M BEGINNING TO SEE WHY YOU'RE HERE...
HAHAHAHAHAHA! A SMART-ARSE, eh?
uh-HUH. JOHN'S THE NAME.
CHEERS, JOHN. I'M MATT. YOU VISITING SOMEONE?
FOR JUST A MOMENT I THOUGHT OF TELLING HIM THE AUNT DOLLY STORY, BUT I LIKED THIS OLD BLOKE.
NO LIES.
NAH. WAS THINKING OF MOVING IN MYSELF IN A WEEK OR TWO, MATT.
WE FELL EASILY INTO CONVERSATION AFTER THAT. I TOLD HIM ABOUT THE SPITTING AND YESTERDAY'S SHOCK DISCOVERY.
AS FOR HIM, HE'D BEEN WITH THE DESERT RATS AT ALAMEIN, COME HOME TO A LIFE THAT COULD NEVER QUITE EQUAL THE THRILL OF HIS ARMY DAYS, DRUNK AND SMOKED ENOUGH TO KILL HIM--AND ENDED UP HERE.
DYING IN A COUNTRY THAT HE DIDN'T KNOW ANYMORE, BECAUSE ALL THE MONEY WAS SPENT ON GETTING A WHORE INTO OFFICE EVERY FOUR YEARS.

SO, WHAT'RE YOU GOING TO DO, SON? I GET THE FEELING YOU'RE NOT LOOKING FORWARD TO LIFE IN THE SHITHOLE, HERE.

NURSES ARE NICE, MIND.

HEH. YOU'RE RIGHT, THOUGH. DON'T THINK I'LL BE MOVING IN WITH YOU.

YOU WOULDN'T *TOP* YOURSELF, I HOPE. MORTAL SIN, THAT.

ABOUT AS MORTAL AS YOU CAN GET... BUT NO, I DON'T THINK I'LL DO MYSELF IN, EITHER. TELL YOU THE TRUTH, I HAVEN'T GOT A BLOODY CLUE WHAT I'LL DO.

WE LEFT IT AT THAT, BUT I PROMISED I'D COME BACK AND VISIT. I DIDN'T SAY "SOON," BECAUSE THAT WAS OBVIOUS. NEITHER OF US HAD VERY LONG TO GO.

BUT I'D MADE A FRIEND.

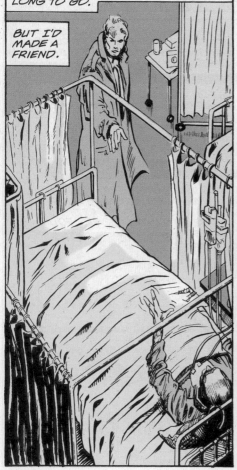

OUTSIDE, I STILL DIDN'T KNOW WHAT TO DO. I FELT ANNOYED, AS IF MY INDECISION WAS WHAT WAS KILLING ME, AND NOT THE CANCER.

I'D KNOWN ALL ALONG THAT THERE WERE SEVERAL THINGS I *MIGHT* TRY TO GET ME OUT OF THIS.

I WAS ALSO SURE THAT NONE OF THEM WOULD ACTUALLY *WORK*, SO I'D NO REAL INCLINATION TO TRY THEM.

THEN, BACK AT THE FLAT, I GOT THE *PHONE CALL*.

YEAH?

MISTER CONSTANTINE? DOCTOR ELLIS HERE-- WE SPOKE YESTERDAY, REMEMBER?

YOU DON'T THINK I'M GONNA FORGET *THAT*, DO YOU?

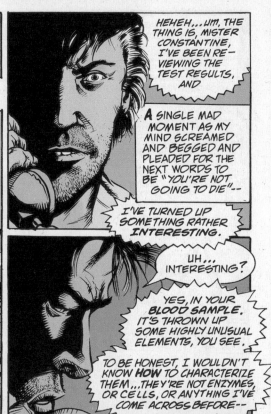

HEHEH...UM, THE THING IS, MISTER CONSTANTINE, I'VE BEEN RE-VIEWING THE TEST RESULTS, AND

A SINGLE MAD MOMENT AS MY MIND SCREAMED AND BEGGED AND PLEADED FOR THE NEXT WORDS TO BE "YOU'RE NOT GOING TO DIE"--

I'VE TURNED UP SOMETHING RATHER *INTERESTING.*

UH... INTERESTING?

YES, IN YOUR BLOOD SAMPLE. IT'S THROWN UP SOME HIGHLY UNUSUAL ELEMENTS, YOU SEE.

TO BE HONEST, I WOULDN'T KNOW *HOW* TO CHARACTERIZE THEM...THEY'RE NOT ENZYMES, OR CELLS, OR ANYTHING I'VE COME ACROSS BEFORE--

I WAS WONDERING IF YOU COULD COME IN FOR SOME MORE TESTS, MISTER CONSTANTINE...

SHIT.

MISTER CONSTANTINE?

IT'S *DEMON BLOOD*

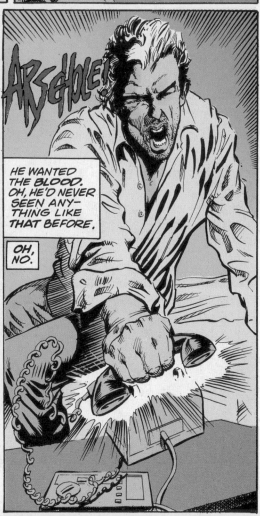

ARSEHOLE!

HE WANTED THE BLOOD. OH, HE'D NEVER SEEN ANY-THING LIKE THAT BEFORE.

OH, NO.

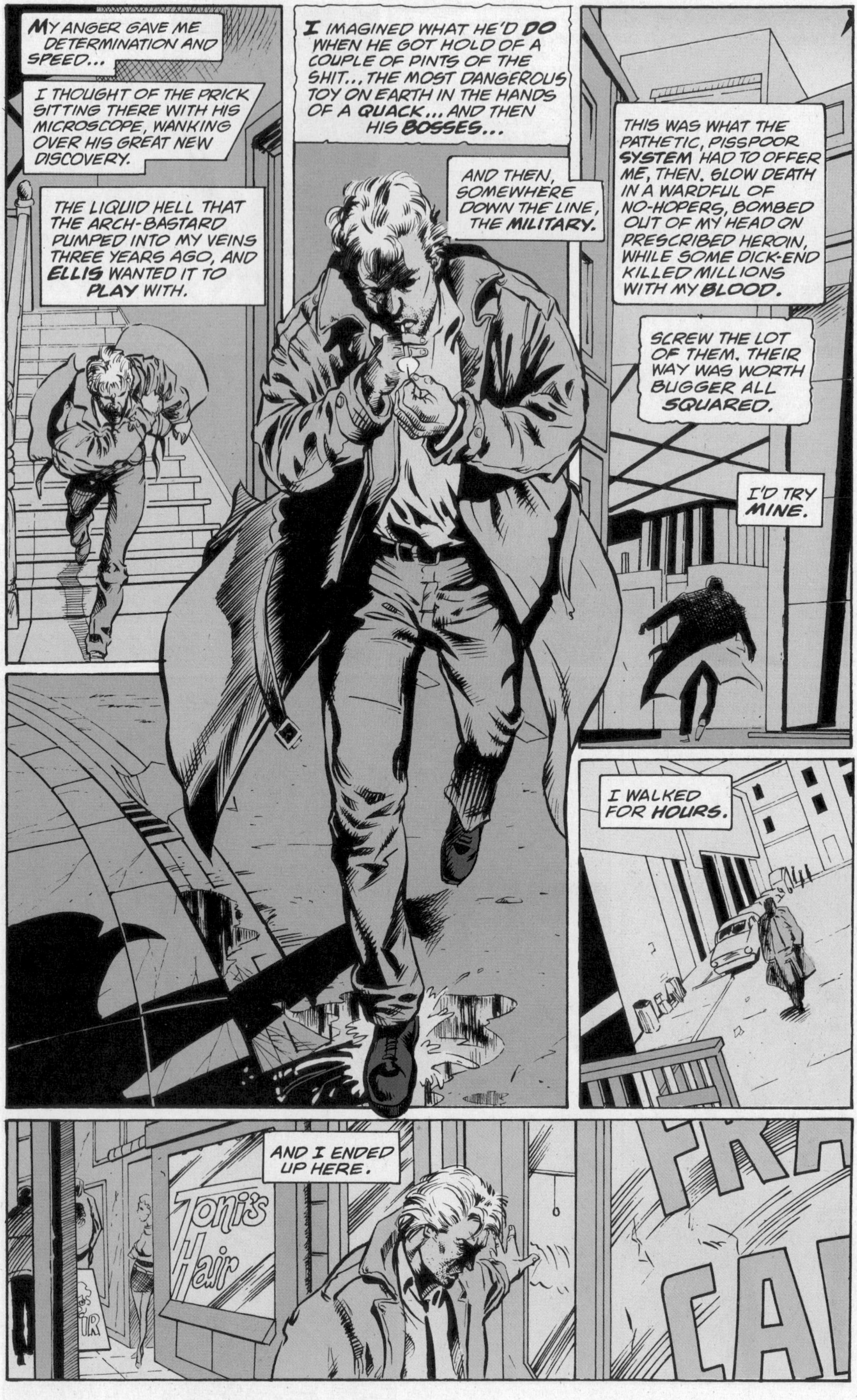
MY ANGER GAVE ME DETERMINATION AND SPEED...
I THOUGHT OF THE PRICK SITTING THERE WITH HIS MICROSCOPE, WANKING OVER HIS GREAT NEW DISCOVERY.
THE LIQUID HELL THAT THE ARCH-BASTARD PUMPED INTO MY VEINS THREE YEARS AGO, AND ELLIS WANTED IT TO PLAY WITH.
I IMAGINED WHAT HE'D DO WHEN HE GOT HOLD OF A COUPLE OF PINTS OF THE SHIT... THE MOST DANGEROUS TOY ON EARTH IN THE HANDS OF A QUACK... AND THEN HIS BOSSES...
AND THEN, SOMEWHERE DOWN THE LINE, THE MILITARY.
THIS WAS WHAT THE PATHETIC, PISSPOOR SYSTEM HAD TO OFFER ME, THEN. SLOW DEATH IN A WARDFUL OF NO-HOPERS, BOMBED OUT OF MY HEAD ON PRESCRIBED HEROIN, WHILE SOME DICK-END KILLED MILLIONS WITH MY BLOOD.
SCREW THE LOT OF THEM. THEIR WAY WAS WORTH BUGGER ALL SQUARED.
I'D TRY MINE.
I WALKED FOR HOURS.
AND I ENDED UP HERE.
Toni's Hair

I'VE BEEN HERE TWO HOURS, NOW. IT WAS **MEANT** TO BE A PLANNING SESSION, BUT...

...THE ANGER'S GONE, AND THE FEAR'S COME BACK.

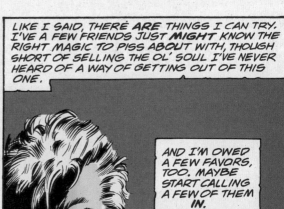

LIKE I SAID, THERE **ARE** THINGS I CAN TRY. I'VE A FEW FRIENDS JUST **MIGHT** KNOW THE RIGHT MAGIC TO PISS ABOUT WITH, THOUGH SHORT OF SELLING THE OL' SOUL I'VE NEVER HEARD OF A WAY OF GETTING OUT OF THIS ONE.

AND I'M OWED A FEW FAVORS, TOO. MAYBE START CALLING A FEW OF THEM **IN**.

THING IS--

RIGHT, SUNSHINE...

HUH?

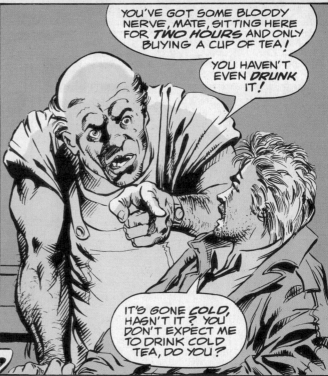

YOU'VE GOT SOME BLOODY NERVE, MATE, SITTING HERE FOR **TWO HOURS** AND ONLY BUYING A CUP OF TEA!

YOU HAVEN'T EVEN **DRUNK** IT!

IT'S GONE **COLD,** HASN'T IT? YOU DON'T EXPECT ME TO DRINK COLD TEA, DO YOU?

WELL, IT'S **BOUND** TO GO COLD IF YOU LEAVE IT FOR TWO HOURS, ISN'T IT?

NO CHANCE OF A REFILL, THEN?

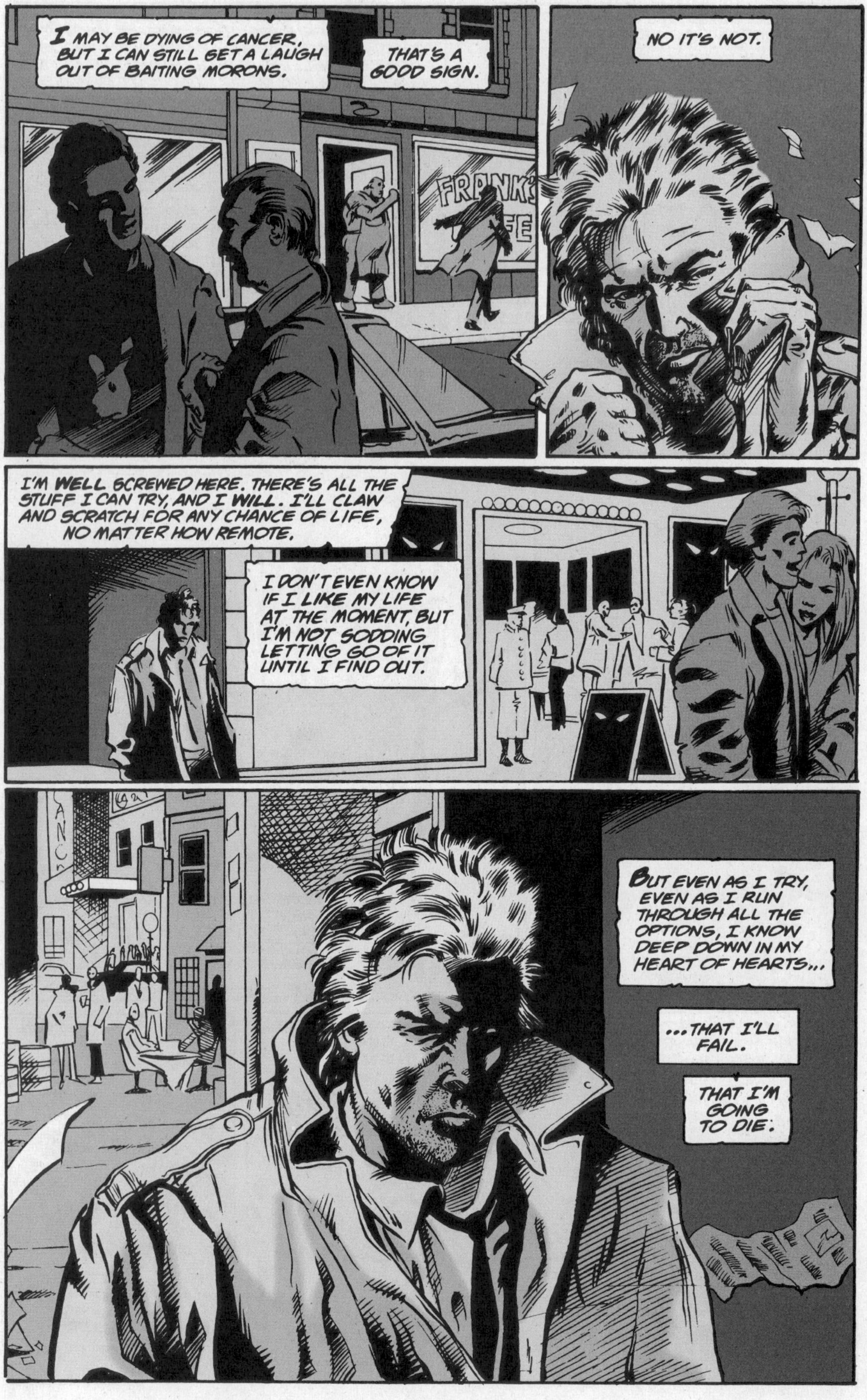
I MAY BE DYING OF CANCER, BUT I CAN STILL GET A LAUGH OUT OF BAITING MORONS.
THAT'S A GOOD SIGN.
FRANK'S
NO IT'S NOT.
I'M WELL SCREWED HERE. THERE'S ALL THE STUFF I CAN TRY, AND I WILL. I'LL CLAW AND SCRATCH FOR ANY CHANCE OF LIFE, NO MATTER HOW REMOTE.
I DON'T EVEN KNOW IF I LIKE MY LIFE AT THE MOMENT, BUT I'M NOT SODDING LETTING GO OF IT UNTIL I FIND OUT.
BUT EVEN AS I TRY, EVEN AS I RUN THROUGH ALL THE OPTIONS, I KNOW DEEP DOWN IN MY HEART OF HEARTS...
...THAT I'LL FAIL.
THAT I'M GOING TO DIE.

a

drop

of

the

hard

stuff

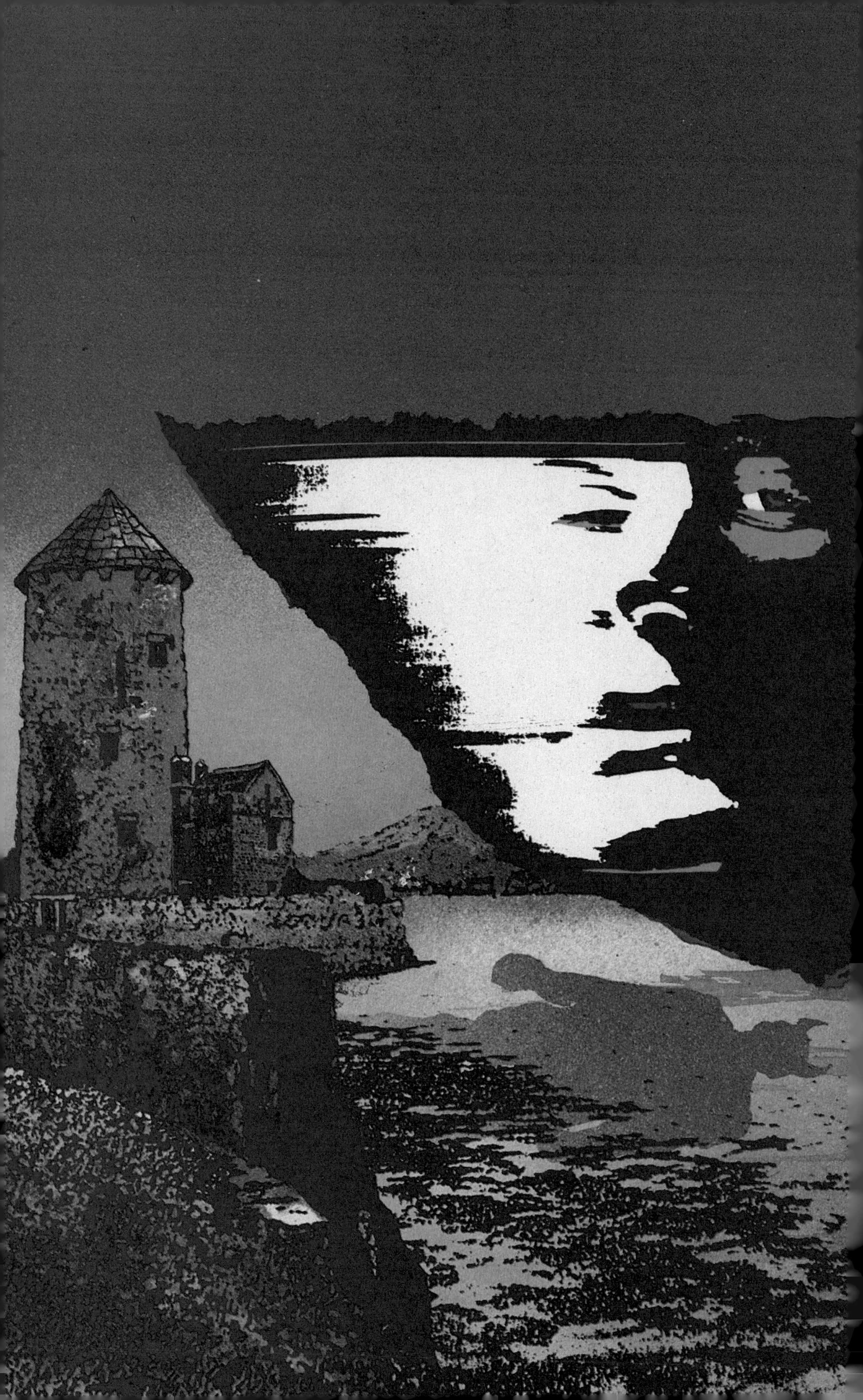

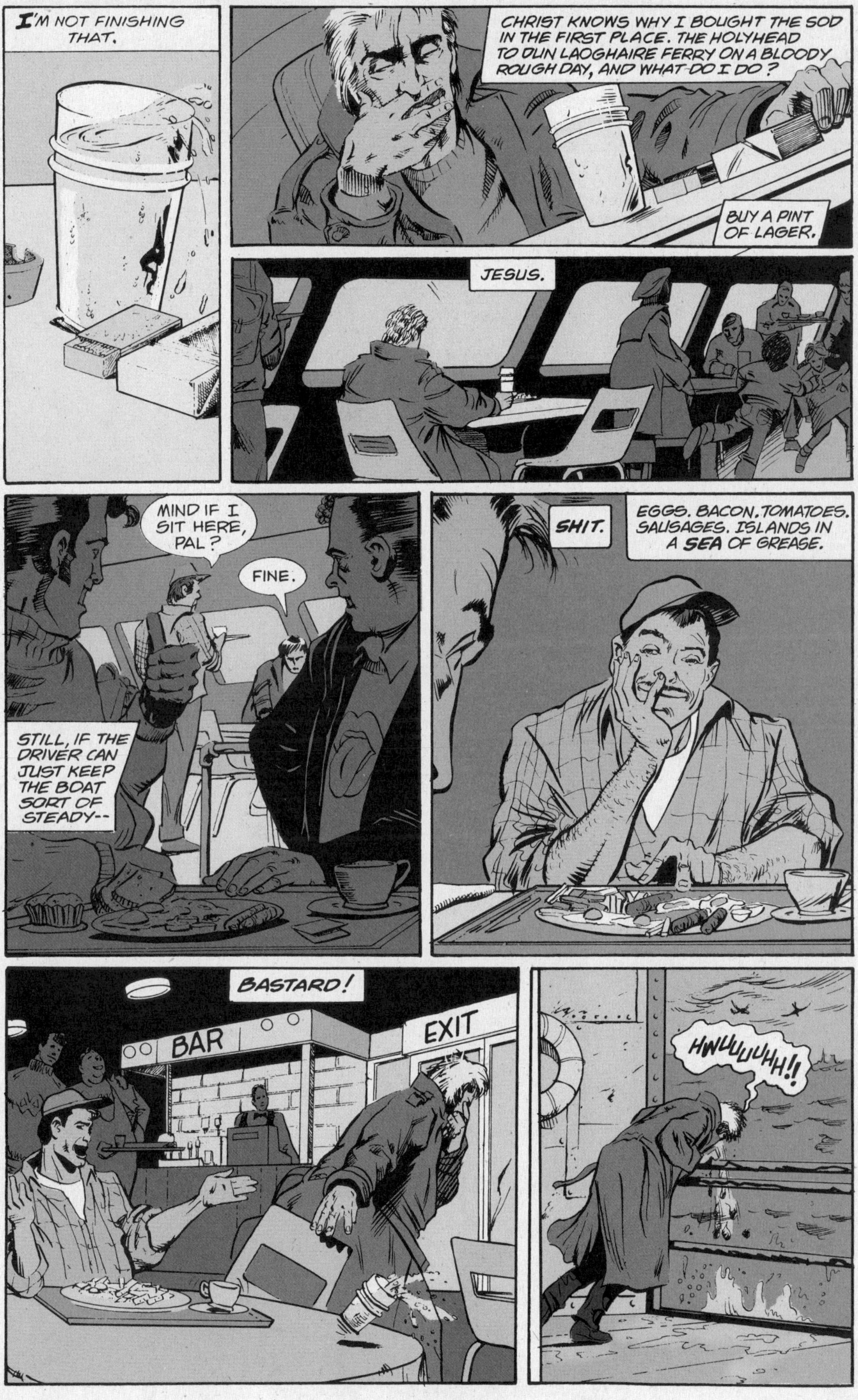
I'M NOT FINISHING THAT.
CHRIST KNOWS WHY I BOUGHT THE SOD IN THE FIRST PLACE. THE HOLYHEAD TO DUN LAOGHAIRE FERRY ON A BLOODY ROUGH DAY, AND WHAT DO I DO?
BUY A PINT OF LAGER.
JESUS.
MIND IF I SIT HERE, PAL?
FINE.
STILL, IF THE DRIVER CAN JUST KEEP THE BOAT SORT OF STEADY--
SHIT.
EGGS. BACON. TOMATOES. SAUSAGES. ISLANDS IN A SEA OF GREASE.
BASTARD!
BAR
EXIT
HWUUUUHH!!

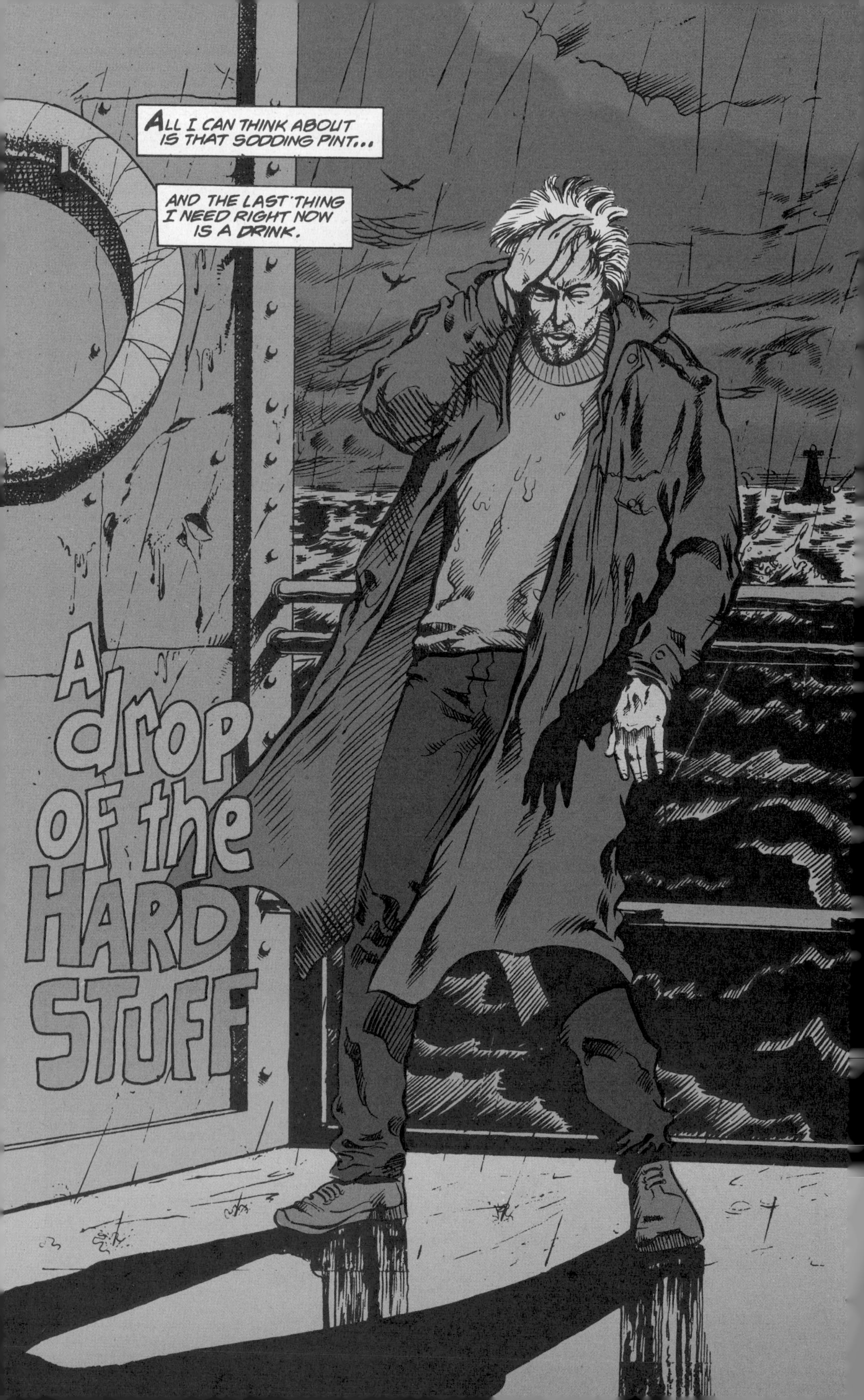

ALL I CAN THINK ABOUT IS THAT SODDING PINT...
AND THE LAST THING I NEED RIGHT NOW IS A DRINK.
A drop of the HARD STUFF

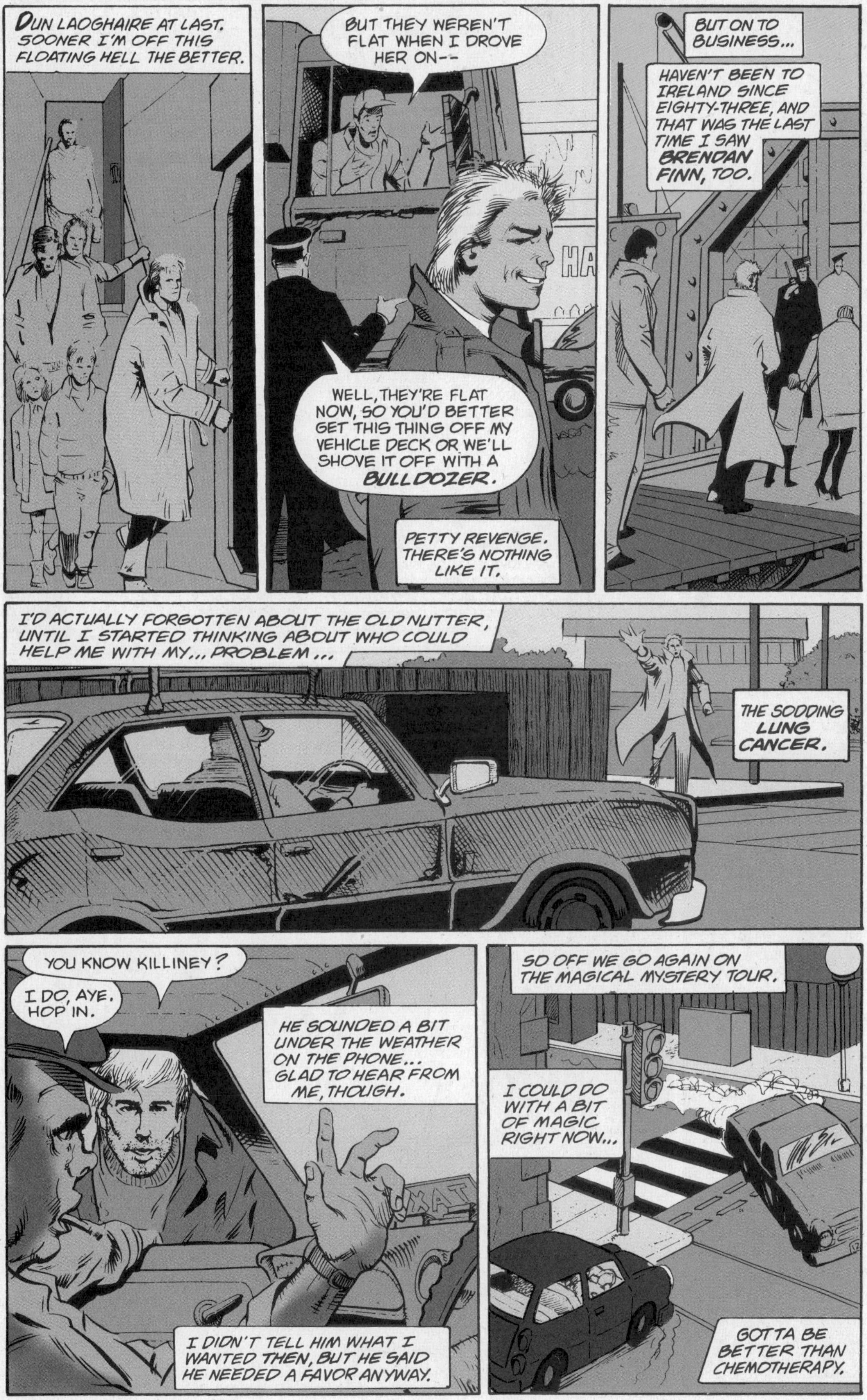
DUN LAOGHAIRE AT LAST. SOONER I'M OFF THIS FLOATING HELL THE BETTER.
BUT THEY WEREN'T FLAT WHEN I DROVE HER ON--
WELL, THEY'RE FLAT NOW, SO YOU'D BETTER GET THIS THING OFF MY VEHICLE DECK OR WE'LL SHOVE IT OFF WITH A BULLDOZER.
PETTY REVENGE. THERE'S NOTHING LIKE IT.
BUT ON TO BUSINESS...
HAVEN'T BEEN TO IRELAND SINCE EIGHTY-THREE, AND THAT WAS THE LAST TIME I SAW BRENDAN FINN, TOO.
I'D ACTUALLY FORGOTTEN ABOUT THE OLD NUTTER, UNTIL I STARTED THINKING ABOUT WHO COULD HELP ME WITH MY... PROBLEM...
THE SODDING LUNG CANCER.
YOU KNOW KILLINEY?
I DO, AYE. HOP IN.
HE SOUNDED A BIT UNDER THE WEATHER ON THE PHONE... GLAD TO HEAR FROM ME, THOUGH.
I DIDN'T TELL HIM WHAT I WANTED THEN, BUT HE SAID HE NEEDED A FAVOR ANYWAY.
SO OFF WE GO AGAIN ON THE MAGICAL MYSTERY TOUR.
I COULD DO WITH A BIT OF MAGIC RIGHT NOW...
GOTTA BE BETTER THAN CHEMOTHERAPY.

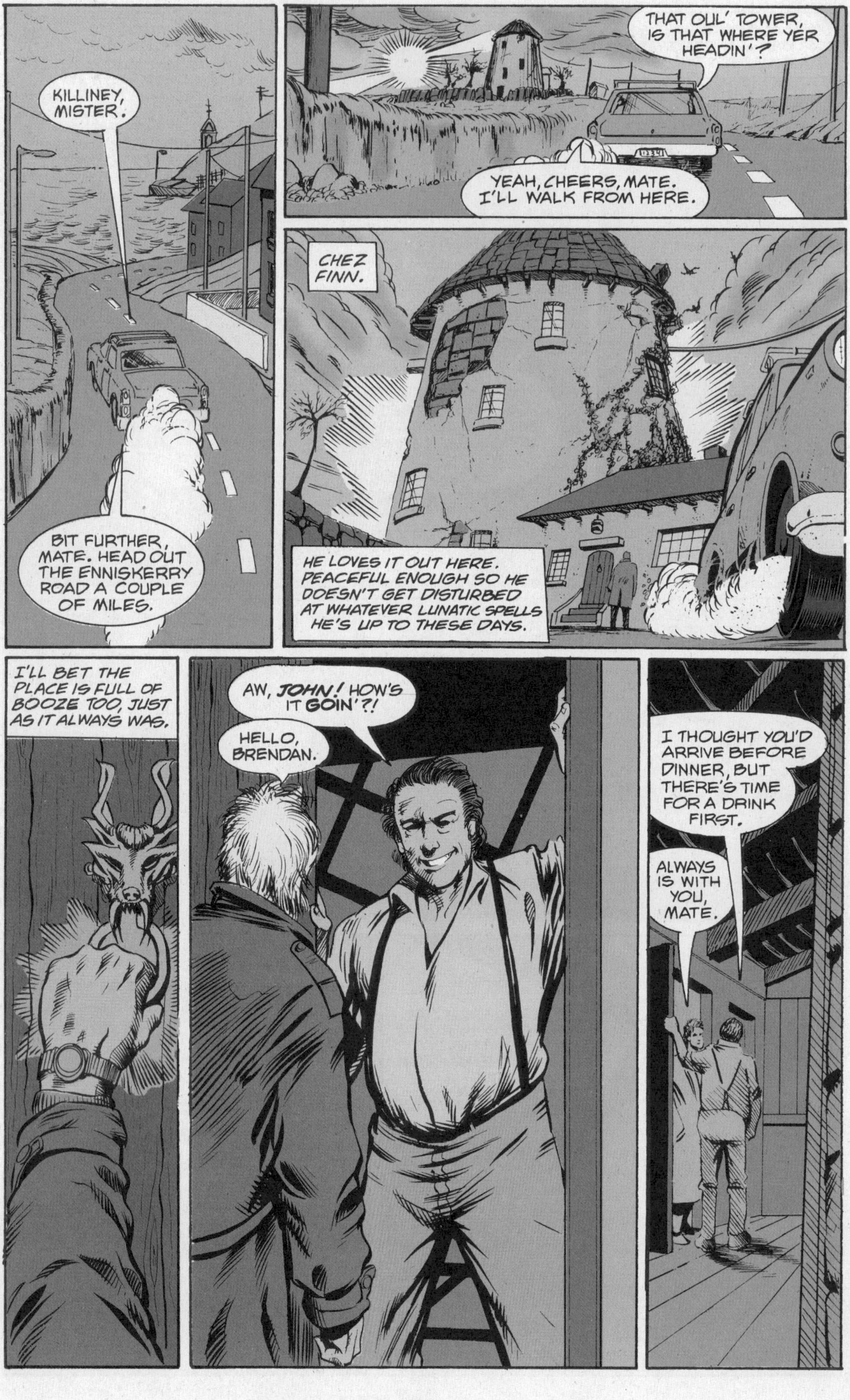
KILLINEY, MISTER.
BIT FURTHER, MATE. HEAD OUT THE ENNISKERRY ROAD A COUPLE OF MILES.
THAT OUL' TOWER, IS THAT WHERE YER HEADIN'?
YEAH, CHEERS, MATE. I'LL WALK FROM HERE.
CHEZ FINN.
HE LOVES IT OUT HERE. PEACEFUL ENOUGH SO HE DOESN'T GET DISTURBED AT WHATEVER LUNATIC SPELLS HE'S UP TO THESE DAYS.
I'LL BET THE PLACE IS FULL OF BOOZE TOO, JUST AS IT ALWAYS WAS.
AW, JOHN! HOW'S IT GOIN'?!
HELLO, BRENDAN.
I THOUGHT YOU'D ARRIVE BEFORE DINNER, BUT THERE'S TIME FOR A DRINK FIRST.
ALWAYS IS WITH YOU, MATE.

YOU'RE STILL A CONNOISSEUR OF THE FINEST LIQUOR, I SEE...

mmm... THIS LOT'S NOT SO BAD, BUT I'VE THE BEST STUFF HIDDEN ALL ROUND THE PLACE.

AND I WOULDN'T GO DRINKIN' THAT POTEEN 'TIL YOU'VE HAD SOME WHISKEY TO SEASON YOUR GUTS.

CHEERS.

SLAINTE.

SO, BRENDAN... TO BUSINESS?

eh? AW, THAT'LL KEEP FOR A WHILE. HAVEN'T WE A BIT O' CATCHIN' UP TO DO?

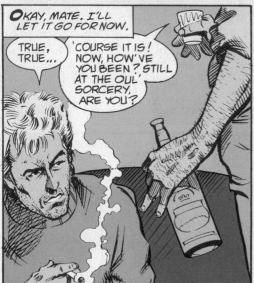

OKAY, MATE. I'LL LET IT GO FOR NOW.

TRUE, TRUE...

'COURSE IT IS! NOW, HOW'VE YOU BEEN? STILL AT THE OUL' SORCERY, ARE YOU?

HAVEN'T HEARD IT CALLED *THAT* IN A WHILE, MATE.

NO, I'D IMAGINE YOU HAVEN'T. BUT YOU KNOW *ME*, JOHN.

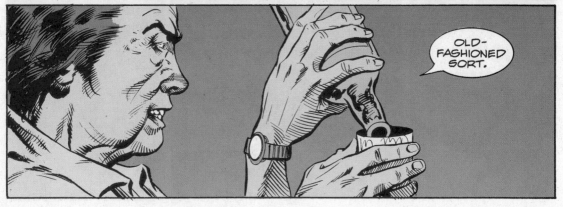

OLD-FASHIONED SORT.

HE'S NOT LOOKING SO GOOD... HE'S PALE AND DRAWN, AND HIS FACE IS A SPIDER'S WEB OF BURST BLOOD VESSELS.

THE NEVER ENDING BOOZING, I SUPPOSE. HOW MUCH *DOES* HE DRINK?

YOU STILL SEEING THAT YOUNG ONE FROM NEW YORK, THEN? ANNA?

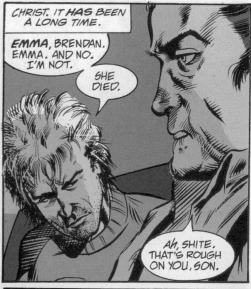

CHRIST. IT *HAS* BEEN A LONG TIME.

EMMA, BRENDAN. EMMA. AND NO. I'M NOT.

SHE DIED.

AH, SHITE. THAT'S ROUGH ON YOU, SON.

I, AH, I HEARD ABOUT YOUR FATHER, JOHN. I'M SORRY FOR YOUR TROUBLE.

YEAH.

HAVEN'T BEEN HAVING MUCH LUCK IN THE PAST COUPLE OF YEARS, TO TELL THE TRUTH. WITH FRIENDS, I MEAN.

RITCHIE AND GARY DIED AND ALL.

JESUS... WELL, I'M NOT DOIN' ALL THAT WELL MYSELF, IT HAS TO BE SAID.

TACTFUL SOUL THAT YOU ARE, JOHN, I NOTICE YOU'VE NOT MENTIONED *KIT*.

I... WELL, I THOUGHT YOU'D GET AROUND TO IT IN YOUR OWN TIME, Y'KNOW?

SHE'S AWAY.

GONE FOUR YEARS, NOW.

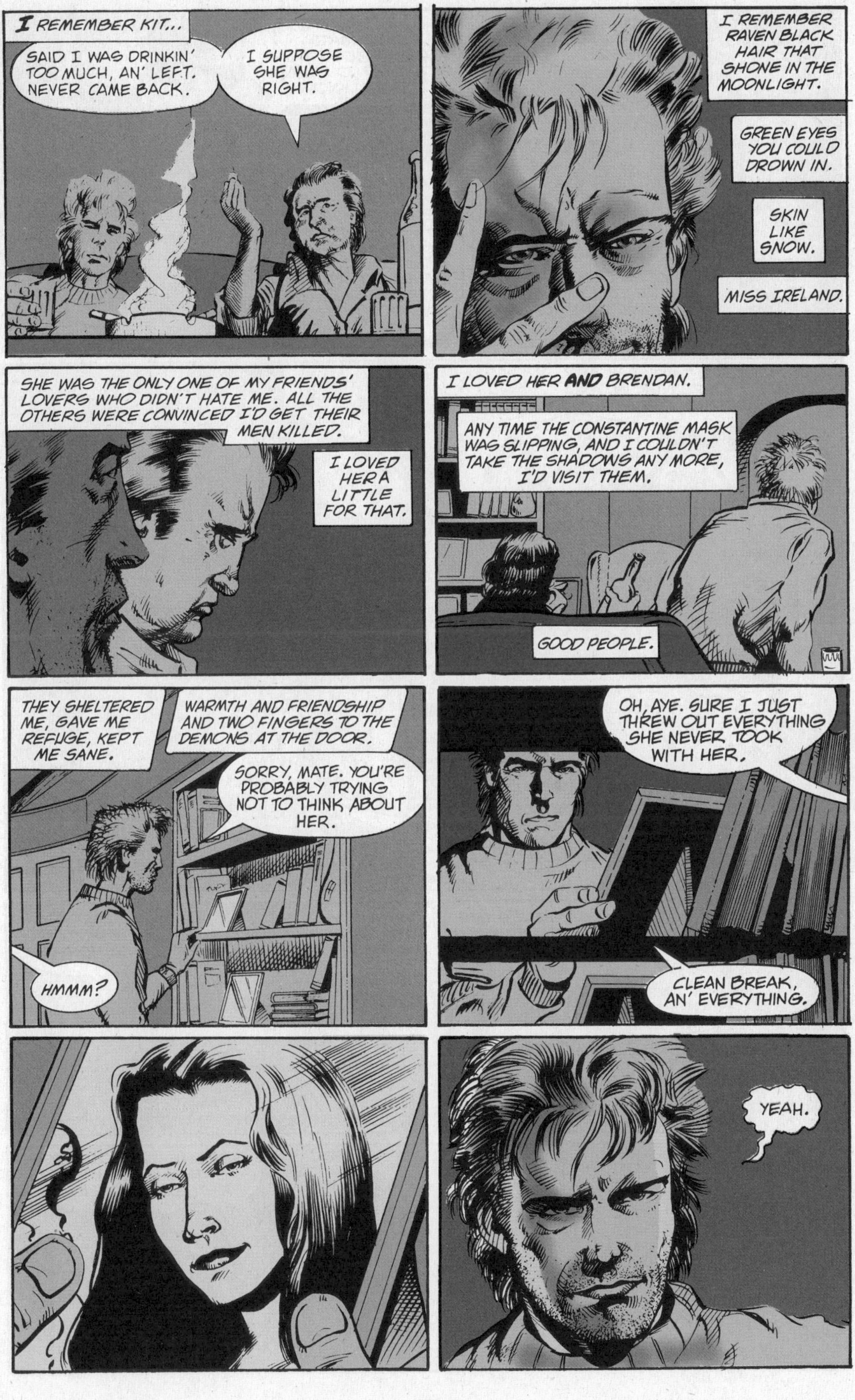
I REMEMBER KIT...
SAID I WAS DRINKIN' TOO MUCH, AN' LEFT. NEVER CAME BACK.
I SUPPOSE SHE WAS RIGHT.
I REMEMBER RAVEN BLACK HAIR THAT SHONE IN THE MOONLIGHT.
GREEN EYES YOU COULD DROWN IN.
SKIN LIKE SNOW.
MISS IRELAND.
SHE WAS THE ONLY ONE OF MY FRIENDS' LOVERS WHO DIDN'T HATE ME. ALL THE OTHERS WERE CONVINCED I'D GET THEIR MEN KILLED.
I LOVED HER A LITTLE FOR THAT.
I LOVED HER AND BRENDAN.
ANY TIME THE CONSTANTINE MASK WAS SLIPPING, AND I COULDN'T TAKE THE SHADOWS ANY MORE, I'D VISIT THEM.
GOOD PEOPLE.
THEY SHELTERED ME, GAVE ME REFUGE, KEPT ME SANE.
WARMTH AND FRIENDSHIP AND TWO FINGERS TO THE DEMONS AT THE DOOR.
SORRY, MATE. YOU'RE PROBABLY TRYING NOT TO THINK ABOUT HER.
HMMM?
OH, AYE. SURE I JUST THREW OUT EVERYTHING SHE NEVER TOOK WITH HER.
CLEAN BREAK, AN' EVERYTHING.
YEAH.

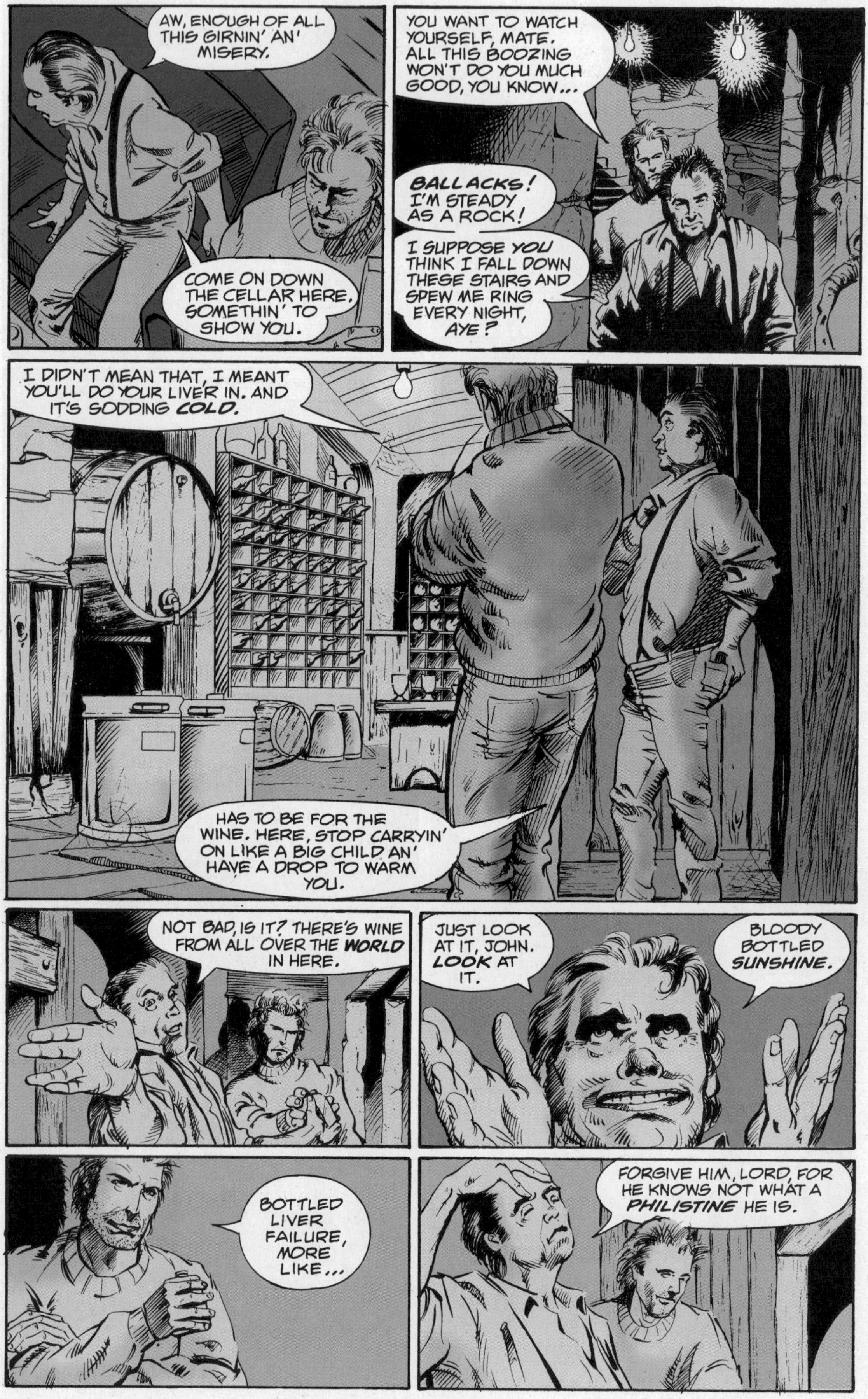
AW, ENOUGH OF ALL THIS GIRNIN' AN' MISERY.
COME ON DOWN THE CELLAR HERE. SOMETHIN' TO SHOW YOU.
YOU WANT TO WATCH YOURSELF, MATE. ALL THIS BOOZING WON'T DO YOU MUCH GOOD, YOU KNOW...
BALLACKS! I'M STEADY AS A ROCK!
I SUPPOSE YOU THINK I FALL DOWN THESE STAIRS AND SPEW ME RING EVERY NIGHT, AYE?
I DIDN'T MEAN THAT, I MEANT YOU'LL DO YOUR LIVER IN. AND IT'S SODDING COLD.
HAS TO BE FOR THE WINE. HERE, STOP CARRYIN' ON LIKE A BIG CHILD AN' HAVE A DROP TO WARM YOU.
NOT BAD, IS IT? THERE'S WINE FROM ALL OVER THE WORLD IN HERE.
JUST LOOK AT IT, JOHN. LOOK AT IT.
BLOODY BOTTLED SUNSHINE.
BOTTLED LIVER FAILURE, MORE LIKE...
FORGIVE HIM, LORD, FOR HE KNOWS NOT WHAT A PHILISTINE HE IS.

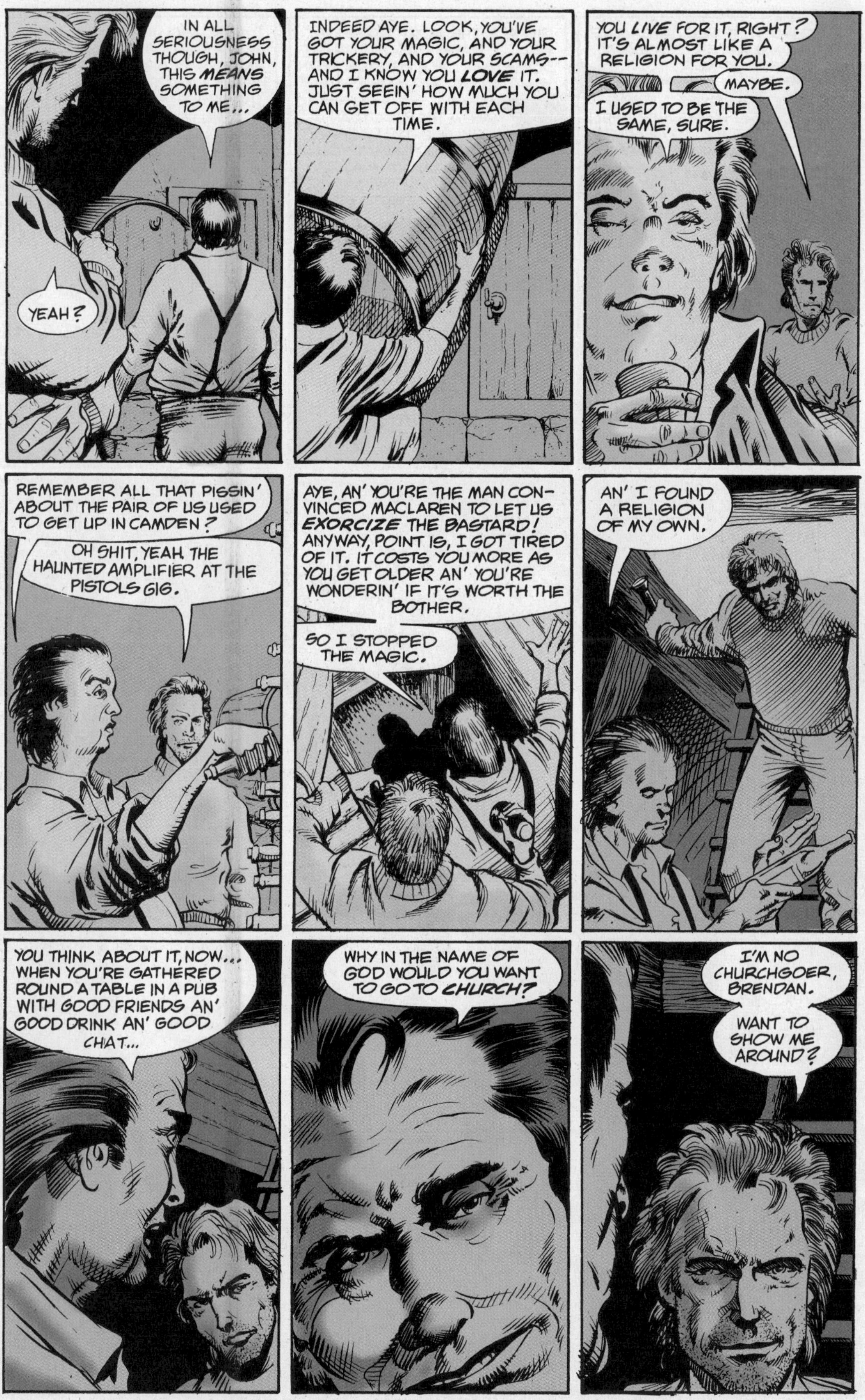
IN ALL SERIOUSNESS THOUGH, JOHN, THIS MEANS SOMETHING TO ME...
YEAH?
INDEED AYE. LOOK, YOU'VE GOT YOUR MAGIC, AND YOUR TRICKERY, AND YOUR SCAMS-- AND I KNOW YOU LOVE IT. JUST SEEIN' HOW MUCH YOU CAN GET OFF WITH EACH TIME.
YOU LIVE FOR IT, RIGHT? IT'S ALMOST LIKE A RELIGION FOR YOU.
MAYBE.
I USED TO BE THE SAME, SURE.
REMEMBER ALL THAT PISSIN' ABOUT THE PAIR OF US USED TO GET UP IN CAMDEN?
OH SHIT, YEAH. THE HAUNTED AMPLIFIER AT THE PISTOLS GIG.
AYE, AN' YOU'RE THE MAN CONVINCED MACLAREN TO LET US EXORCIZE THE BASTARD! ANYWAY, POINT IS, I GOT TIRED OF IT. IT COSTS YOU MORE AS YOU GET OLDER AN' YOU'RE WONDERIN' IF IT'S WORTH THE BOTHER.
SO I STOPPED THE MAGIC.
AN' I FOUND A RELIGION OF MY OWN.
YOU THINK ABOUT IT, NOW... WHEN YOU'RE GATHERED ROUND A TABLE IN A PUB WITH GOOD FRIENDS AN' GOOD DRINK AN' GOOD CHAT...
WHY IN THE NAME OF GOD WOULD YOU WANT TO GO TO CHURCH?
I'M NO CHURCHGOER, BRENDAN.
WANT TO SHOW ME AROUND?

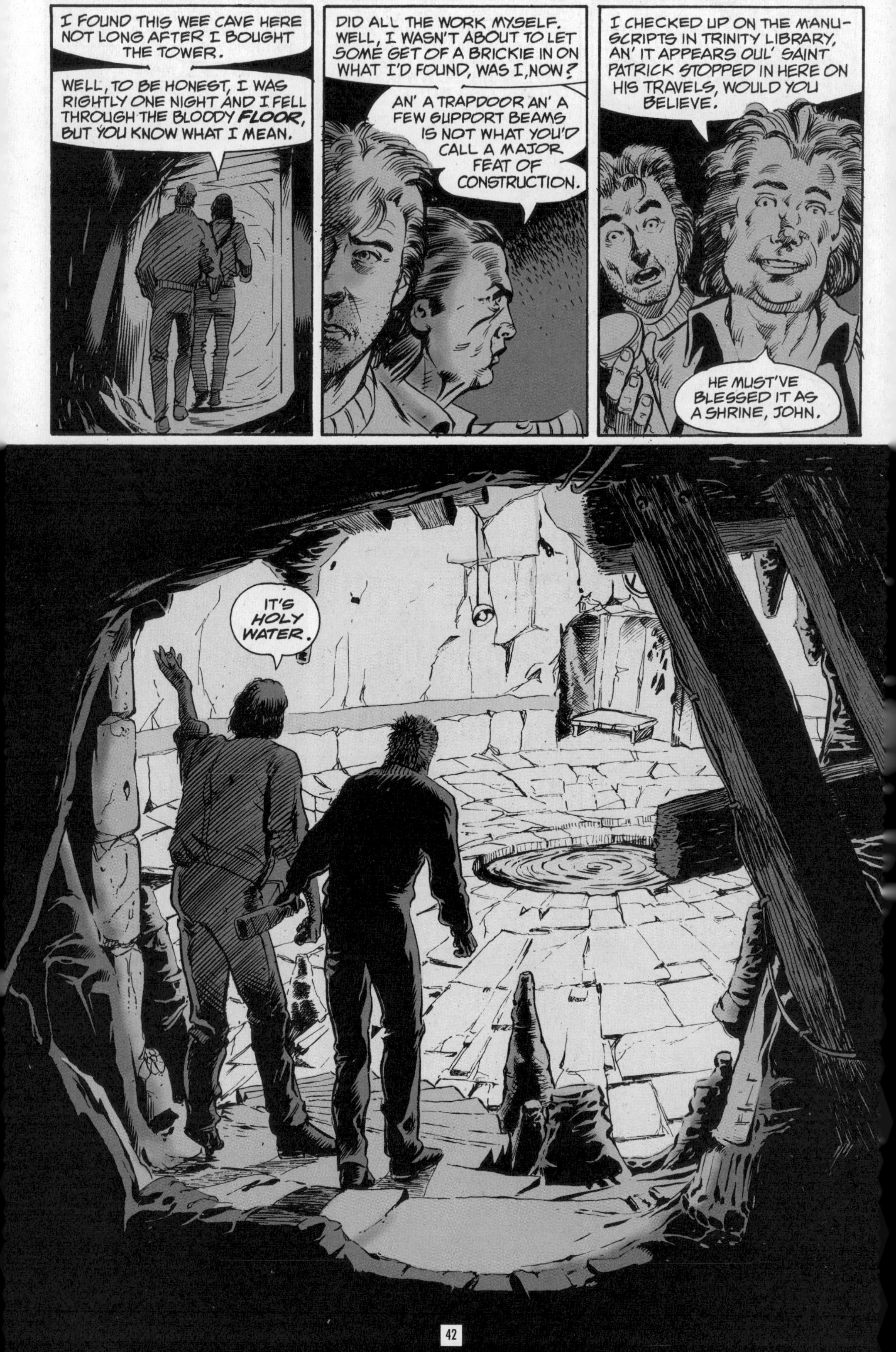
I FOUND THIS WEE CAVE HERE NOT LONG AFTER I BOUGHT THE TOWER.
WELL, TO BE HONEST, I WAS RIGHTLY ONE NIGHT AND I FELL THROUGH THE BLOODY FLOOR, BUT YOU KNOW WHAT I MEAN.
DID ALL THE WORK MYSELF. WELL, I WASN'T ABOUT TO LET SOME GET OF A BRICKIE IN ON WHAT I'D FOUND, WAS I, NOW?
AN' A TRAPDOOR AN' A FEW SUPPORT BEAMS IS NOT WHAT YOU'D CALL A MAJOR FEAT OF CONSTRUCTION.
I CHECKED UP ON THE MANU-SCRIPTS IN TRINITY LIBRARY, AN' IT APPEARS OUL' SAINT PATRICK STOPPED IN HERE ON HIS TRAVELS, WOULD YOU BELIEVE.
HE MUST'VE BLESSED IT AS A SHRINE, JOHN.
IT'S HOLY WATER.

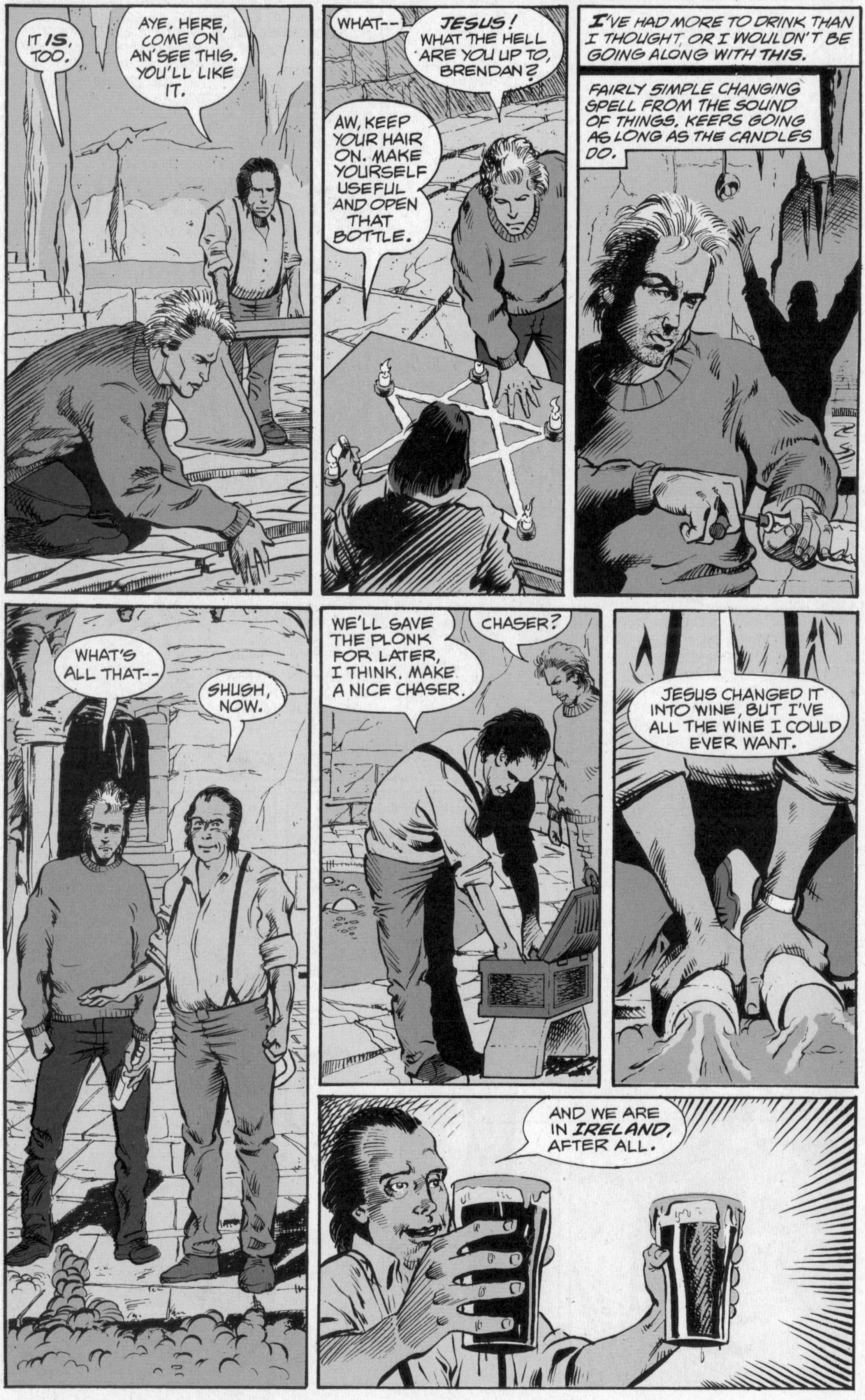

IT IS, TOO.
AYE. HERE, COME ON AN' SEE THIS. YOU'LL LIKE IT.
WHAT--
JESUS! WHAT THE HELL ARE YOU UP TO, BRENDAN?
AW, KEEP YOUR HAIR ON. MAKE YOURSELF USEFUL AND OPEN THAT BOTTLE.
I'VE HAD MORE TO DRINK THAN I THOUGHT, OR I WOULDN'T BE GOING ALONG WITH THIS.
FAIRLY SIMPLE CHANGING SPELL FROM THE SOUND OF THINGS. KEEPS GOING AS LONG AS THE CANDLES DO.
WHAT'S ALL THAT--
SHUSH, NOW.
WE'LL SAVE THE PLONK FOR LATER, I THINK. MAKE A NICE CHASER.
CHASER?
JESUS CHANGED IT INTO WINE, BUT I'VE ALL THE WINE I COULD EVER WANT.
AND WE ARE IN IRELAND, AFTER ALL.

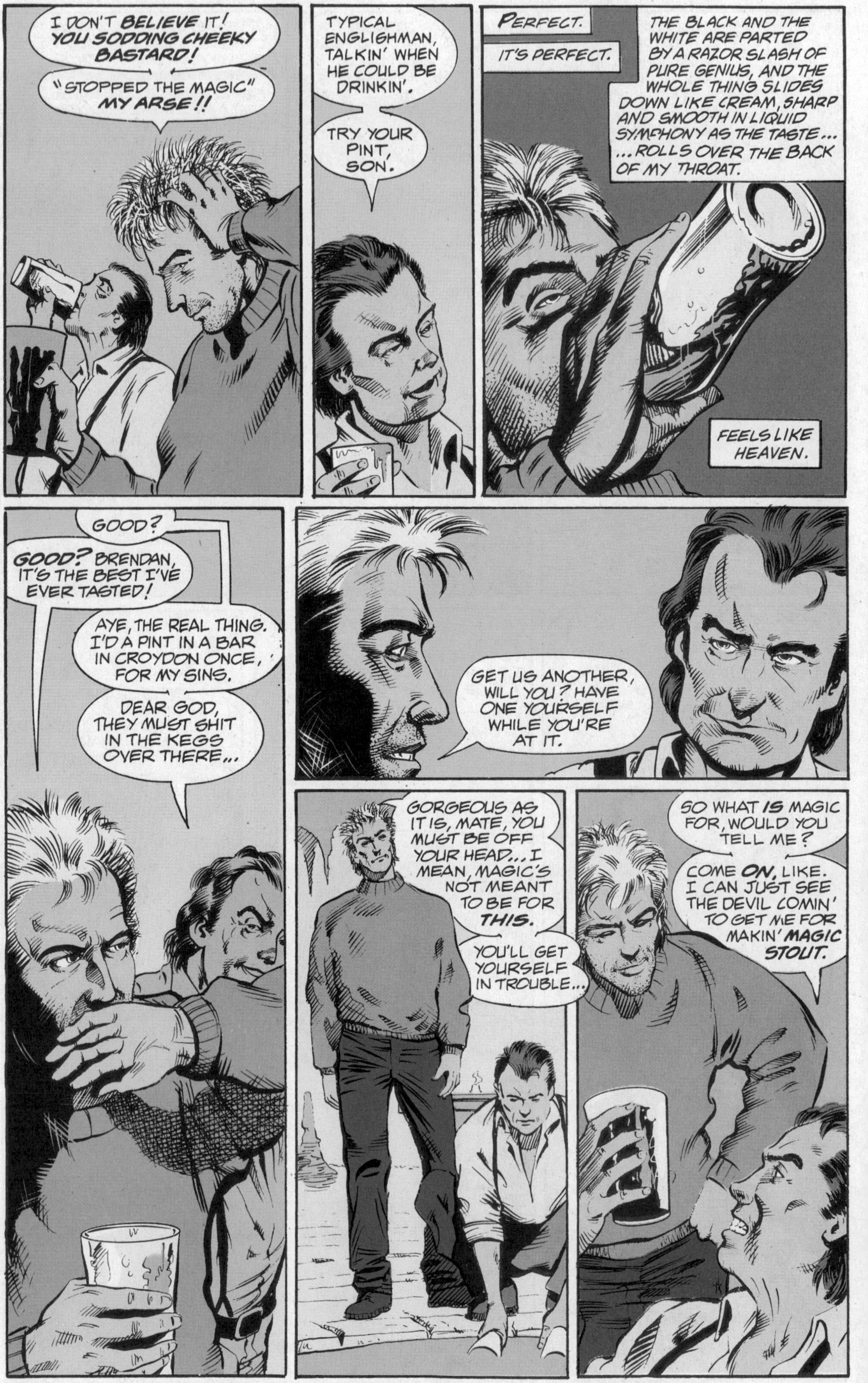
I DON'T BELIEVE IT! YOU SODDING CHEEKY BASTARD!
"STOPPED THE MAGIC" MY ARSE!!
TYPICAL ENGLISHMAN, TALKIN' WHEN HE COULD BE DRINKIN'.
TRY YOUR PINT, SON.
PERFECT.
IT'S PERFECT.
THE BLACK AND THE WHITE ARE PARTED BY A RAZOR SLASH OF PURE GENIUS, AND THE WHOLE THING SLIDES DOWN LIKE CREAM, SHARP AND SMOOTH IN LIQUID SYMPHONY AS THE TASTE... ...ROLLS OVER THE BACK OF MY THROAT.
FEELS LIKE HEAVEN.
GOOD?
GOOD? BRENDAN, IT'S THE BEST I'VE EVER TASTED!
AYE, THE REAL THING. I'D A PINT IN A BAR IN CROYDON ONCE, FOR MY SINS.
DEAR GOD, THEY MUST SHIT IN THE KEGS OVER THERE...
GET US ANOTHER, WILL YOU? HAVE ONE YOURSELF WHILE YOU'RE AT IT.
GORGEOUS AS IT IS, MATE, YOU MUST BE OFF YOUR HEAD... I MEAN, MAGIC'S NOT MEANT TO BE FOR THIS.
YOU'LL GET YOURSELF IN TROUBLE...
SO WHAT IS MAGIC FOR, WOULD YOU TELL ME?
COME ON, LIKE. I CAN JUST SEE THE DEVIL COMIN' TO GET ME FOR MAKIN' MAGIC STOUT.

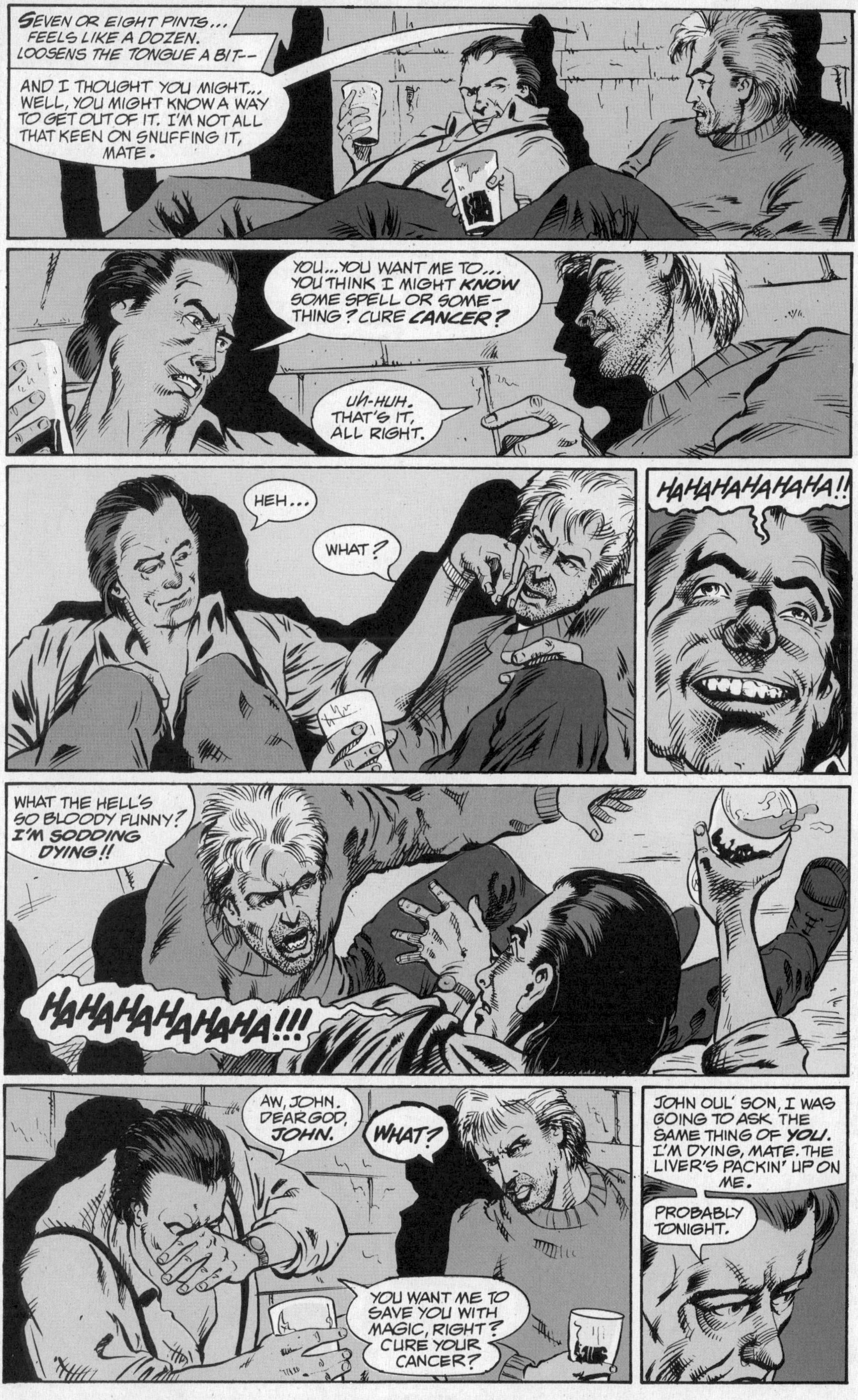
SEVEN OR EIGHT PINTS... FEELS LIKE A DOZEN. LOOSENS THE TONGUE A BIT--
AND I THOUGHT YOU MIGHT... WELL, YOU MIGHT KNOW A WAY TO GET OUT OF IT. I'M NOT ALL THAT KEEN ON SNUFFING IT, MATE.
YOU...YOU WANT ME TO... YOU THINK I MIGHT KNOW SOME SPELL OR SOMETHING? CURE CANCER?
UH-HUH. THAT'S IT, ALL RIGHT.
HEH...
WHAT?
HAHAHAHAHAHA!!
WHAT THE HELL'S SO BLOODY FUNNY? I'M SODDING DYING!!
HAHAHAHAHAHA!!!
AW, JOHN. DEAR GOD, JOHN.
WHAT?
YOU WANT ME TO SAVE YOU WITH MAGIC, RIGHT? CURE YOUR CANCER?
JOHN OUL' SON, I WAS GOING TO ASK THE SAME THING OF YOU. I'M DYING, MATE. THE LIVER'S PACKIN' UP ON ME.
PROBABLY TONIGHT.

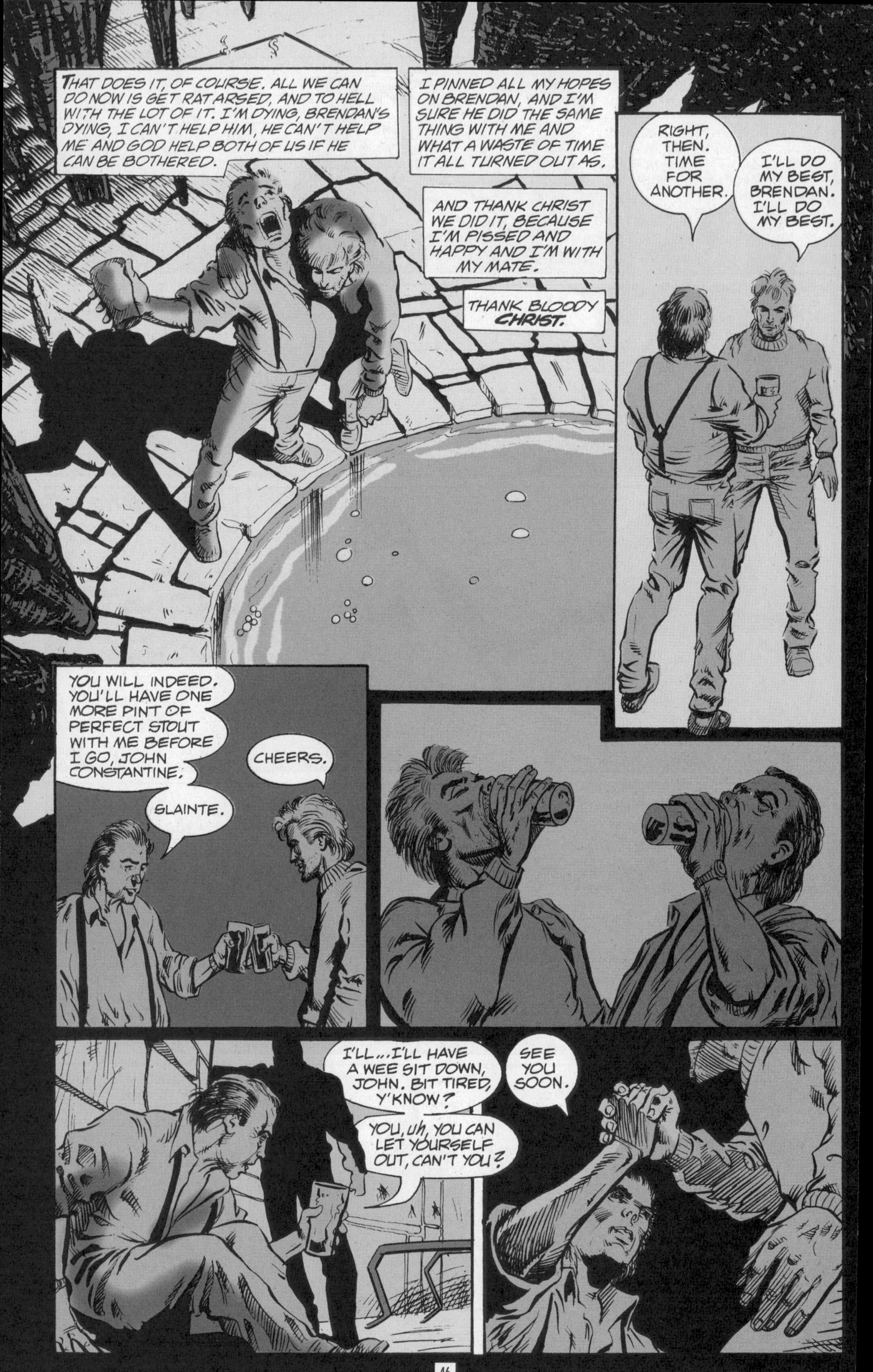
THAT DOES IT, OF COURSE. ALL WE CAN DO NOW IS GET RAT ARSED, AND TO HELL WITH THE LOT OF IT. I'M DYING, BRENDAN'S DYING, I CAN'T HELP HIM, HE CAN'T HELP ME AND GOD HELP BOTH OF US IF HE CAN BE BOTHERED.
I PINNED ALL MY HOPES ON BRENDAN, AND I'M SURE HE DID THE SAME THING WITH ME AND WHAT A WASTE OF TIME IT ALL TURNED OUT AS.
AND THANK CHRIST WE DID IT, BECAUSE I'M PISSED AND HAPPY AND I'M WITH MY MATE.
THANK BLOODY CHRIST.
RIGHT, THEN. TIME FOR ANOTHER.
I'LL DO MY BEST, BRENDAN. I'LL DO MY BEST.
YOU WILL INDEED. YOU'LL HAVE ONE MORE PINT OF PERFECT STOUT WITH ME BEFORE I GO, JOHN CONSTANTINE.
CHEERS.
SLAINTE.
I'LL... I'LL HAVE A WEE SIT DOWN, JOHN. BIT TIRED, Y'KNOW?
YOU, UH, YOU CAN LET YOURSELF OUT, CAN'T YOU?
SEE YOU SOON.

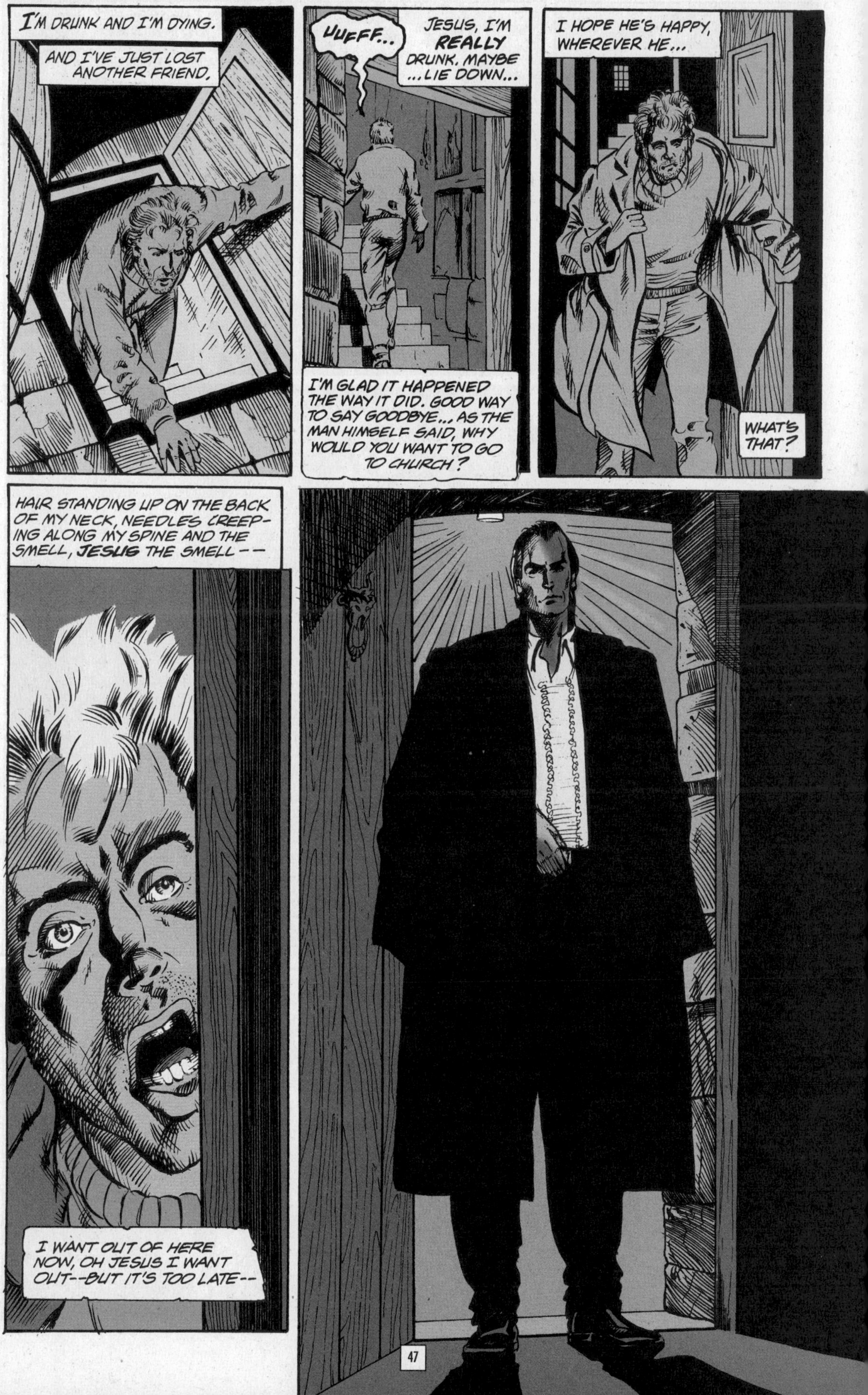
I'M DRUNK AND I'M DYING.
AND I'VE JUST LOST ANOTHER FRIEND.
UUFFF...
JESUS, I'M REALLY DRUNK. MAYBE ...LIE DOWN...
I'M GLAD IT HAPPENED THE WAY IT DID. GOOD WAY TO SAY GOODBYE... AS THE MAN HIMSELF SAID, WHY WOULD YOU WANT TO GO TO CHURCH?
I HOPE HE'S HAPPY, WHEREVER HE...
WHAT'S THAT?
HAIR STANDING UP ON THE BACK OF MY NECK, NEEDLES CREEP-ING ALONG MY SPINE AND THE SMELL, JESUS THE SMELL--
I WANT OUT OF HERE NOW, OH JESUS I WANT OUT--BUT IT'S TOO LATE--

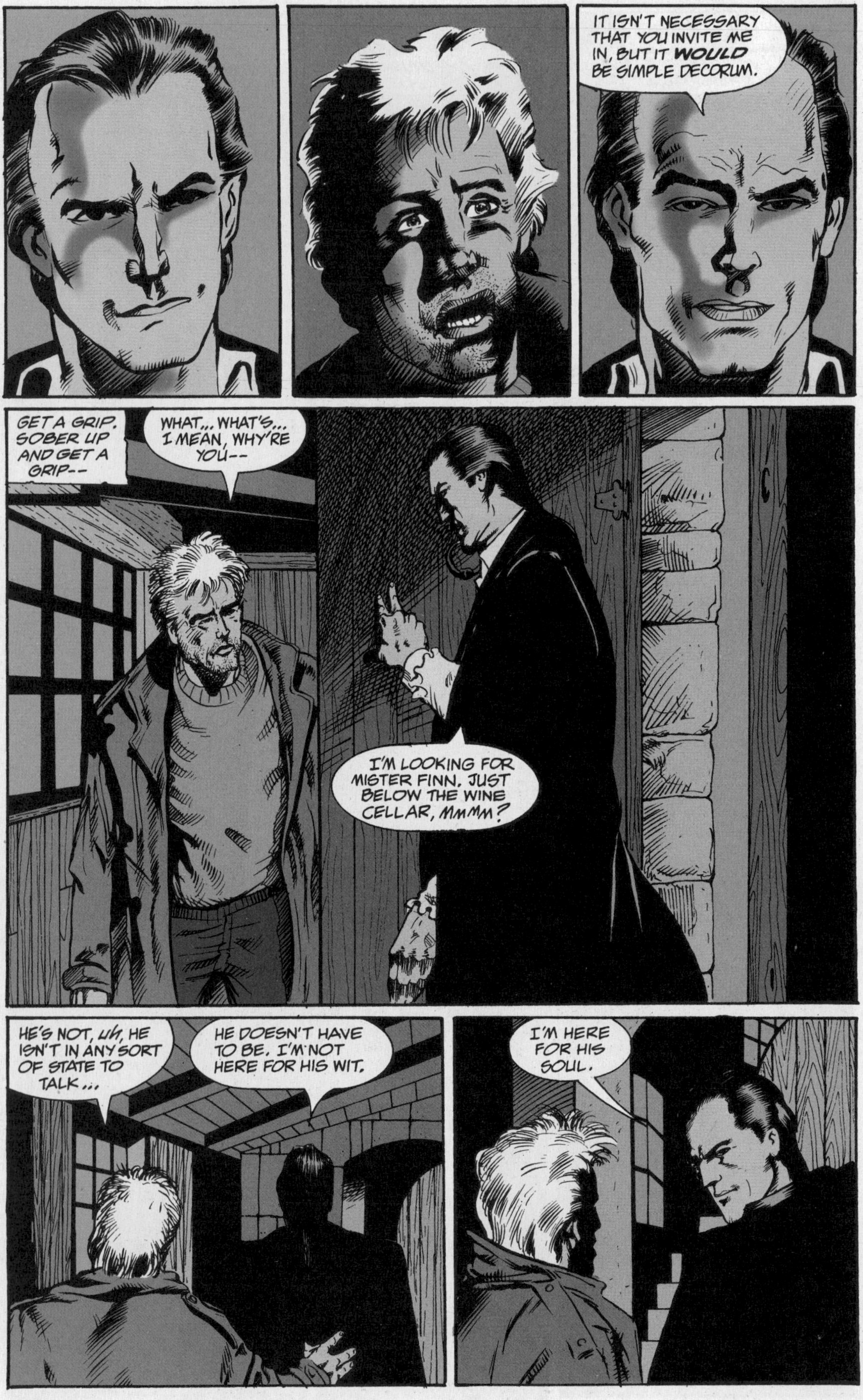
IT ISN'T NECESSARY THAT YOU INVITE ME IN, BUT IT WOULD BE SIMPLE DECORUM.
GET A GRIP. SOBER UP AND GET A GRIP--
WHAT... WHAT'S... I MEAN, WHY'RE YOU--
I'M LOOKING FOR MISTER FINN. JUST BELOW THE WINE CELLAR, MMMM?
HE'S NOT, UH, HE ISN'T IN ANY SORT OF STATE TO TALK...
HE DOESN'T HAVE TO BE. I'M NOT HERE FOR HIS WIT.
I'M HERE FOR HIS SOUL.

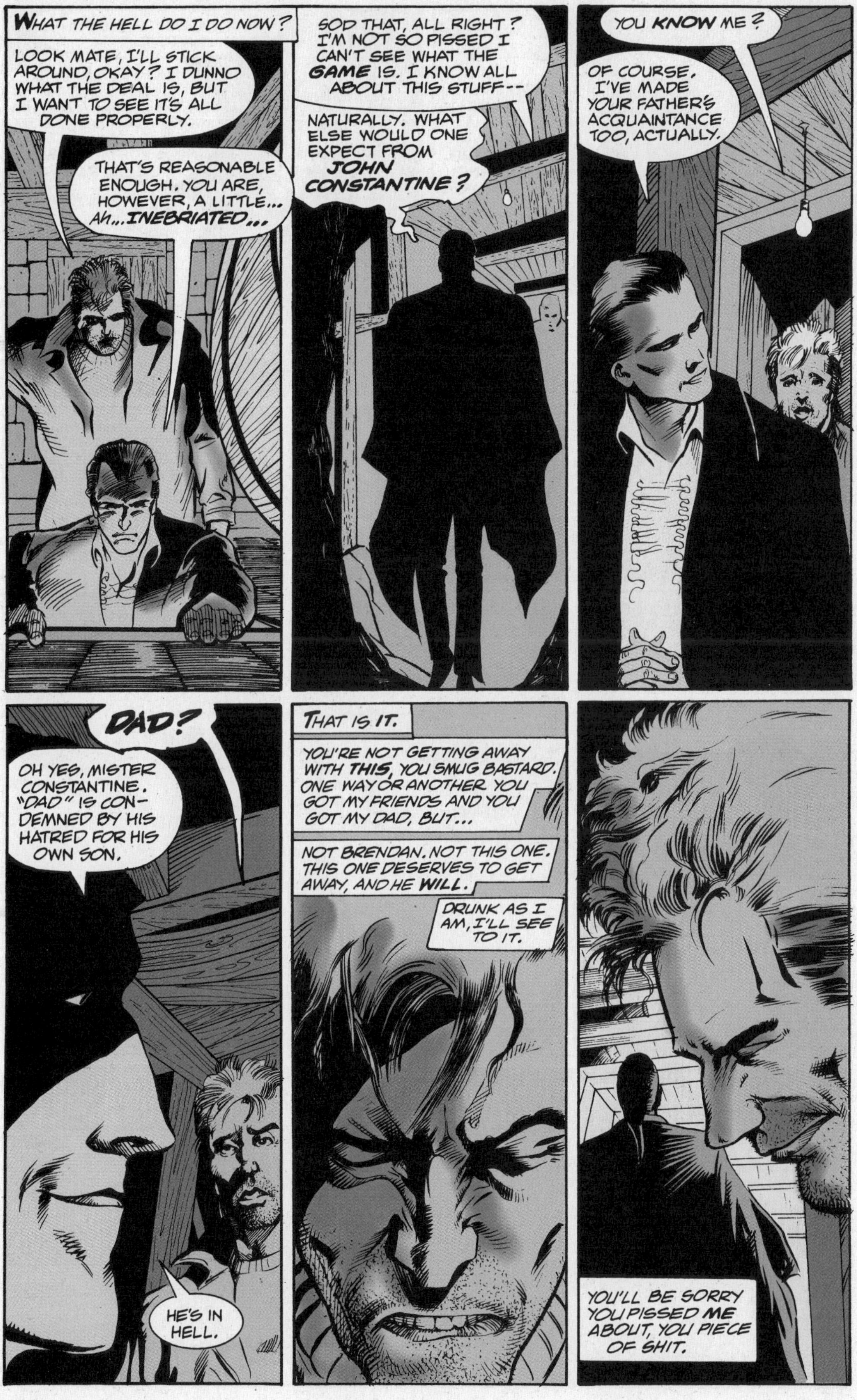

WHAT THE HELL DO I DO NOW?
LOOK MATE, I'LL STICK AROUND, OKAY? I DUNNO WHAT THE DEAL IS, BUT I WANT TO SEE IT'S ALL DONE PROPERLY.
THAT'S REASONABLE ENOUGH. YOU ARE, HOWEVER, A LITTLE... AH... INEBRIATED...
SOD THAT, ALL RIGHT? I'M NOT SO PISSED I CAN'T SEE WHAT THE GAME IS. I KNOW ALL ABOUT THIS STUFF--
NATURALLY. WHAT ELSE WOULD ONE EXPECT FROM JOHN CONSTANTINE?
YOU KNOW ME?
OF COURSE. I'VE MADE YOUR FATHER'S ACQUAINTANCE TOO, ACTUALLY.
DAD?
OH YES, MISTER CONSTANTINE. "DAD" IS CONDEMNED BY HIS HATRED FOR HIS OWN SON.
HE'S IN HELL.
THAT IS IT.
YOU'RE NOT GETTING AWAY WITH THIS, YOU SMUG BASTARD. ONE WAY OR ANOTHER YOU GOT MY FRIENDS AND YOU GOT MY DAD, BUT...
NOT BRENDAN. NOT THIS ONE. THIS ONE DESERVES TO GET AWAY, AND HE WILL.
DRUNK AS I AM, I'LL SEE TO IT.
YOU'LL BE SORRY YOU PISSED ME ABOUT, YOU PIECE OF SHIT.

ESSENTIALLY, THE ARRANGEMENT WAS THAT BRENDAN FINN WOULD GAIN THE EXPERTISE AND POWER TO AMASS A COLLECTION OF THE FINEST DRINK EVER TASTED.

I THINK YOU'LL AGREE HE DID PRECISELY THAT.

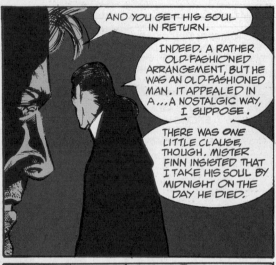

AND YOU GET HIS SOUL IN RETURN.

INDEED. A RATHER OLD-FASHIONED ARRANGEMENT, BUT HE WAS AN OLD-FASHIONED MAN. IT APPEALED IN A...A NOSTALGIC WAY, I SUPPOSE.

THERE WAS *ONE* LITTLE CLAUSE, THOUGH. MISTER FINN INSISTED THAT I TAKE HIS SOUL BY MIDNIGHT ON THE DAY HE DIED.

IF I DIDN'T, THE WHOLE ARRANGEMENT WOULD BE NULL AND VOID, AND HE COULD GO TO HEAVEN.

I IMAGINE HE THOUGHT HIMSELF A GREAT MAN INDEED TO BARGAIN WITH THE DEVIL.

THAT APPEALED TOO, AND I INDULGED HIM, IF ONLY TO SWEETEN THE DEAL. A LITTLE EXTRA INCENTIVE. I'M SURE HE DREAMED OF SOMEHOW OUTSMARTING ME... MANY MORTALS THINK THAT WAY, AS I'M SURE YOU'RE AWARE.

BUT THEY DON'T OUTSMART ME. AND I'LL TELL YOU WHY.

THEY'RE MORTAL.

AND TO BE MORTAL IS TO BE STUPID, PROUD, CONCEITED-- AND ULTIMATELY PATHETIC.

AND THERE'S NOTHING MORE PATHETIC THAN A *DRUNKARD*.

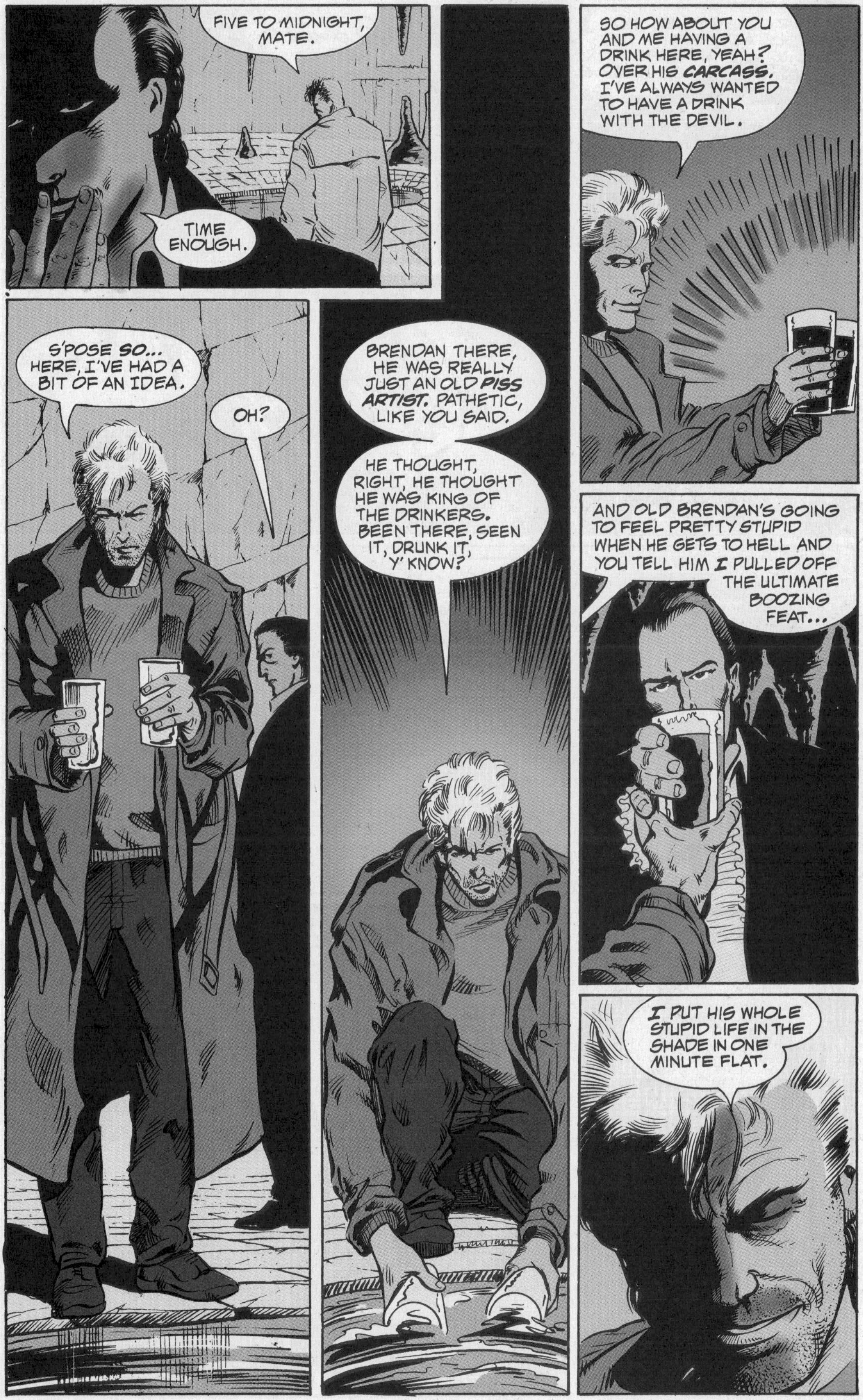
FIVE TO MIDNIGHT, MATE.
TIME ENOUGH.
S'POSE SO... HERE, I'VE HAD A BIT OF AN IDEA.
OH?
BRENDAN THERE, HE WAS REALLY JUST AN OLD PISS ARTIST. PATHETIC, LIKE YOU SAID.
HE THOUGHT, RIGHT, HE THOUGHT HE WAS KING OF THE DRINKERS. BEEN THERE, SEEN IT, DRUNK IT, Y' KNOW?
SO HOW ABOUT YOU AND ME HAVING A DRINK HERE, YEAH? OVER HIS CARCASS. I'VE ALWAYS WANTED TO HAVE A DRINK WITH THE DEVIL.
AND OLD BRENDAN'S GOING TO FEEL PRETTY STUPID WHEN HE GETS TO HELL AND YOU TELL HIM I PULLED OFF THE ULTIMATE BOOZING FEAT...
I PUT HIS WHOLE STUPID LIFE IN THE SHADE IN ONE MINUTE FLAT.

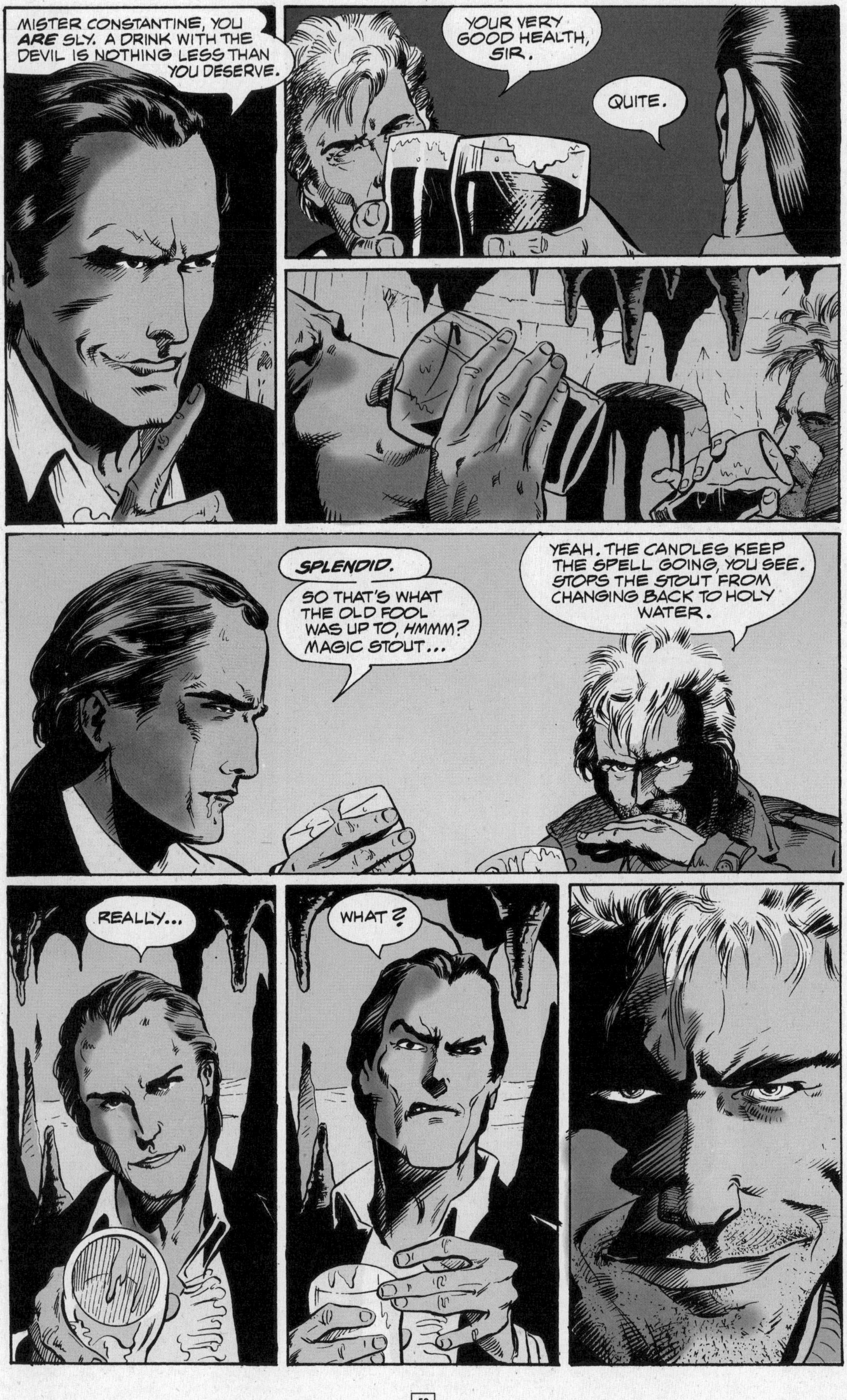
MISTER CONSTANTINE, YOU **ARE** SLY. A DRINK WITH THE DEVIL IS NOTHING LESS THAN YOU DESERVE.
YOUR VERY GOOD HEALTH, SIR.
QUITE.
SPLENDID.
SO THAT'S WHAT THE OLD FOOL WAS UP TO, *HMMM?* MAGIC STOUT...
YEAH. THE CANDLES KEEP THE SPELL GOING, YOU SEE. STOPS THE STOUT FROM CHANGING BACK TO HOLY WATER.
REALLY...
WHAT?

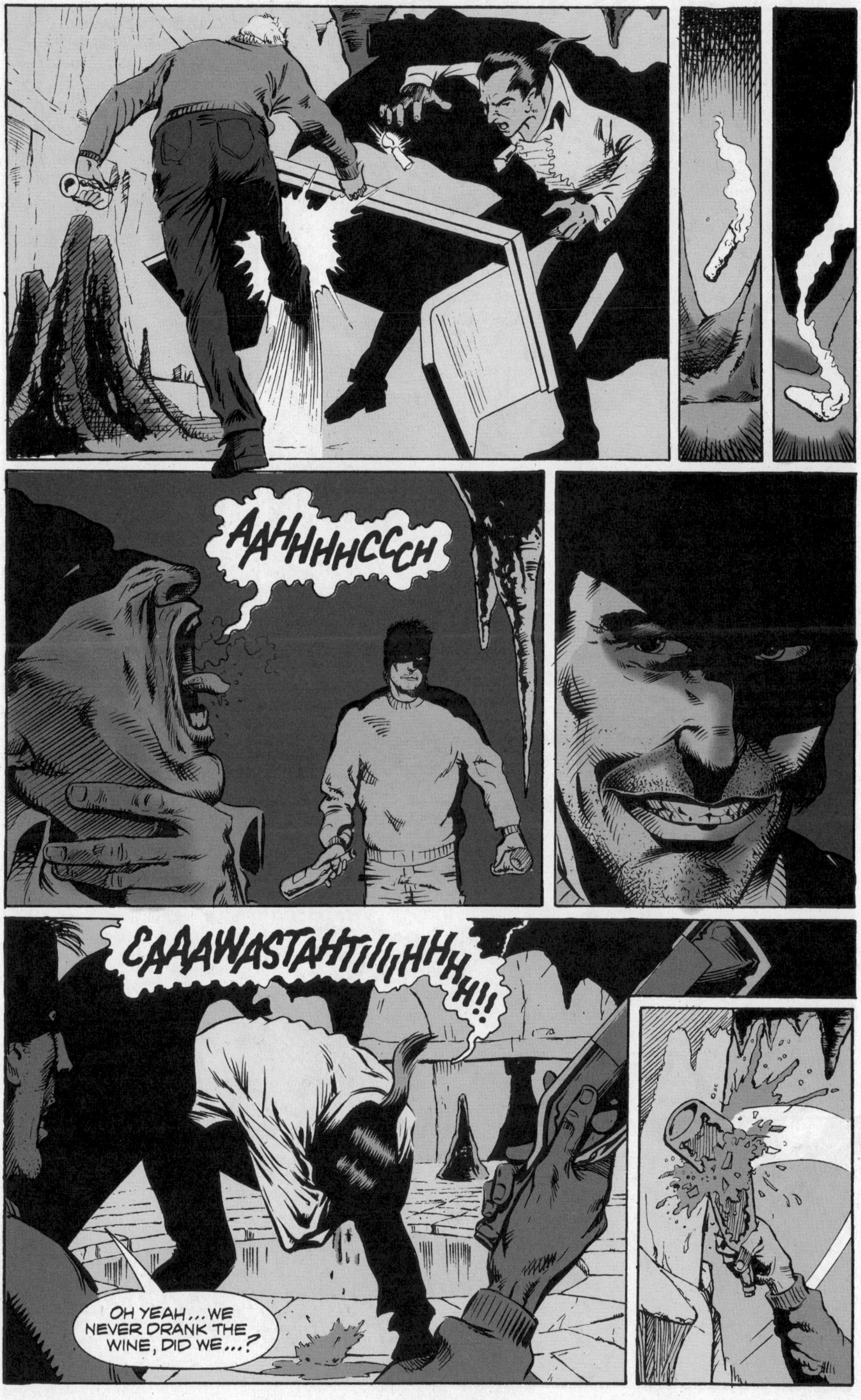
AAHHHHCCCCH
CAAAWASTAHTIIIIHHHH!!
OH YEAH... WE NEVER DRANK THE WINE, DID WE...?

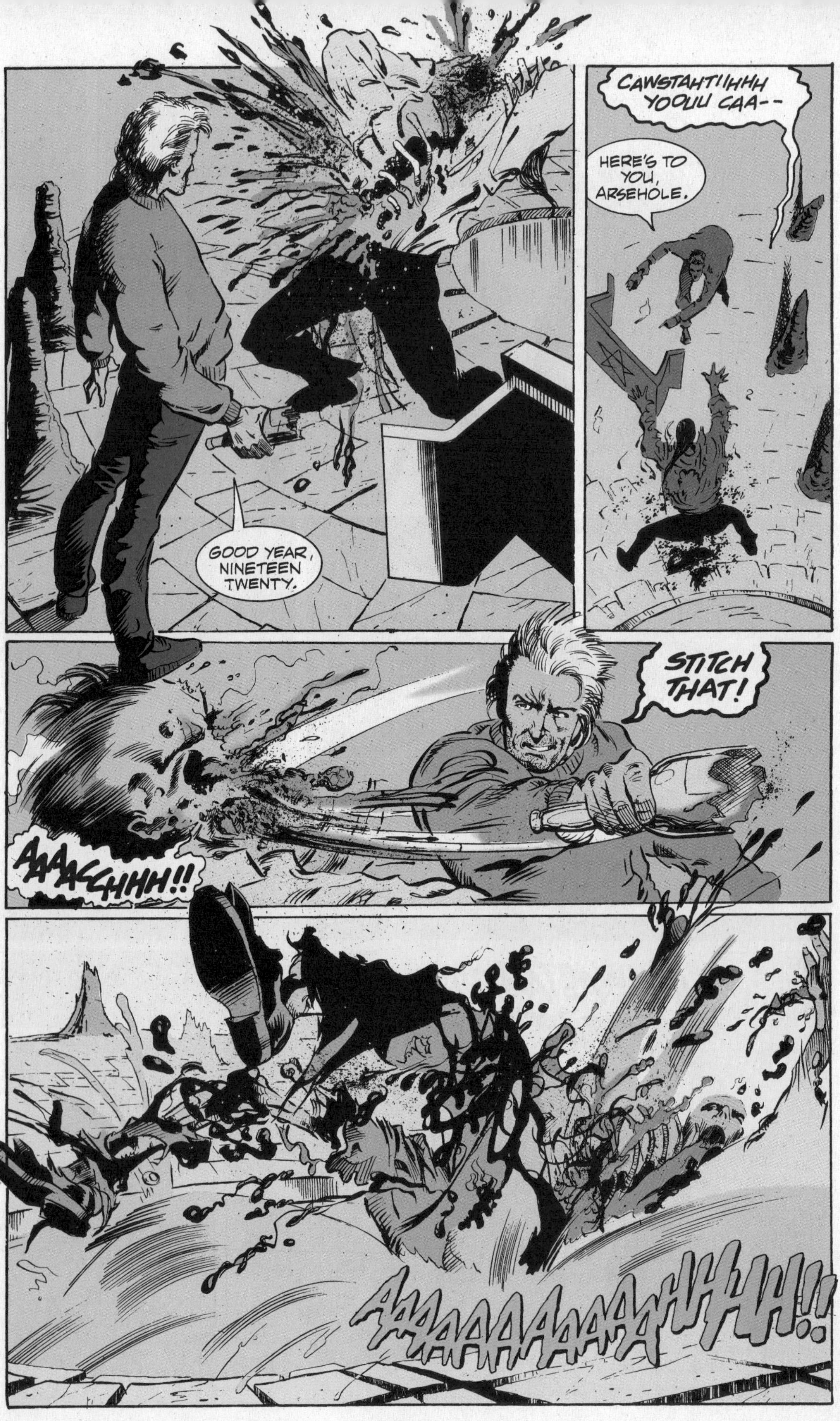
GOOD YEAR, NINETEEN TWENTY.
CAWSTAHT!!HHH YOOUU CAA--
HERE'S TO YOU, ARSEHOLE.
STITCH THAT!
AAAACCHHH!!
AAAAAAAAAAAHHHHH!!

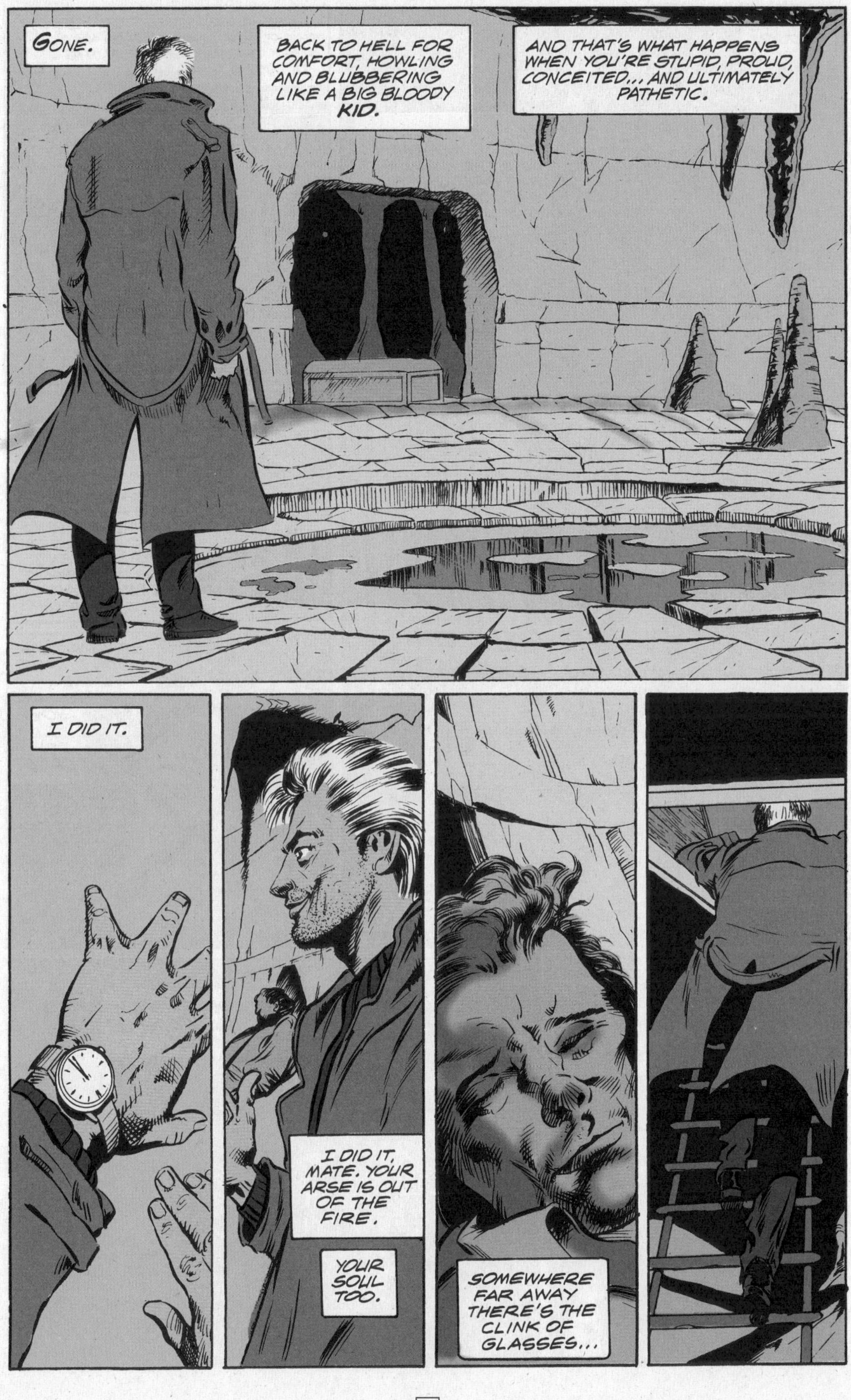
GONE.
BACK TO HELL FOR COMFORT, HOWLING AND BLUBBERING LIKE A BIG BLOODY KID.
AND THAT'S WHAT HAPPENS WHEN YOU'RE STUPID, PROUD, CONCEITED... AND ULTIMATELY PATHETIC.
I DID IT.
I DID IT, MATE. YOUR ARSE IS OUT OF THE FIRE.
YOUR SOUL TOO.
SOMEWHERE FAR AWAY THERE'S THE CLINK OF GLASSES...

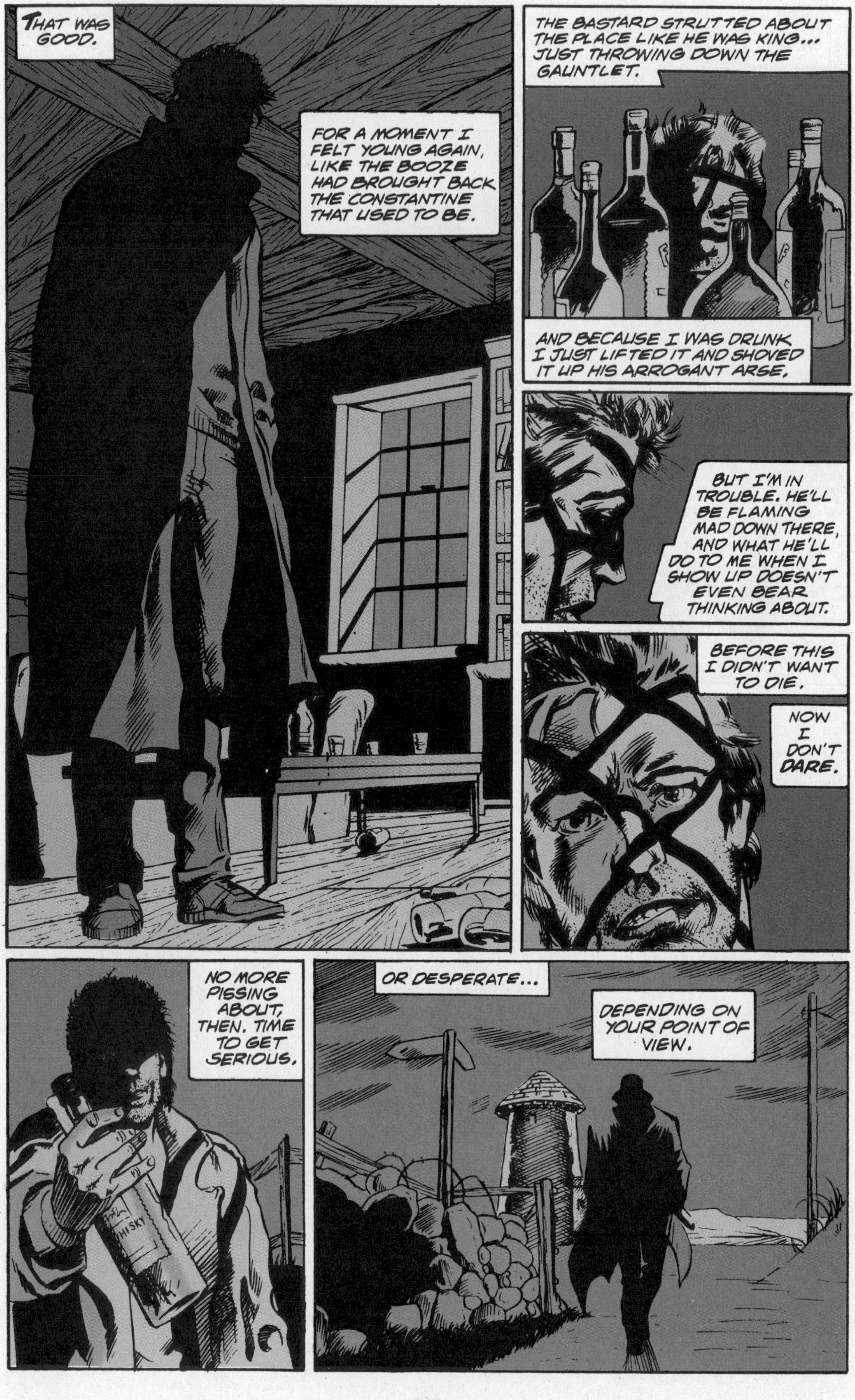
THAT WAS GOOD.
FOR A MOMENT I FELT YOUNG AGAIN, LIKE THE BOOZE HAD BROUGHT BACK THE CONSTANTINE THAT USED TO BE.
THE BASTARD STRUTTED ABOUT THE PLACE LIKE HE WAS KING... JUST THROWING DOWN THE GAUNTLET.
AND BECAUSE I WAS DRUNK I JUST LIFTED IT AND SHOVED IT UP HIS ARROGANT ARSE.
BUT I'M IN TROUBLE. HE'LL BE FLAMING MAD DOWN THERE, AND WHAT HE'LL DO TO ME WHEN I SHOW UP DOESN'T EVEN BEAR THINKING ABOUT.
BEFORE THIS I DIDN'T WANT TO DIE.
NOW I DON'T DARE.
NO MORE PISSING ABOUT, THEN. TIME TO GET SERIOUS.
OR DESPERATE...
DEPENDING ON YOUR POINT OF VIEW.

friends in high places

II

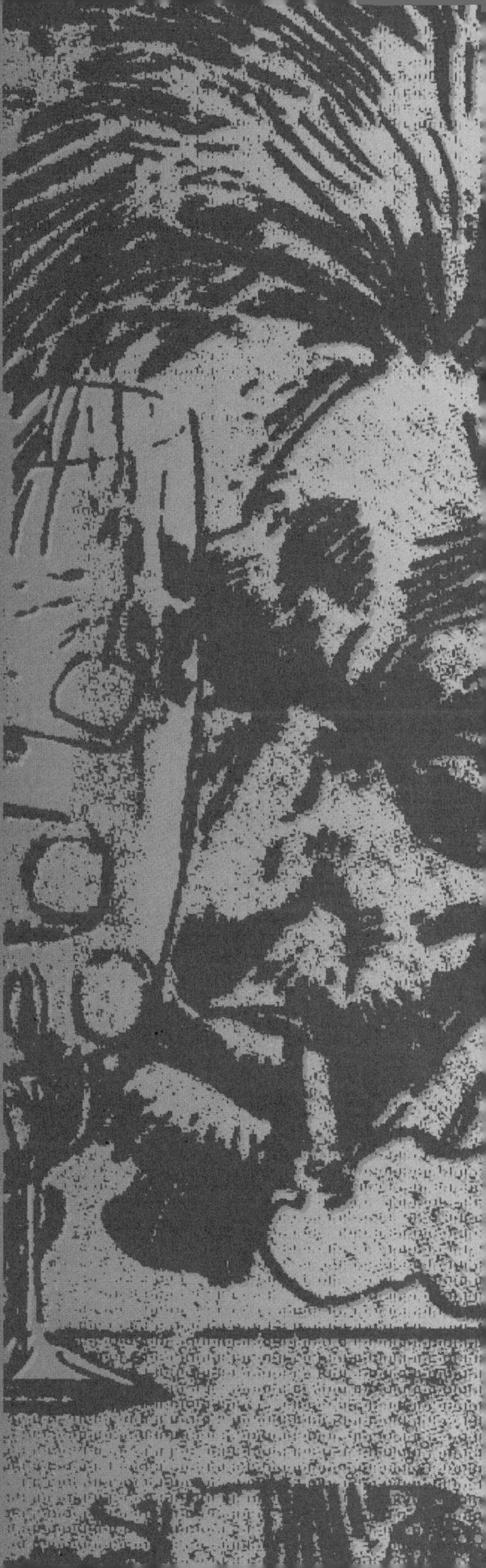

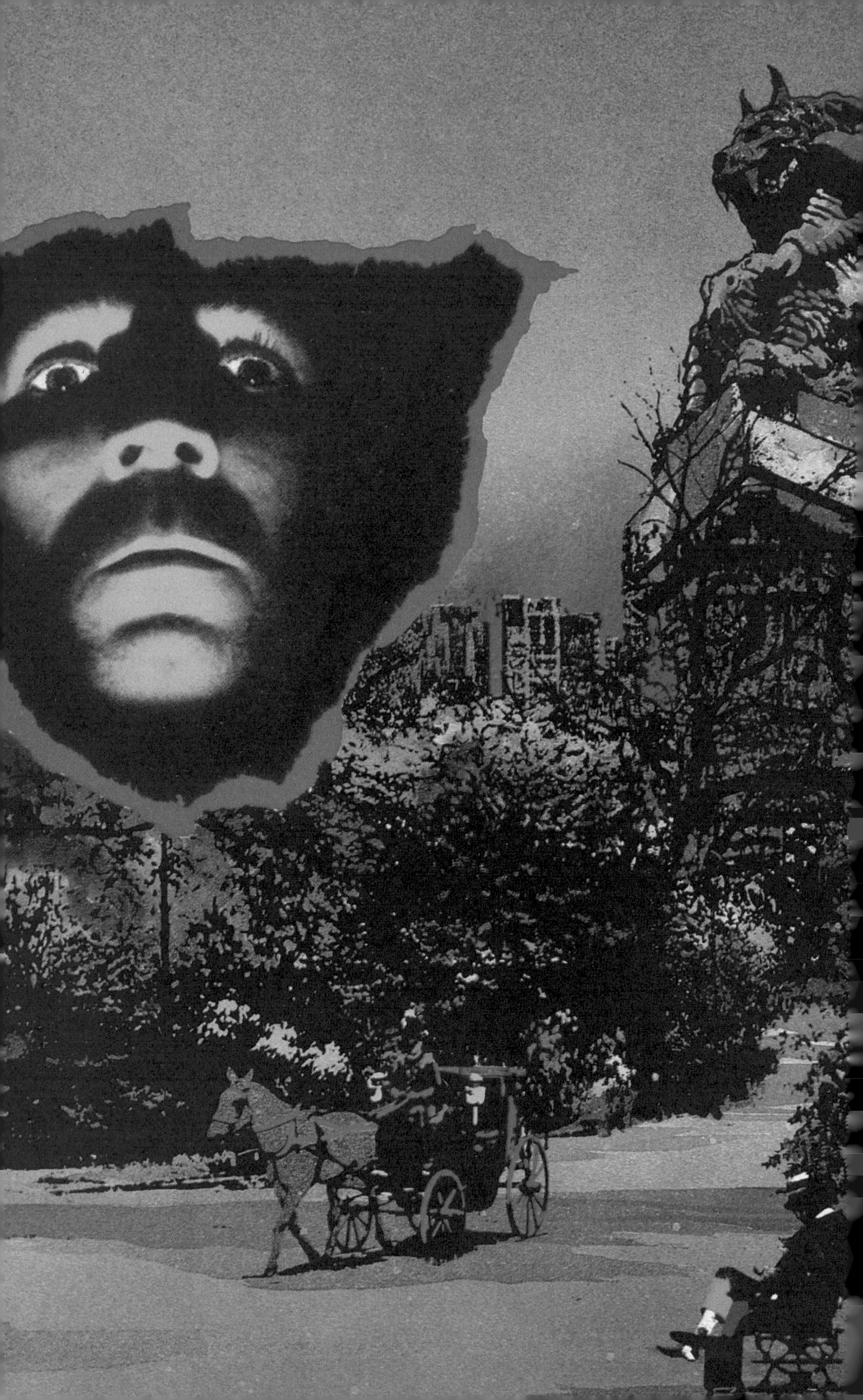

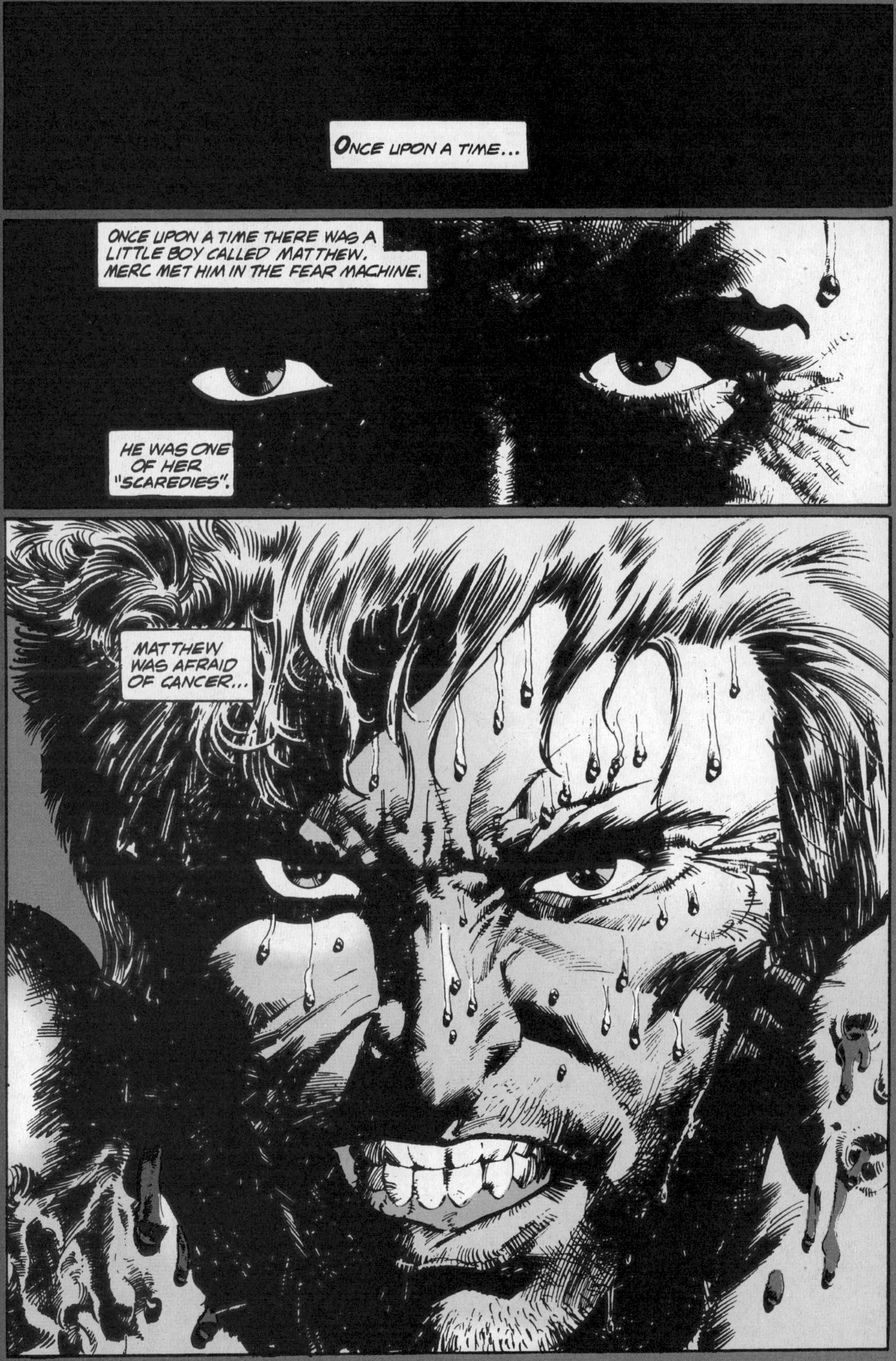

ONCE UPON A TIME...
ONCE UPON A TIME THERE WAS A LITTLE BOY CALLED MATTHEW. MERC MET HIM IN THE FEAR MACHINE.
HE WAS ONE OF HER "SCAREDIES".
MATTHEW WAS AFRAID OF CANCER...

I CAN SEE WHY.
FRIENDS IN HIGH PLACES
DANGEROUS HABITS, PART THREE

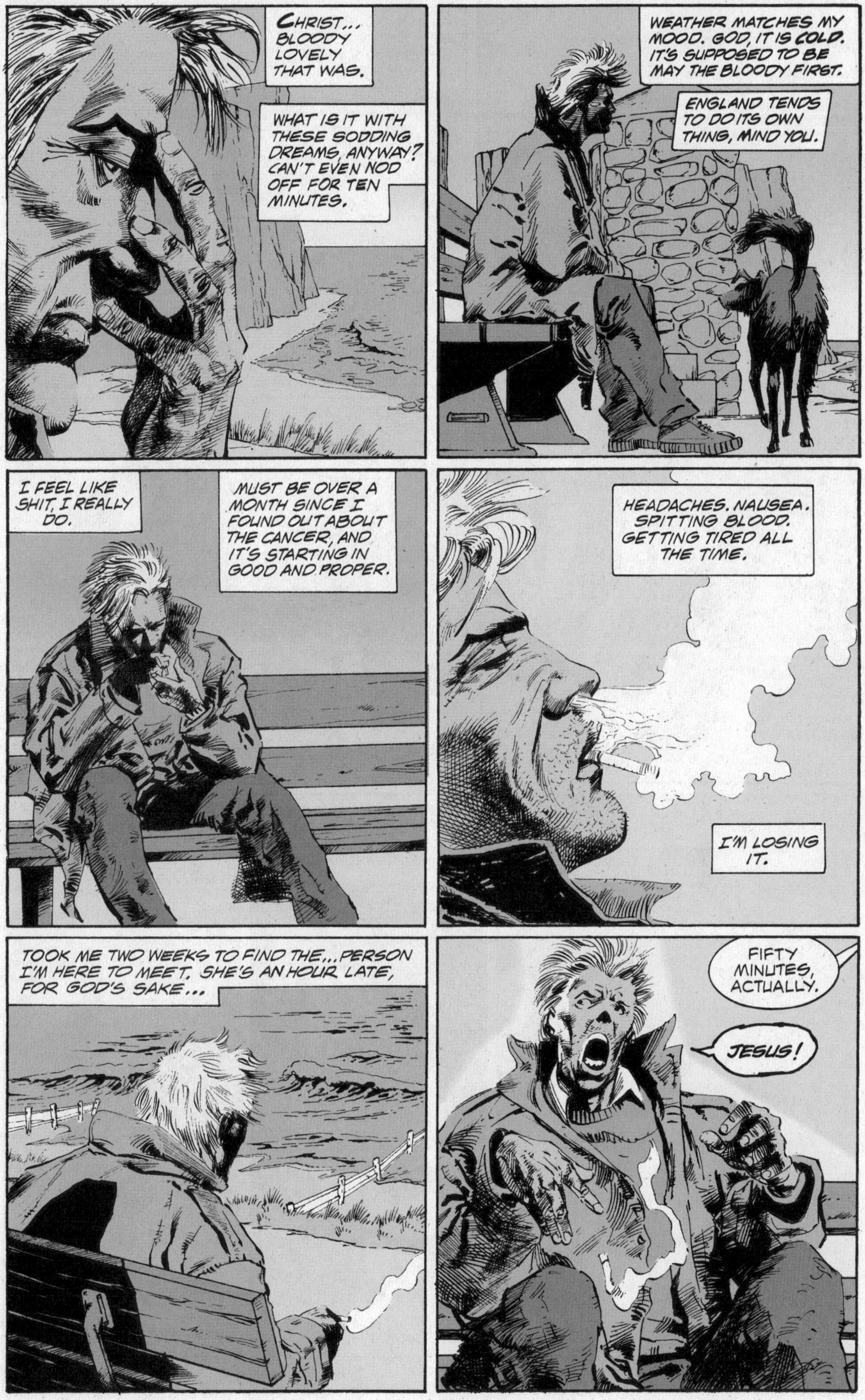
CHRIST... BLOODY LOVELY THAT WAS.
WHAT IS IT WITH THESE SODDING DREAMS, ANYWAY? CAN'T EVEN NOD OFF FOR TEN MINUTES.
WEATHER MATCHES MY MOOD. GOD, IT IS COLD. IT'S SUPPOSED TO BE MAY THE BLOODY FIRST.
ENGLAND TENDS TO DO ITS OWN THING, MIND YOU.
I FEEL LIKE SHIT, I REALLY DO.
MUST BE OVER A MONTH SINCE I FOUND OUT ABOUT THE CANCER, AND IT'S STARTING IN GOOD AND PROPER.
HEADACHES. NAUSEA. SPITTING BLOOD. GETTING TIRED ALL THE TIME.
I'M LOSING IT.
TOOK ME TWO WEEKS TO FIND THE... PERSON I'M HERE TO MEET. SHE'S AN HOUR LATE, FOR GOD'S SAKE...
FIFTY MINUTES, ACTUALLY.
JESUS!

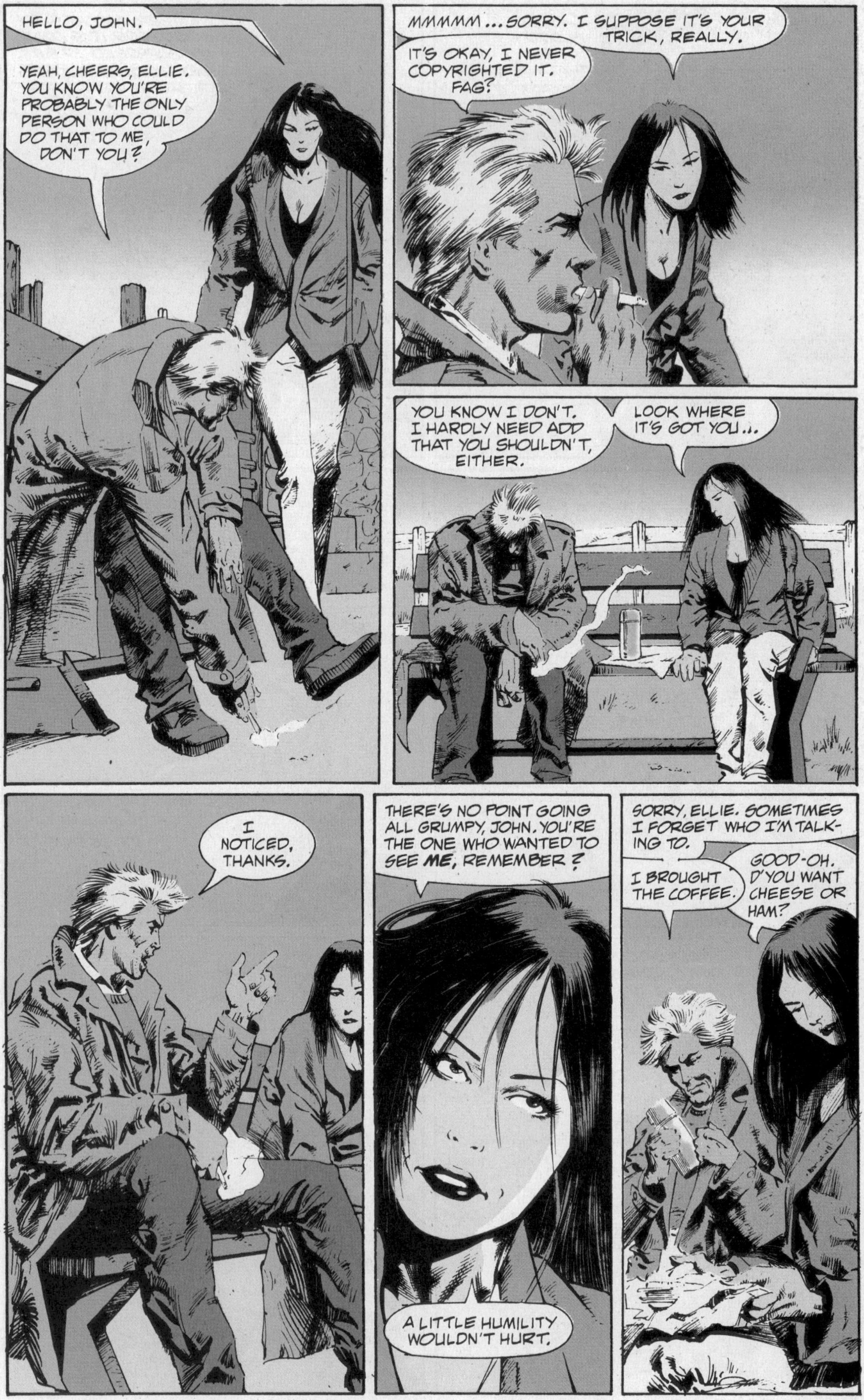

HELLO, JOHN.
YEAH, CHEERS, ELLIE. YOU KNOW YOU'RE PROBABLY THE ONLY PERSON WHO COULD DO THAT TO ME, DON'T YOU?
MMMMM... SORRY. I SUPPOSE IT'S YOUR TRICK, REALLY.
IT'S OKAY, I NEVER COPYRIGHTED IT. FAG?
YOU KNOW I DON'T. I HARDLY NEED ADD THAT YOU SHOULDN'T, EITHER.
LOOK WHERE IT'S GOT YOU...
I NOTICED, THANKS.
THERE'S NO POINT GOING ALL GRUMPY, JOHN. YOU'RE THE ONE WHO WANTED TO SEE ME, REMEMBER?
A LITTLE HUMILITY WOULDN'T HURT.
SORRY, ELLIE. SOMETIMES I FORGET WHO I'M TALKING TO.
I BROUGHT THE COFFEE.
GOOD-OH. D'YOU WANT CHEESE OR HAM?

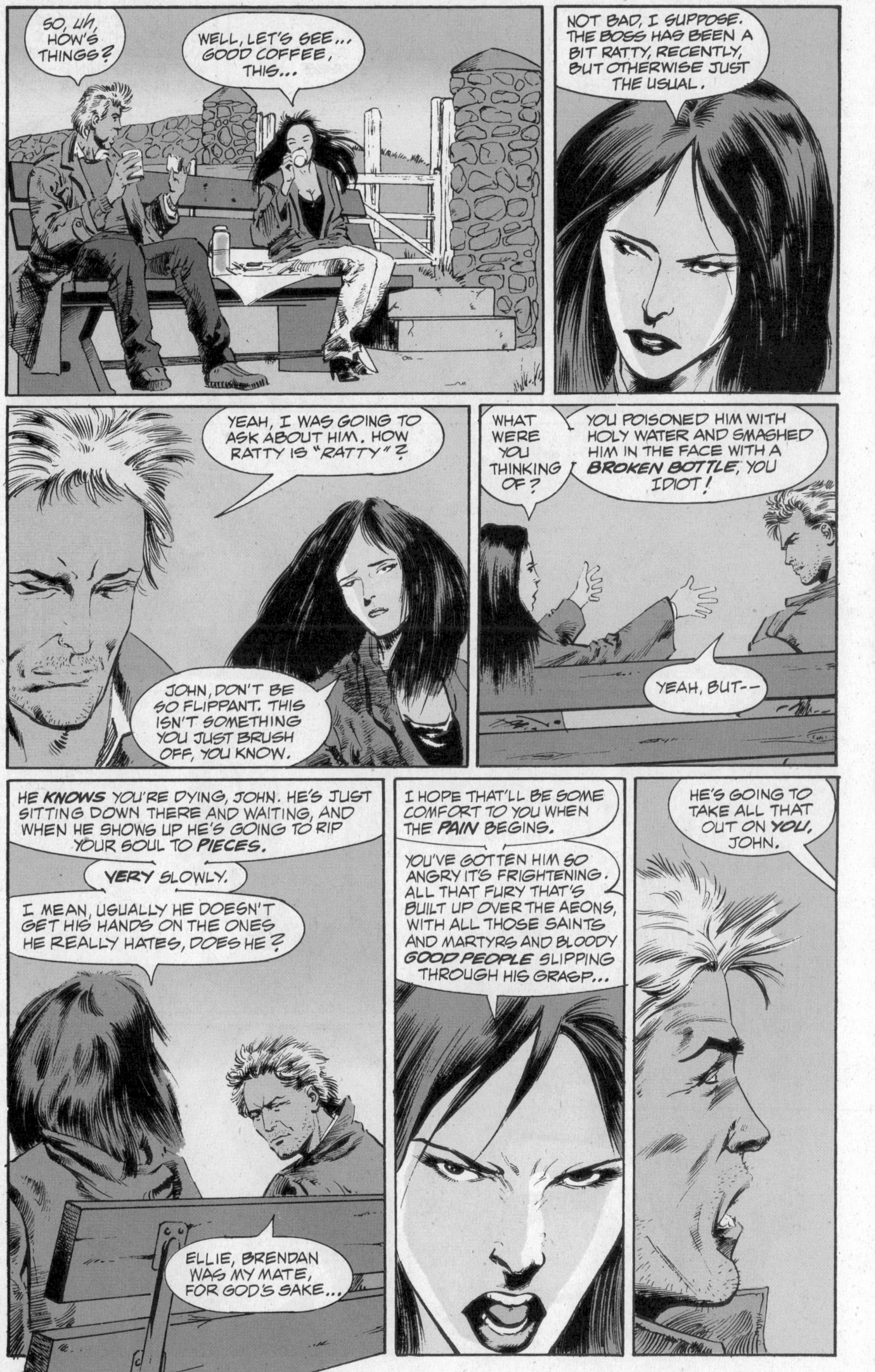
SO, UH, HOW'S THINGS?
WELL, LET'S SEE... GOOD COFFEE, THIS...
NOT BAD, I SUPPOSE. THE BOSS HAS BEEN A BIT RATTY, RECENTLY, BUT OTHERWISE JUST THE USUAL.
YEAH, I WAS GOING TO ASK ABOUT HIM. HOW RATTY IS "RATTY"?
JOHN, DON'T BE SO FLIPPANT. THIS ISN'T SOMETHING YOU JUST BRUSH OFF, YOU KNOW.
WHAT WERE YOU THINKING OF?
YOU POISONED HIM WITH HOLY WATER AND SMASHED HIM IN THE FACE WITH A BROKEN BOTTLE, YOU IDIOT!
YEAH, BUT--
HE KNOWS YOU'RE DYING, JOHN. HE'S JUST SITTING DOWN THERE AND WAITING, AND WHEN HE SHOWS UP HE'S GOING TO RIP YOUR SOUL TO PIECES.
VERY SLOWLY.
I MEAN, USUALLY HE DOESN'T GET HIS HANDS ON THE ONES HE REALLY HATES, DOES HE?
ELLIE, BRENDAN WAS MY MATE, FOR GOD'S SAKE...
I HOPE THAT'LL BE SOME COMFORT TO YOU WHEN THE PAIN BEGINS.
YOU'VE GOTTEN HIM SO ANGRY IT'S FRIGHTENING. ALL THAT FURY THAT'S BUILT UP OVER THE AEONS, WITH ALL THOSE SAINTS AND MARTYRS AND BLOODY GOOD PEOPLE SLIPPING THROUGH HIS GRASP...
HE'S GOING TO TAKE ALL THAT OUT ON YOU, JOHN.

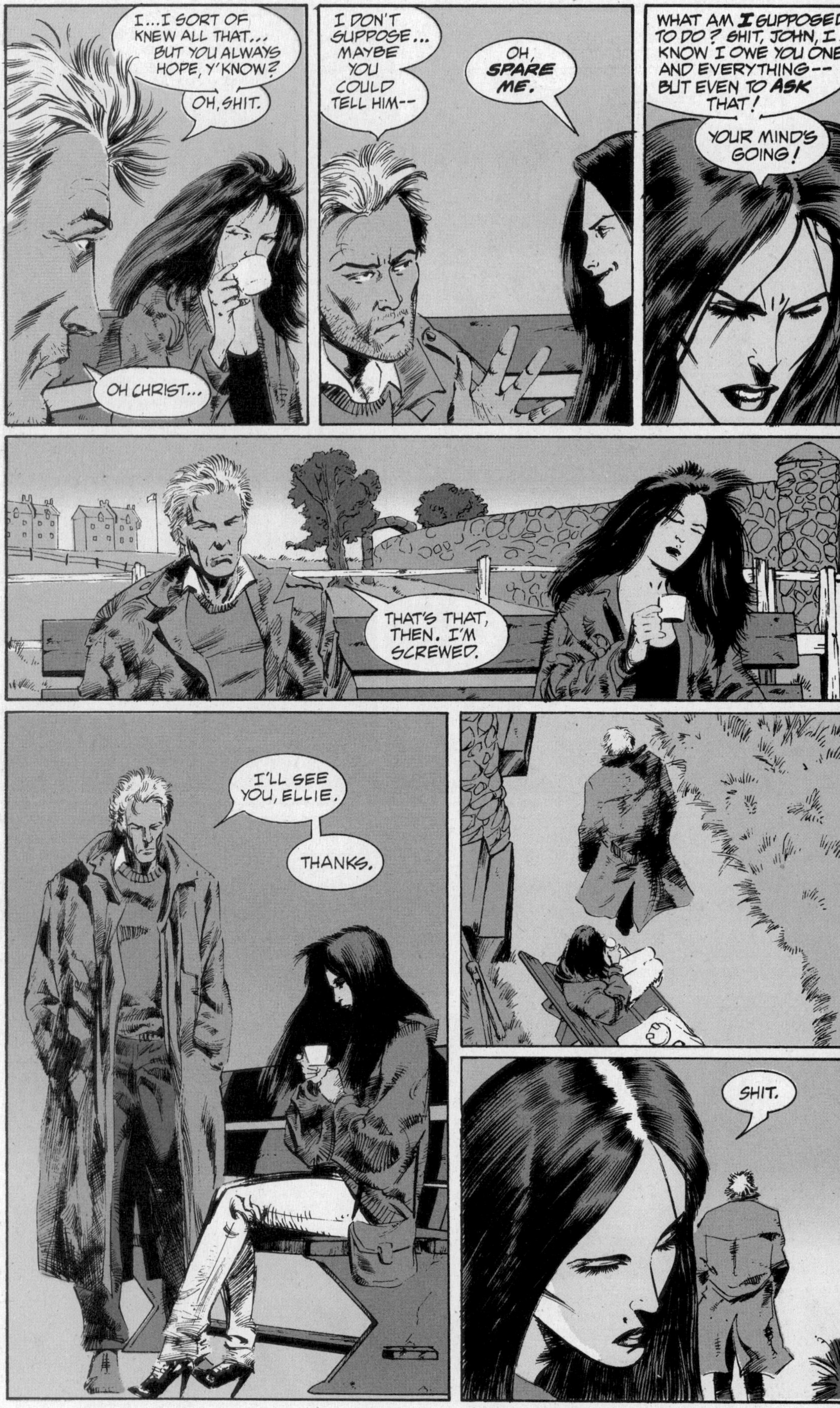
I...I SORT OF KNEW ALL THAT... BUT YOU ALWAYS HOPE, Y'KNOW?
OH, SHIT.
OH CHRIST...
I DON'T SUPPOSE... MAYBE YOU COULD TELL HIM--
OH, SPARE ME.
WHAT AM I SUPPOSED TO DO? SHIT, JOHN, I KNOW I OWE YOU ONE AND EVERYTHING-- BUT EVEN TO ASK THAT!
YOUR MIND'S GOING!
THAT'S THAT, THEN. I'M SCREWED.
I'LL SEE YOU, ELLIE.
THANKS.
SHIT.

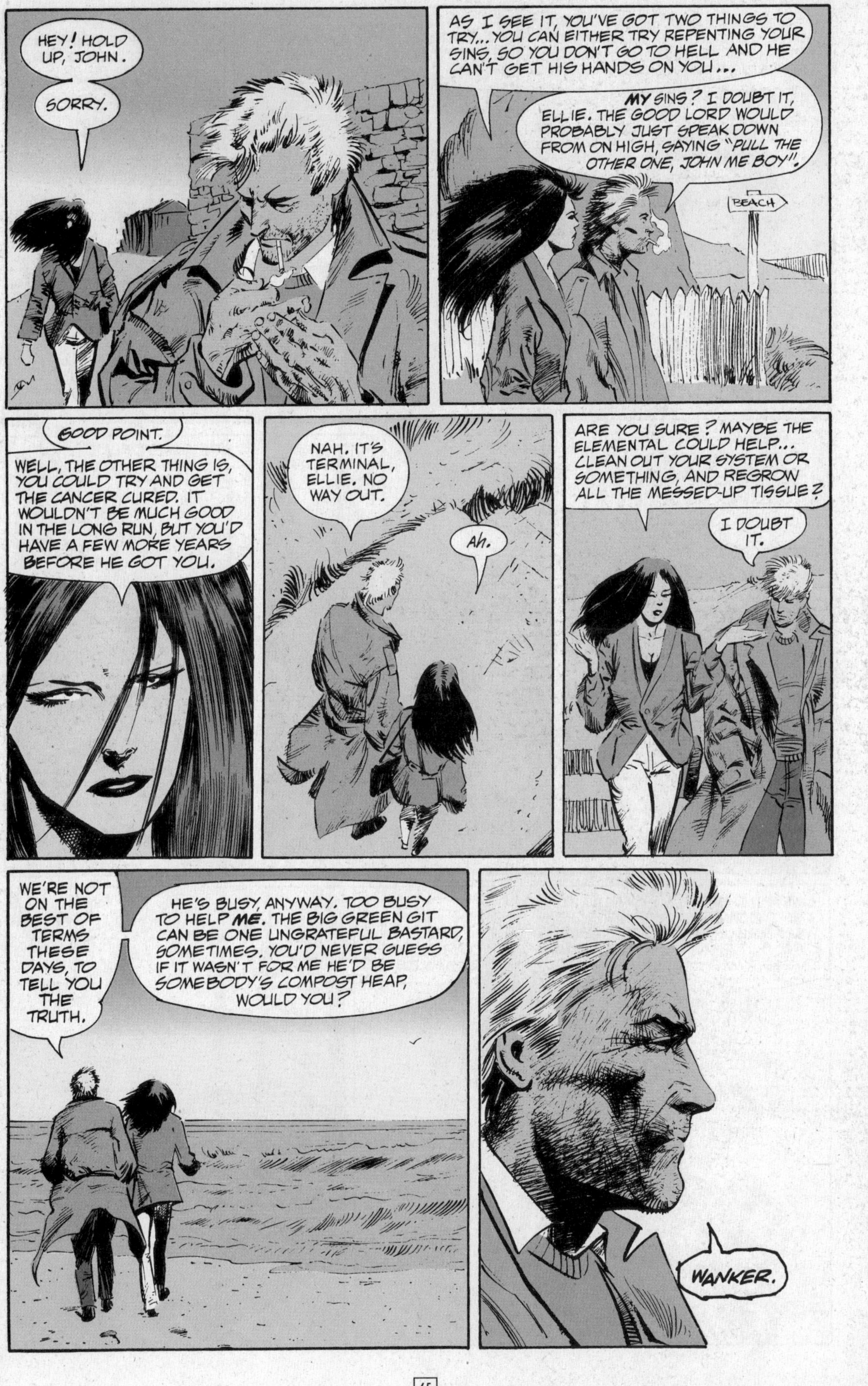
HEY! HOLD UP, JOHN.
SORRY.
AS I SEE IT, YOU'VE GOT TWO THINGS TO TRY... YOU CAN EITHER TRY REPENTING YOUR SINS, SO YOU DON'T GO TO HELL AND HE CAN'T GET HIS HANDS ON YOU...
MY SINS? I DOUBT IT, ELLIE. THE GOOD LORD WOULD PROBABLY JUST SPEAK DOWN FROM ON HIGH, SAYING "PULL THE OTHER ONE, JOHN ME BOY".
BEACH
GOOD POINT.
WELL, THE OTHER THING IS, YOU COULD TRY AND GET THE CANCER CURED. IT WOULDN'T BE MUCH GOOD IN THE LONG RUN, BUT YOU'D HAVE A FEW MORE YEARS BEFORE HE GOT YOU.
NAH. IT'S TERMINAL, ELLIE. NO WAY OUT.
Ah.
ARE YOU SURE? MAYBE THE ELEMENTAL COULD HELP... CLEAN OUT YOUR SYSTEM OR SOMETHING, AND REGROW ALL THE MESSED-UP TISSUE?
I DOUBT IT.
WE'RE NOT ON THE BEST OF TERMS THESE DAYS, TO TELL YOU THE TRUTH.
HE'S BUSY, ANYWAY. TOO BUSY TO HELP ME. THE BIG GREEN GIT CAN BE ONE UNGRATEFUL BASTARD, SOMETIMES. YOU'D NEVER GUESS IF IT WASN'T FOR ME HE'D BE SOMEBODY'S COMPOST HEAP, WOULD YOU?
WANKER.

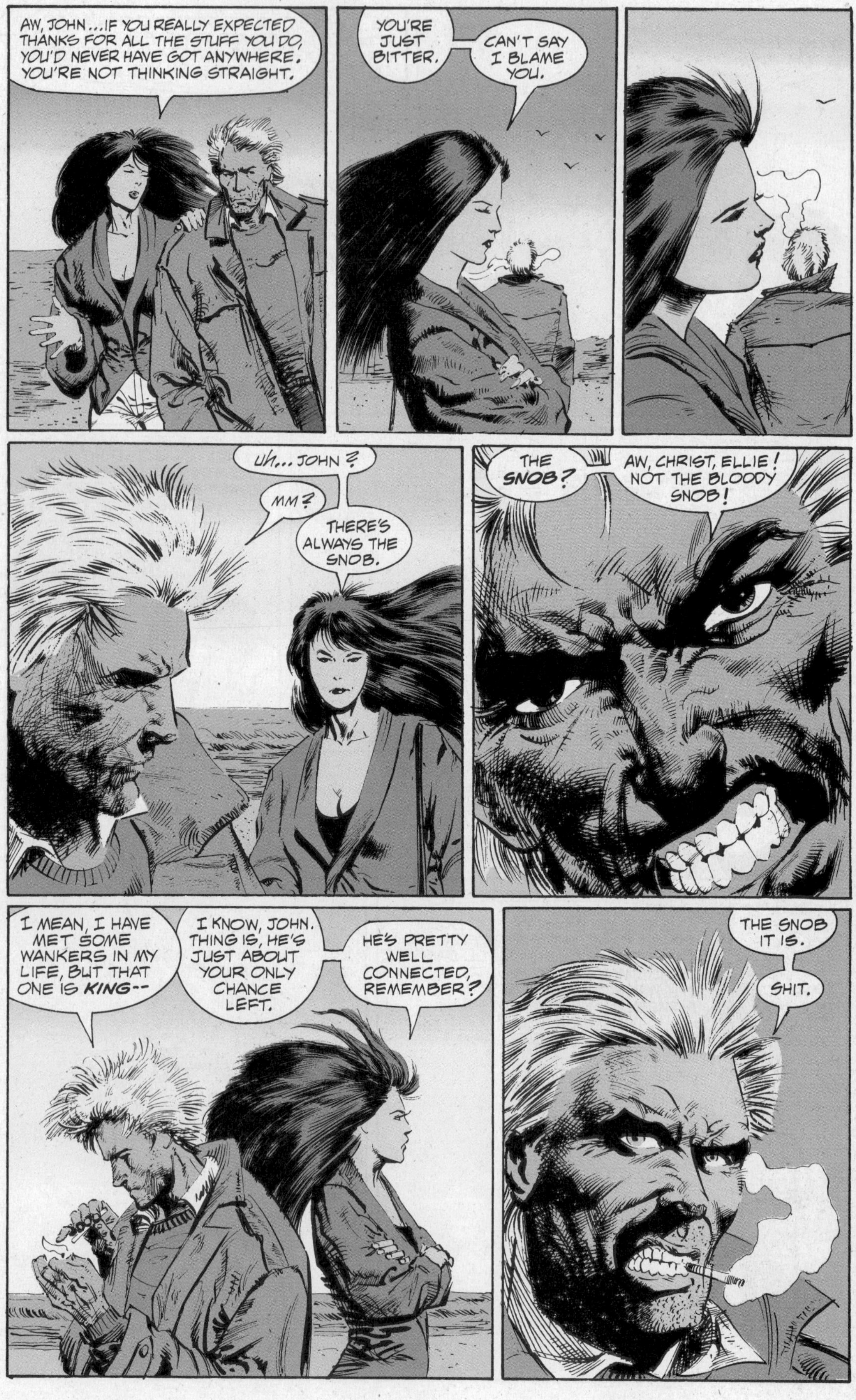
AW, JOHN...IF YOU REALLY EXPECTED THANKS FOR ALL THE STUFF YOU DO, YOU'D NEVER HAVE GOT ANYWHERE. YOU'RE NOT THINKING STRAIGHT.
YOU'RE JUST BITTER.
CAN'T SAY I BLAME YOU.
uh... JOHN?
MM?
THERE'S ALWAYS THE SNOB.
THE SNOB?
AW, CHRIST, ELLIE! NOT THE BLOODY SNOB!
I MEAN, I HAVE MET SOME WANKERS IN MY LIFE, BUT THAT ONE IS KING--
I KNOW, JOHN. THING IS, HE'S JUST ABOUT YOUR ONLY CHANCE LEFT.
HE'S PRETTY WELL CONNECTED, REMEMBER?
THE SNOB IT IS.
SHIT.

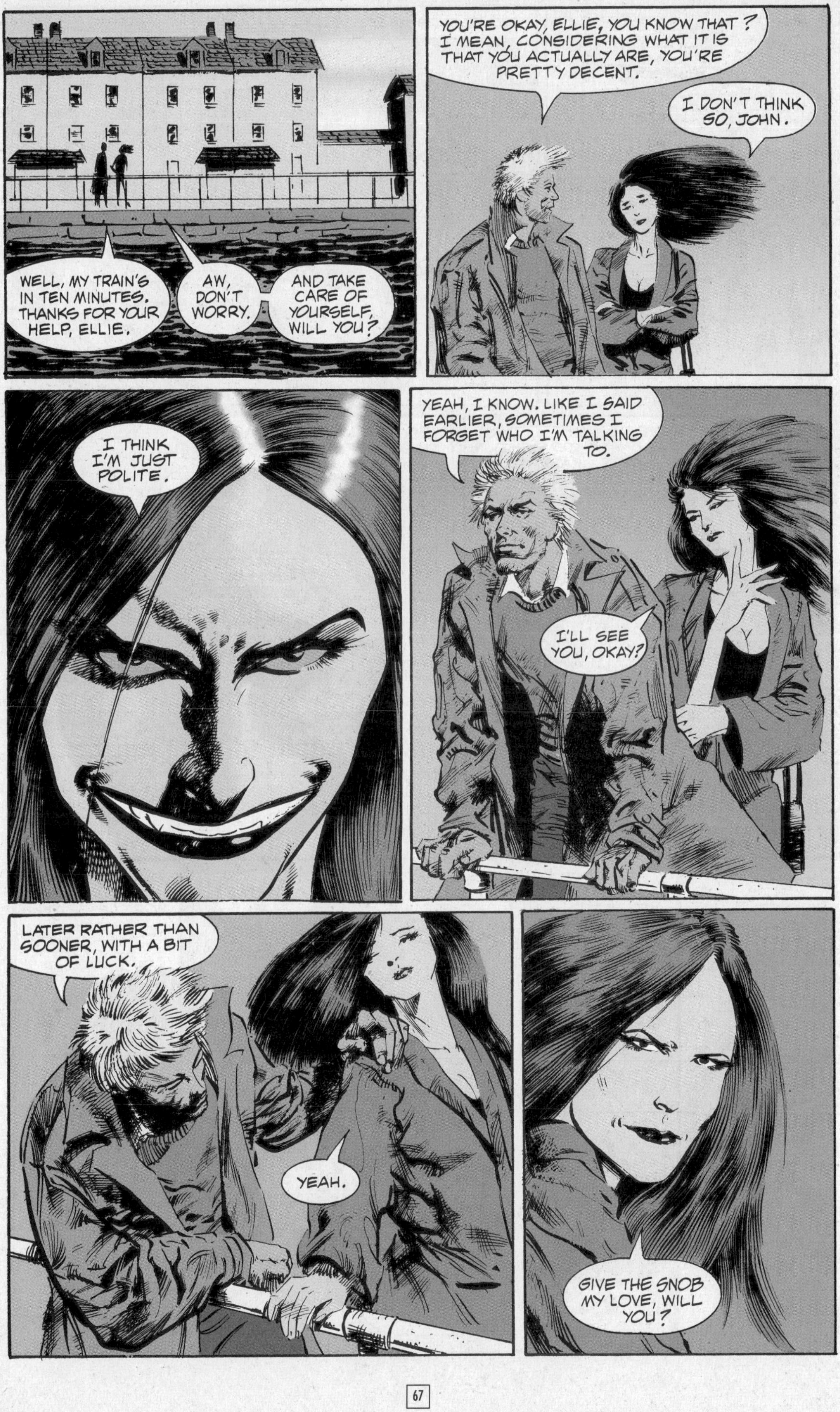
WELL, MY TRAIN'S IN TEN MINUTES. THANKS FOR YOUR HELP, ELLIE.
AW, DON'T WORRY.
AND TAKE CARE OF YOURSELF, WILL YOU?
YOU'RE OKAY, ELLIE, YOU KNOW THAT? I MEAN, CONSIDERING WHAT IT IS THAT YOU ACTUALLY ARE, YOU'RE PRETTY DECENT.
I DON'T THINK SO, JOHN.
I THINK I'M JUST POLITE.
YEAH, I KNOW. LIKE I SAID EARLIER, SOMETIMES I FORGET WHO I'M TALKING TO.
I'LL SEE YOU, OKAY?
LATER RATHER THAN SOONER, WITH A BIT OF LUCK.
YEAH.
GIVE THE SNOB MY LOVE, WILL YOU?

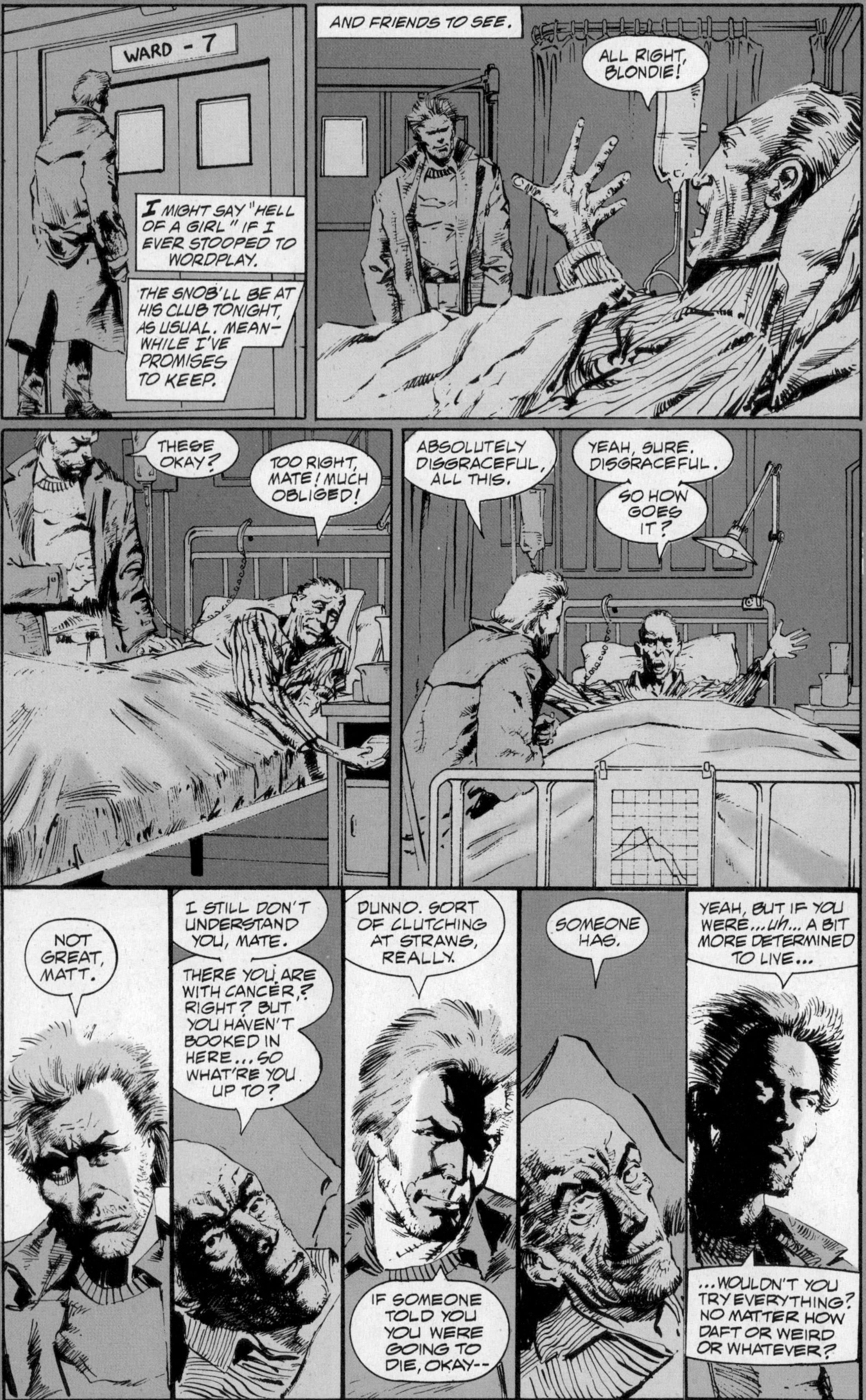
WARD - 7
I MIGHT SAY "HELL OF A GIRL" IF I EVER STOOPED TO WORDPLAY.
THE SNOB'LL BE AT HIS CLUB TONIGHT, AS USUAL. MEAN-WHILE I'VE PROMISES TO KEEP.
AND FRIENDS TO SEE.
ALL RIGHT, BLONDIE!
THESE OKAY?
TOO RIGHT, MATE! MUCH OBLIGED!
ABSOLUTELY DISGRACEFUL, ALL THIS.
YEAH, SURE. DISGRACEFUL.
SO HOW GOES IT?
NOT GREAT, MATT.
I STILL DON'T UNDERSTAND YOU, MATE.
THERE YOU ARE WITH CANCER,? RIGHT? BUT YOU HAVEN'T BOOKED IN HERE... SO WHAT'RE YOU UP TO?
DUNNO. SORT OF CLUTCHING AT STRAWS, REALLY.
IF SOMEONE TOLD YOU YOU WERE GOING TO DIE, OKAY--
SOMEONE HAS.
YEAH, BUT IF YOU WERE... uh... A BIT MORE DETERMINED TO LIVE...
...WOULDN'T YOU TRY EVERYTHING? NO MATTER HOW DAFT OR WEIRD OR WHATEVER?

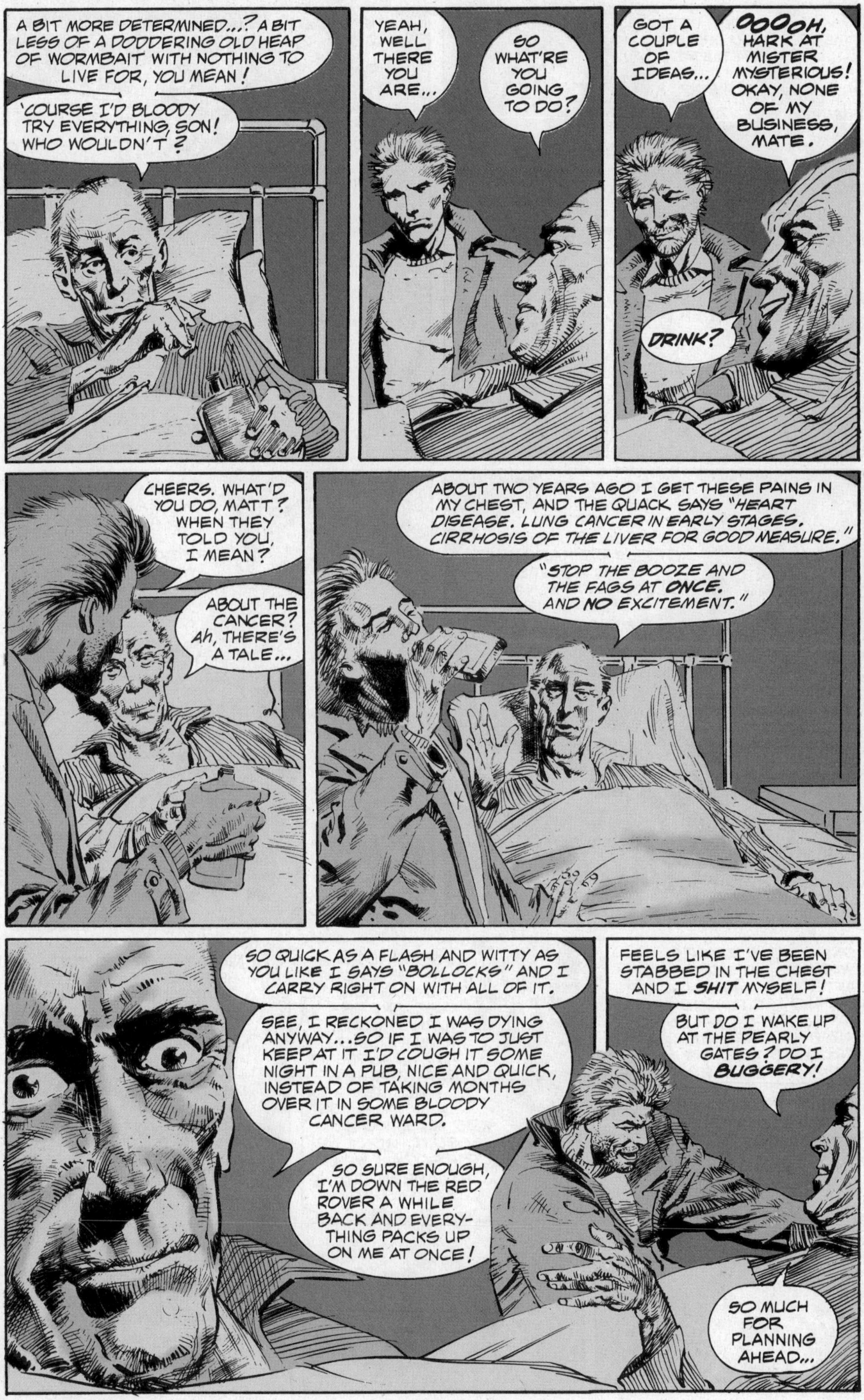

A BIT MORE DETERMINED...? A BIT LESS OF A DODDERING OLD HEAP OF WORMBAIT WITH NOTHING TO LIVE FOR, YOU MEAN!
'COURSE I'D BLOODY TRY EVERYTHING, SON! WHO WOULDN'T?
YEAH, WELL THERE YOU ARE...
SO WHAT'RE YOU GOING TO DO?
GOT A COUPLE OF IDEAS...
OOOOH, HARK AT MISTER MYSTERIOUS! OKAY, NONE OF MY BUSINESS, MATE.
DRINK?
CHEERS. WHAT'D YOU DO, MATT? WHEN THEY TOLD YOU, I MEAN?
ABOUT THE CANCER? Ah, THERE'S A TALE...
ABOUT TWO YEARS AGO I GET THESE PAINS IN MY CHEST, AND THE QUACK SAYS "HEART DISEASE. LUNG CANCER IN EARLY STAGES. CIRRHOSIS OF THE LIVER FOR GOOD MEASURE."
"STOP THE BOOZE AND THE FAGS AT ONCE. AND NO EXCITEMENT."
SO QUICK AS A FLASH AND WITTY AS YOU LIKE I SAYS "BOLLOCKS" AND I CARRY RIGHT ON WITH ALL OF IT.
SEE, I RECKONED I WAS DYING ANYWAY...SO IF I WAS TO JUST KEEP AT IT I'D COUGH IT SOME NIGHT IN A PUB, NICE AND QUICK, INSTEAD OF TAKING MONTHS OVER IT IN SOME BLOODY CANCER WARD.
SO SURE ENOUGH, I'M DOWN THE RED ROVER A WHILE BACK AND EVERYTHING PACKS UP ON ME AT ONCE!
FEELS LIKE I'VE BEEN STABBED IN THE CHEST AND I SHIT MYSELF!
BUT DO I WAKE UP AT THE PEARLY GATES? DO I BUGGERY!
SO MUCH FOR PLANNING AHEAD...

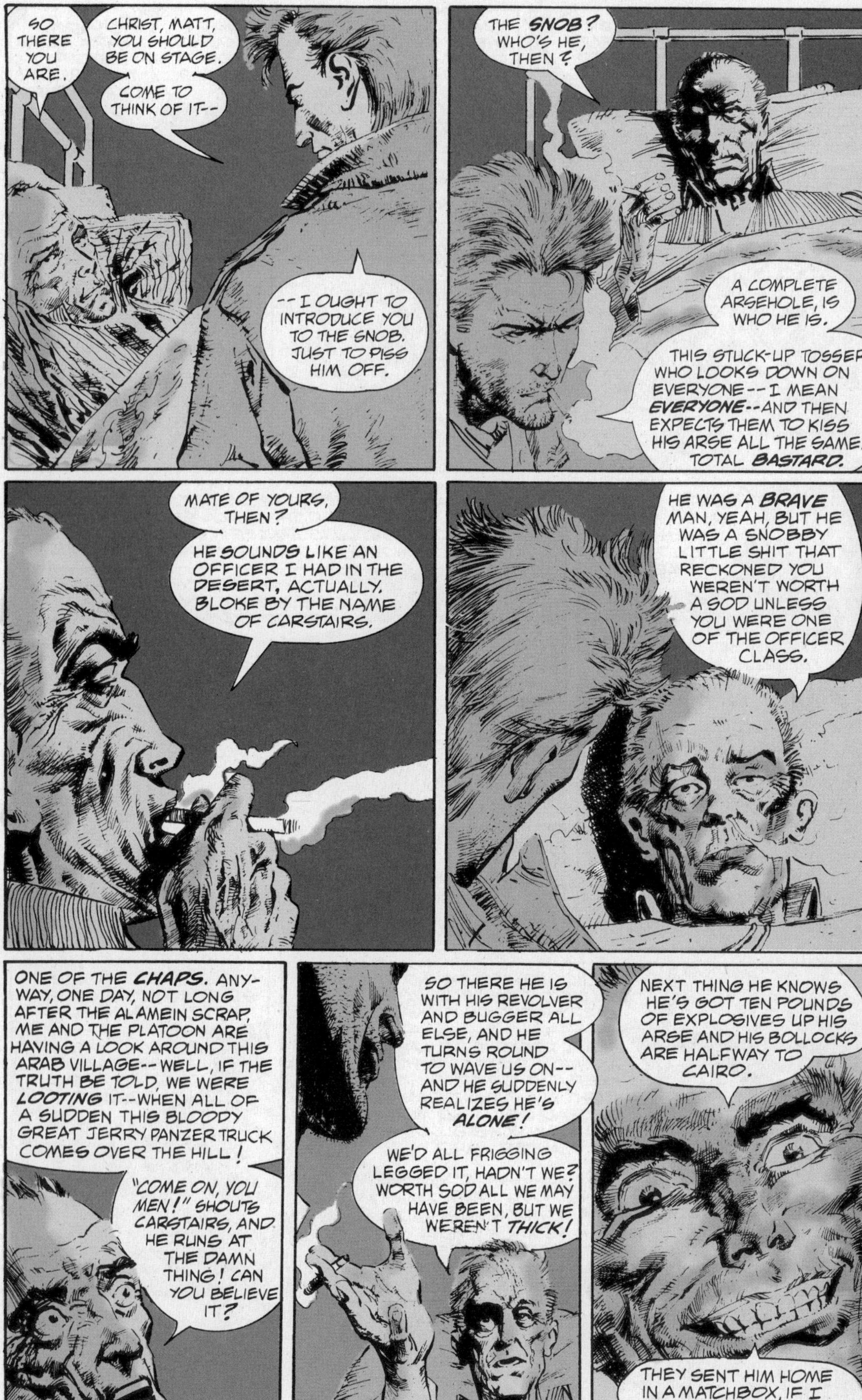
SO THERE YOU ARE.
CHRIST, MATT, YOU SHOULD BE ON STAGE.
COME TO THINK OF IT--
--I OUGHT TO INTRODUCE YOU TO THE SNOB. JUST TO PISS HIM OFF.
THE SNOB? WHO'S HE, THEN?
A COMPLETE ARSEHOLE, IS WHO HE IS.
THIS STUCK-UP TOSSER WHO LOOKS DOWN ON EVERYONE--I MEAN EVERYONE--AND THEN EXPECTS THEM TO KISS HIS ARSE ALL THE SAME. TOTAL BASTARD.
MATE OF YOURS, THEN?
HE SOUNDS LIKE AN OFFICER I HAD IN THE DESERT, ACTUALLY. BLOKE BY THE NAME OF CARSTAIRS.
HE WAS A BRAVE MAN, YEAH, BUT HE WAS A SNOBBY LITTLE SHIT THAT RECKONED YOU WEREN'T WORTH A SOD UNLESS YOU WERE ONE OF THE OFFICER CLASS.
ONE OF THE CHAPS. ANYWAY, ONE DAY, NOT LONG AFTER THE ALAMEIN SCRAP, ME AND THE PLATOON ARE HAVING A LOOK AROUND THIS ARAB VILLAGE--WELL, IF THE TRUTH BE TOLD, WE WERE LOOTING IT--WHEN ALL OF A SUDDEN THIS BLOODY GREAT JERRY PANZER TRUCK COMES OVER THE HILL!
"COME ON, YOU MEN!" SHOUTS CARSTAIRS, AND HE RUNS AT THE DAMN THING! CAN YOU BELIEVE IT?
SO THERE HE IS WITH HIS REVOLVER AND BUGGER ALL ELSE, AND HE TURNS ROUND TO WAVE US ON--AND HE SUDDENLY REALIZES HE'S ALONE!
WE'D ALL FRIGGING LEGGED IT, HADN'T WE? WORTH SOD ALL WE MAY HAVE BEEN, BUT WE WEREN'T THICK!
NEXT THING HE KNOWS HE'S GOT TEN POUNDS OF EXPLOSIVES UP HIS ARSE AND HIS BOLLOCKS ARE HALFWAY TO CAIRO.
THEY SENT HIM HOME IN A MATCHBOX, IF I REMEMBER RIGHTLY...

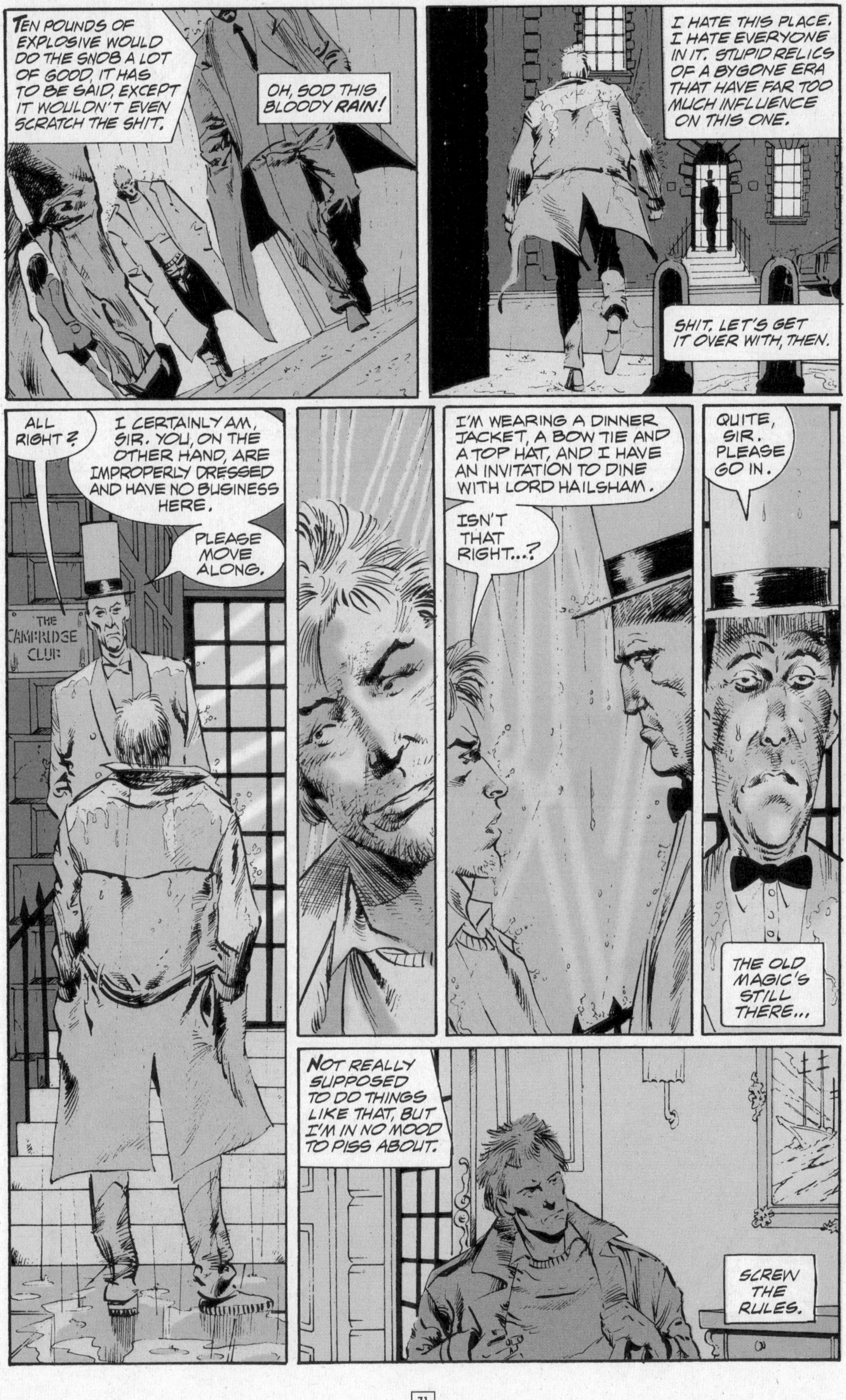
TEN POUNDS OF EXPLOSIVE WOULD DO THE SNOB A LOT OF GOOD, IT HAS TO BE SAID, EXCEPT IT WOULDN'T EVEN SCRATCH THE SHIT.
OH, SOD THIS BLOODY RAIN!
I HATE THIS PLACE. I HATE EVERYONE IN IT. STUPID RELICS OF A BYGONE ERA THAT HAVE FAR TOO MUCH INFLUENCE ON THIS ONE.
SHIT. LET'S GET IT OVER WITH, THEN.
ALL RIGHT?
I CERTAINLY AM, SIR. YOU, ON THE OTHER HAND, ARE IMPROPERLY DRESSED AND HAVE NO BUSINESS HERE.
PLEASE MOVE ALONG.
THE CAMBRIDGE CLUB
I'M WEARING A DINNER JACKET, A BOW TIE AND A TOP HAT, AND I HAVE AN INVITATION TO DINE WITH LORD HAILSHAM.
ISN'T THAT RIGHT...?
QUITE, SIR. PLEASE GO IN.
THE OLD MAGIC'S STILL THERE...
NOT REALLY SUPPOSED TO DO THINGS LIKE THAT, BUT I'M IN NO MOOD TO PISS ABOUT.
SCREW THE RULES.

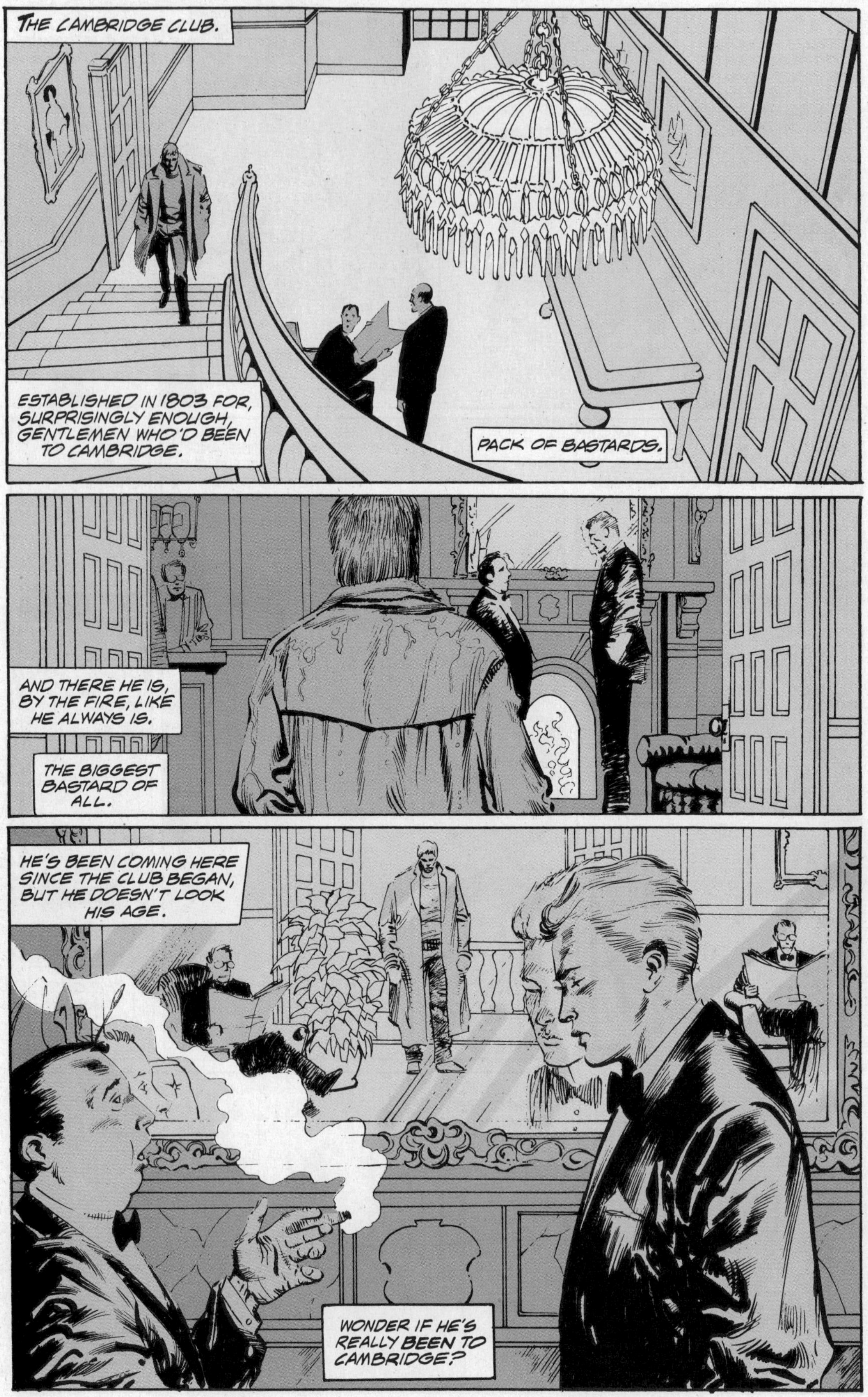
THE CAMBRIDGE CLUB.
ESTABLISHED IN 1803 FOR, SURPRISINGLY ENOUGH, GENTLEMEN WHO'D BEEN TO CAMBRIDGE.
PACK OF BASTARDS.
AND THERE HE IS, BY THE FIRE, LIKE HE ALWAYS IS.
THE BIGGEST BASTARD OF ALL.
HE'S BEEN COMING HERE SINCE THE CLUB BEGAN, BUT HE DOESN'T LOOK HIS AGE.
WONDER IF HE'S REALLY BEEN TO CAMBRIDGE?

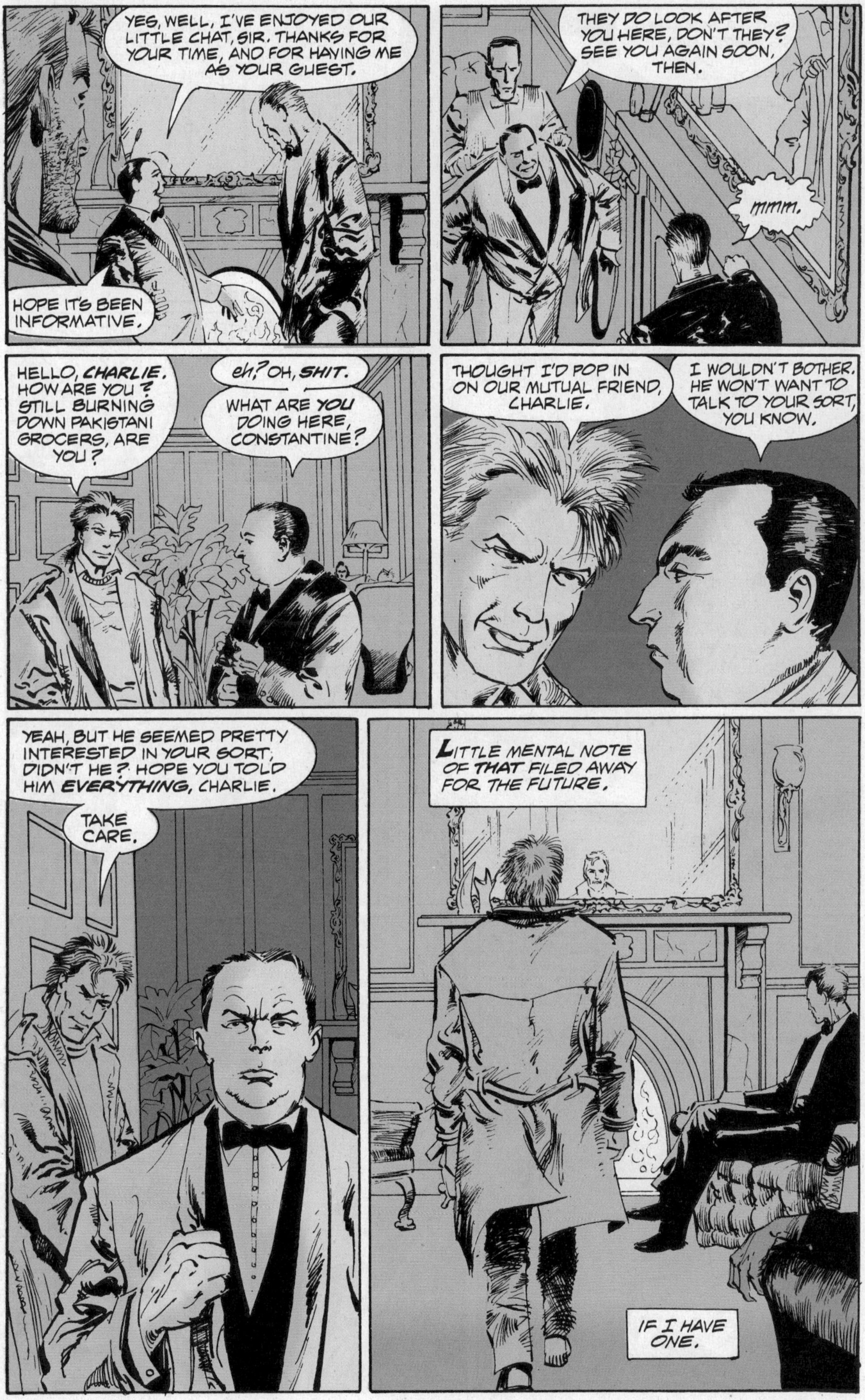
YES, WELL, I'VE ENJOYED OUR LITTLE CHAT, SIR. THANKS FOR YOUR TIME, AND FOR HAVING ME AS YOUR GUEST.
HOPE IT'S BEEN INFORMATIVE.
THEY DO LOOK AFTER YOU HERE, DON'T THEY? SEE YOU AGAIN SOON, THEN.
mmm.
HELLO, CHARLIE. HOW ARE YOU? STILL BURNING DOWN PAKISTANI GROCERS, ARE YOU?
eh? OH, SHIT.
WHAT ARE YOU DOING HERE, CONSTANTINE?
THOUGHT I'D POP IN ON OUR MUTUAL FRIEND, CHARLIE.
I WOULDN'T BOTHER. HE WON'T WANT TO TALK TO YOUR SORT, YOU KNOW.
YEAH, BUT HE SEEMED PRETTY INTERESTED IN YOUR SORT, DIDN'T HE? HOPE YOU TOLD HIM EVERYTHING, CHARLIE.
TAKE CARE.
LITTLE MENTAL NOTE OF THAT FILED AWAY FOR THE FUTURE.
IF I HAVE ONE.

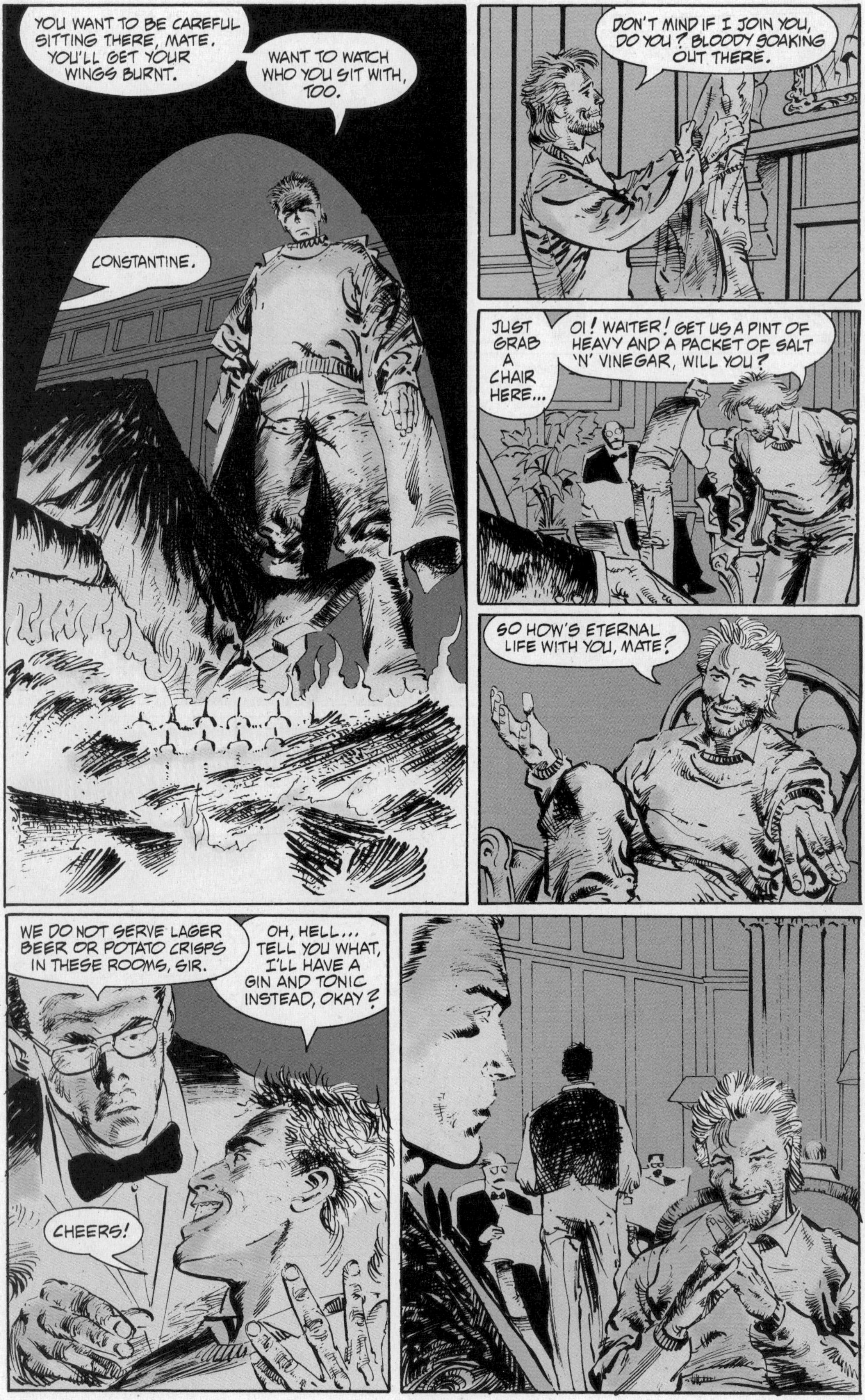
YOU WANT TO BE CAREFUL SITTING THERE, MATE. YOU'LL GET YOUR WINGS BURNT.
WANT TO WATCH WHO YOU SIT WITH, TOO.
CONSTANTINE.
DON'T MIND IF I JOIN YOU, DO YOU? BLOODY SOAKING OUT THERE.
JUST GRAB A CHAIR HERE...
OI! WAITER! GET US A PINT OF HEAVY AND A PACKET OF SALT 'N' VINEGAR, WILL YOU?
SO HOW'S ETERNAL LIFE WITH YOU, MATE?
WE DO NOT SERVE LAGER BEER OR POTATO CRISPS IN THESE ROOMS, SIR.
OH, HELL... TELL YOU WHAT, I'LL HAVE A GIN AND TONIC INSTEAD, OKAY?
CHEERS!

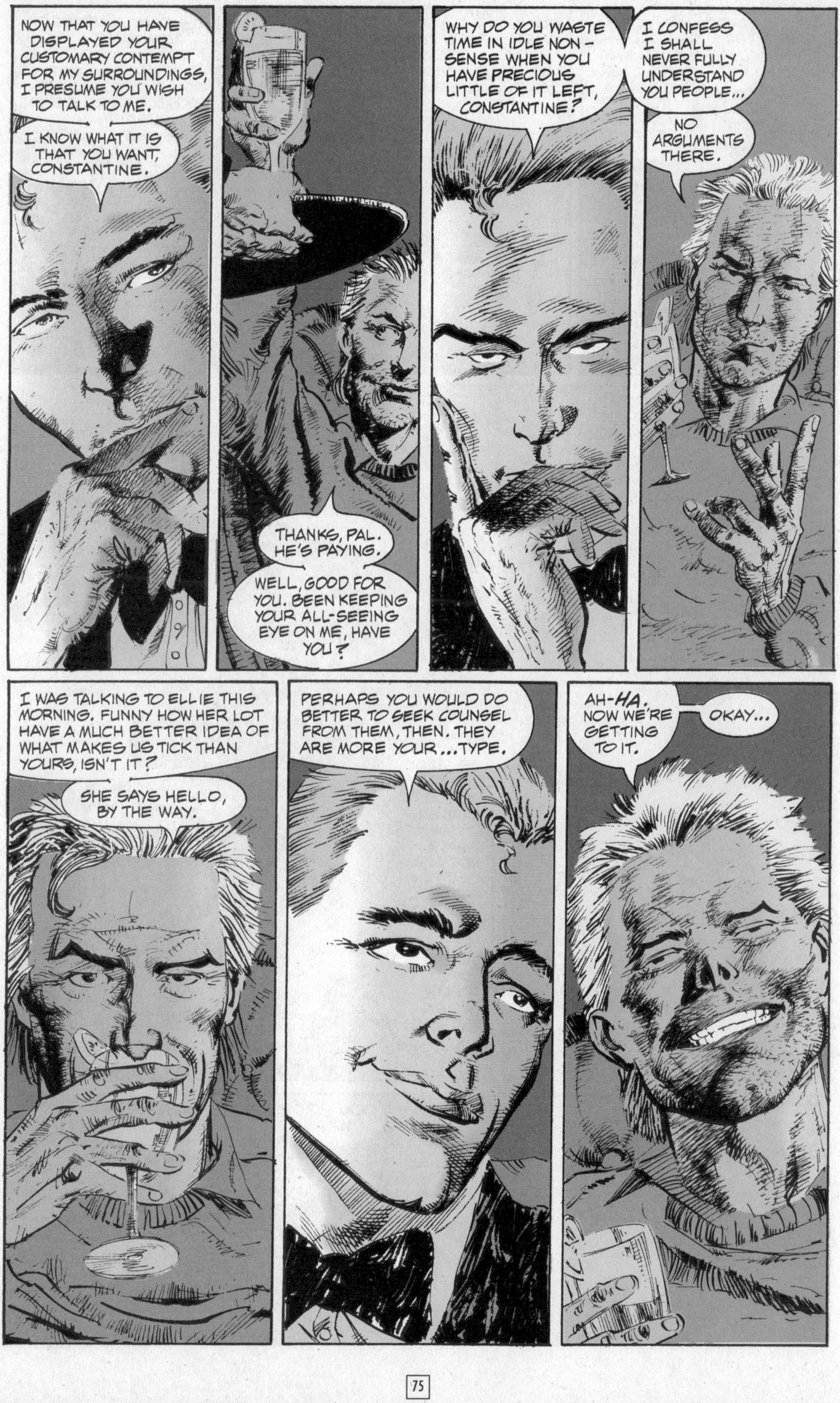
NOW THAT YOU HAVE DISPLAYED YOUR CUSTOMARY CONTEMPT FOR MY SURROUNDINGS, I PRESUME YOU WISH TO TALK TO ME.
I KNOW WHAT IT IS THAT YOU WANT, CONSTANTINE.
THANKS, PAL. HE'S PAYING.
WELL, GOOD FOR YOU. BEEN KEEPING YOUR ALL-SEEING EYE ON ME, HAVE YOU?
WHY DO YOU WASTE TIME IN IDLE NON-SENSE WHEN YOU HAVE PRECIOUS LITTLE OF IT LEFT, CONSTANTINE?
I CONFESS I SHALL NEVER FULLY UNDERSTAND YOU PEOPLE...
NO ARGUMENTS THERE.
I WAS TALKING TO ELLIE THIS MORNING. FUNNY HOW HER LOT HAVE A MUCH BETTER IDEA OF WHAT MAKES US TICK THAN YOURS, ISN'T IT?
SHE SAYS HELLO, BY THE WAY.
PERHAPS YOU WOULD DO BETTER TO SEEK COUNSEL FROM THEM, THEN. THEY ARE MORE YOUR...TYPE.
AH-HA. NOW WE'RE GETTING TO IT.
OKAY...

YOU GOING TO HELP ME, THEN?

OF COURSE NOT.

WHY NOT? YOU ARE AT THE VERY LEAST A CUNNING MAN, CONSTANTINE.

DO NOT OVER-RATE YOUR-SELF.

IT WOULD NOT DO FOR YOU TO START BELIEVING YOUR OWN LIES.

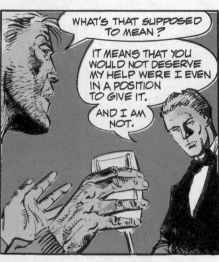

WHAT'S THAT SUPPOSED TO MEAN?

IT MEANS THAT YOU WOULD NOT DESERVE MY HELP WERE I EVEN IN A POSITION TO GIVE IT.

AND I AM NOT.

WHAT D'YOU MEAN I DON'T DESERVE IT? YOU OWE ME ONE--CHRIST, MORE THAN ONE--

I DO NOT OWE YOU ANY-THING. DEBTS MEAN NOTHING TO MY KIND.

YOU WANKER! YOU TOTAL FU--

QUIET.

BE QUIET, CONSTANTINE. AND BE CAREFUL.

I HAVE NOT FOR-GOTTEN WHAT YOU HAVE DONE IN THE PAST, BUT AS I SAID, DEBTS MEAN NOTHING.

YOU DO OVERRATE YOURSELF. YOU SHOULD UNDERSTAND, CONSTANTINE...

YOU TOO MEAN NOTHING.

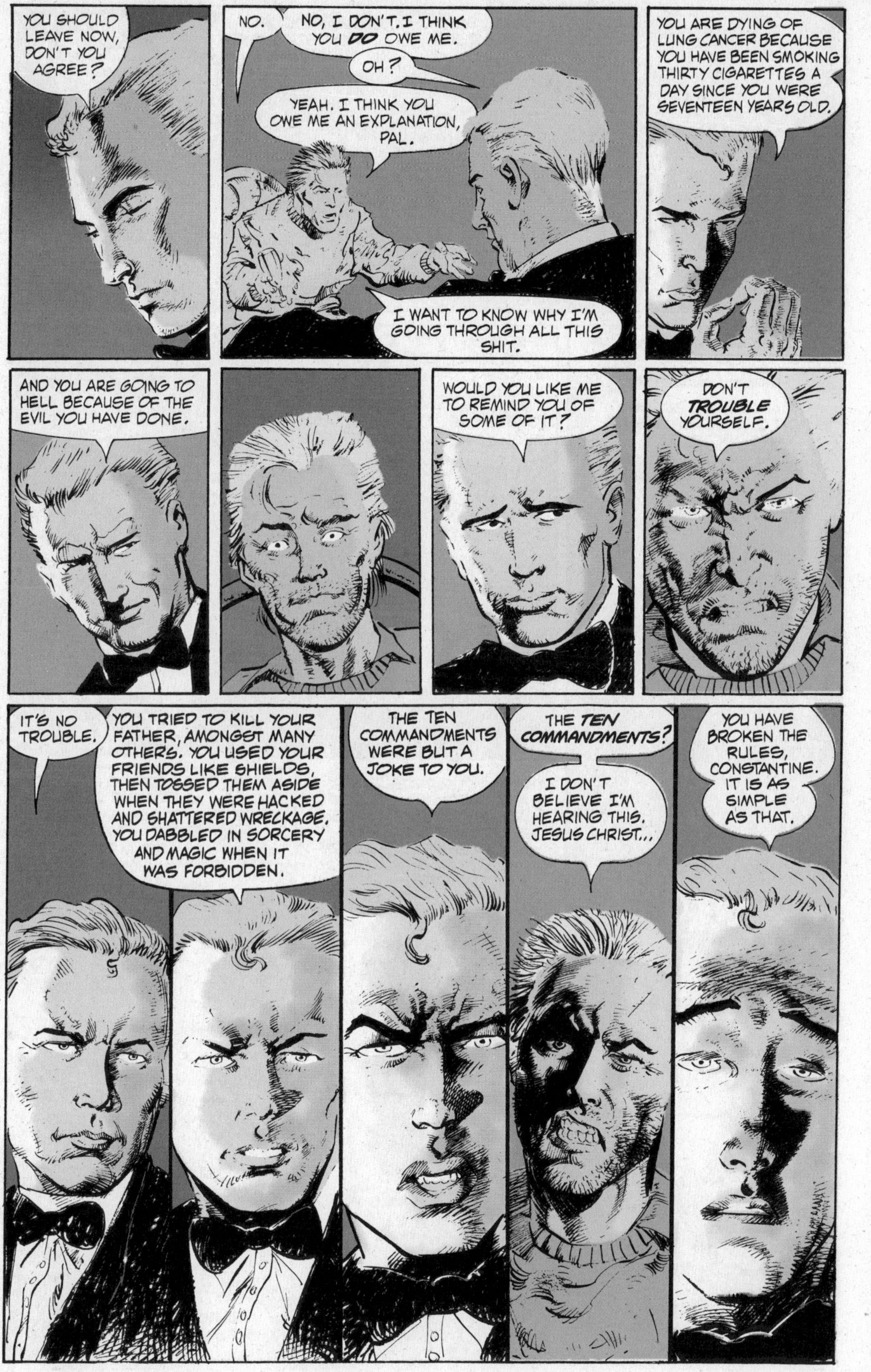
YOU SHOULD LEAVE NOW, DON'T YOU AGREE?
NO.
NO, I DON'T. I THINK YOU DO OWE ME.
OH?
YEAH. I THINK YOU OWE ME AN EXPLANATION, PAL.
I WANT TO KNOW WHY I'M GOING THROUGH ALL THIS SHIT.
YOU ARE DYING OF LUNG CANCER BECAUSE YOU HAVE BEEN SMOKING THIRTY CIGARETTES A DAY SINCE YOU WERE SEVENTEEN YEARS OLD.
AND YOU ARE GOING TO HELL BECAUSE OF THE EVIL YOU HAVE DONE.
WOULD YOU LIKE ME TO REMIND YOU OF SOME OF IT?
DON'T TROUBLE YOURSELF.
IT'S NO TROUBLE.
YOU TRIED TO KILL YOUR FATHER, AMONGST MANY OTHERS. YOU USED YOUR FRIENDS LIKE SHIELDS, THEN TOSSED THEM ASIDE WHEN THEY WERE HACKED AND SHATTERED WRECKAGE. YOU DABBLED IN SORCERY AND MAGIC WHEN IT WAS FORBIDDEN.
THE TEN COMMANDMENTS WERE BUT A JOKE TO YOU.
THE TEN COMMANDMENTS?
I DON'T BELIEVE I'M HEARING THIS. JESUS CHRIST...
YOU HAVE BROKEN THE RULES, CONSTANTINE. IT IS AS SIMPLE AS THAT.

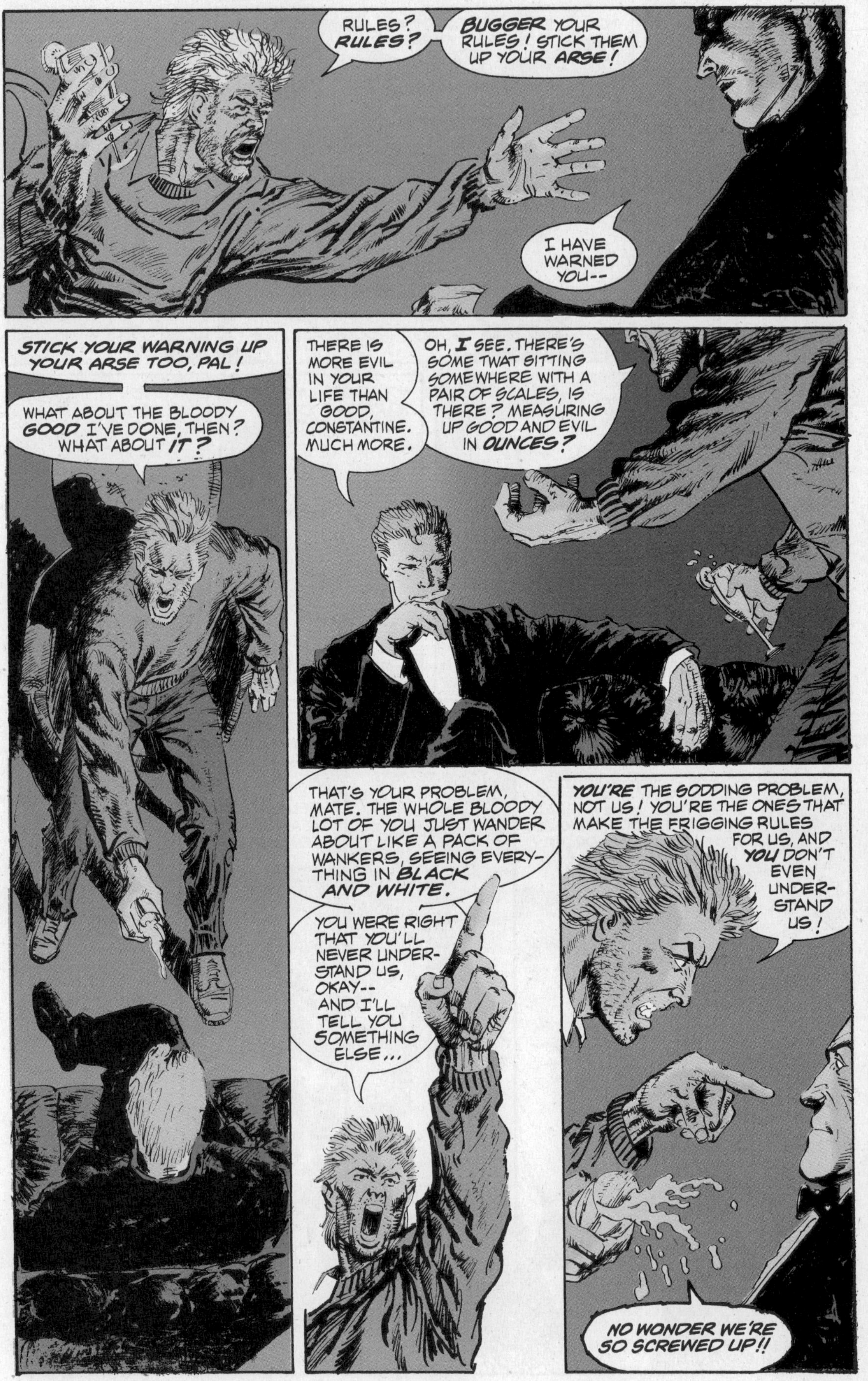
RULES? RULES?
BUGGER YOUR RULES! STICK THEM UP YOUR ARSE!
I HAVE WARNED YOU--
STICK YOUR WARNING UP YOUR ARSE TOO, PAL!
WHAT ABOUT THE BLOODY GOOD I'VE DONE, THEN? WHAT ABOUT IT?
THERE IS MORE EVIL IN YOUR LIFE THAN GOOD, CONSTANTINE. MUCH MORE.
OH, I SEE. THERE'S SOME TWAT SITTING SOMEWHERE WITH A PAIR OF SCALES, IS THERE? MEASURING UP GOOD AND EVIL IN OUNCES?
THAT'S YOUR PROBLEM, MATE. THE WHOLE BLOODY LOT OF YOU JUST WANDER ABOUT LIKE A PACK OF WANKERS, SEEING EVERY-THING IN BLACK AND WHITE.
YOU WERE RIGHT THAT YOU'LL NEVER UNDER-STAND US, OKAY-- AND I'LL TELL YOU SOMETHING ELSE...
YOU'RE THE SODDING PROBLEM, NOT US! YOU'RE THE ONES THAT MAKE THE FRIGGING RULES FOR US, AND YOU DON'T EVEN UNDER-STAND US!
NO WONDER WE'RE SO SCREWED UP!!

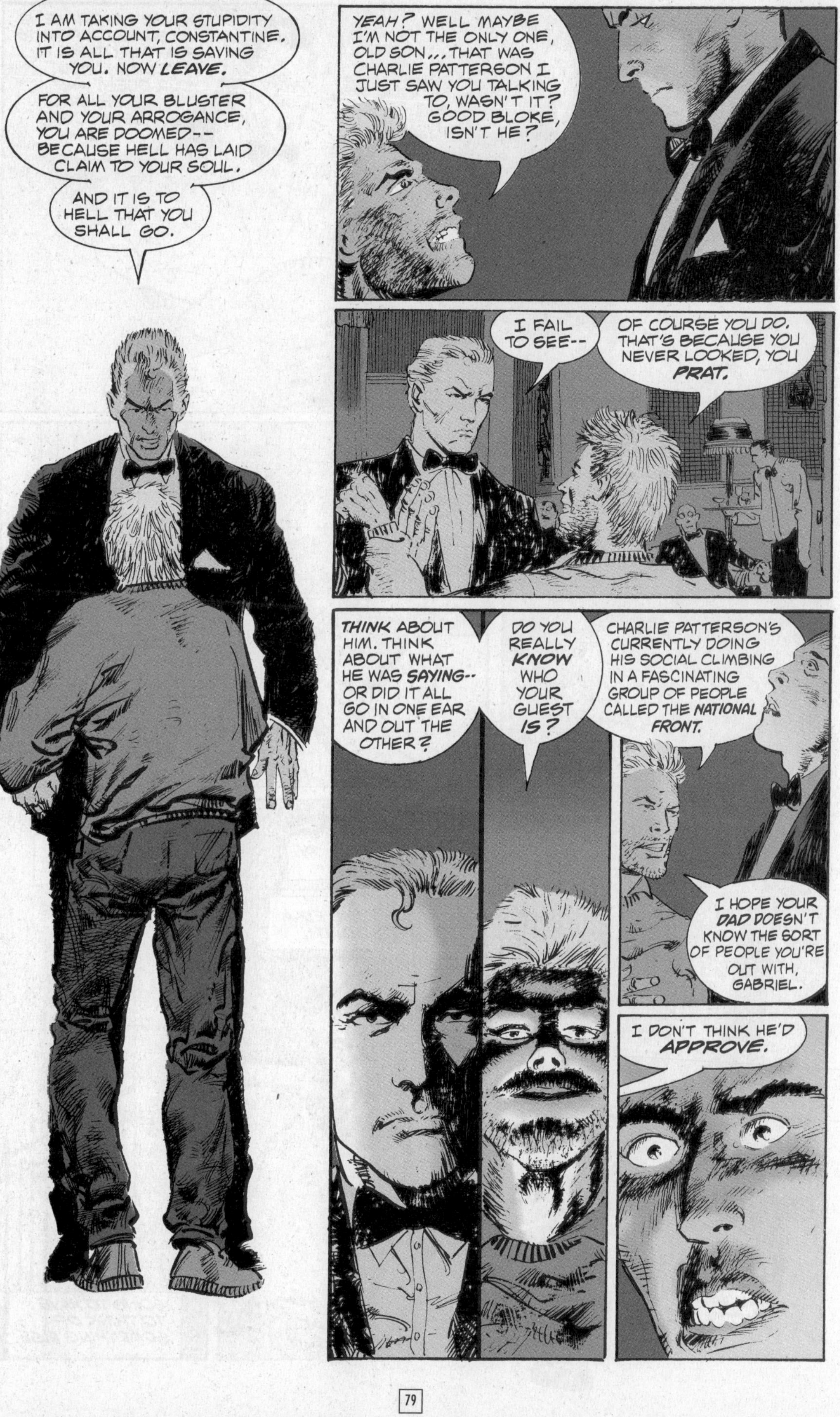

I AM TAKING YOUR STUPIDITY INTO ACCOUNT, CONSTANTINE. IT IS ALL THAT IS SAVING YOU. NOW LEAVE.
FOR ALL YOUR BLUSTER AND YOUR ARROGANCE, YOU ARE DOOMED-- BECAUSE HELL HAS LAID CLAIM TO YOUR SOUL.
AND IT IS TO HELL THAT YOU SHALL GO.
YEAH? WELL MAYBE I'M NOT THE ONLY ONE, OLD SON... THAT WAS CHARLIE PATTERSON I JUST SAW YOU TALKING TO, WASN'T IT? GOOD BLOKE, ISN'T HE?
I FAIL TO SEE--
OF COURSE YOU DO. THAT'S BECAUSE YOU NEVER LOOKED, YOU PRAT.
THINK ABOUT HIM. THINK ABOUT WHAT HE WAS SAYING-- OR DID IT ALL GO IN ONE EAR AND OUT THE OTHER?
DO YOU REALLY KNOW WHO YOUR GUEST IS?
CHARLIE PATTERSON'S CURRENTLY DOING HIS SOCIAL CLIMBING IN A FASCINATING GROUP OF PEOPLE CALLED THE NATIONAL FRONT.
I HOPE YOUR DAD DOESN'T KNOW THE SORT OF PEOPLE YOU'RE OUT WITH, GABRIEL.
I DON'T THINK HE'D APPROVE.

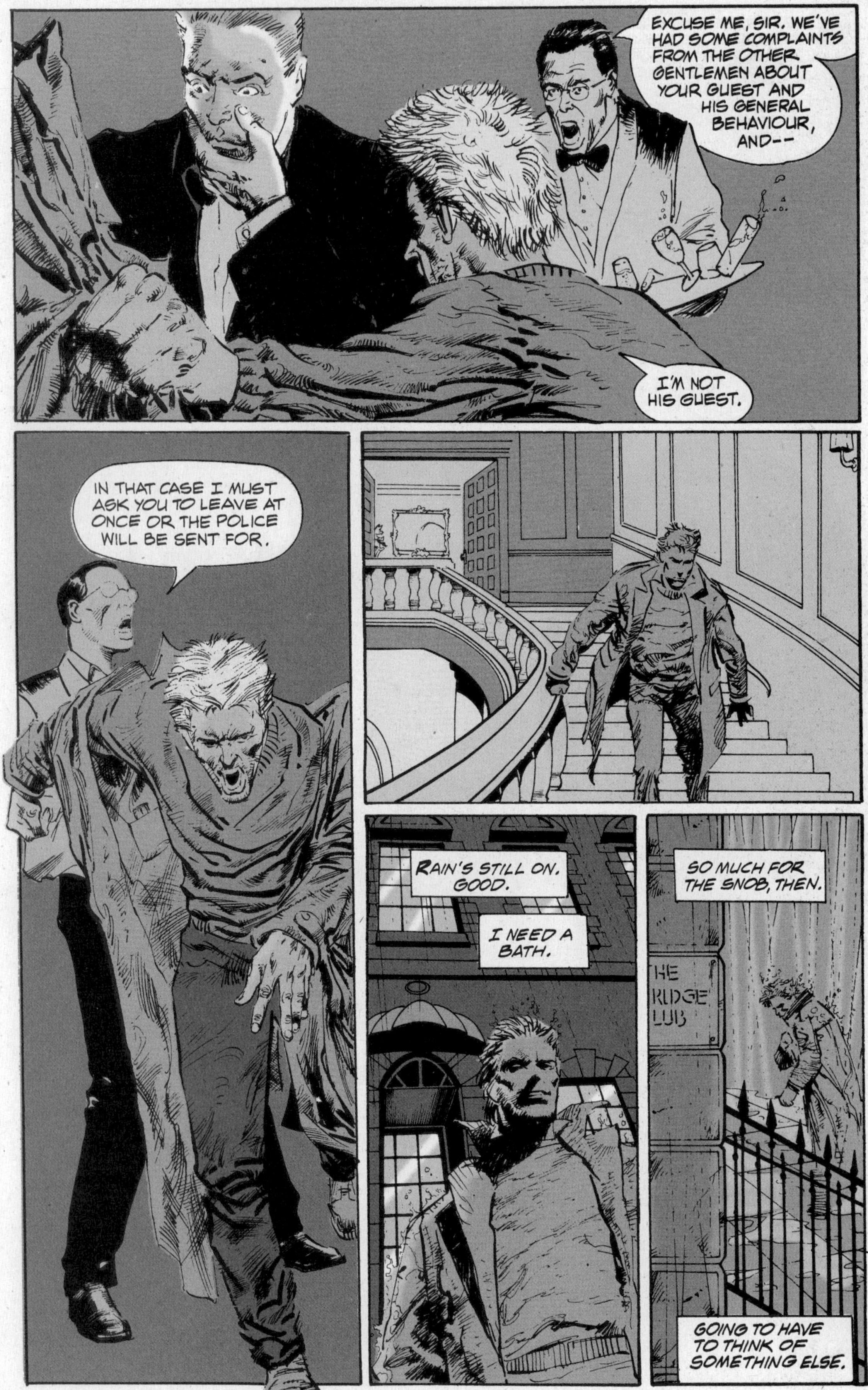

EXCUSE ME, SIR. WE'VE HAD SOME COMPLAINTS FROM THE OTHER GENTLEMEN ABOUT YOUR GUEST AND HIS GENERAL BEHAVIOUR, AND--
I'M NOT HIS GUEST.
IN THAT CASE I MUST ASK YOU TO LEAVE AT ONCE OR THE POLICE WILL BE SENT FOR.
RAIN'S STILL ON. GOOD.
I NEED A BATH.
SO MUCH FOR THE SNOB, THEN.
GOING TO HAVE TO THINK OF SOMETHING ELSE.

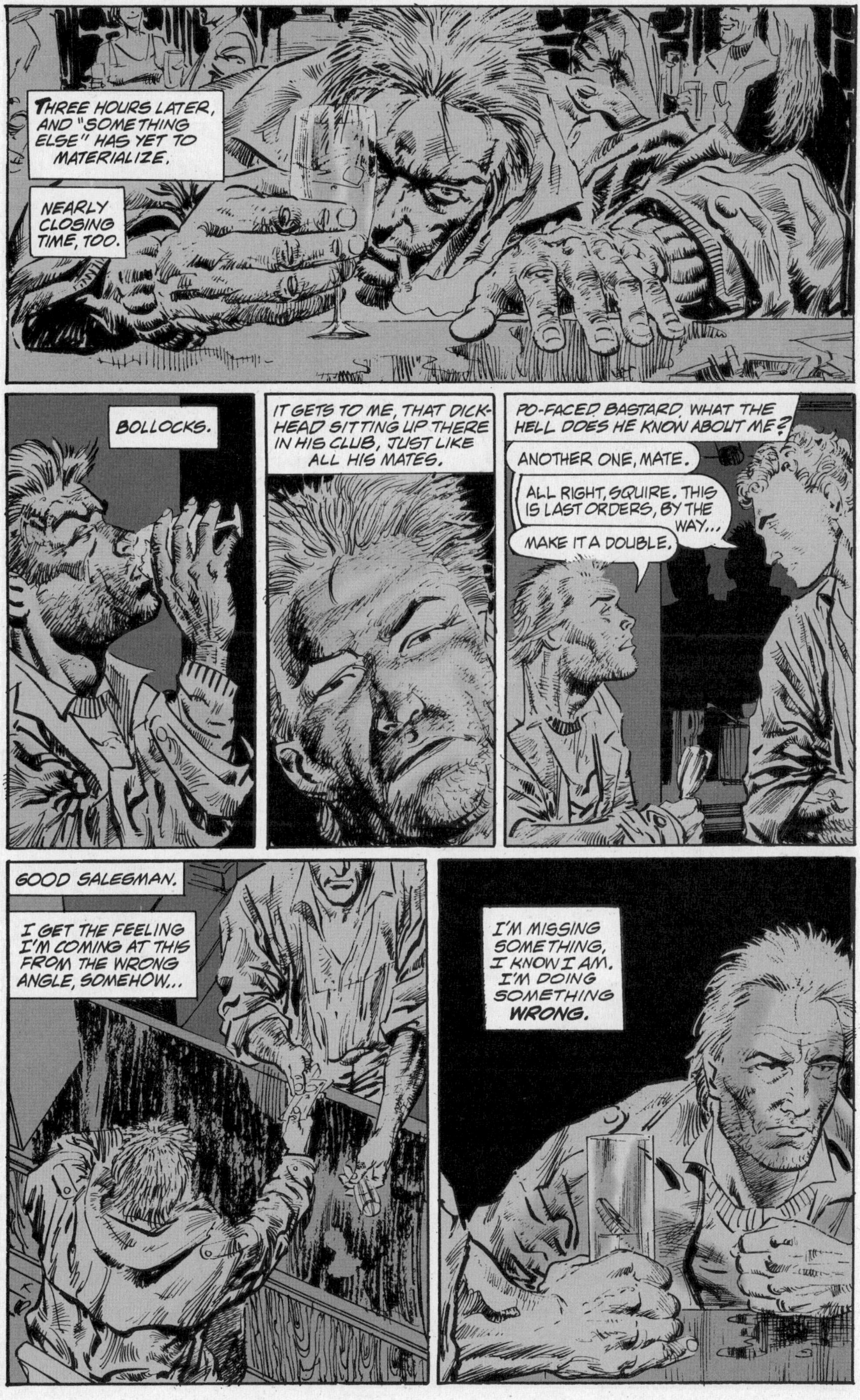
THREE HOURS LATER, AND "SOMETHING ELSE" HAS YET TO MATERIALIZE.
NEARLY CLOSING TIME, TOO.
BOLLOCKS.
IT GETS TO ME, THAT DICK-HEAD SITTING UP THERE IN HIS CLUB, JUST LIKE ALL HIS MATES.
PO-FACED BASTARD, WHAT THE HELL DOES HE KNOW ABOUT ME?
ANOTHER ONE, MATE.
ALL RIGHT, SQUIRE. THIS IS LAST ORDERS, BY THE WAY...
MAKE IT A DOUBLE.
GOOD SALESMAN.
I GET THE FEELING I'M COMING AT THIS FROM THE WRONG ANGLE, SOMEHOW...
I'M MISSING SOMETHING, I KNOW I AM. I'M DOING SOMETHING WRONG.

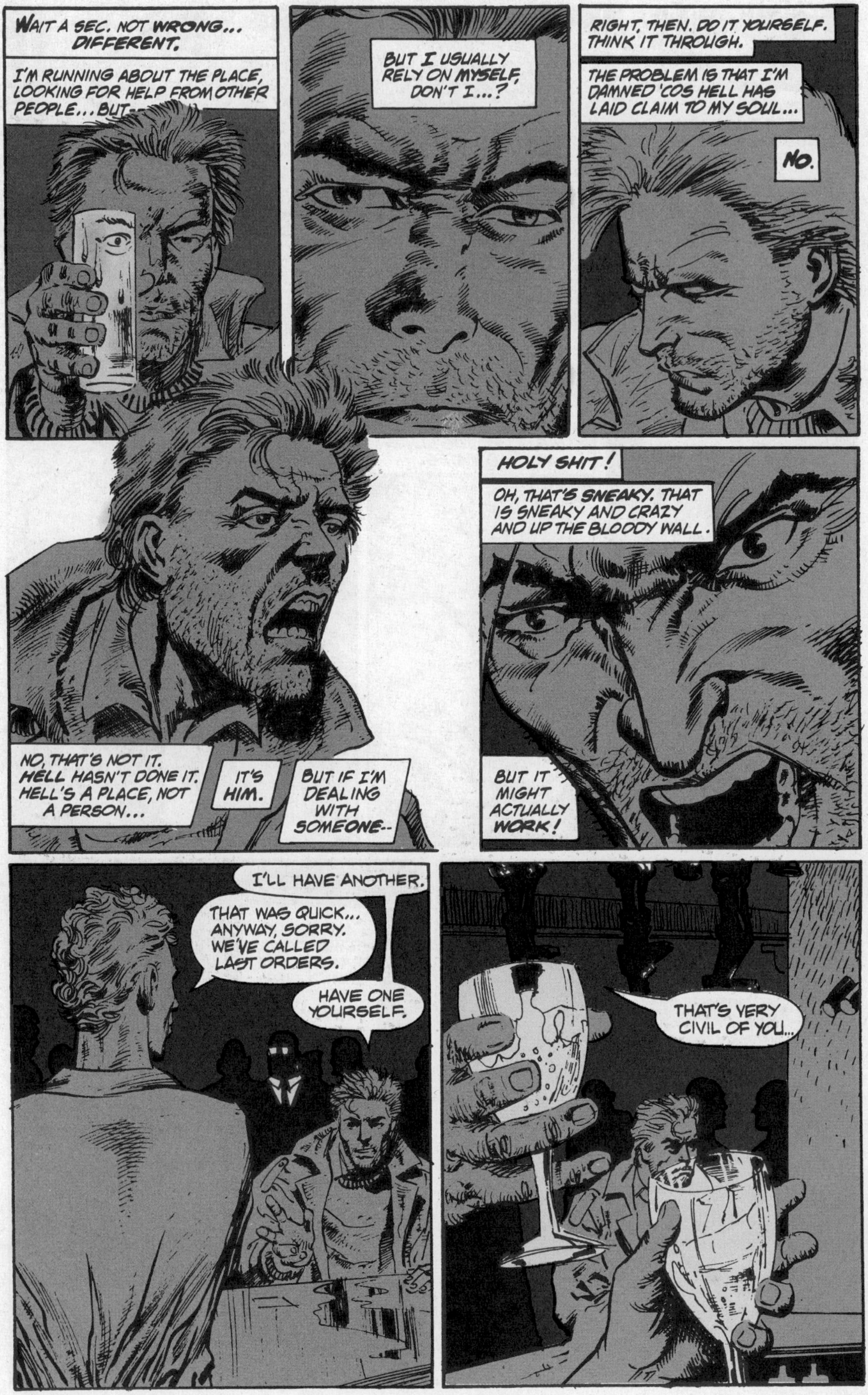

WAIT A SEC. NOT WRONG... DIFFERENT.
I'M RUNNING ABOUT THE PLACE, LOOKING FOR HELP FROM OTHER PEOPLE... BUT--
BUT I USUALLY RELY ON MYSELF, DON'T I...?
RIGHT, THEN. DO IT YOURSELF. THINK IT THROUGH.
THE PROBLEM IS THAT I'M DAMNED 'COS HELL HAS LAID CLAIM TO MY SOUL...
NO.
NO, THAT'S NOT IT. HELL HASN'T DONE IT. HELL'S A PLACE, NOT A PERSON...
IT'S HIM.
BUT IF I'M DEALING WITH SOMEONE--
HOLY SHIT!
OH, THAT'S SNEAKY. THAT IS SNEAKY AND CRAZY AND UP THE BLOODY WALL.
BUT IT MIGHT ACTUALLY WORK!
I'LL HAVE ANOTHER.
THAT WAS QUICK... ANYWAY, SORRY. WE'VE CALLED LAST ORDERS.
HAVE ONE YOURSELF.
THAT'S VERY CIVIL OF YOU...

my

way

V

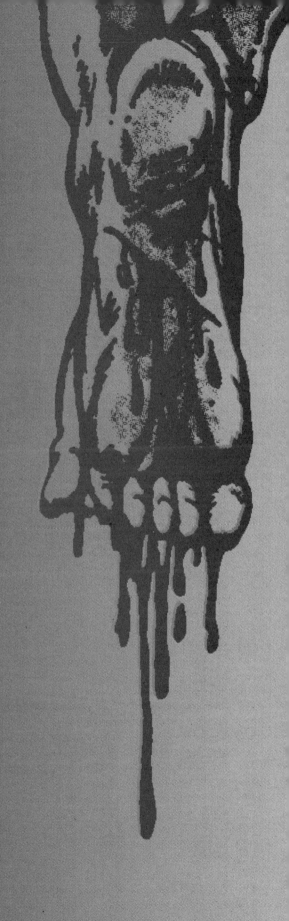

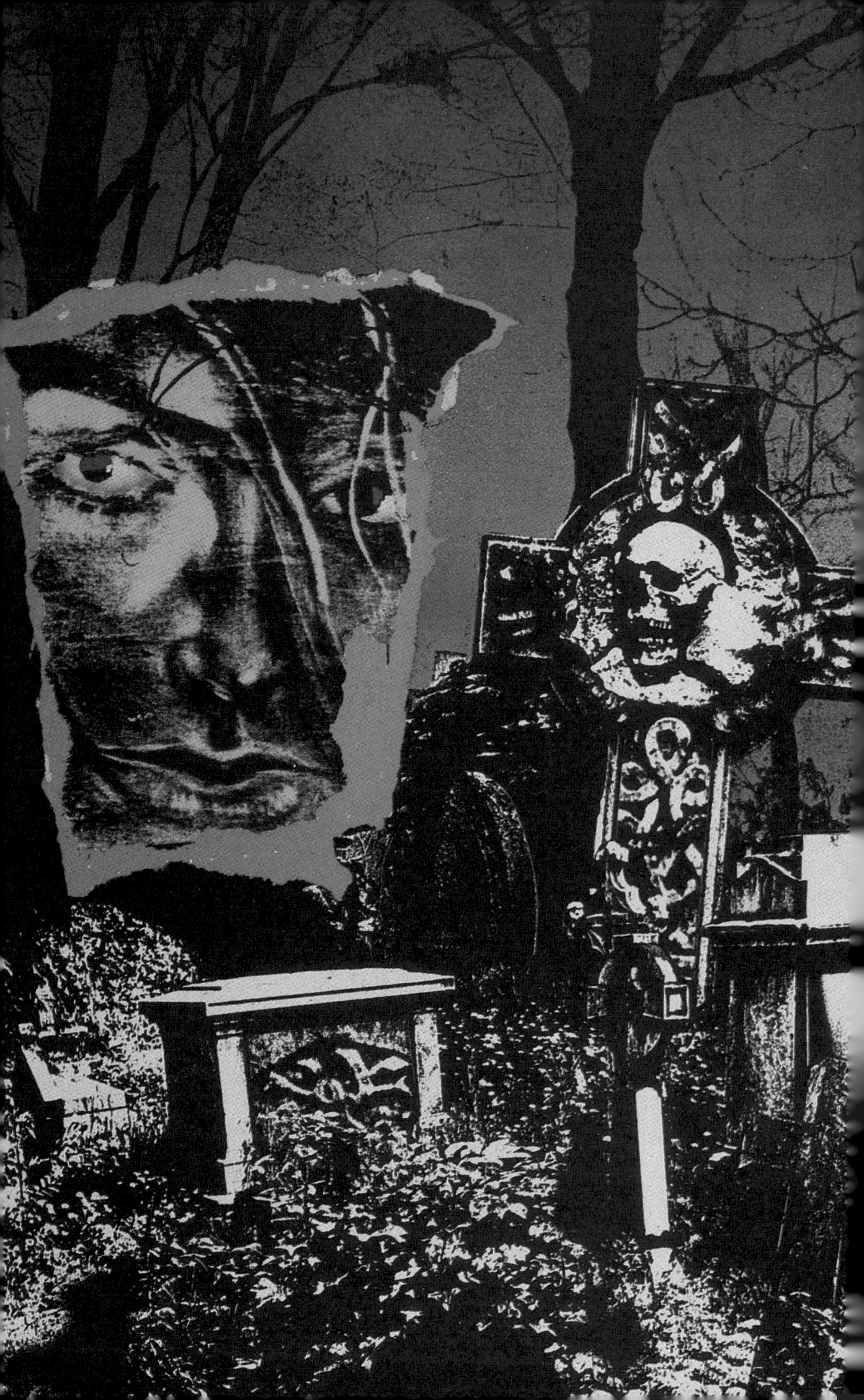

IT'S GOING TO BE SOON. COUPLE OF DAYS AT THE MOST, FROM THE WAY I KEEP GETTING THE SHAKES.

CAN'T EVEN OPEN A SODDING FAG PACKET--

SHIT.

YOU ENJOYED THAT, DIDN'T YOU? YOU'LL BE LAUGHING YOUR BOLLOCKS OFF AT ME, RIGHT THIS MINUTE.

I'VE BEEN TRYING NOT TO THINK ABOUT WHERE HE SAID YOU WERE. I KNOW HOW MUCH YOU LOVED MUM. CHERYL DIDN'T NEED TO EXPLAIN IT.

I'D LIKE TO THINK YOU'RE WITH HER NOW, WHEREVER SHE IS.

WELL THEN, DAD. HERE WE ARE.

I'VE SPENT A FORTNIGHT PLANNING, CHECKING AND DOUBLE CHECKING. AND THERE'S NO GETTING AWAY FROM IT...

MARY AN
Beloved
THOMA
and moth
CHERYL
who died
JOHN

October 1923-10

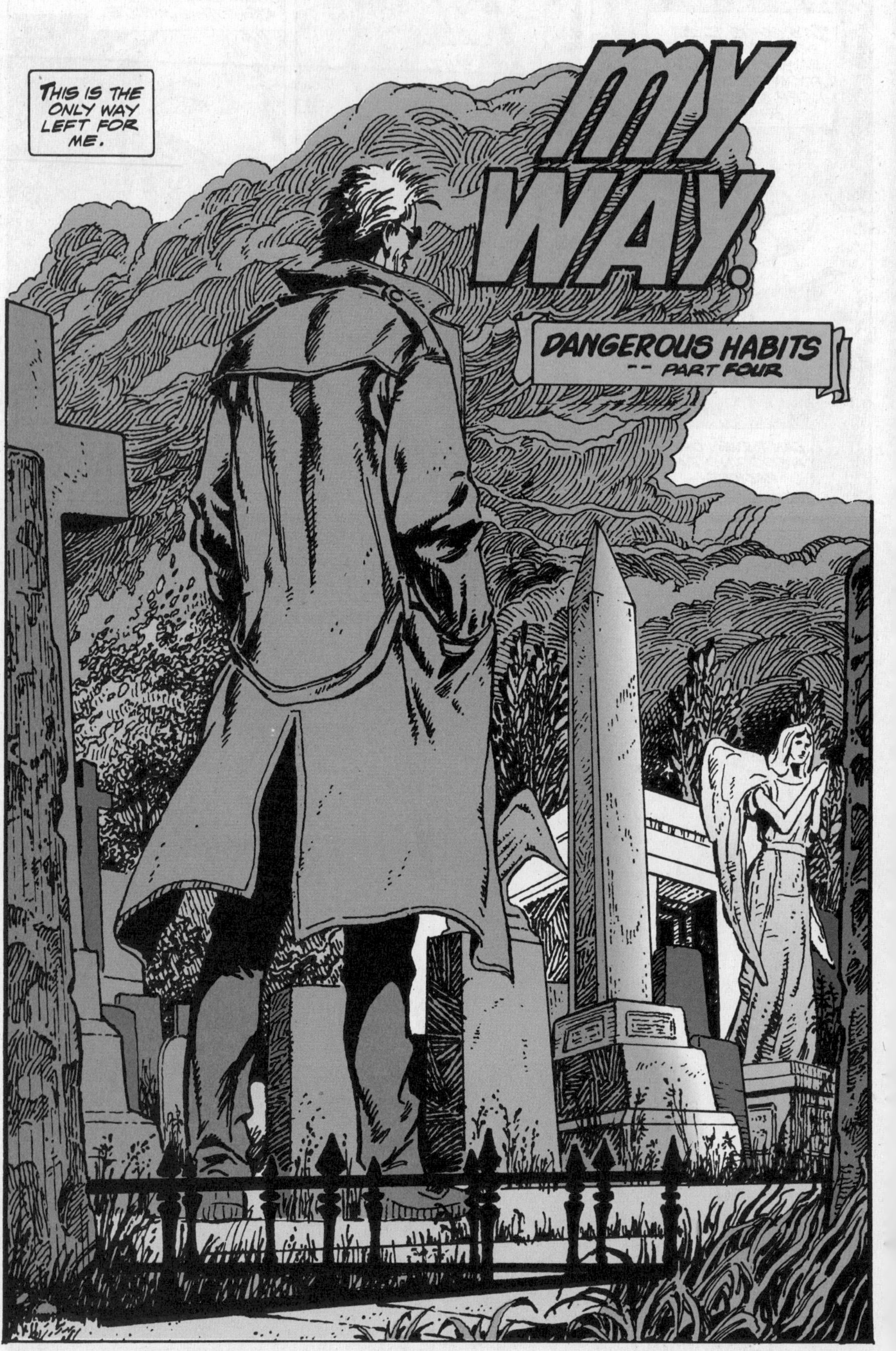
THIS IS THE ONLY WAY LEFT FOR ME.
MY WAY.
DANGEROUS HABITS
-- PART FOUR

NEVER MEANT TO DO THAT. I'M SUPPOSED TO BE IN LIVERPOOL TO SAY GOODBYE TO CHERYL AND GEMMA, BUT...

CHRIST, THIS IS MY LAST DAY HERE AND I THOUGHT, "WHAT THE HELL, LET'S GO AND BE A PRAT IN A GRAVEYARD."

AW WELL.

ALL RIGHT? CHERYL?

IN HERE!

WHY ON EARTH ARE YOU WEARING YOUR COAT, JOHN? IT'S THE MIDDLE OF MAY!

GOT A BIT OF A CHILL, SIS. FLU COMING ON, PROBABLY.

WELL, ACTUALLY, I'VE BEEN MEANING TO SAY...YOU'RE A BIT PALE. WE HEARD YOU COUGHING LAST NIGHT.

IT'S NOTHING SERIOUS, IS IT?

NAH. WELL, NOTHING A CUPPA WOULDN'T HELP.

LAZY SOD.

JOHN, IT'S BEEN NICE HAVING YOU THE LAST COUPLE OF DAYS. I JUST WISH YOU COULD COME UP MORE OFTEN, THAT'S ALL.

mmmm?

YEAH. IT'S GEMMA, REALLY. SHE...SHE NEEDS AN UNCLE RIGHT NOW...

THIS WOULDN'T BE BECAUSE HER DAD SPENDS MOST OF HIS TIME ON VALIUM AFTER A HARD DAYS SCREWING CAPS ONTO TOOTHPASTE TUBES, WOULDN'T IT?

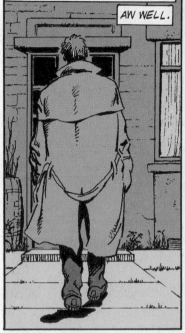

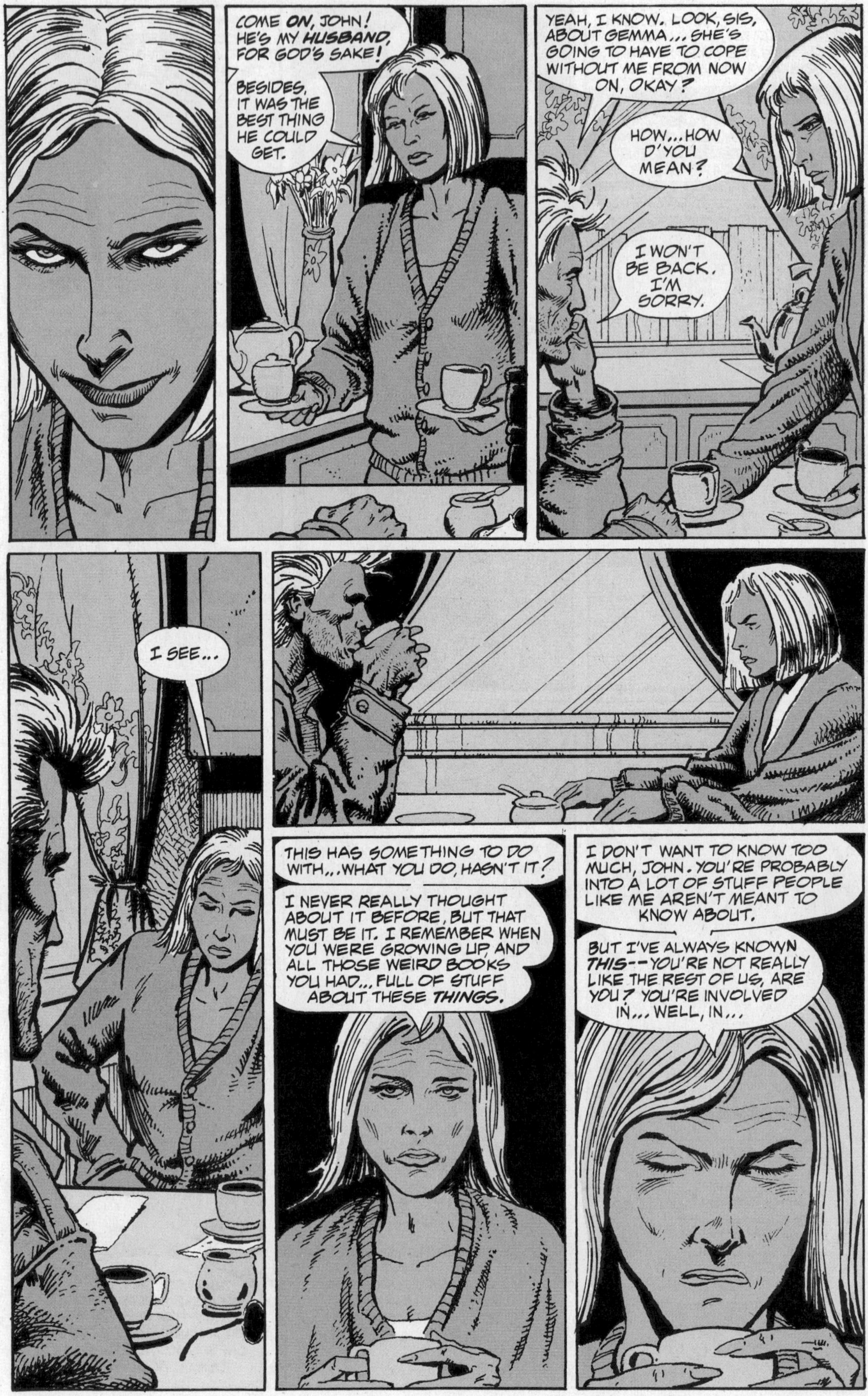
COME ON, JOHN! HE'S MY HUSBAND, FOR GOD'S SAKE!
BESIDES, IT WAS THE BEST THING HE COULD GET.
YEAH, I KNOW. LOOK, SIS, ABOUT GEMMA... SHE'S GOING TO HAVE TO COPE WITHOUT ME FROM NOW ON, OKAY?
HOW... HOW D'YOU MEAN?
I WON'T BE BACK. I'M SORRY.
I SEE...
THIS HAS SOMETHING TO DO WITH... WHAT YOU DO, HASN'T IT?
I NEVER REALLY THOUGHT ABOUT IT BEFORE, BUT THAT MUST BE IT. I REMEMBER WHEN YOU WERE GROWING UP, AND ALL THOSE WEIRD BOOKS YOU HAD... FULL OF STUFF ABOUT THESE THINGS.
I DON'T WANT TO KNOW TOO MUCH, JOHN. YOU'RE PROBABLY INTO A LOT OF STUFF PEOPLE LIKE ME AREN'T MEANT TO KNOW ABOUT.
BUT I'VE ALWAYS KNOWN THIS-- YOU'RE NOT REALLY LIKE THE REST OF US, ARE YOU? YOU'RE INVOLVED IN... WELL, IN...

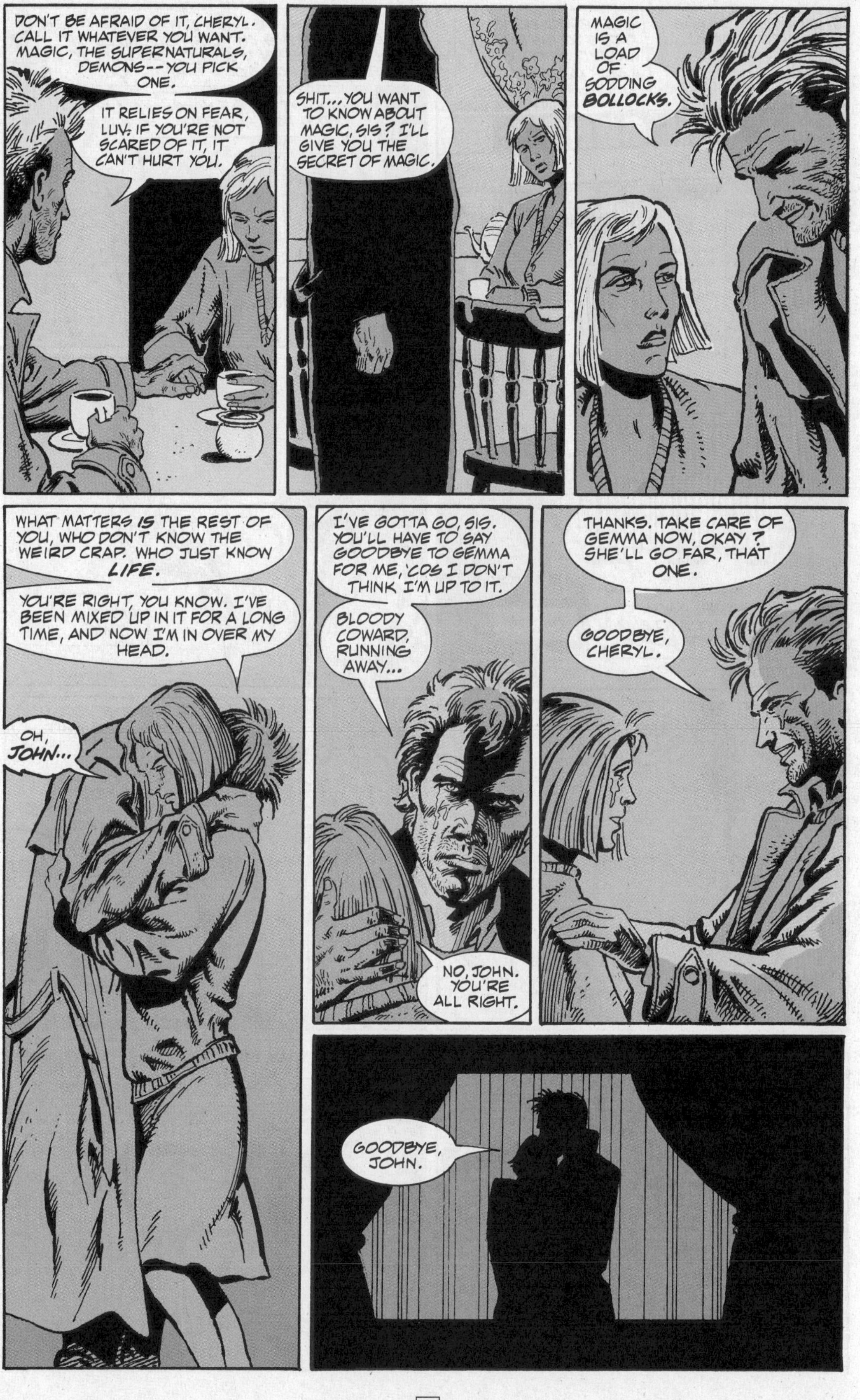

DON'T BE AFRAID OF IT, CHERYL. CALL IT WHATEVER YOU WANT. MAGIC, THE SUPERNATURALS, DEMONS--YOU PICK ONE.
IT RELIES ON FEAR, LUV. IF YOU'RE NOT SCARED OF IT, IT CAN'T HURT YOU.
SHIT... YOU WANT TO KNOW ABOUT MAGIC, SIS? I'LL GIVE YOU THE SECRET OF MAGIC.
MAGIC IS A LOAD OF SODDING BOLLOCKS.
WHAT MATTERS IS THE REST OF YOU, WHO DON'T KNOW THE WEIRD CRAP. WHO JUST KNOW LIFE.
YOU'RE RIGHT, YOU KNOW. I'VE BEEN MIXED UP IN IT FOR A LONG TIME, AND NOW I'M IN OVER MY HEAD.
OH, JOHN...
I'VE GOTTA GO, SIS. YOU'LL HAVE TO SAY GOODBYE TO GEMMA FOR ME, 'COS I DON'T THINK I'M UP TO IT.
BLOODY COWARD, RUNNING AWAY...
NO, JOHN. YOU'RE ALL RIGHT.
THANKS. TAKE CARE OF GEMMA NOW, OKAY? SHE'LL GO FAR, THAT ONE.
GOODBYE, CHERYL.
GOODBYE, JOHN.

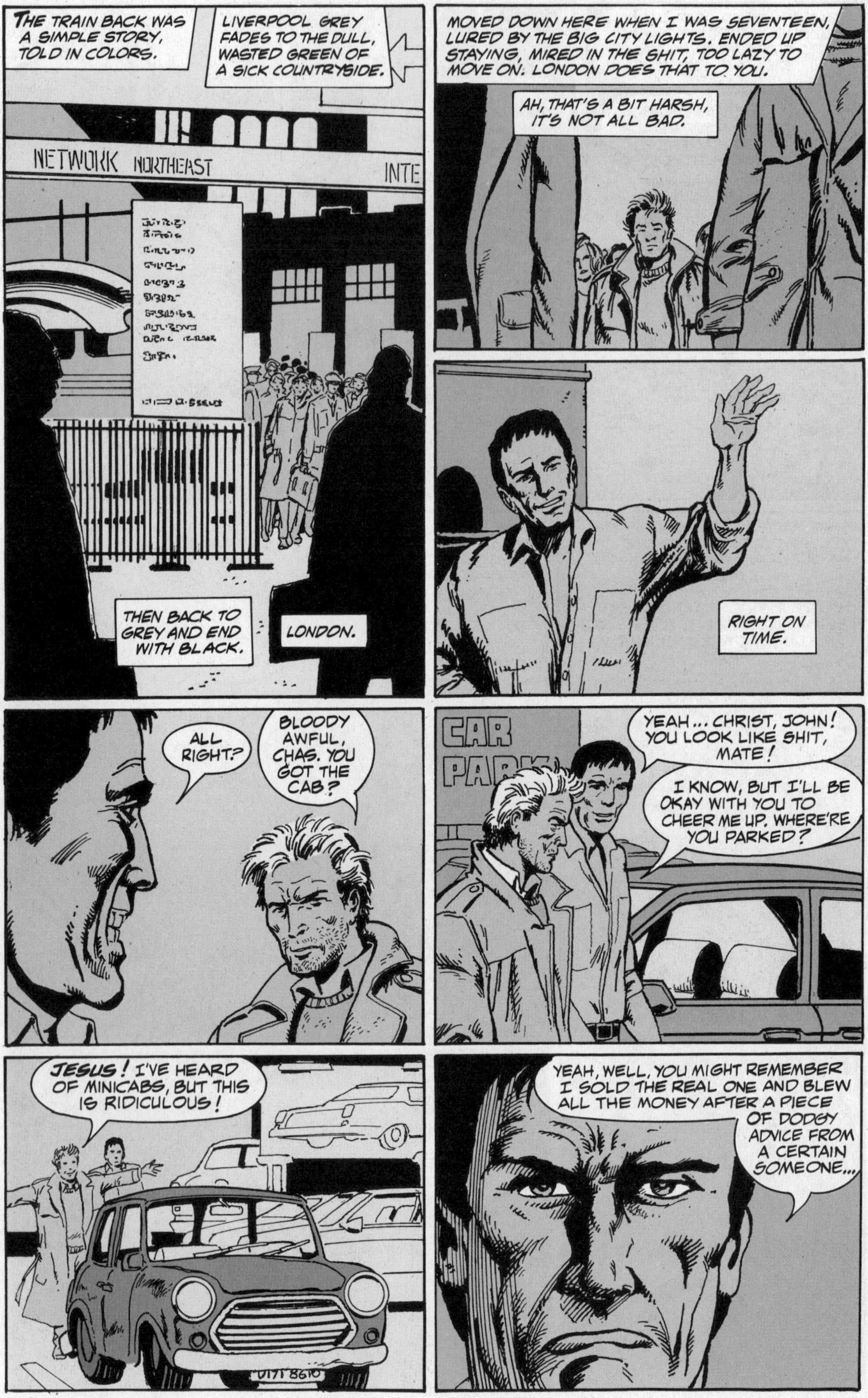
THE TRAIN BACK WAS A SIMPLE STORY, TOLD IN COLORS.
LIVERPOOL GREY FADES TO THE DULL, WASTED GREEN OF A SICK COUNTRYSIDE.
NETWORK NORTHEAST
INTE
THEN BACK TO GREY AND END WITH BLACK.
LONDON.
MOVED DOWN HERE WHEN I WAS SEVENTEEN, LURED BY THE BIG CITY LIGHTS. ENDED UP STAYING, MIRED IN THE SHIT, TOO LAZY TO MOVE ON. LONDON DOES THAT TO YOU.
AH, THAT'S A BIT HARSH, IT'S NOT ALL BAD.
RIGHT ON TIME.
ALL RIGHT?
BLOODY AWFUL, CHAS. YOU GOT THE CAB?
CAR PARK
YEAH... CHRIST, JOHN! YOU LOOK LIKE SHIT, MATE!
I KNOW, BUT I'LL BE OKAY WITH YOU TO CHEER ME UP. WHERE'RE YOU PARKED?
JESUS! I'VE HEARD OF MINICABS, BUT THIS IS RIDICULOUS!
YEAH, WELL, YOU MIGHT REMEMBER I SOLD THE REAL ONE AND BLEW ALL THE MONEY AFTER A PIECE OF DODGY ADVICE FROM A CERTAIN SOMEONE...

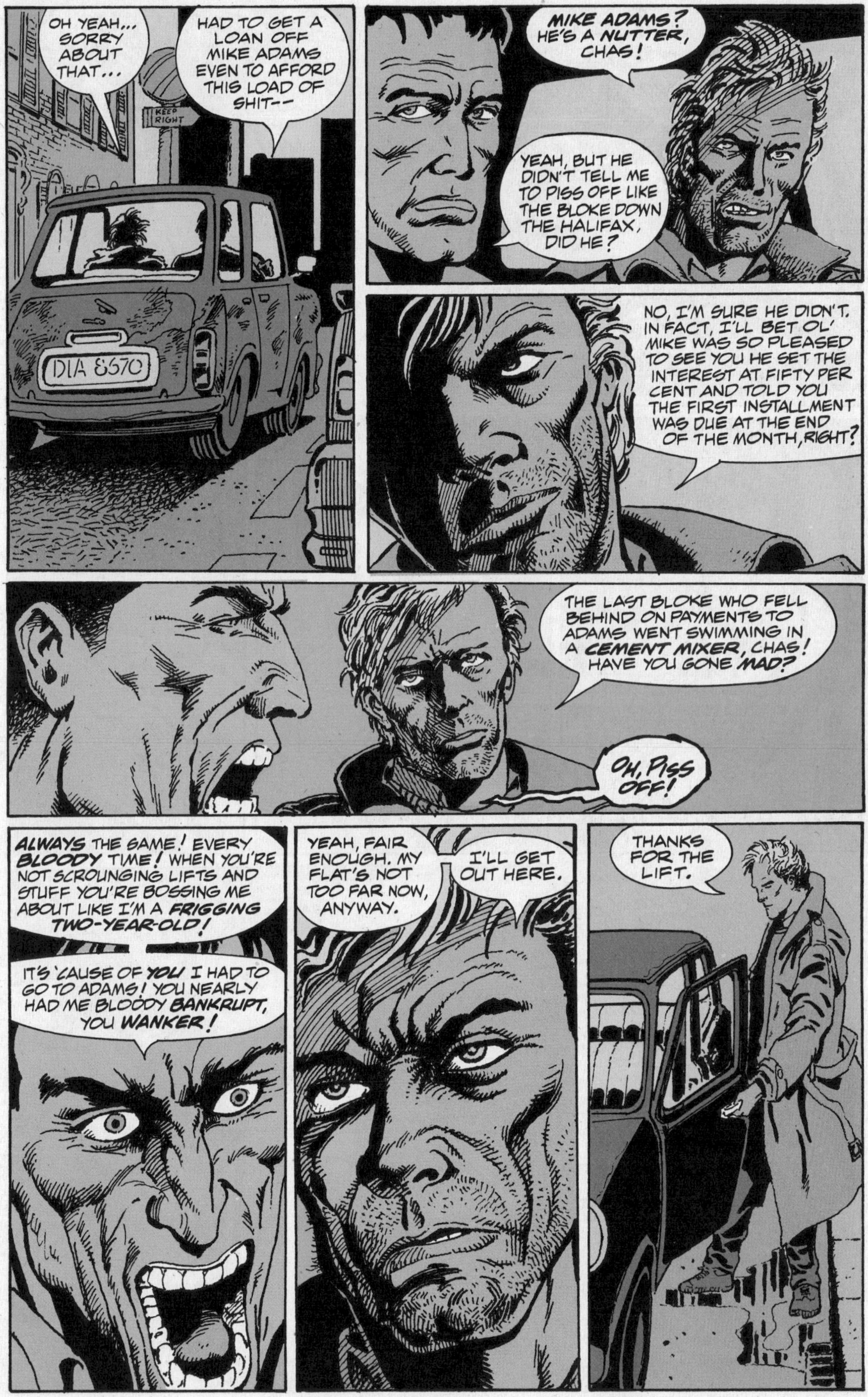

OH YEAH... SORRY ABOUT THAT...
HAD TO GET A LOAN OFF MIKE ADAMS EVEN TO AFFORD THIS LOAD OF SHIT--
KEEP RIGHT
DIA 857O
MIKE ADAMS? HE'S A NUTTER, CHAS!
YEAH, BUT HE DIDN'T TELL ME TO PISS OFF LIKE THE BLOKE DOWN THE HALIFAX, DID HE?
NO, I'M SURE HE DIDN'T. IN FACT, I'LL BET OL' MIKE WAS SO PLEASED TO SEE YOU HE SET THE INTEREST AT FIFTY PER CENT AND TOLD YOU THE FIRST INSTALLMENT WAS DUE AT THE END OF THE MONTH, RIGHT?
THE LAST BLOKE WHO FELL BEHIND ON PAYMENTS TO ADAMS WENT SWIMMING IN A CEMENT MIXER, CHAS! HAVE YOU GONE MAD?
OH, PISS OFF!
ALWAYS THE SAME! EVERY BLOODY TIME! WHEN YOU'RE NOT SCROUNGING LIFTS AND STUFF YOU'RE BOSSING ME ABOUT LIKE I'M A FRIGGING TWO-YEAR-OLD!
IT'S 'CAUSE OF YOU I HAD TO GO TO ADAMS! YOU NEARLY HAD ME BLOODY BANKRUPT, YOU WANKER!
YEAH, FAIR ENOUGH. MY FLAT'S NOT TOO FAR NOW, ANYWAY.
I'LL GET OUT HERE.
THANKS FOR THE LIFT.

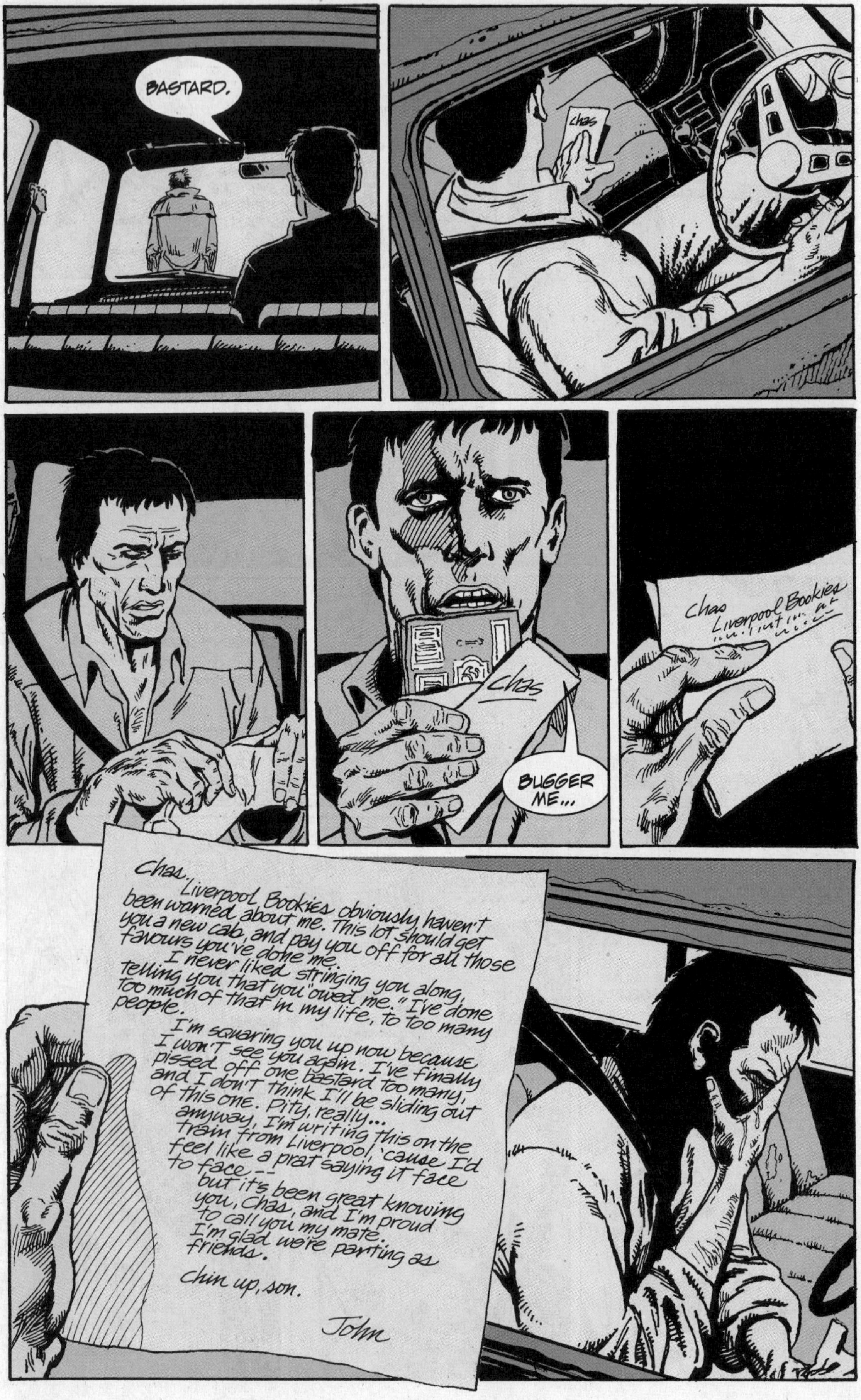
BASTARD.
Chas
Chas
BUGGER ME...
Chas
Liverpool Bookies
Chas,
Liverpool Bookies obviously haven't
been warned about me. This lot should get
you a new cab, and pay you off for all those
favours you've done me.
I never liked stringing you along,
telling you that you "owed me." I've done
too much of that in my life, to too many
people.
I'm squaring you up now because
I won't see you again. I've finally
pissed off one bastard too many,
and I don't think I'll be sliding out
of this one. Pity, really...
anyway, I'm writing this on the
train from Liverpool, 'cause I'd
feel like a prat saying it face
to face --
but it's been great knowing
you, Chas, and I'm proud
to call you my mate.
I'm glad we're parting as
friends.
Chin up, son.
John

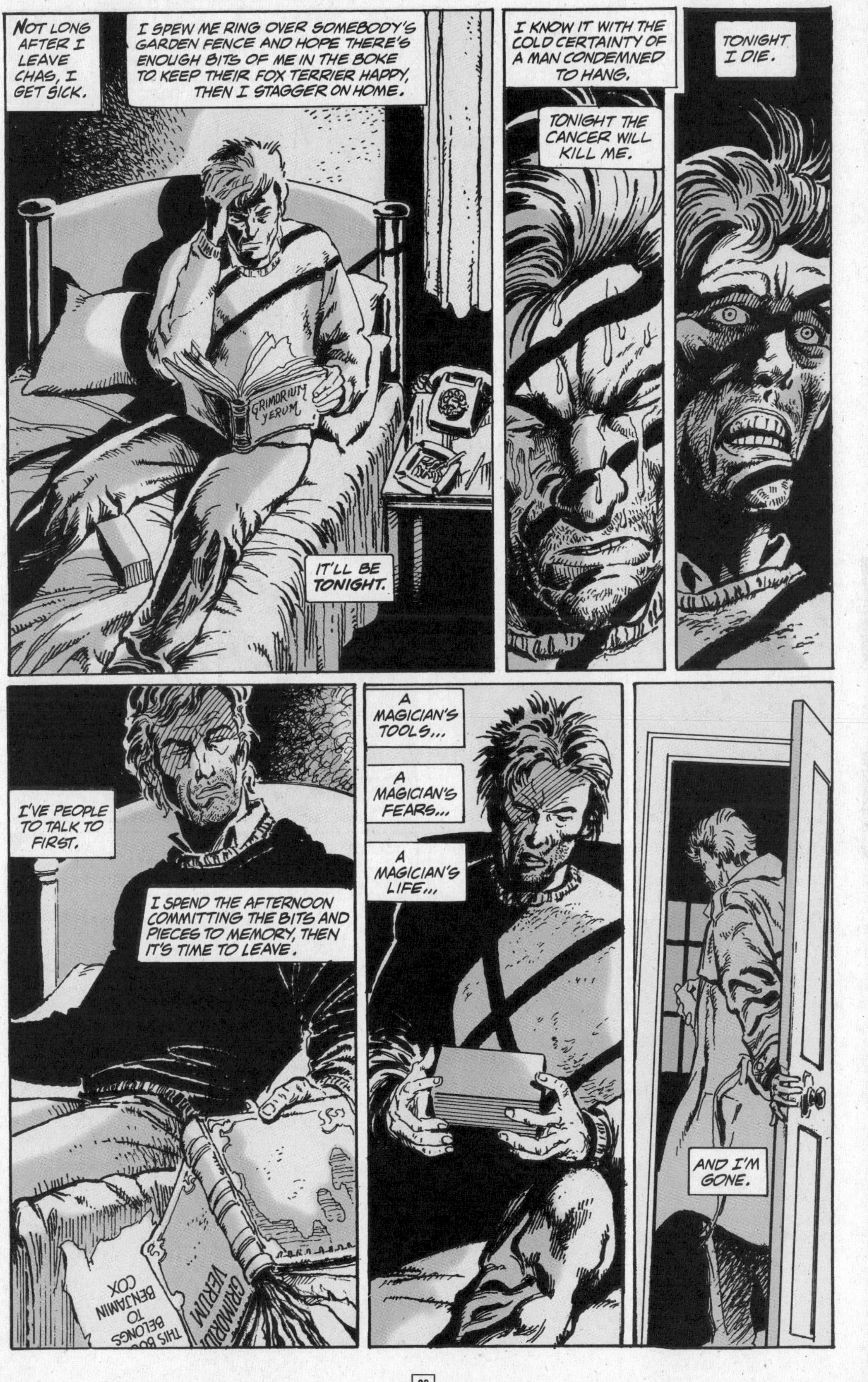
NOT LONG AFTER I LEAVE CHAS, I GET SICK.
I SPEW ME RING OVER SOMEBODY'S GARDEN FENCE AND HOPE THERE'S ENOUGH BITS OF ME IN THE BOKE TO KEEP THEIR FOX TERRIER HAPPY, THEN I STAGGER ON HOME.
GRIMORIUM VERUM
IT'LL BE TONIGHT.
I KNOW IT WITH THE COLD CERTAINTY OF A MAN CONDEMNED TO HANG.
TONIGHT THE CANCER WILL KILL ME.
TONIGHT I DIE.
I'VE PEOPLE TO TALK TO FIRST.
I SPEND THE AFTERNOON COMMITTING THE BITS AND PIECES TO MEMORY, THEN IT'S TIME TO LEAVE.
GRIMORIUM VERUM
THIS BOOK BELONGS TO BENJAMIN COX
A MAGICIAN'S TOOLS...
A MAGICIAN'S FEARS...
A MAGICIAN'S LIFE...
AND I'M GONE.

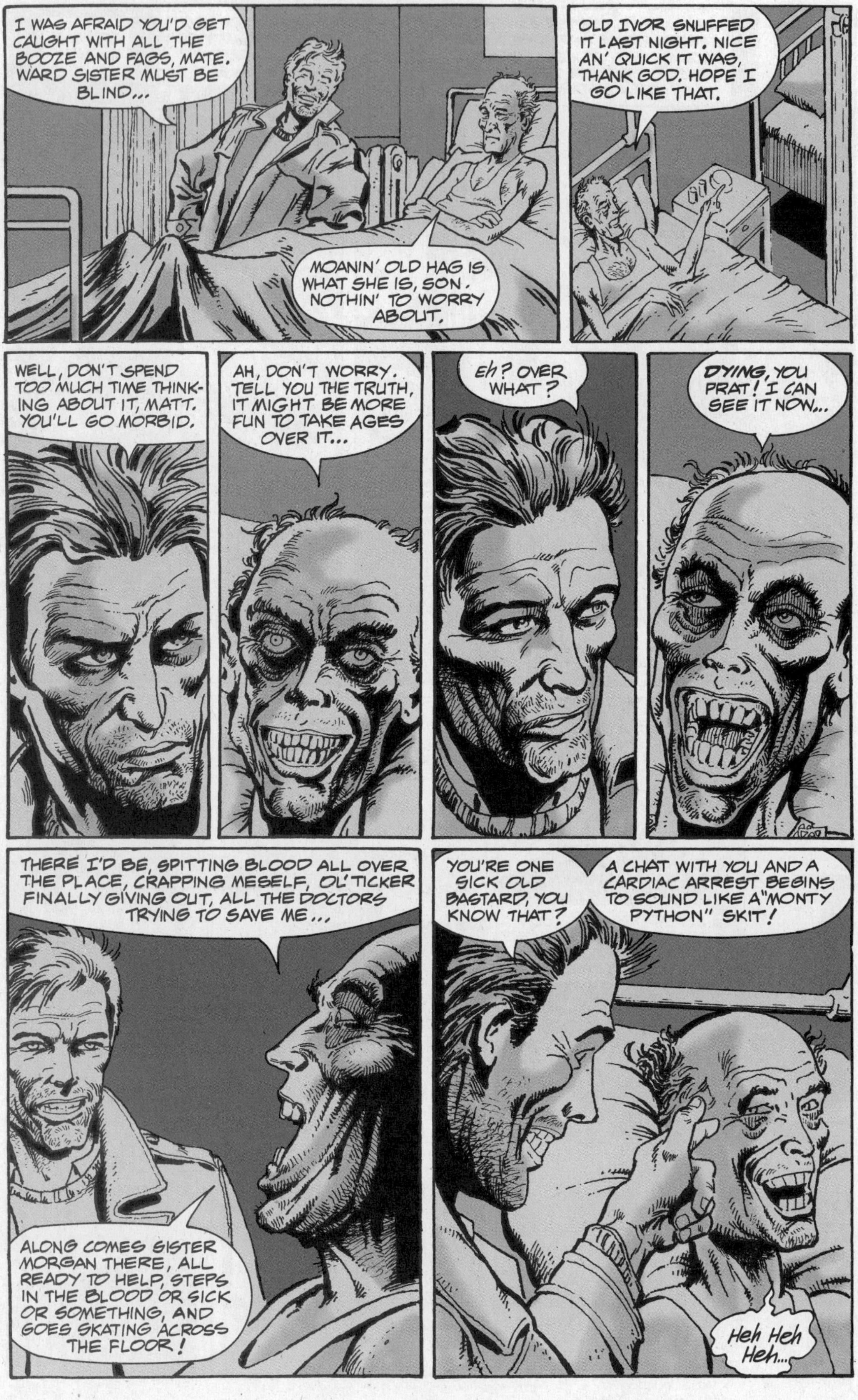
I WAS AFRAID YOU'D GET CAUGHT WITH ALL THE BOOZE AND FAGS, MATE. WARD SISTER MUST BE BLIND...
MOANIN' OLD HAG IS WHAT SHE IS, SON. NOTHIN' TO WORRY ABOUT.
OLD IVOR SNUFFED IT LAST NIGHT. NICE AN' QUICK IT WAS, THANK GOD. HOPE I GO LIKE THAT.
WELL, DON'T SPEND TOO MUCH TIME THINKING ABOUT IT, MATT. YOU'LL GO MORBID.
AH, DON'T WORRY. TELL YOU THE TRUTH, IT MIGHT BE MORE FUN TO TAKE AGES OVER IT...
Eh? OVER WHAT?
DYING, YOU PRAT! I CAN SEE IT NOW...
THERE I'D BE, SPITTING BLOOD ALL OVER THE PLACE, CRAPPING MESELF, OL' TICKER FINALLY GIVING OUT, ALL THE DOCTORS TRYING TO SAVE ME...
ALONG COMES SISTER MORGAN THERE, ALL READY TO HELP, STEPS IN THE BLOOD OR SICK OR SOMETHING, AND GOES SKATING ACROSS THE FLOOR!
YOU'RE ONE SICK OLD BASTARD, YOU KNOW THAT?
A CHAT WITH YOU AND A CARDIAC ARREST BEGINS TO SOUND LIKE A "MONTY PYTHON" SKIT!
Heh Heh Heh...

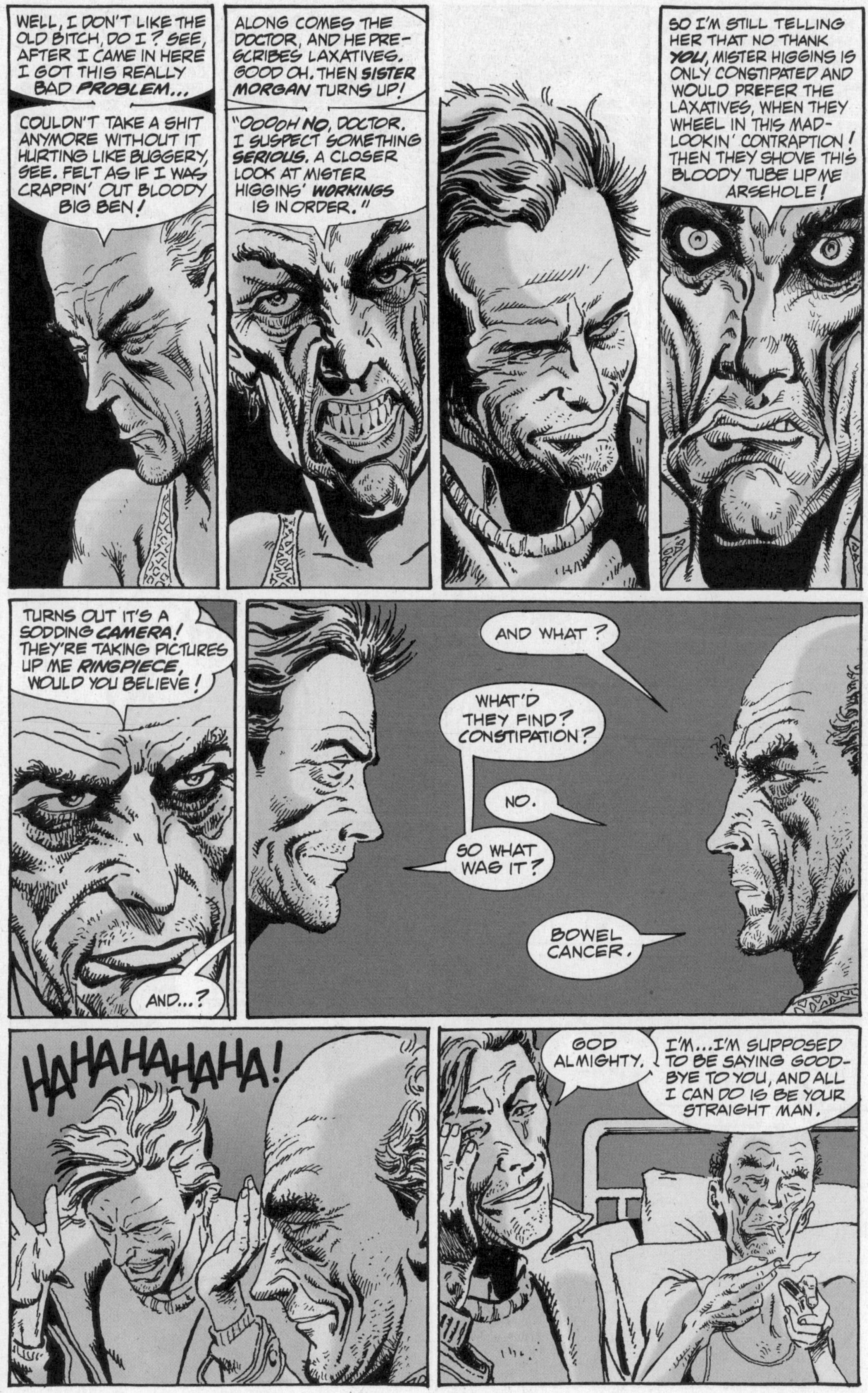
WELL, I DON'T LIKE THE OLD BITCH, DO I? SEE, AFTER I CAME IN HERE I GOT THIS REALLY BAD PROBLEM...
COULDN'T TAKE A SHIT ANYMORE WITHOUT IT HURTING LIKE BUGGERY, SEE. FELT AS IF I WAS CRAPPIN' OUT BLOODY BIG BEN!
ALONG COMES THE DOCTOR, AND HE PRESCRIBES LAXATIVES. GOOD OH. THEN SISTER MORGAN TURNS UP!
"OOOOH NO, DOCTOR. I SUSPECT SOMETHING SERIOUS. A CLOSER LOOK AT MISTER HIGGINS' WORKINGS IS IN ORDER."
SO I'M STILL TELLING HER THAT NO THANK YOU, MISTER HIGGINS IS ONLY CONSTIPATED AND WOULD PREFER THE LAXATIVES, WHEN THEY WHEEL IN THIS MAD-LOOKIN' CONTRAPTION! THEN THEY SHOVE THIS BLOODY TUBE UP ME ARSEHOLE!
TURNS OUT IT'S A SODDING CAMERA! THEY'RE TAKING PICTURES UP ME RINGPIECE, WOULD YOU BELIEVE!
AND...?
AND WHAT?
WHAT'D THEY FIND? CONSTIPATION?
NO.
SO WHAT WAS IT?
BOWEL CANCER.
HAHAHAHAHA!
GOD ALMIGHTY.
I'M...I'M SUPPOSED TO BE SAYING GOOD-BYE TO YOU, AND ALL I CAN DO IS BE YOUR STRAIGHT MAN.

HERE, HOLD ON... WHAT D'YOU MEAN, "SAYING GOODBYE"? WHAT YOU ON ABOUT?

WELL, JUST THAT, REALLY.

I'M GOING TO BE...WELL, I WON'T BE BACK. I'M SORRY.

LISTEN, SON. YOU DON'T HAVE TO SAY YOU'RE SORRY TO ME. YOU CAME TO SEE ME AND BROUGHT ME STUFF AND TALKED TO ME.

YOU DON'T OWE ME ANY APOLOGIES.

NNNNG--

HEY, MATT! TAKE IT EASY--

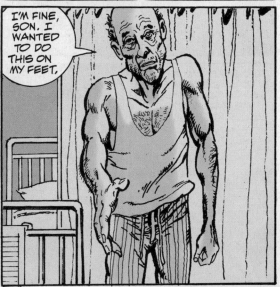

I'M FINE, SON. I WANTED TO DO THIS ON MY FEET.

GOODBYE NOW, JOHN.

'BYE, MATT. TAKE CARE.

YEAH...LOOK, DON'T EVER BE SORRY, SON. REGRETS AREN'T WORTH A BUGGER.

SEE YOU.

96

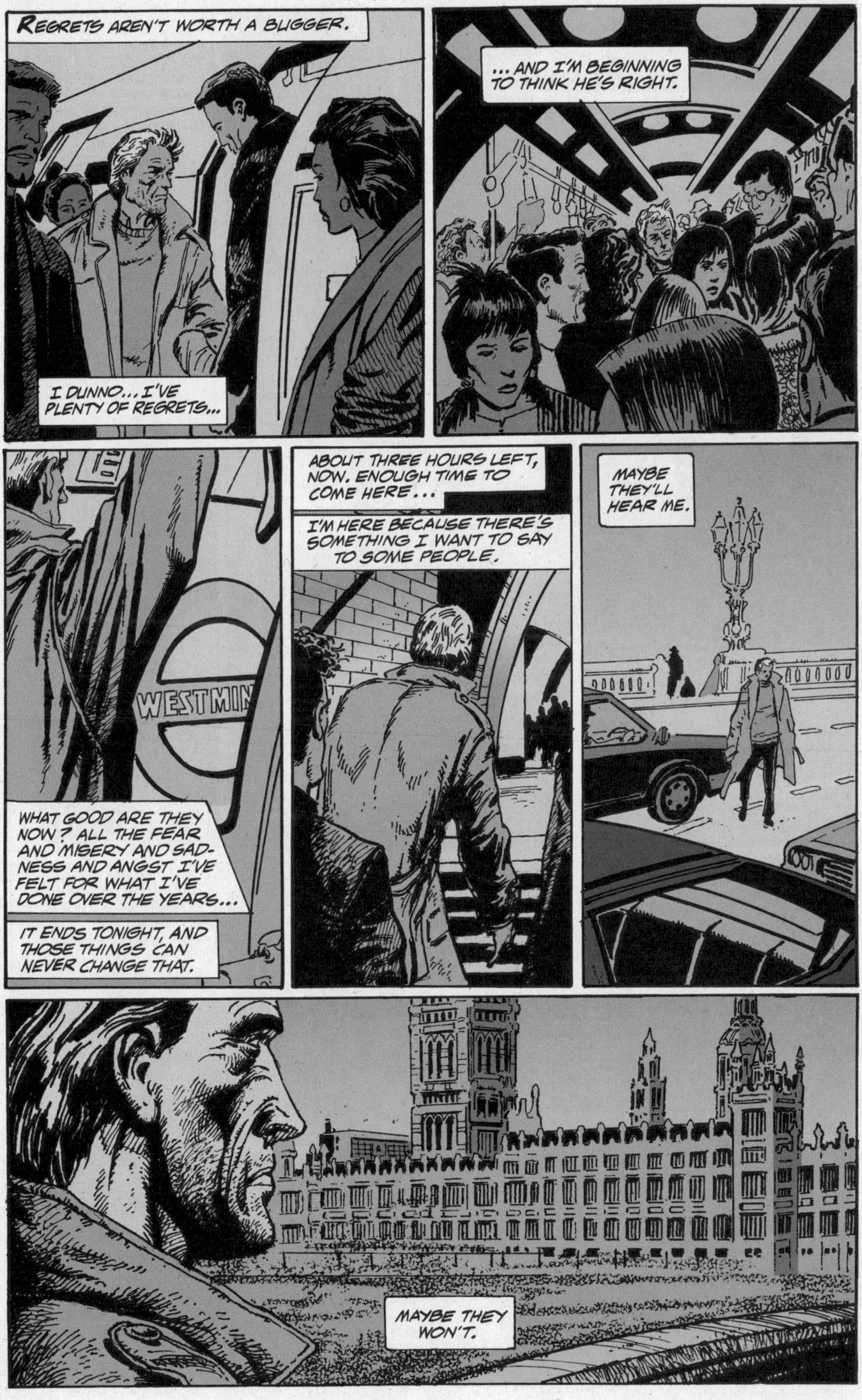
REGRETS AREN'T WORTH A BUGGER.
I DUNNO... I'VE PLENTY OF REGRETS...
...AND I'M BEGINNING TO THINK HE'S RIGHT.
WESTMIN
WHAT GOOD ARE THEY NOW? ALL THE FEAR AND MISERY AND SADNESS AND ANGST I'VE FELT FOR WHAT I'VE DONE OVER THE YEARS...
IT ENDS TONIGHT, AND THOSE THINGS CAN NEVER CHANGE THAT.
ABOUT THREE HOURS LEFT, NOW. ENOUGH TIME TO COME HERE...
I'M HERE BECAUSE THERE'S SOMETHING I WANT TO SAY TO SOME PEOPLE.
MAYBE THEY'LL HEAR ME.
MAYBE THEY WON'T.

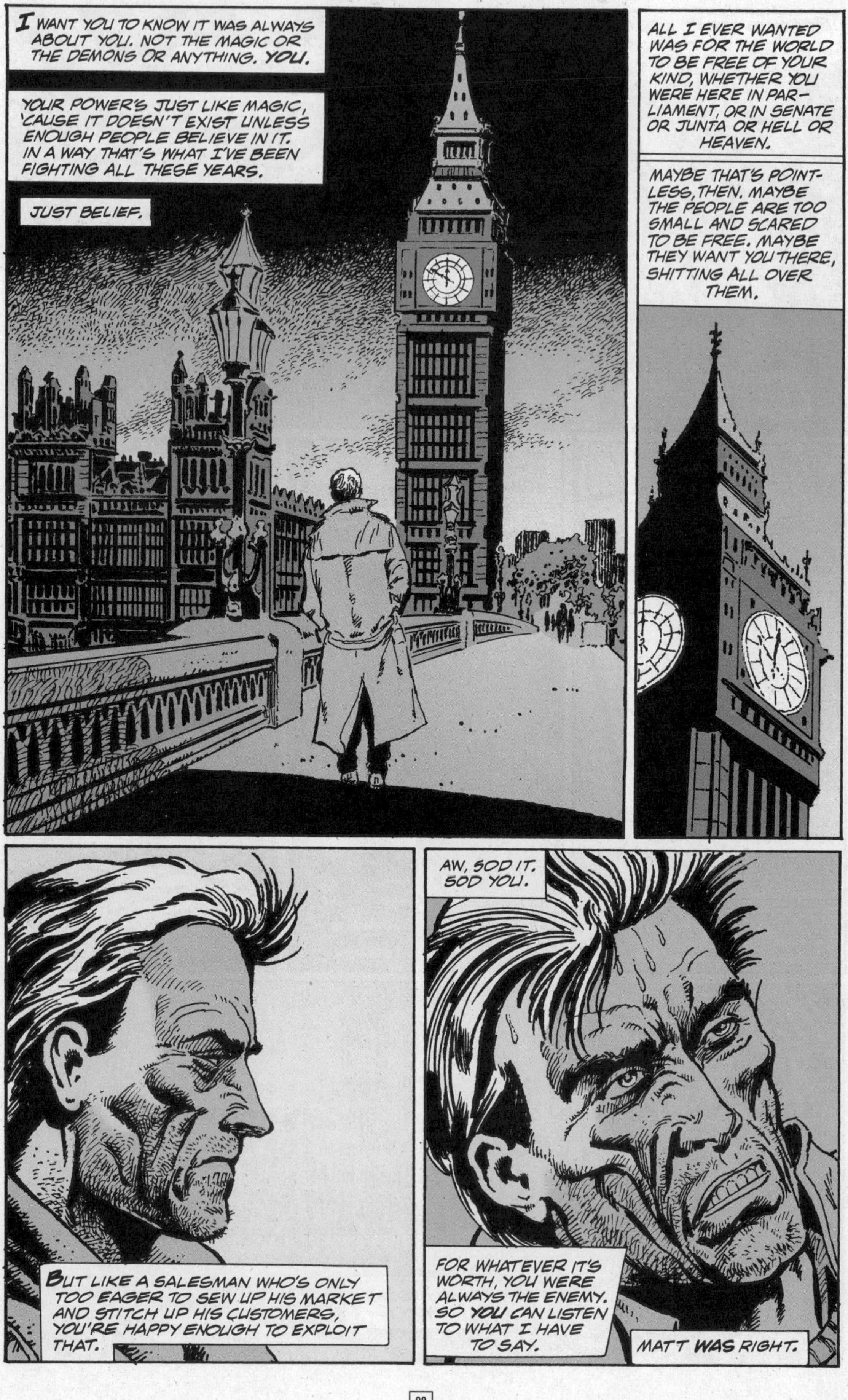
I WANT YOU TO KNOW IT WAS ALWAYS ABOUT YOU. NOT THE MAGIC OR THE DEMONS OR ANYTHING. YOU.
YOUR POWER'S JUST LIKE MAGIC, 'CAUSE IT DOESN'T EXIST UNLESS ENOUGH PEOPLE BELIEVE IN IT. IN A WAY THAT'S WHAT I'VE BEEN FIGHTING ALL THESE YEARS.
JUST BELIEF.
ALL I EVER WANTED WAS FOR THE WORLD TO BE FREE OF YOUR KIND, WHETHER YOU WERE HERE IN PARLIAMENT, OR IN SENATE OR JUNTA OR HELL OR HEAVEN.
MAYBE THAT'S POINTLESS, THEN. MAYBE THE PEOPLE ARE TOO SMALL AND SCARED TO BE FREE. MAYBE THEY WANT YOU THERE, SHITTING ALL OVER THEM.
BUT LIKE A SALESMAN WHO'S ONLY TOO EAGER TO SEW UP HIS MARKET AND STITCH UP HIS CUSTOMERS, YOU'RE HAPPY ENOUGH TO EXPLOIT THAT.
AW, SOD IT. SOD YOU.
FOR WHATEVER IT'S WORTH, YOU WERE ALWAYS THE ENEMY. SO YOU CAN LISTEN TO WHAT I HAVE TO SAY.
MATT WAS RIGHT.

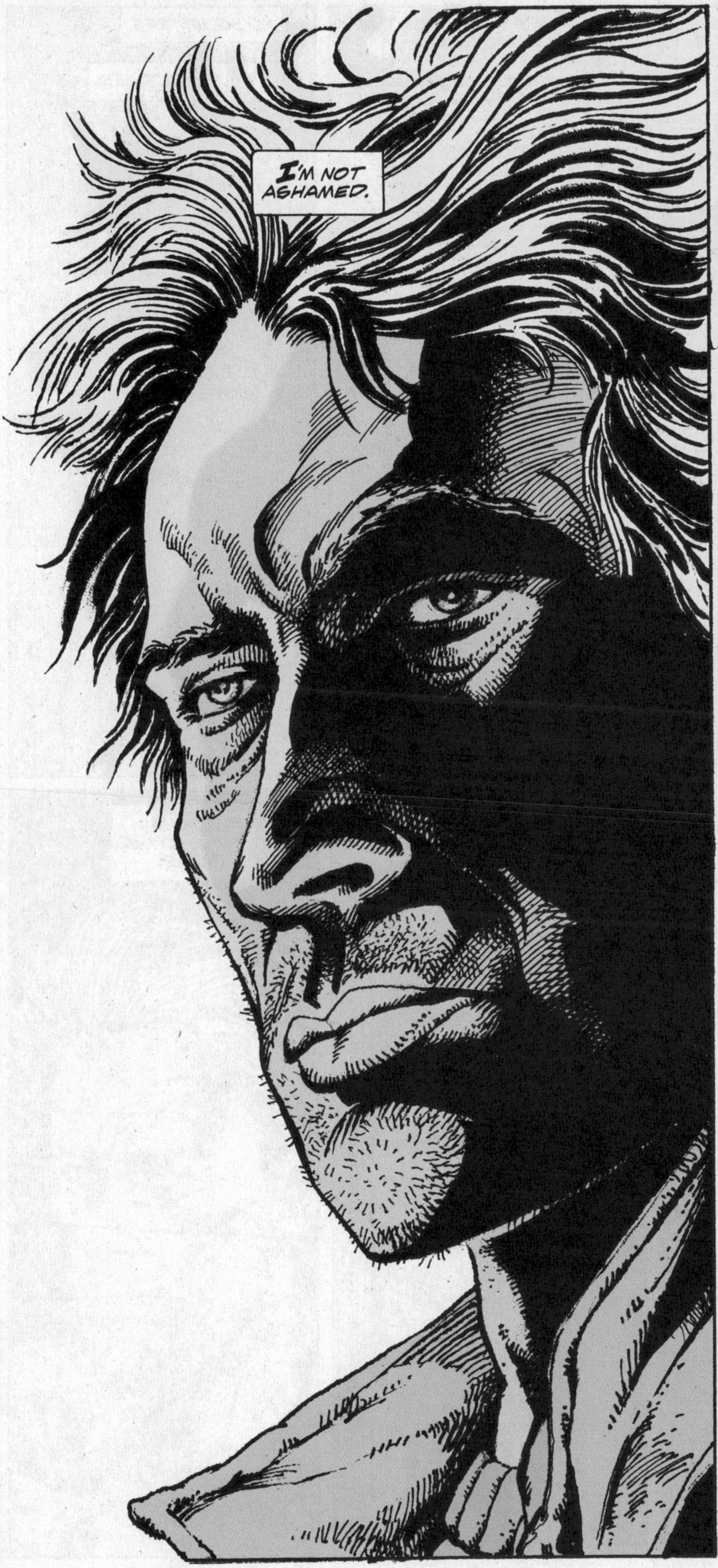
I'M NOT ASHAMED.

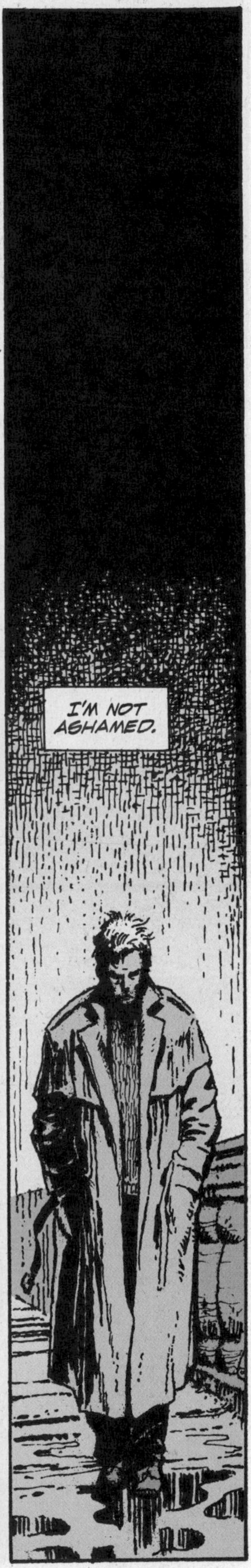
I'M NOT ASHAMED.

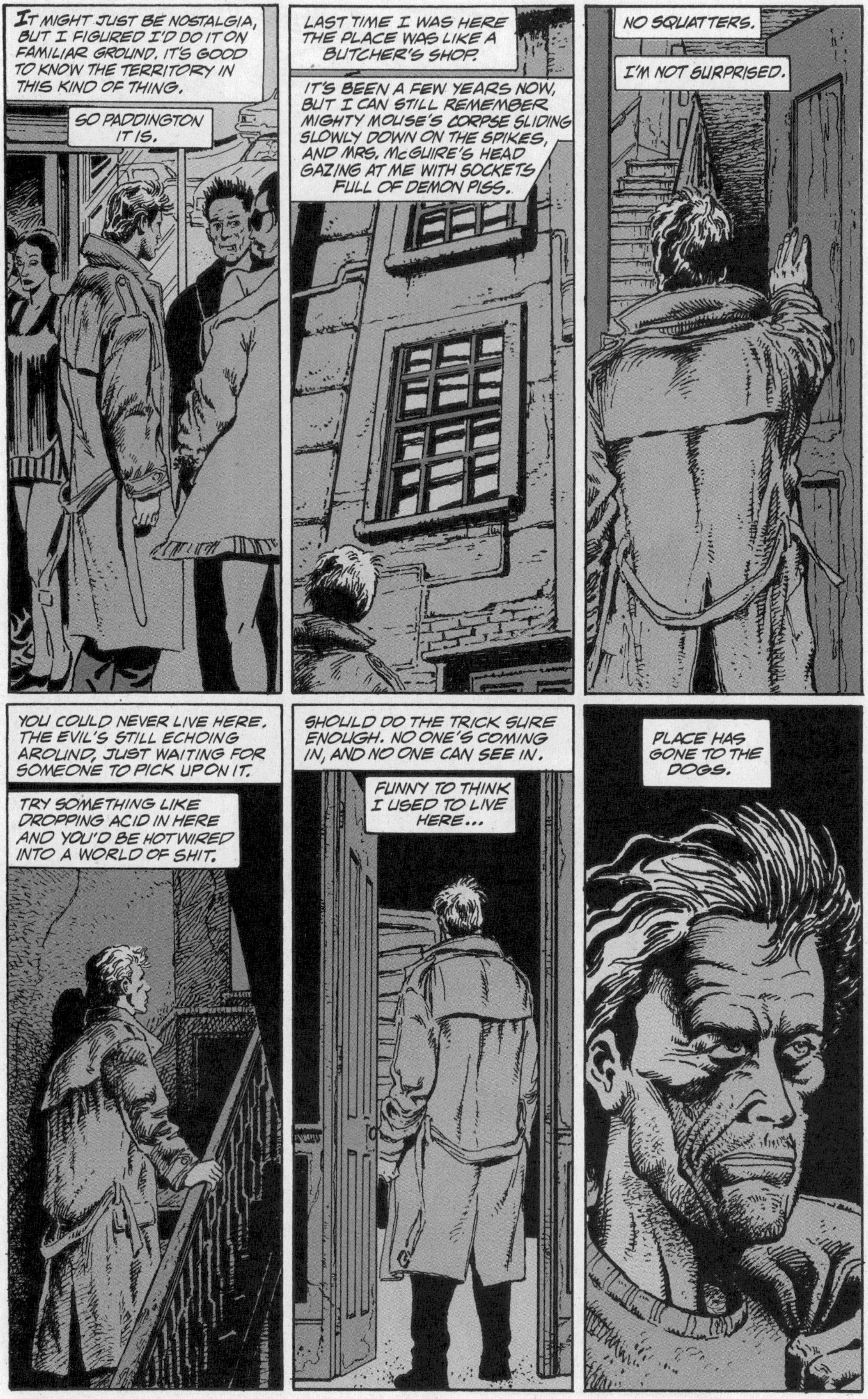
IT MIGHT JUST BE NOSTALGIA, BUT I FIGURED I'D DO IT ON FAMILIAR GROUND. IT'S GOOD TO KNOW THE TERRITORY IN THIS KIND OF THING.
SO PADDINGTON IT IS.
LAST TIME I WAS HERE THE PLACE WAS LIKE A BUTCHER'S SHOP.
IT'S BEEN A FEW YEARS NOW, BUT I CAN STILL REMEMBER MIGHTY MOUSE'S CORPSE SLIDING SLOWLY DOWN ON THE SPIKES, AND MRS. McGUIRE'S HEAD GAZING AT ME WITH SOCKETS FULL OF DEMON PISS.
NO SQUATTERS.
I'M NOT SURPRISED.
YOU COULD NEVER LIVE HERE. THE EVIL'S STILL ECHOING AROUND, JUST WAITING FOR SOMEONE TO PICK UPON IT.
TRY SOMETHING LIKE DROPPING ACID IN HERE AND YOU'D BE HOTWIRED INTO A WORLD OF SHIT.
SHOULD DO THE TRICK SURE ENOUGH. NO ONE'S COMING IN, AND NO ONE CAN SEE IN.
FUNNY TO THINK I USED TO LIVE HERE...
PLACE HAS GONE TO THE DOGS.

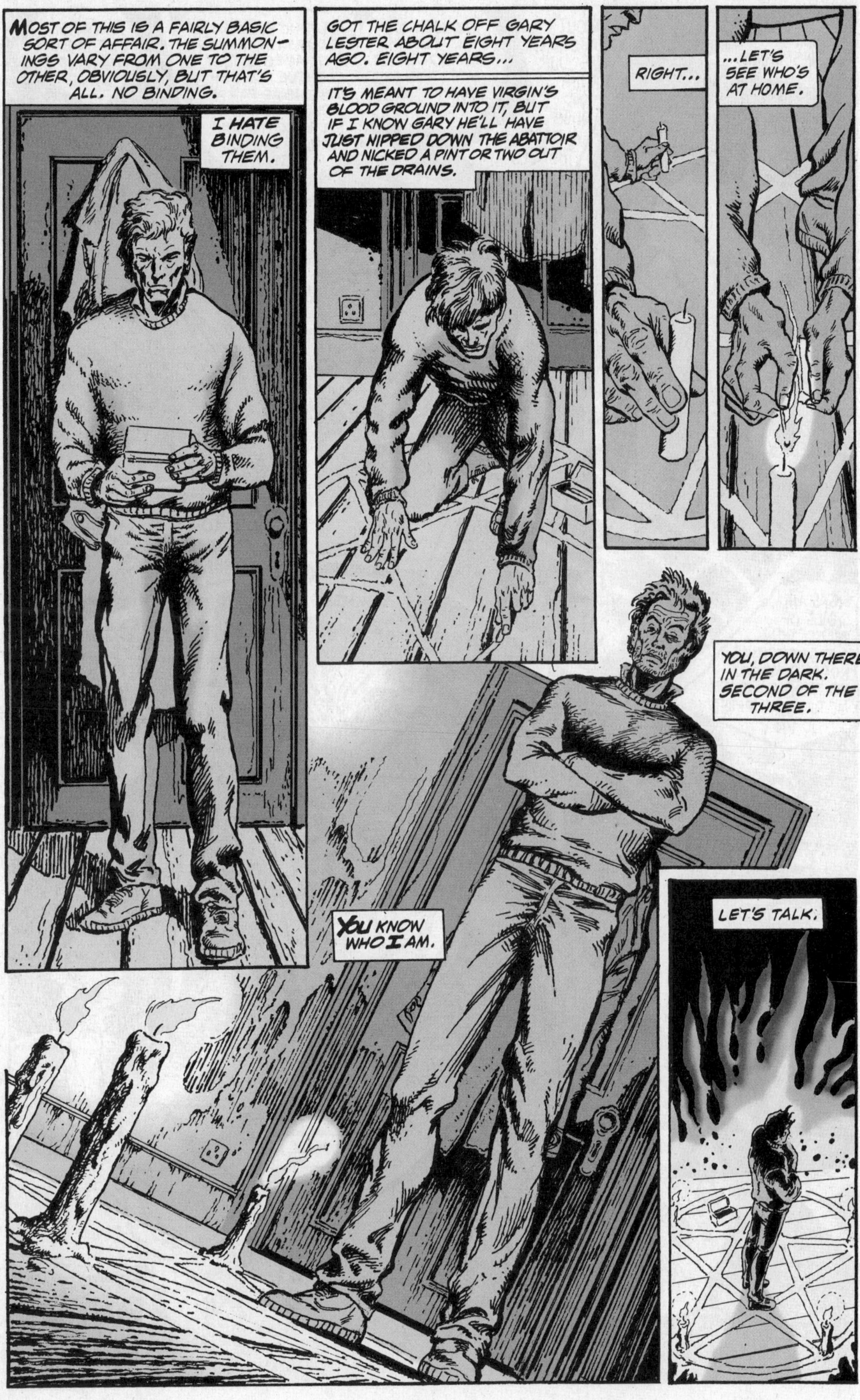
MOST OF THIS IS A FAIRLY BASIC SORT OF AFFAIR. THE SUMMONINGS VARY FROM ONE TO THE OTHER, OBVIOUSLY, BUT THAT'S ALL. NO BINDING.
I HATE BINDING THEM.
GOT THE CHALK OFF GARY LESTER ABOUT EIGHT YEARS AGO. EIGHT YEARS...
IT'S MEANT TO HAVE VIRGIN'S BLOOD GROUND INTO IT, BUT IF I KNOW GARY HE'LL HAVE JUST NIPPED DOWN THE ABATTOIR AND NICKED A PINT OR TWO OUT OF THE DRAINS.
RIGHT...
...LET'S SEE WHO'S AT HOME.
YOU, DOWN THERE IN THE DARK. SECOND OF THE THREE.
YOU KNOW WHO I AM.
LET'S TALK.

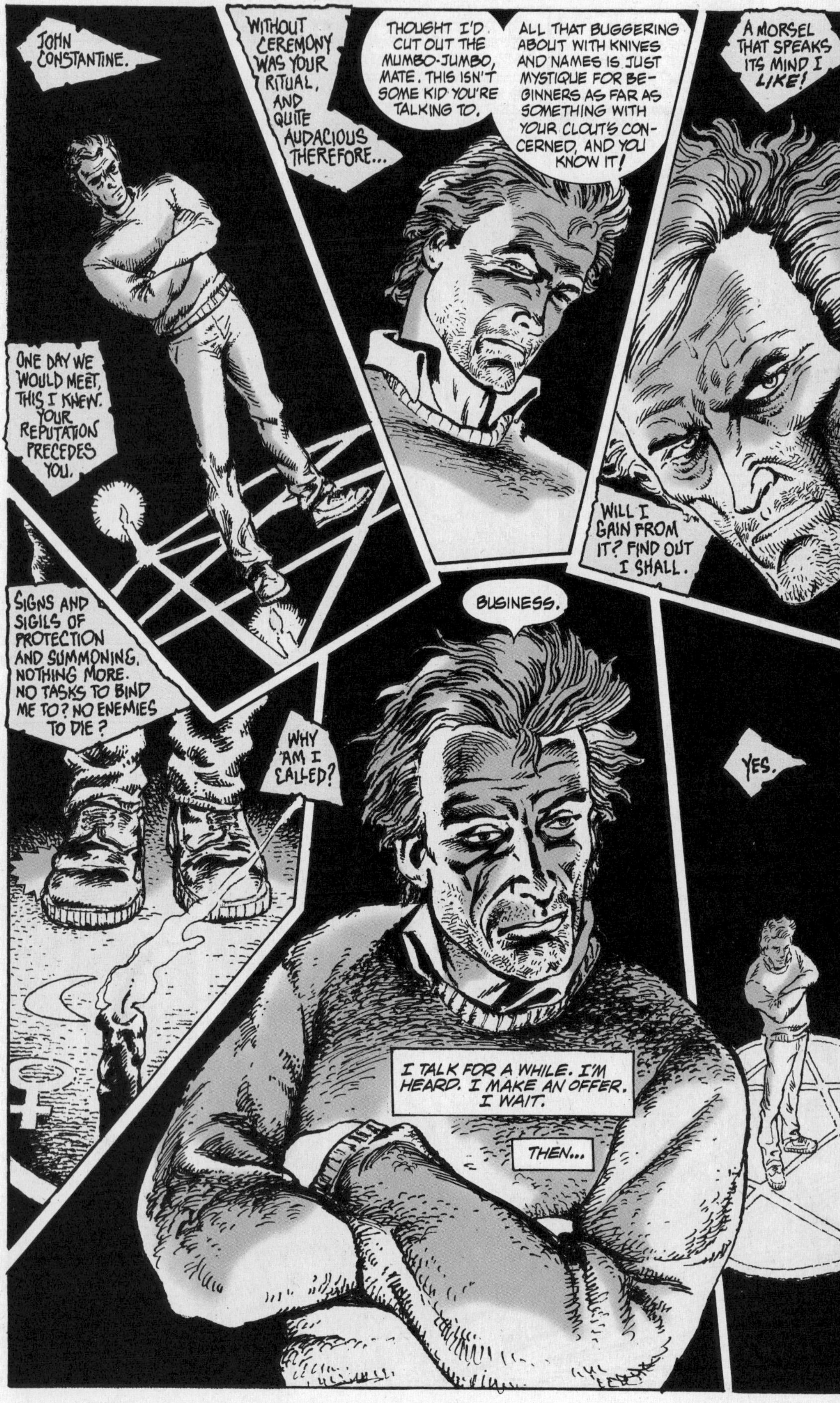
JOHN CONSTANTINE.
WITHOUT CEREMONY WAS YOUR RITUAL, AND QUITE AUDACIOUS THEREFORE...
THOUGHT I'D CUT OUT THE MUMBO-JUMBO, MATE. THIS ISN'T SOME KID YOU'RE TALKING TO.
ALL THAT BUGGERING ABOUT WITH KNIVES AND NAMES IS JUST MYSTIQUE FOR BEGINNERS AS FAR AS SOMETHING WITH YOUR CLOUT'S CONCERNED, AND YOU KNOW IT!
A MORSEL THAT SPEAKS ITS MIND I LIKE!
WILL I GAIN FROM IT? FIND OUT I SHALL.
ONE DAY WE WOULD MEET, THIS I KNEW. YOUR REPUTATION PRECEDES YOU.
SIGNS AND SIGILS OF PROTECTION AND SUMMONING. NOTHING MORE. NO TASKS TO BIND ME TO? NO ENEMIES TO DIE?
WHY AM I CALLED?
BUSINESS.
YES.
I TALK FOR A WHILE. I'M HEARD. I MAKE AN OFFER. I WAIT.
THEN...

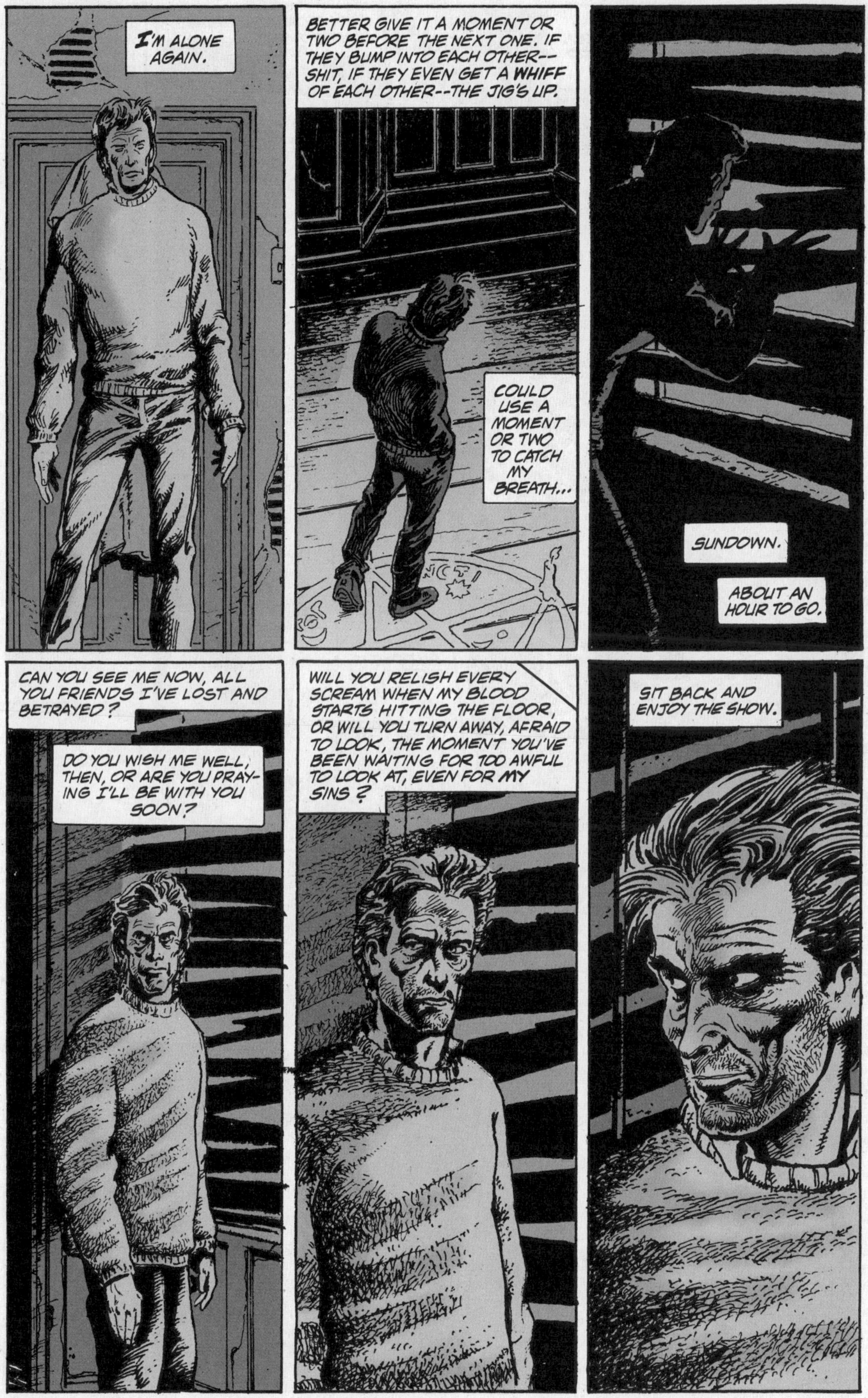
I'M ALONE AGAIN.
BETTER GIVE IT A MOMENT OR TWO BEFORE THE NEXT ONE. IF THEY BUMP INTO EACH OTHER-- SHIT, IF THEY EVEN GET A WHIFF OF EACH OTHER--THE JIG'S UP.
COULD USE A MOMENT OR TWO TO CATCH MY BREATH...
SUNDOWN.
ABOUT AN HOUR TO GO.
CAN YOU SEE ME NOW, ALL YOU FRIENDS I'VE LOST AND BETRAYED?
DO YOU WISH ME WELL, THEN, OR ARE YOU PRAYING I'LL BE WITH YOU SOON?
WILL YOU RELISH EVERY SCREAM WHEN MY BLOOD STARTS HITTING THE FLOOR, OR WILL YOU TURN AWAY, AFRAID TO LOOK, THE MOMENT YOU'VE BEEN WAITING FOR TOO AWFUL TO LOOK AT, EVEN FOR MY SINS?
SIT BACK AND ENJOY THE SHOW.

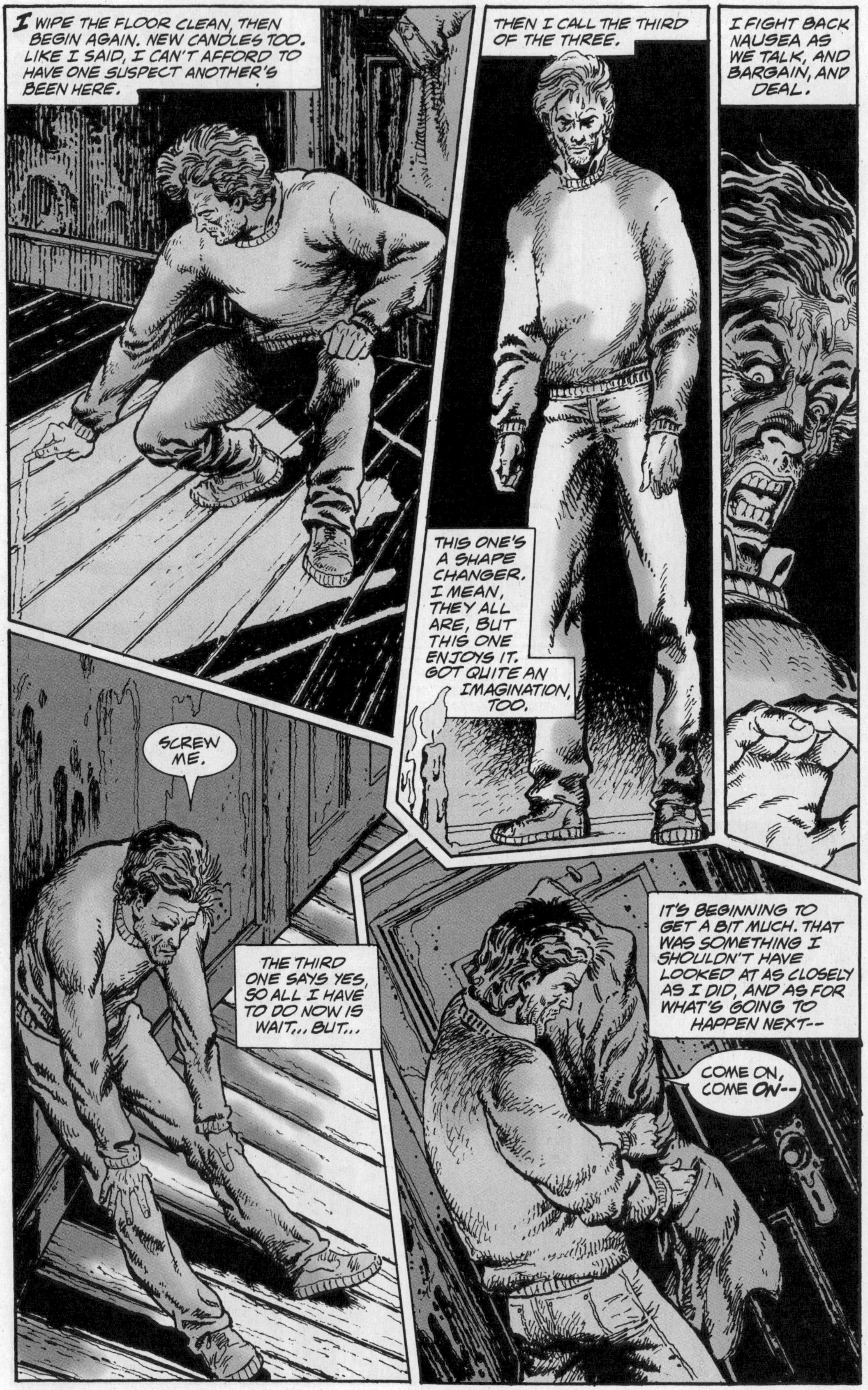
I WIPE THE FLOOR CLEAN, THEN BEGIN AGAIN. NEW CANDLES TOO. LIKE I SAID, I CAN'T AFFORD TO HAVE ONE SUSPECT ANOTHER'S BEEN HERE.
THEN I CALL THE THIRD OF THE THREE.
THIS ONE'S A SHAPE CHANGER. I MEAN, THEY ALL ARE, BUT THIS ONE ENJOYS IT. GOT QUITE AN IMAGINATION, TOO.
I FIGHT BACK NAUSEA AS WE TALK, AND BARGAIN, AND DEAL.
SCREW ME.
THE THIRD ONE SAYS YES, SO ALL I HAVE TO DO NOW IS WAIT... BUT...
IT'S BEGINNING TO GET A BIT MUCH. THAT WAS SOMETHING I SHOULDN'T HAVE LOOKED AT AS CLOSELY AS I DID, AND AS FOR WHAT'S GOING TO HAPPEN NEXT--
COME ON, COME ON--

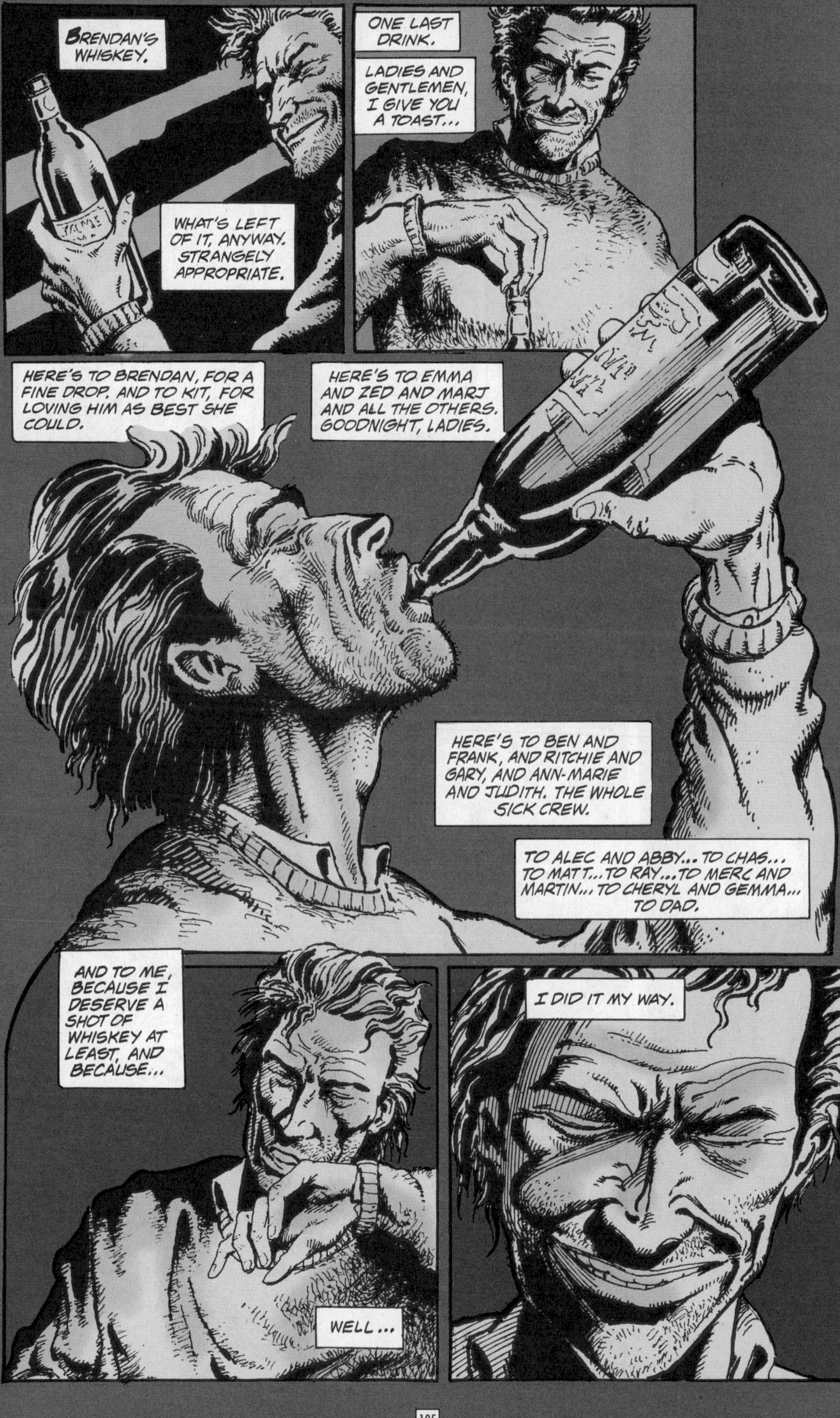
BRENDAN'S WHISKEY.
WHAT'S LEFT OF IT, ANYWAY. STRANGELY APPROPRIATE.
ONE LAST DRINK.
LADIES AND GENTLEMEN, I GIVE YOU A TOAST...
HERE'S TO BRENDAN, FOR A FINE DROP. AND TO KIT, FOR LOVING HIM AS BEST SHE COULD.
HERE'S TO EMMA AND ZED AND MARJ AND ALL THE OTHERS. GOODNIGHT, LADIES.
HERE'S TO BEN AND FRANK, AND RITCHIE AND GARY, AND ANN-MARIE AND JUDITH. THE WHOLE SICK CREW.
TO ALEC AND ABBY... TO CHAS... TO MATT... TO RAY... TO MERC AND MARTIN... TO CHERYL AND GEMMA... TO DAD.
AND TO ME, BECAUSE I DESERVE A SHOT OF WHISKEY AT LEAST, AND BECAUSE...
WELL...
I DID IT MY WAY.

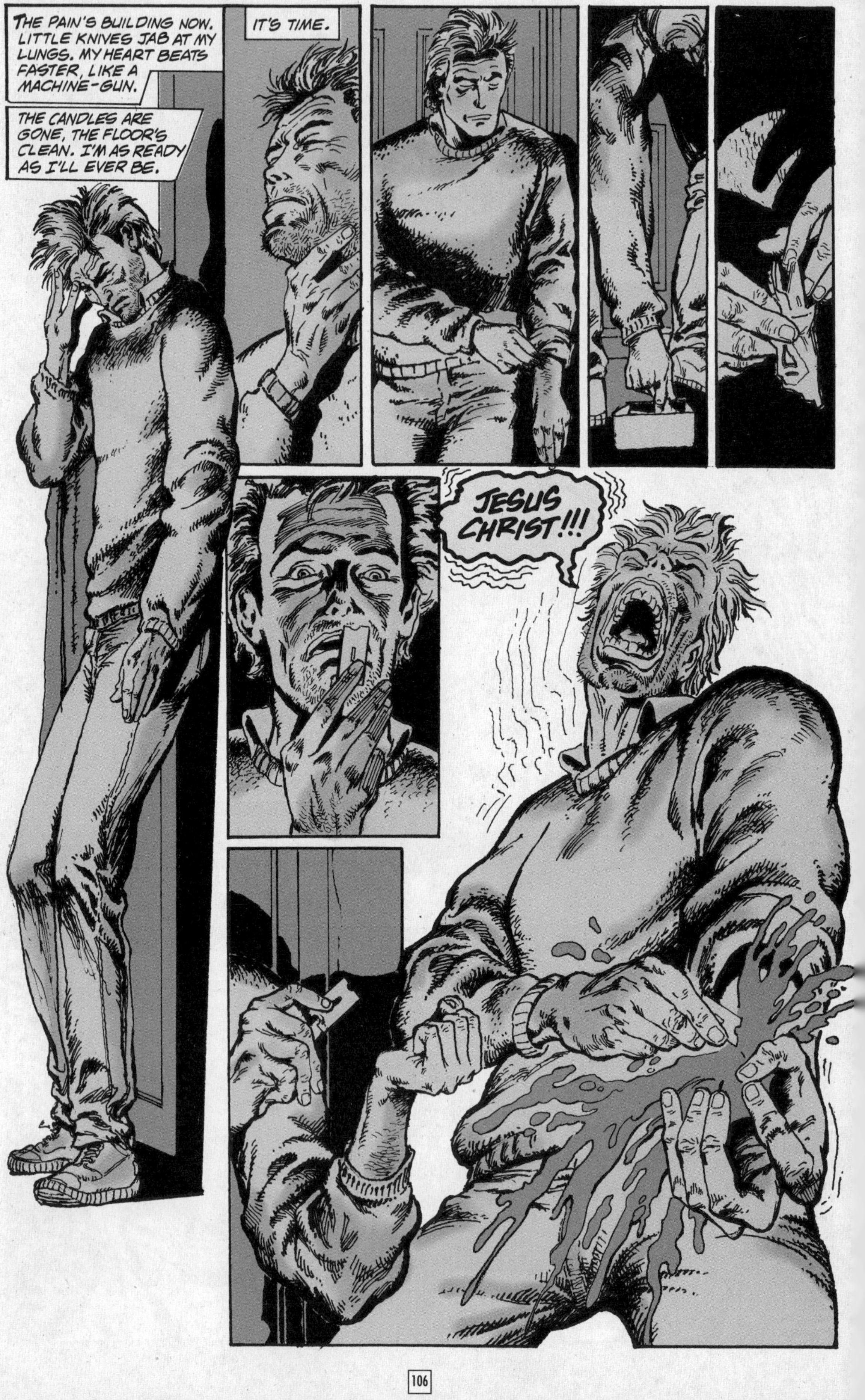
THE PAIN'S BUILDING NOW. LITTLE KNIVES JAB AT MY LUNGS. MY HEART BEATS FASTER, LIKE A MACHINE-GUN.
THE CANDLES ARE GONE, THE FLOOR'S CLEAN. I'M AS READY AS I'LL EVER BE.
IT'S TIME.
JESUS CHRIST!!!

JESUS... CHRIST...!

EVEN AS I REALIZE I'LL BE DEAD IN FIVE MINUTES, CANCER OR NOT, I FEEL HIM IN THE ROOM WITH ME.

THE FIRST OF THE THREE IS HERE.

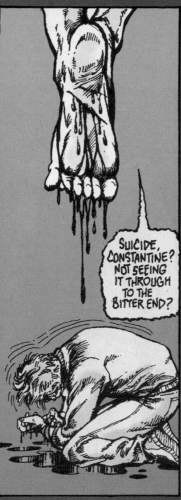

SUICIDE, CONSTANTINE? NOT SEEING IT THROUGH TO THE BITTER END?

IT DOESN'T MATTER. YOU'RE *MINE* NOW. YOU ALWAYS WILL BE.

THE INSULT YOU DEALT ME WITH THE HOLY WATER WAS *IMMENSE,* CONSTANTINE. I SHALL ENJOY SPENDING THE REST OF *ETERNITY* WITH YOU.

LOOK AT ME, CONSTANTINE. LOOK AT MY GARB.

I BRING YOU *DAMNATION.*

VERY... *NICE*... YOU... SON... OF... A... *BITCH*--

AREN'T YOU... SUPPOSED... TO... WAIT... 'TIL... I... *DIE?*

I KNOW YOU'RE DYING, CONSTANTINE.

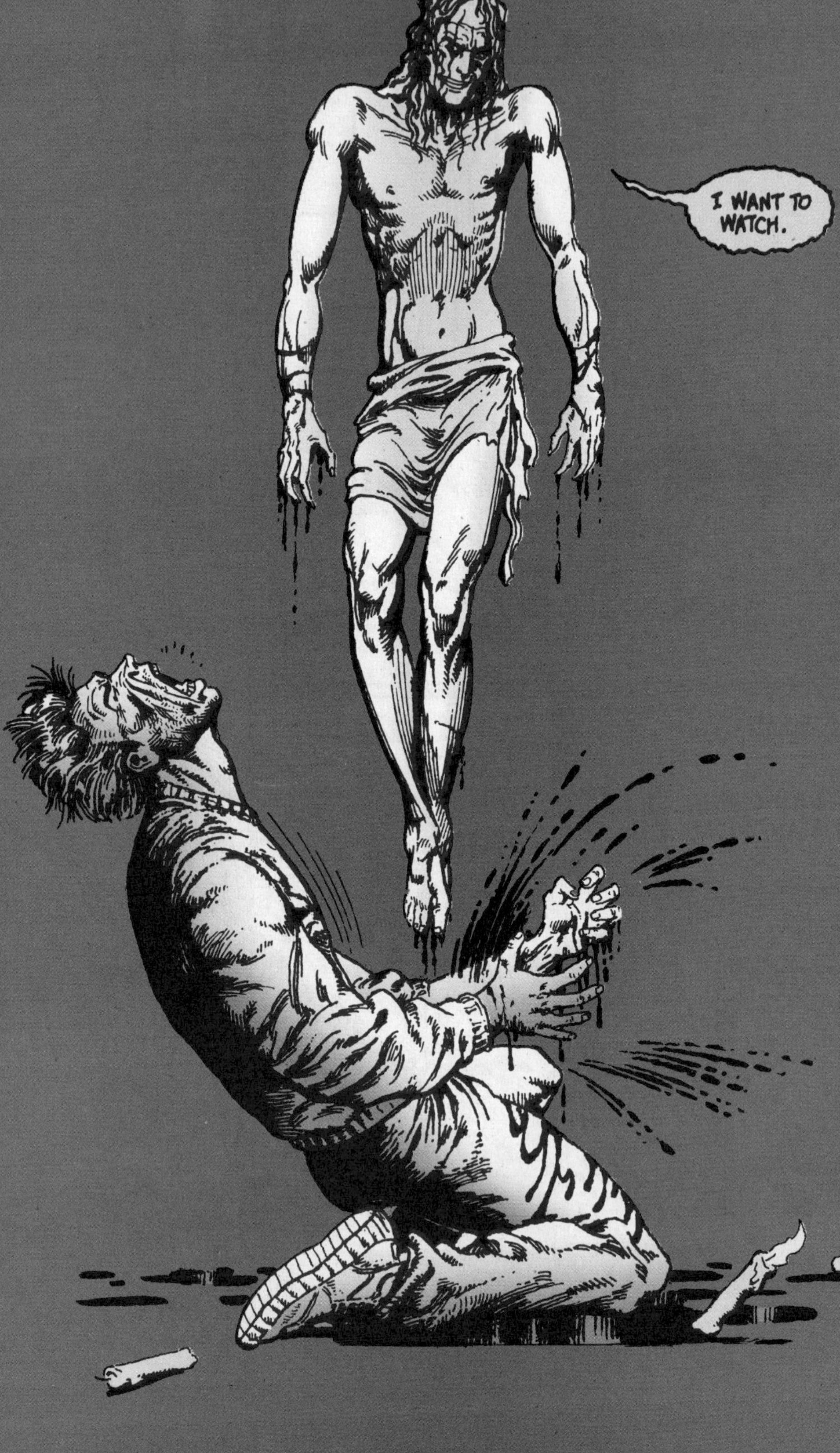
I WANT TO WATCH.

the
sting

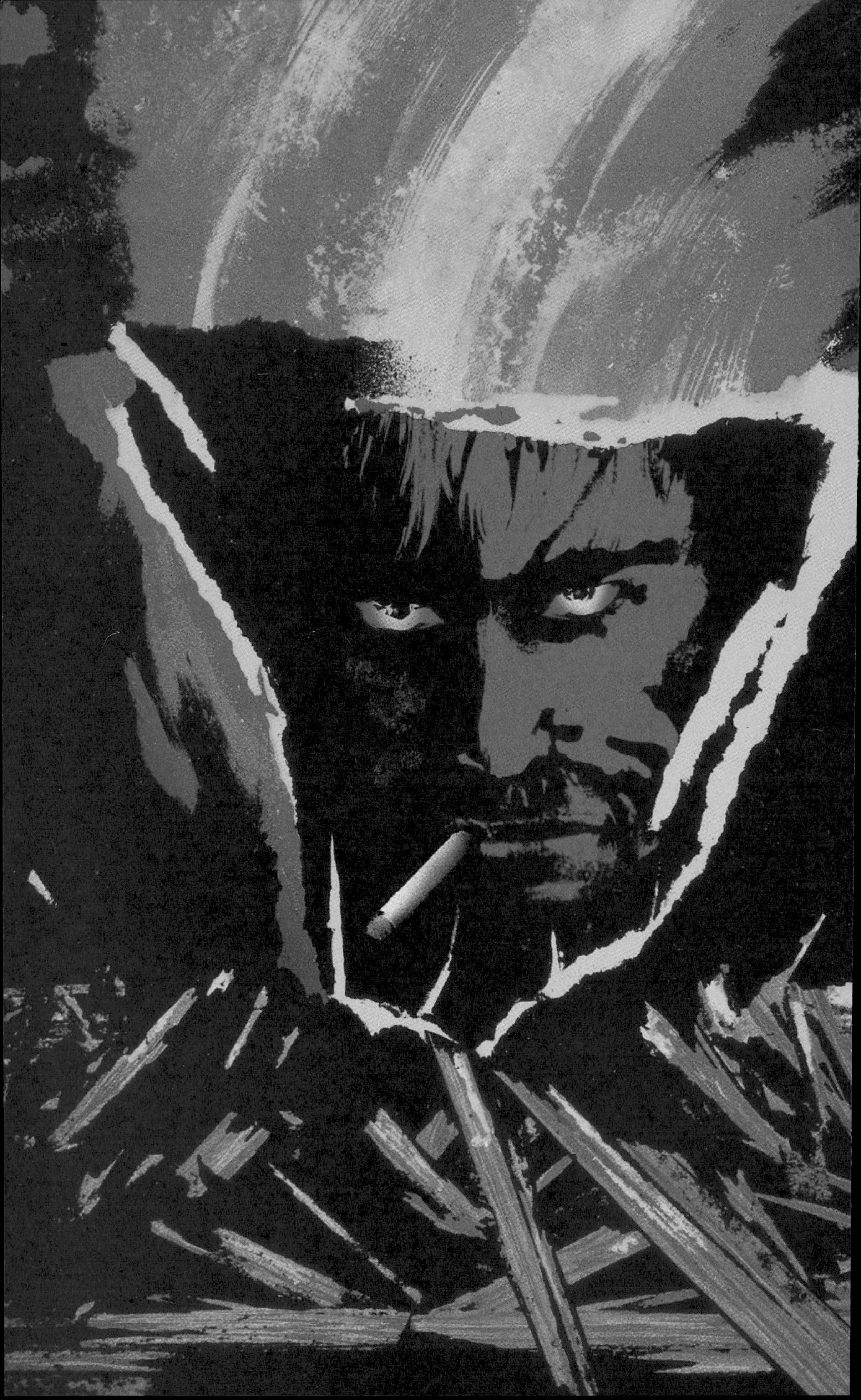

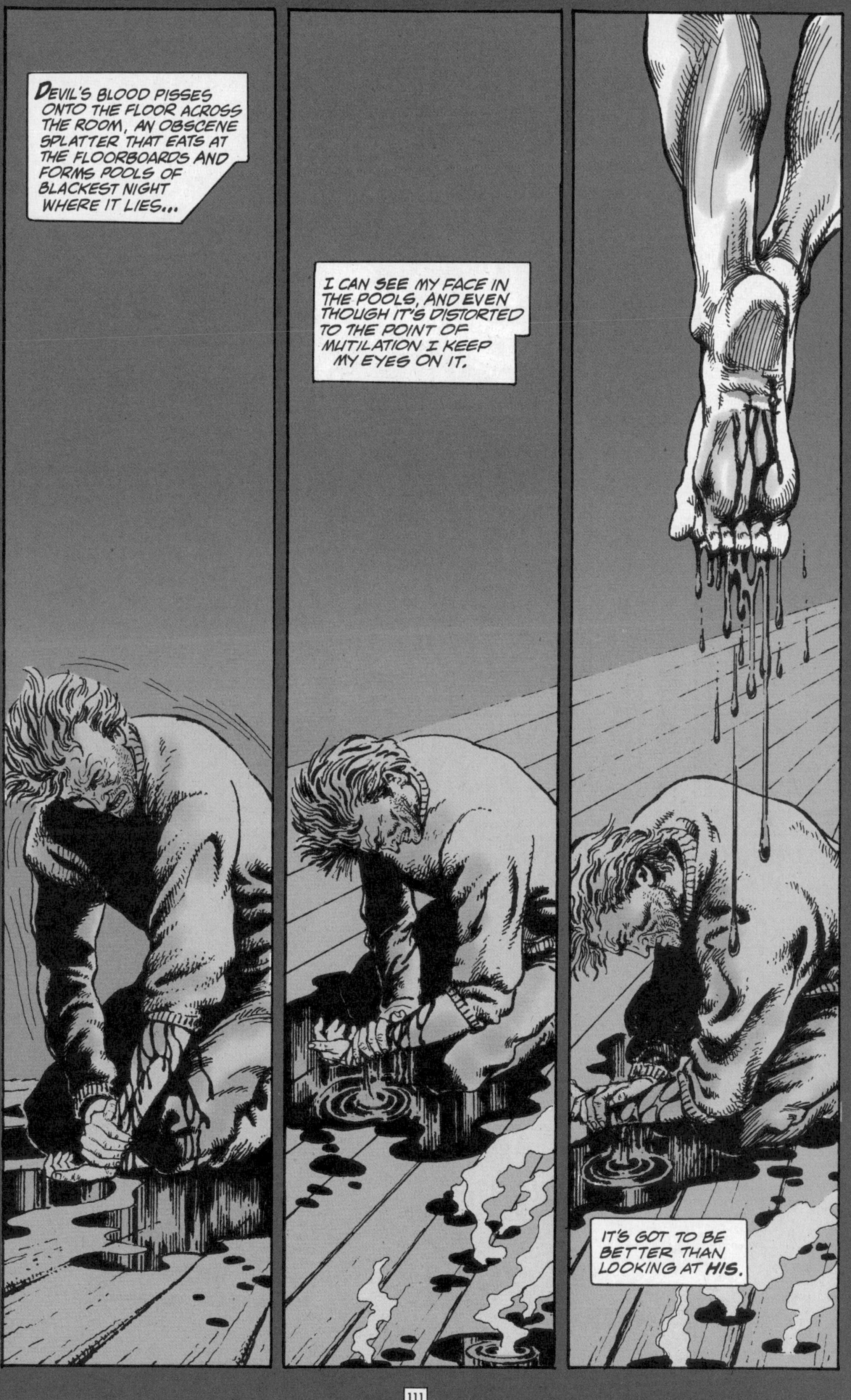
DEVIL'S BLOOD PISSES ONTO THE FLOOR ACROSS THE ROOM, AN OBSCENE SPLATTER THAT EATS AT THE FLOORBOARDS AND FORMS POOLS OF BLACKEST NIGHT WHERE IT LIES...
I CAN SEE MY FACE IN THE POOLS, AND EVEN THOUGH IT'S DISTORTED TO THE POINT OF MUTILATION I KEEP MY EYES ON IT.
IT'S GOT TO BE BETTER THAN LOOKING AT HIS.

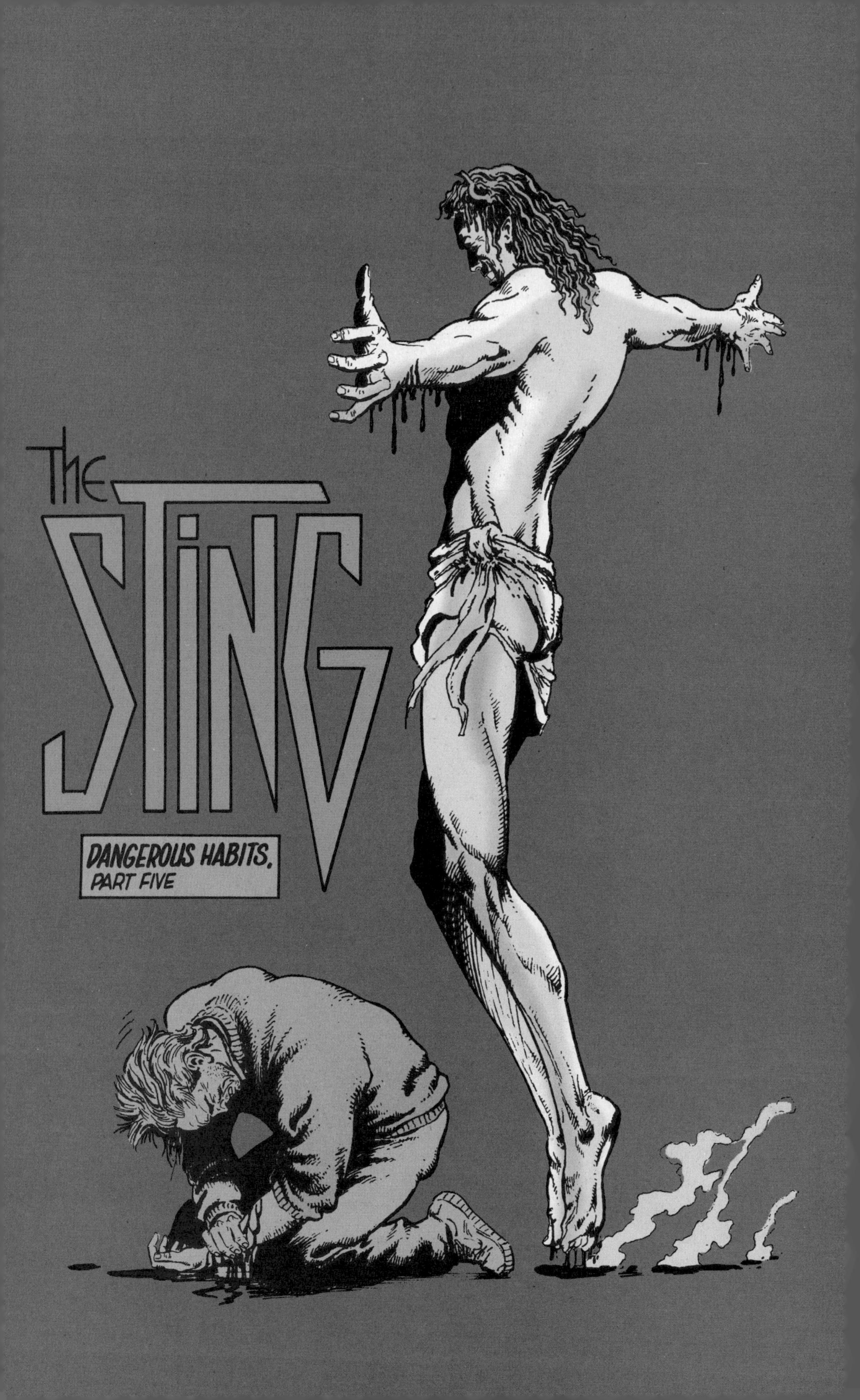
The STING
DANGEROUS HABITS, PART FIVE

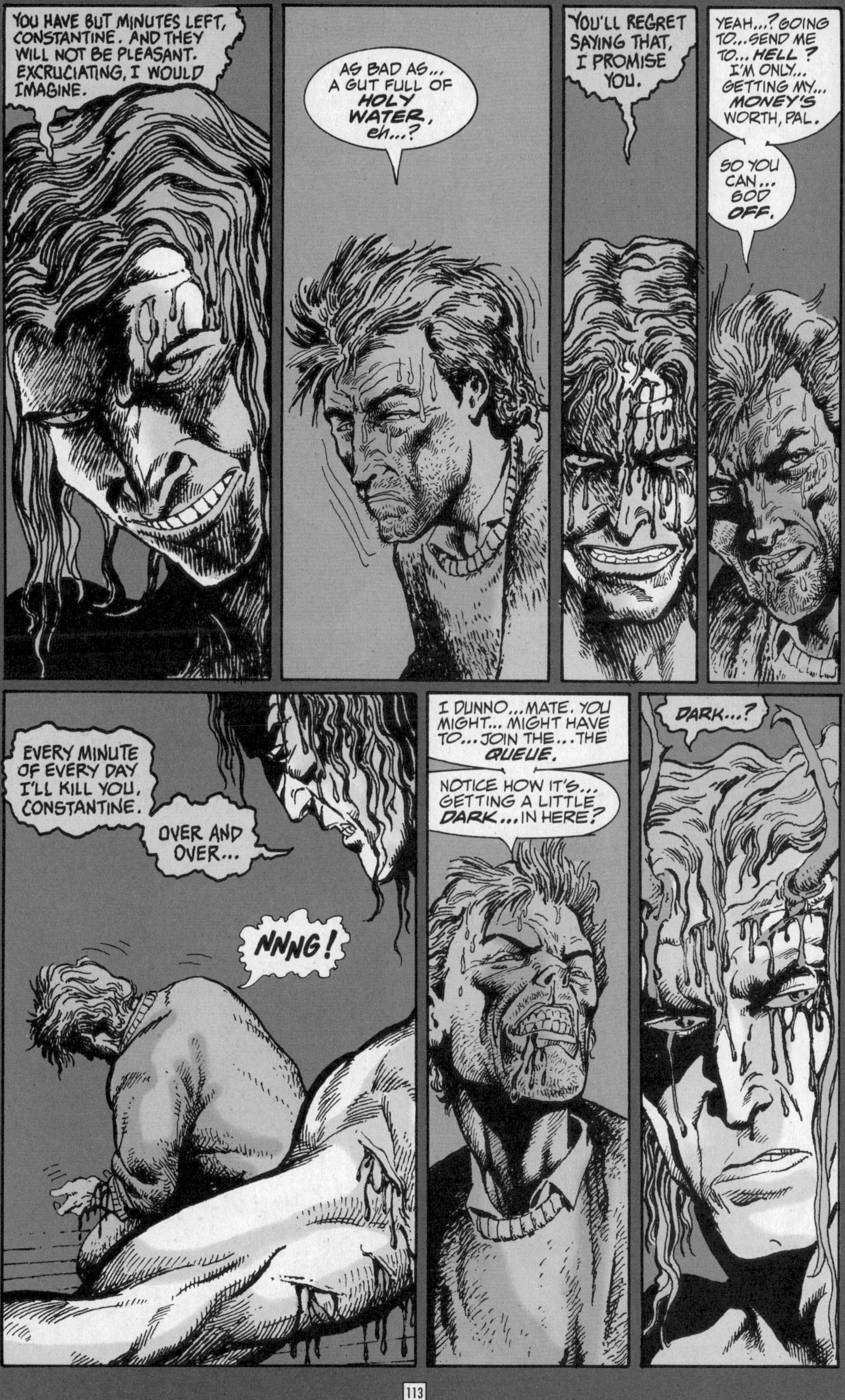
YOU HAVE BUT MINUTES LEFT, CONSTANTINE. AND THEY WILL NOT BE PLEASANT. EXCRUCIATING, I WOULD IMAGINE.
AS BAD AS... A GUT FULL OF HOLY WATER, eh...?
YOU'LL REGRET SAYING THAT, I PROMISE YOU.
YEAH...? GOING TO... SEND ME TO... HELL? I'M ONLY... GETTING MY... MONEY'S WORTH, PAL.
SO YOU CAN... SOD OFF.
EVERY MINUTE OF EVERY DAY I'LL KILL YOU, CONSTANTINE.
OVER AND OVER...
NNNG!
I DUNNO... MATE. YOU MIGHT... MIGHT HAVE TO... JOIN THE... THE QUEUE.
NOTICE HOW IT'S... GETTING A LITTLE DARK... IN HERE?
DARK...?

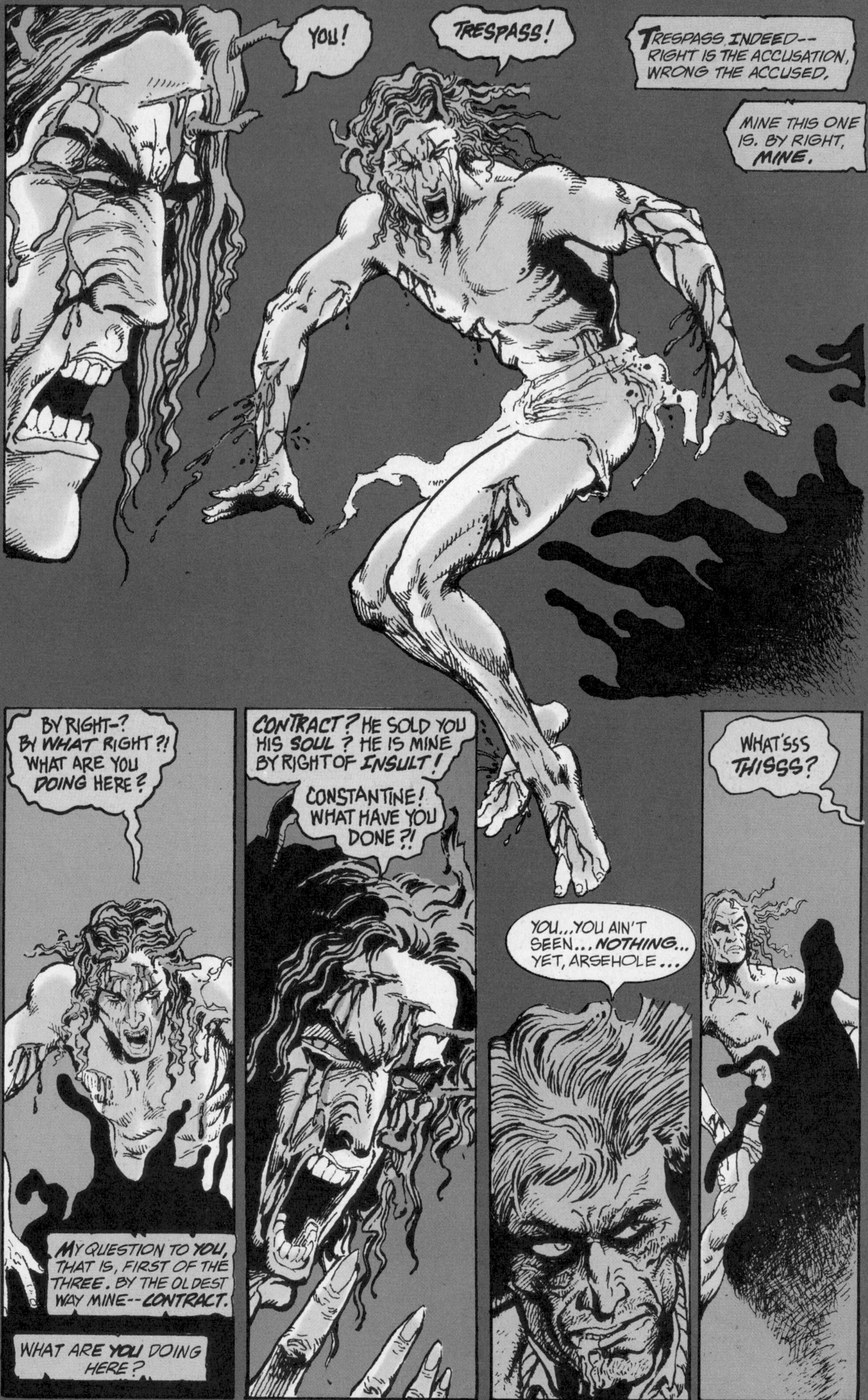
YOU!
TRESPASS!
TRESPASS INDEED-- RIGHT IS THE ACCUSATION, WRONG THE ACCUSED.
MINE THIS ONE IS. BY RIGHT, MINE.
BY RIGHT-? BY WHAT RIGHT?! WHAT ARE YOU DOING HERE?
MY QUESTION TO YOU, THAT IS, FIRST OF THE THREE. BY THE OLDEST WAY MINE--CONTRACT.
WHAT ARE YOU DOING HERE?
CONTRACT? HE SOLD YOU HIS SOUL? HE IS MINE BY RIGHT OF INSULT!
CONSTANTINE! WHAT HAVE YOU DONE?!
YOU...YOU AIN'T SEEN...NOTHING... YET, ARSEHOLE...
WHAT'SSS THISSS?

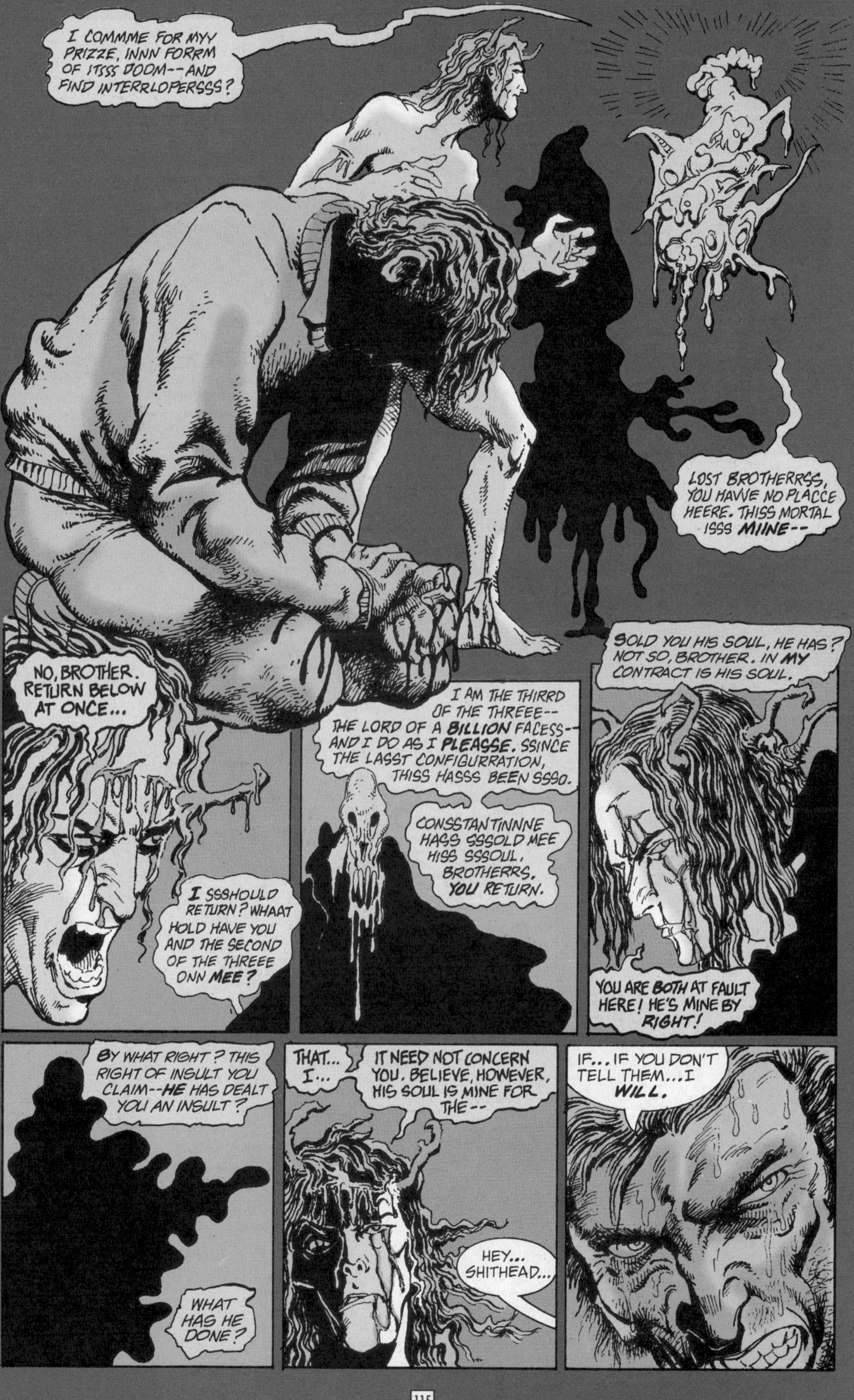
I COMMME FOR MYY PRIZZE, INNN FORRM OF ITSSS DOOM--AND FIND INTERRLOPERSSS?
LOST BROTHERRSS, YOU HAVVE NO PLACCE HEERE. THISS MORTAL ISSS MIINE--
NO, BROTHER. RETURN BELOW AT ONCE...
I SSSHOULD RETURN? WHAAT HOLD HAVE YOU AND THE SECOND OF THE THREEE ONN MEE?
I AM THE THIRRD OF THE THREEE--THE LORD OF A BILLION FACESS--AND I DO AS I PLEASSE. SSINCE THE LASST CONFIGURRATION, THISS HASSS BEEN SSSO.
CONSSTANTINNNE HASS SSSOLD MEE HISS SSSOUL, BROTHERRS. YOU RETURN.
SOLD YOU HIS SOUL, HE HAS? NOT SO, BROTHER. IN MY CONTRACT IS HIS SOUL.
YOU ARE BOTH AT FAULT HERE! HE'S MINE BY RIGHT!
BY WHAT RIGHT? THIS RIGHT OF INSULT YOU CLAIM--HE HAS DEALT YOU AN INSULT?
WHAT HAS HE DONE?
THAT... I...
IT NEED NOT CONCERN YOU. BELIEVE, HOWEVER, HIS SOUL IS MINE FOR THE--
HEY... SHITHEAD...
IF... IF YOU DON'T TELL THEM... I WILL.

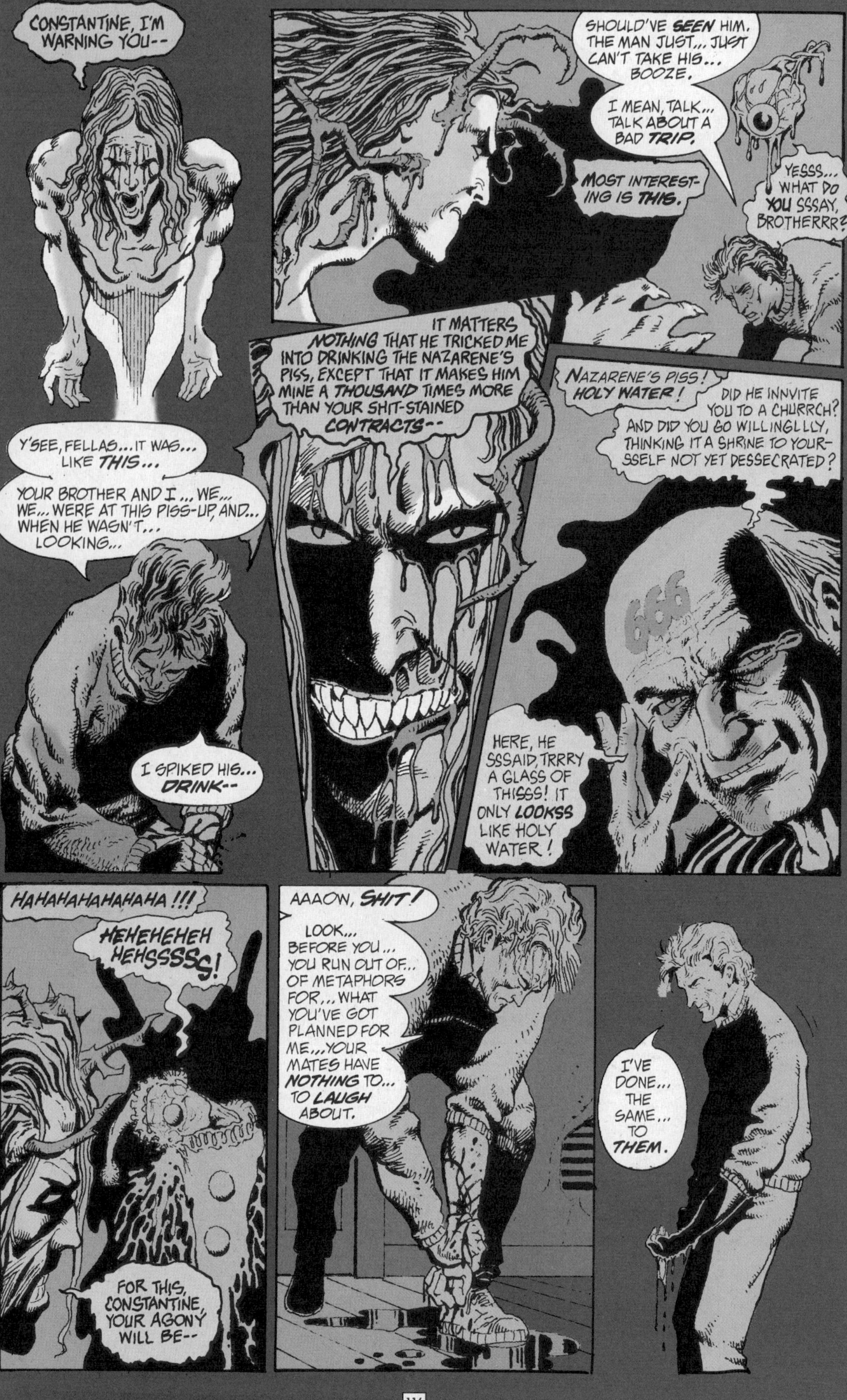
CONSTANTINE, I'M WARNING YOU--
SHOULD'VE SEEN HIM. THE MAN JUST... JUST CAN'T TAKE HIS... BOOZE.
I MEAN, TALK... TALK ABOUT A BAD TRIP.
MOST INTERESTING IS THIS.
YESSS... WHAT DO YOU SSSAY, BROTHERRR?
Y'SEE, FELLAS... IT WAS... LIKE THIS...
YOUR BROTHER AND I... WE... WE... WERE AT THIS PISS-UP, AND... WHEN HE WASN'T... LOOKING...
I SPIKED HIS... DRINK--
IT MATTERS NOTHING THAT HE TRICKED ME INTO DRINKING THE NAZARENE'S PISS, EXCEPT THAT IT MAKES HIM MINE A THOUSAND TIMES MORE THAN YOUR SHIT-STAINED CONTRACTS--
NAZARENE'S PISS! HOLY WATER!
DID HE INNVITE YOU TO A CHURRCH? AND DID YOU GO WILLINGLLY, THINKING IT A SHRINE TO YOURSSELF NOT YET DESSECRATED?
HERE, HE SSSAID, TRRRY A GLASS OF THISSS! IT ONLY LOOKSS LIKE HOLY WATER!
HAHAHAHAHAHAHA!!!
HEHEHEHEH HEHSSSSG!
FOR THIS, CONSTANTINE, YOUR AGONY WILL BE--
AAAOW, SHIT!
LOOK... BEFORE YOU... YOU RUN OUT OF... OF METAPHORS FOR... WHAT YOU'VE GOT PLANNED FOR ME... YOUR MATES HAVE NOTHING TO... TO LAUGH ABOUT.
I'VE DONE... THE SAME... TO THEM.

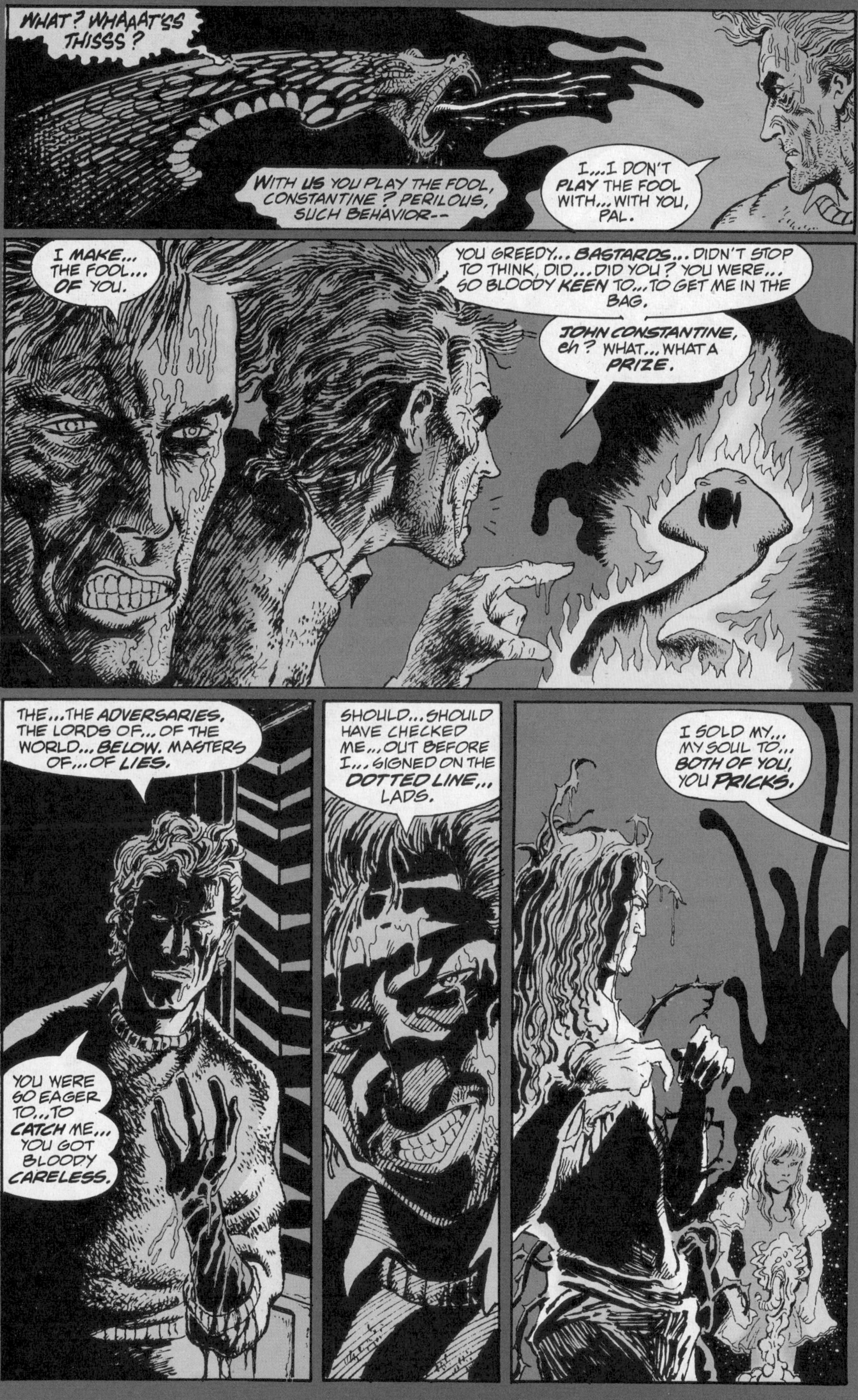

WHAT? WHAAAT'SS THISSS?
WITH US YOU PLAY THE FOOL, CONSTANTINE? PERILOUS, SUCH BEHAVIOR--
I... I DON'T PLAY THE FOOL WITH... WITH YOU, PAL.
I MAKE... THE FOOL... OF YOU.
YOU GREEDY... BASTARDS... DIDN'T STOP TO THINK, DID... DID YOU? YOU WERE... SO BLOODY KEEN TO... TO GET ME IN THE BAG.
JOHN CONSTANTINE, eh? WHAT... WHAT A PRIZE.
THE... THE ADVERSARIES. THE LORDS OF... OF THE WORLD... BELOW. MASTERS OF... OF LIES.
YOU WERE SO EAGER TO... TO CATCH ME... YOU GOT BLOODY CARELESS.
SHOULD... SHOULD HAVE CHECKED ME... OUT BEFORE I... SIGNED ON THE DOTTED LINE... LADS.
I SOLD MY... MY SOUL TO... BOTH OF YOU, YOU PRICKS.

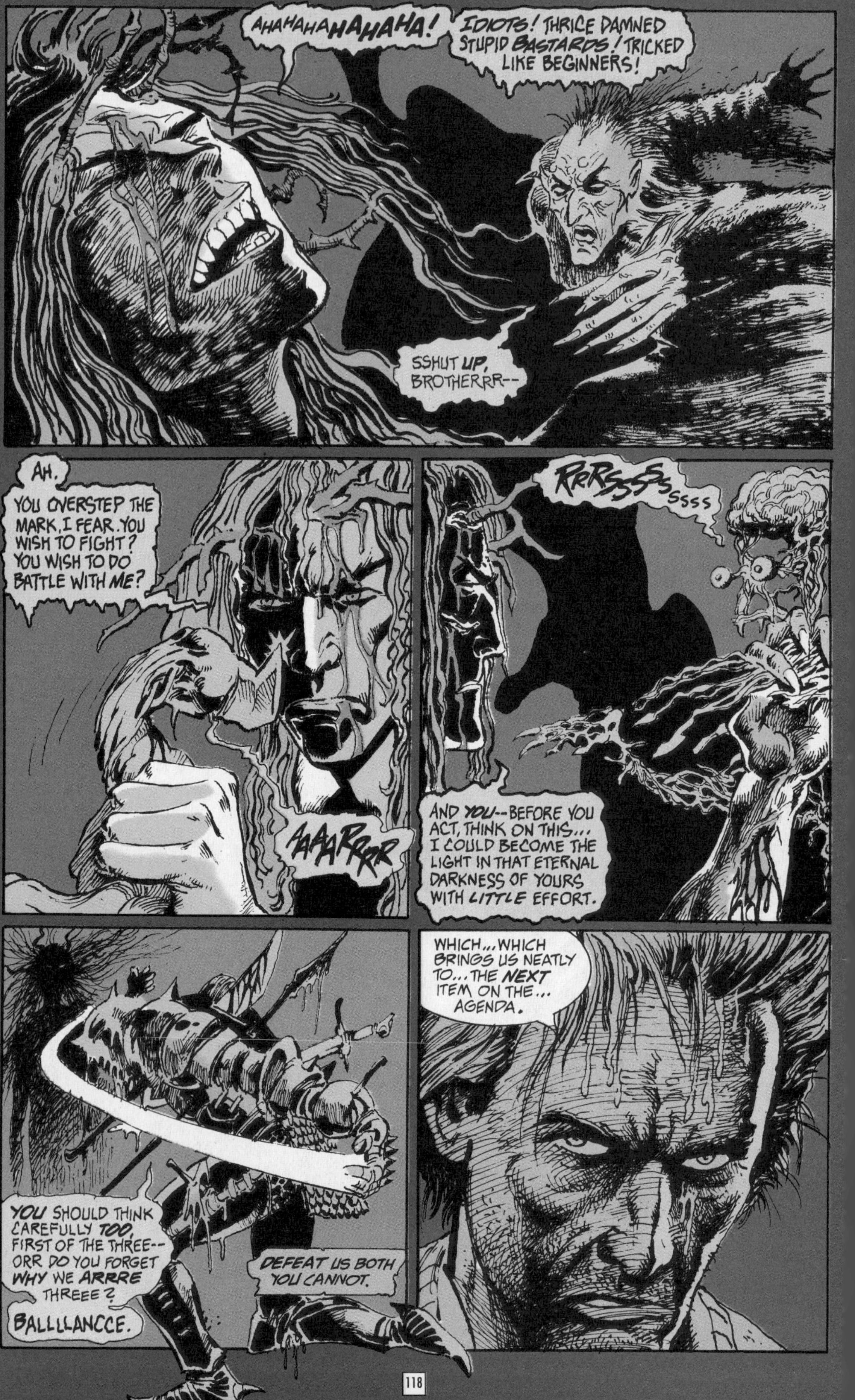
AHAHAHAHAHAHA!
IDIOTS! THRICE DAMNED STUPID BASTARDS! TRICKED LIKE BEGINNERS!
SSHUT UP, BROTHERRR--
AH.
YOU OVERSTEP THE MARK, I FEAR. YOU WISH TO FIGHT? YOU WISH TO DO BATTLE WITH ME?
AAAARRRR
RRRSSSSSssss
AND YOU--BEFORE YOU ACT, THINK ON THIS... I COULD BECOME THE LIGHT IN THAT ETERNAL DARKNESS OF YOURS WITH LITTLE EFFORT.
YOU SHOULD THINK CAREFULLY TOO, FIRST OF THE THREE--ORR DO YOU FORGET WHY WE ARRRE THREEE?
DEFEAT US BOTH YOU CANNOT.
BALLLLANCCE.
WHICH... WHICH BRINGS US NEATLY TO... THE NEXT ITEM ON THE... AGENDA.

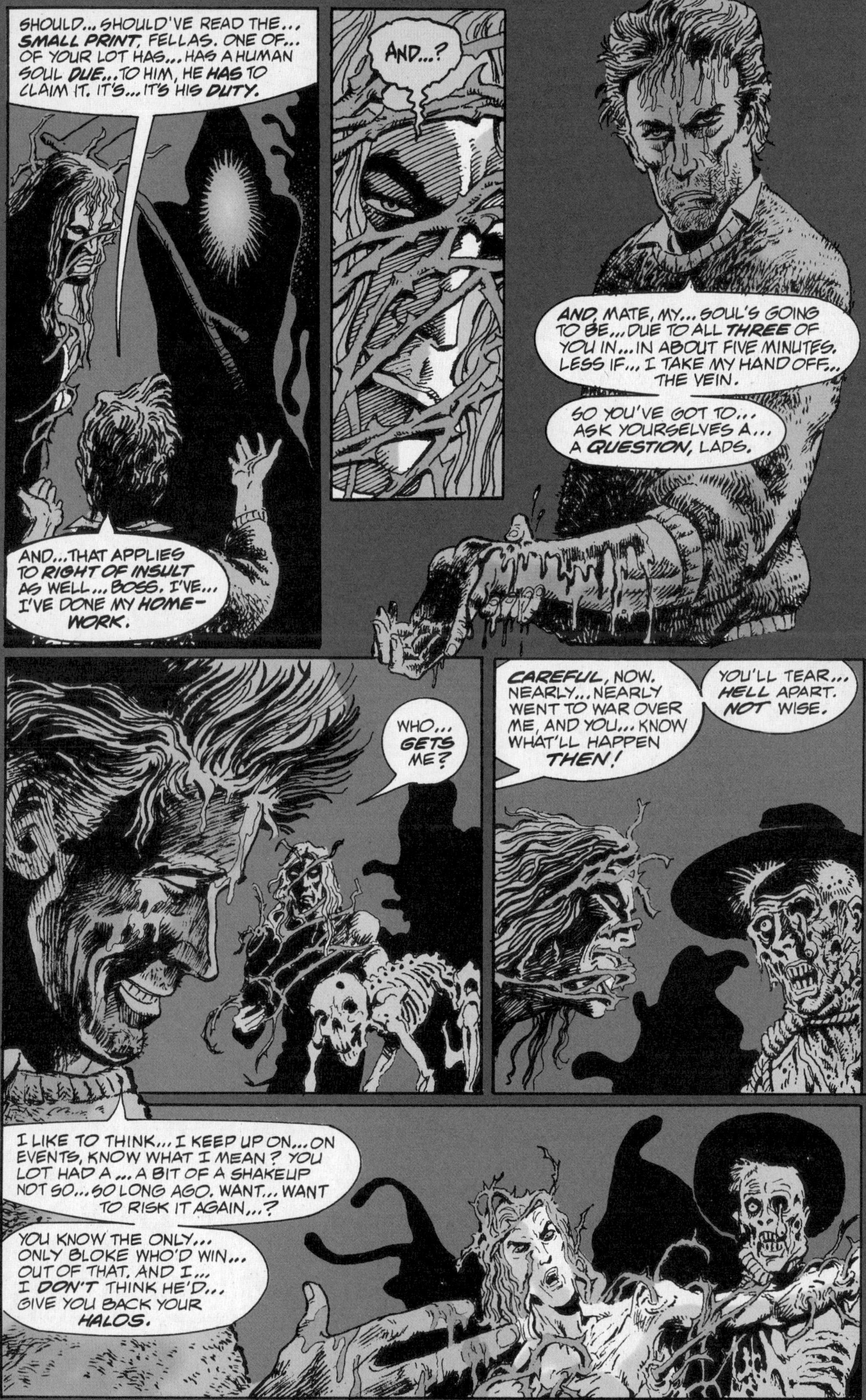
SHOULD... SHOULD'VE READ THE... SMALL PRINT, FELLAS. ONE OF... OF YOUR LOT HAS... HAS A HUMAN SOUL DUE... TO HIM, HE HAS TO CLAIM IT. IT'S... IT'S HIS DUTY.
AND... THAT APPLIES TO RIGHT OF INSULT AS WELL... BOSS. I'VE... I'VE DONE MY HOME-WORK.
AND...?
AND, MATE, MY... SOUL'S GOING TO BE... DUE TO ALL THREE OF YOU IN... IN ABOUT FIVE MINUTES. LESS IF... I TAKE MY HAND OFF... THE VEIN.
SO YOU'VE GOT TO... ASK YOURSELVES A... A QUESTION, LADS.
WHO... GETS ME?
CAREFUL, NOW. NEARLY... NEARLY WENT TO WAR OVER ME, AND YOU... KNOW WHAT'LL HAPPEN THEN!
YOU'LL TEAR... HELL APART. NOT WISE.
I LIKE TO THINK... I KEEP UP ON... ON EVENTS, KNOW WHAT I MEAN? YOU LOT HAD A... A BIT OF A SHAKEUP NOT SO... SO LONG AGO. WANT... WANT TO RISK IT AGAIN...?
YOU KNOW THE ONLY... ONLY BLOKE WHO'D WIN... OUT OF THAT. AND I... I DON'T THINK HE'D... GIVE YOU BACK YOUR HALOS.

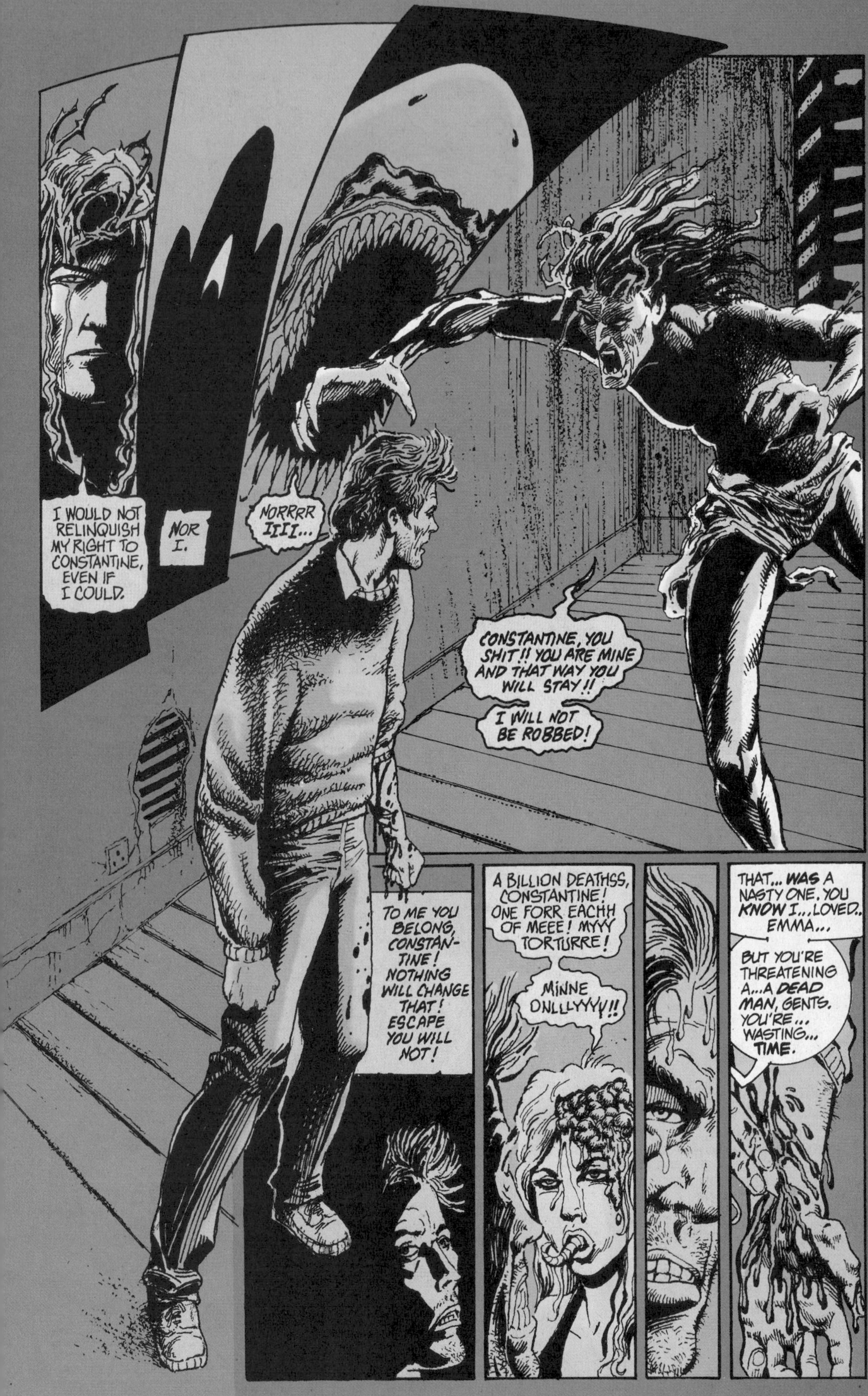
I WOULD NOT RELINQUISH MY RIGHT TO CONSTANTINE, EVEN IF I COULD.
NOR I.
NORRRR IIII...
CONSTANTINE, YOU SHIT!! YOU ARE MINE AND THAT WAY YOU WILL STAY!!
I WILL NOT BE ROBBED!
TO ME YOU BELONG, CONSTAN-TINE! NOTHING WILL CHANGE THAT! ESCAPE YOU WILL NOT!
A BILLION DEATHSS, CONSTANTINE! ONE FORR EACHH OF MEEE! MYYY TORTURRE!
MINNE ONLLLYYYY!!
THAT... WAS A NASTY ONE. YOU KNOW I... LOVED... EMMA...
BUT YOU'RE THREATENING A... A DEAD MAN, GENTS. YOU'RE... WASTING... TIME.

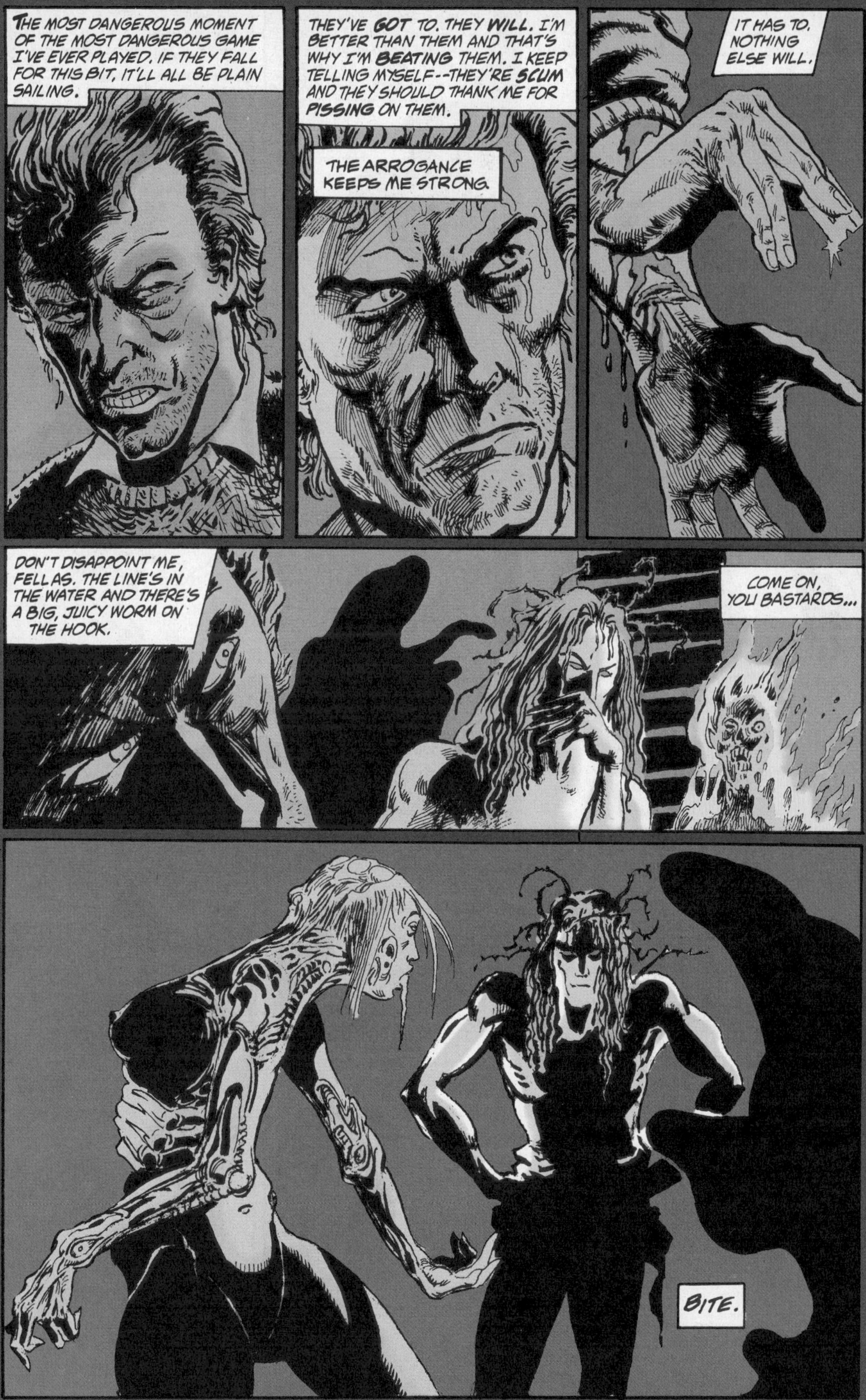
THE MOST DANGEROUS MOMENT OF THE MOST DANGEROUS GAME I'VE EVER PLAYED. IF THEY FALL FOR THIS BIT, IT'LL ALL BE PLAIN SAILING.
THEY'VE GOT TO. THEY WILL. I'M BETTER THAN THEM AND THAT'S WHY I'M BEATING THEM. I KEEP TELLING MYSELF--THEY'RE SCUM AND THEY SHOULD THANK ME FOR PISSING ON THEM.
THE ARROGANCE KEEPS ME STRONG.
IT HAS TO. NOTHING ELSE WILL.
DON'T DISAPPOINT ME, FELLAS. THE LINE'S IN THE WATER AND THERE'S A BIG, JUICY WORM ON THE HOOK.
COME ON, YOU BASTARDS...
BITE.

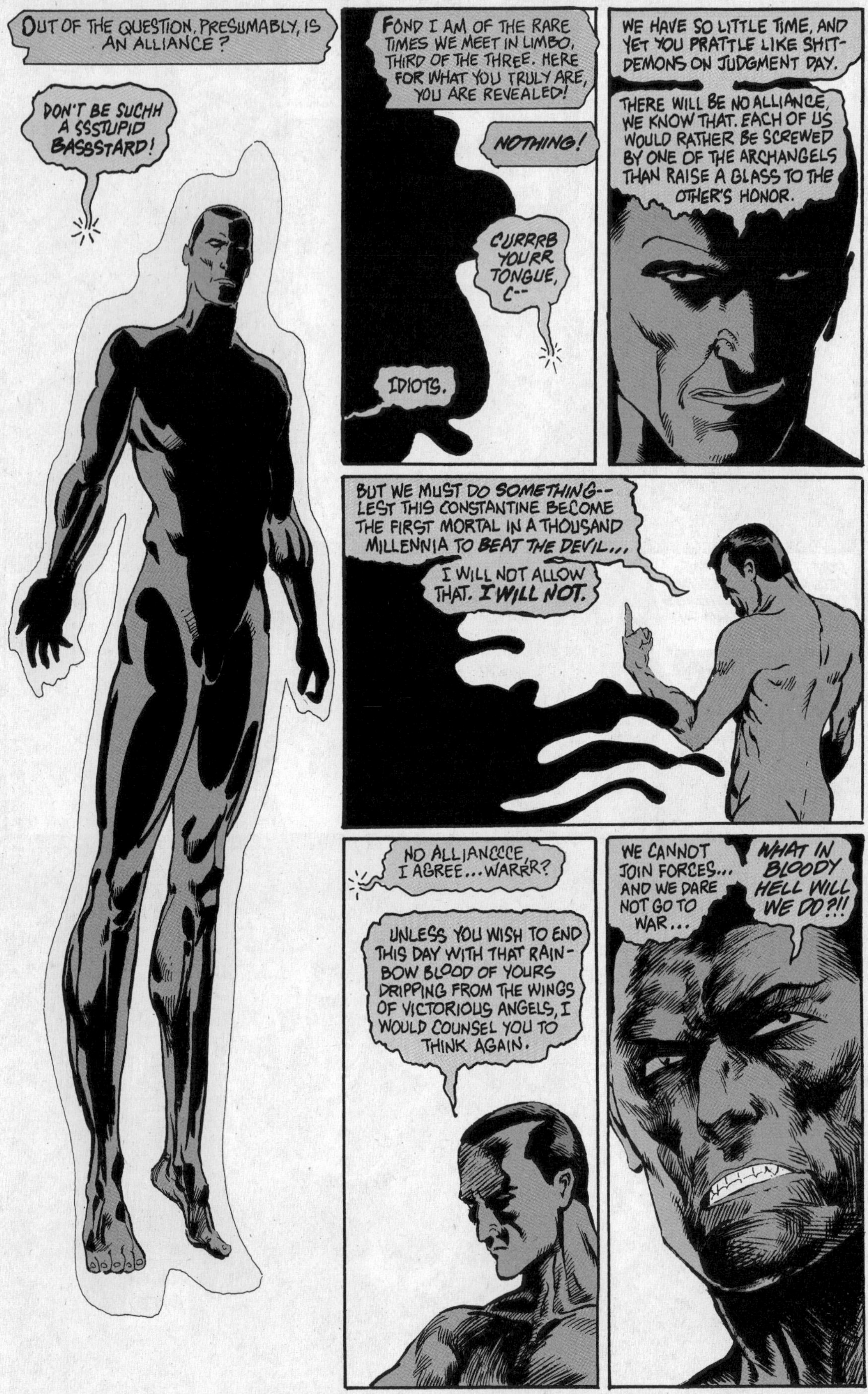

OUT OF THE QUESTION, PRESUMABLY, IS AN ALLIANCE?
DON'T BE SUCHH A SSSTUPID BASSSTARD!
FOND I AM OF THE RARE TIMES WE MEET IN LIMBO, THIRD OF THE THREE. HERE FOR WHAT YOU TRULY ARE, YOU ARE REVEALED!
NOTHING!
CURRRB YOURR TONGUE, C--
IDIOTS.
WE HAVE SO LITTLE TIME, AND YET YOU PRATTLE LIKE SHIT-DEMONS ON JUDGMENT DAY.
THERE WILL BE NO ALLIANCE, WE KNOW THAT. EACH OF US WOULD RATHER BE SCREWED BY ONE OF THE ARCHANGELS THAN RAISE A GLASS TO THE OTHER'S HONOR.
BUT WE MUST DO SOMETHING-- LEST THIS CONSTANTINE BECOME THE FIRST MORTAL IN A THOUSAND MILLENNIA TO BEAT THE DEVIL...
I WILL NOT ALLOW THAT. I WILL NOT.
NO ALLIANCCCE, I AGREE... WARRR?
UNLESS YOU WISH TO END THIS DAY WITH THAT RAIN-BOW BLOOD OF YOURS DRIPPING FROM THE WINGS OF VICTORIOUS ANGELS, I WOULD COUNSEL YOU TO THINK AGAIN.
WE CANNOT JOIN FORCES... AND WE DARE NOT GO TO WAR...
WHAT IN BLOODY HELL WILL WE DO?!!

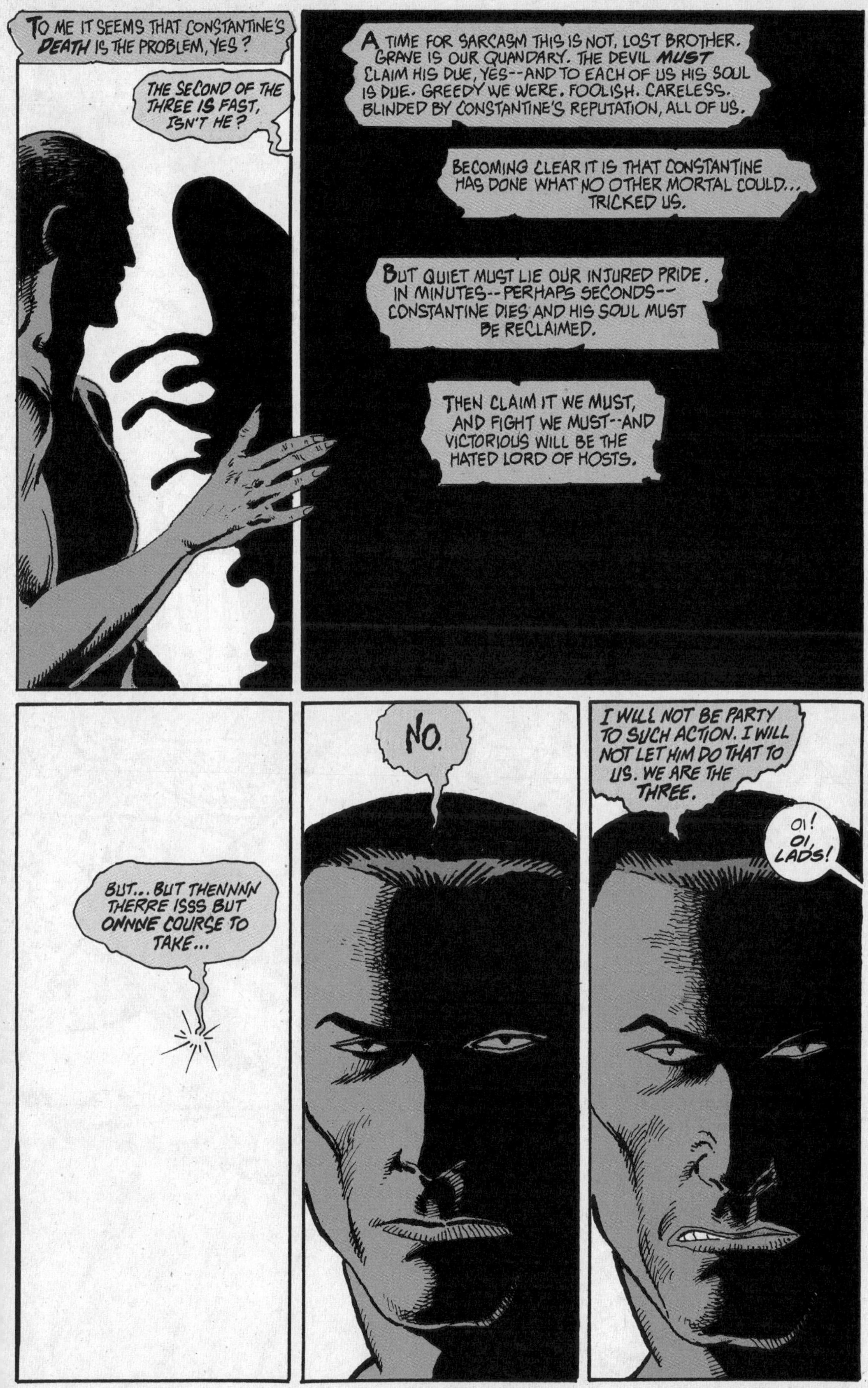
TO ME IT SEEMS THAT CONSTANTINE'S DEATH IS THE PROBLEM, YES?
THE SECOND OF THE THREE IS FAST, ISN'T HE?
A TIME FOR SARCASM THIS IS NOT, LOST BROTHER. GRAVE IS OUR QUANDARY. THE DEVIL MUST CLAIM HIS DUE, YES--AND TO EACH OF US HIS SOUL IS DUE. GREEDY WE WERE. FOOLISH. CARELESS. BLINDED BY CONSTANTINE'S REPUTATION, ALL OF US.
BECOMING CLEAR IT IS THAT CONSTANTINE HAS DONE WHAT NO OTHER MORTAL COULD... TRICKED US.
BUT QUIET MUST LIE OUR INJURED PRIDE. IN MINUTES--PERHAPS SECONDS--CONSTANTINE DIES AND HIS SOUL MUST BE RECLAIMED.
THEN CLAIM IT WE MUST, AND FIGHT WE MUST--AND VICTORIOUS WILL BE THE HATED LORD OF HOSTS.
BUT... BUT THENNNN THERRE ISSS BUT ONNNE COURSE TO TAKE...
NO.
I WILL NOT BE PARTY TO SUCH ACTION. I WILL NOT LET HIM DO THAT TO US. WE ARE THE THREE.
OI! OI, LADS!

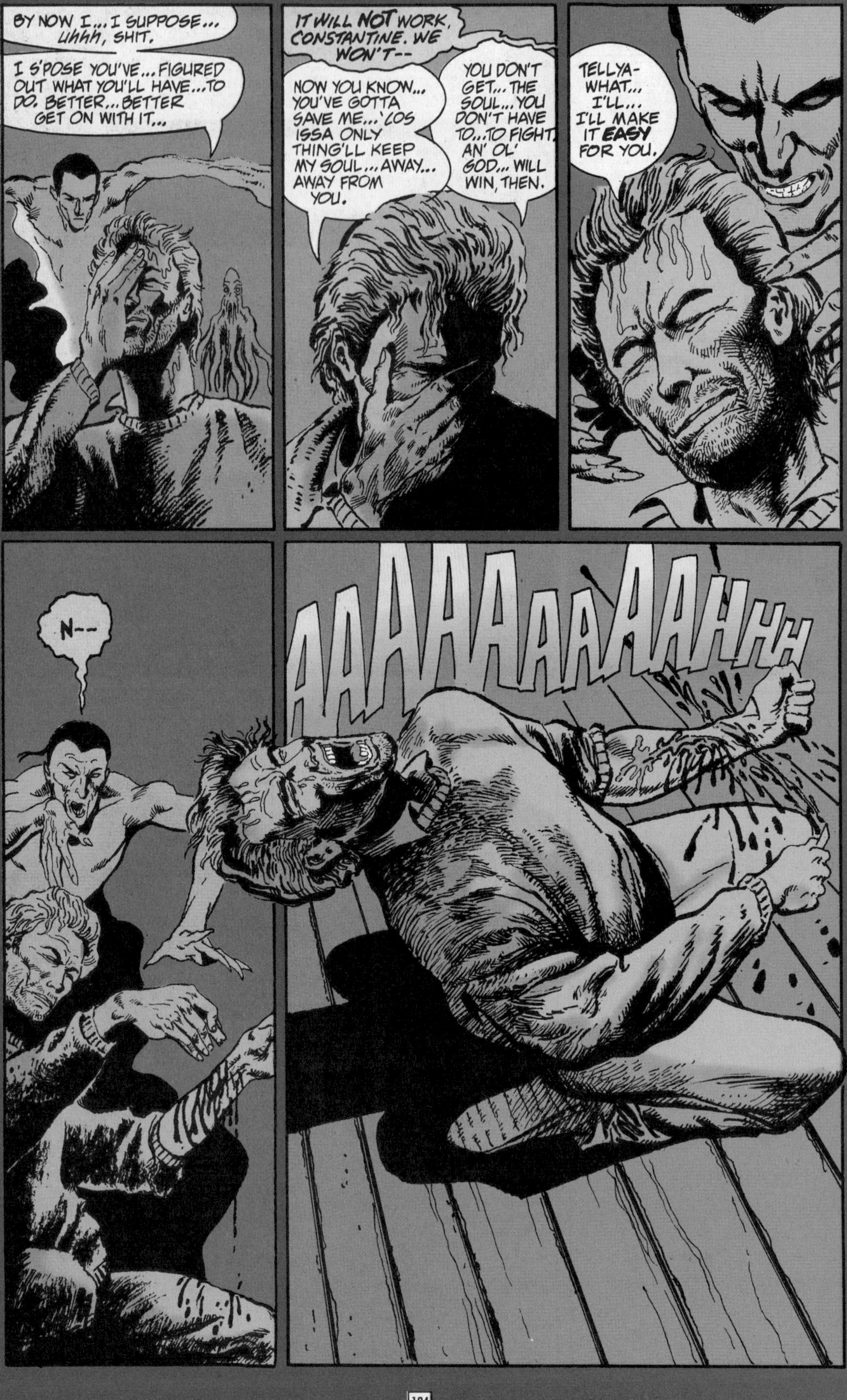

BY NOW I... I SUPPOSE... uhhh, SHIT.
I S'POSE YOU'VE... FIGURED OUT WHAT YOU'LL HAVE... TO DO. BETTER... BETTER GET ON WITH IT...
IT WILL NOT WORK, CONSTANTINE. WE WON'T--
NOW YOU KNOW... YOU'VE GOTTA SAVE ME...'COS ISSA ONLY THING'LL KEEP MY SOUL... AWAY... AWAY FROM YOU.
YOU DON'T GET... THE SOUL... YOU DON'T HAVE TO... TO FIGHT, AN' OL' GOD... WILL WIN, THEN.
TELLYA-WHAT... I'LL... I'LL MAKE IT EASY FOR YOU.
N--
AAAAAAAAAAHHH

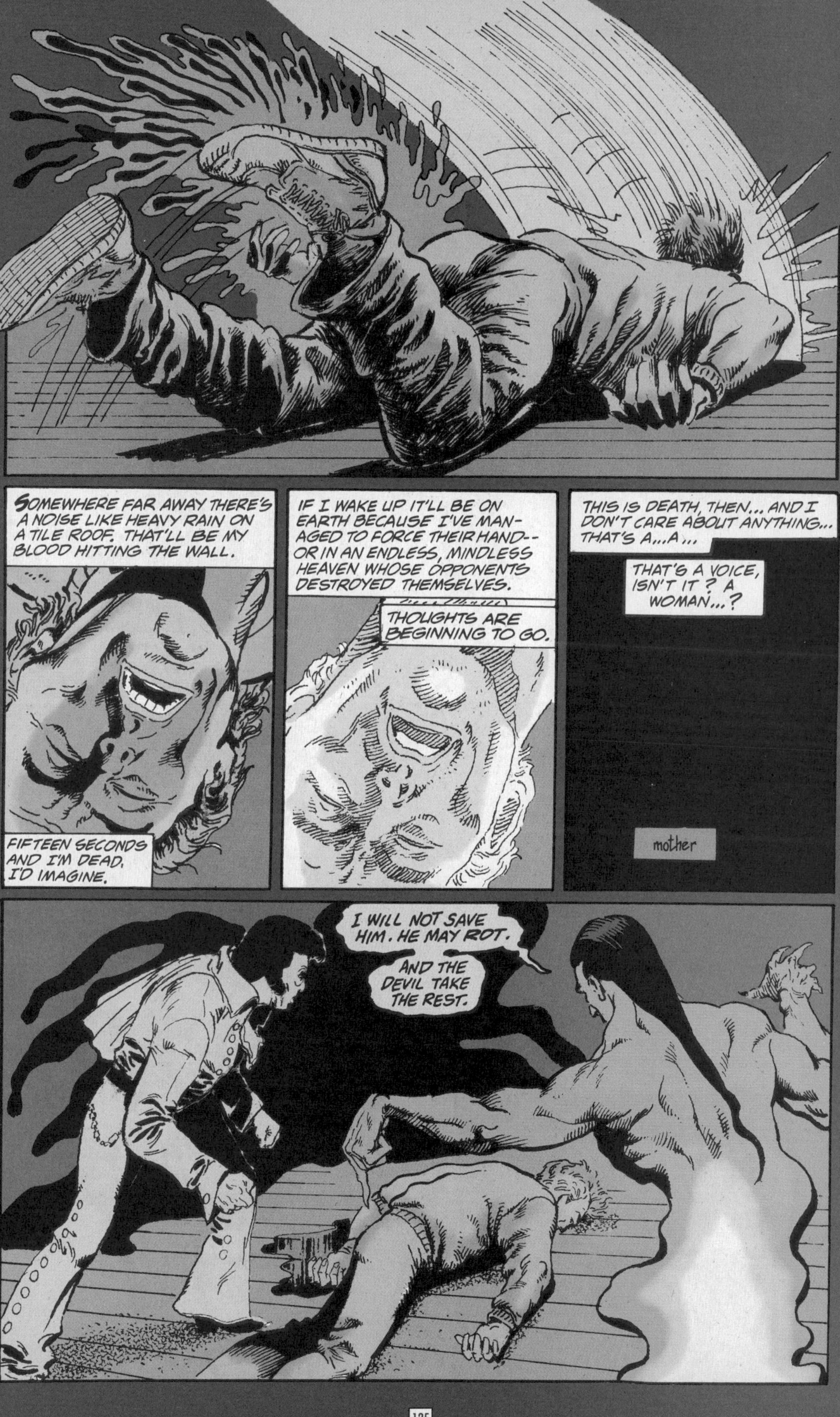
SOMEWHERE FAR AWAY THERE'S A NOISE LIKE HEAVY RAIN ON A TILE ROOF. THAT'LL BE MY BLOOD HITTING THE WALL.
FIFTEEN SECONDS AND I'M DEAD, I'D IMAGINE.
IF I WAKE UP IT'LL BE ON EARTH BECAUSE I'VE MANAGED TO FORCE THEIR HAND-- OR IN AN ENDLESS, MINDLESS HEAVEN WHOSE OPPONENTS DESTROYED THEMSELVES.
THOUGHTS ARE BEGINNING TO GO.
THIS IS DEATH, THEN... AND I DON'T CARE ABOUT ANYTHING... THAT'S A...A...
THAT'S A VOICE, ISN'T IT? A WOMAN...?
mother
I WILL NOT SAVE HIM. HE MAY ROT.
AND THE DEVIL TAKE THE REST.

SAVE HIM WE *MUST!* A WAR *NONE* CAN WIN WILL FOLLOW OTHERWISE!

THEN LET IT BE WAR!

I DO NOT FEAAR WARRR-- BUT WHAT FOLLOWSSS AFTERRR? TO BE THE SSLAVESS OF *HEAVENNN?* HAVE YOU NNOT FORGOTTENNN, FIRSST OF THE THREEE? "BETTER TO REIGN--"

I HAVE NOT FORGOTTEN.

I WILL NOT GIVE CONSTANTINE THE SATISFACTION.

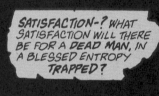

SATISFACTION-? WHAT SATISFACTION WILL THERE BE FOR A *DEAD MAN,* IN A BLESSED ENTROPY TRAPPED?

UNLESS HIS SLAVE *YOU* WISH TO BE--FOR NOT MUCH MORE THAN IN THAT ROLE WILL THE REDEEMER EMPLOY US! PERHAPS THE SLAVES OF *CONSTANTINE* WE WILL BE FOR ETERNITY!

BY LETTING HIM DIE YOU DESTROY US ALONG WITH ALL EXISTENCE, FAR AND NEAR, AND FOR NOTHING BUT PRIDE--

ENOUGH!!!

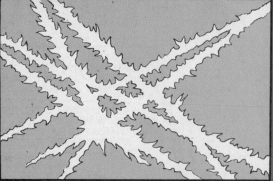

AT LASSST!

SWIFTLY, LOST BROTHER. WE HAVE BUT SECONDS--

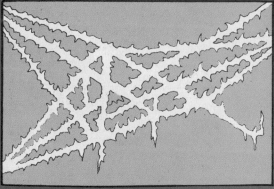

NOW.

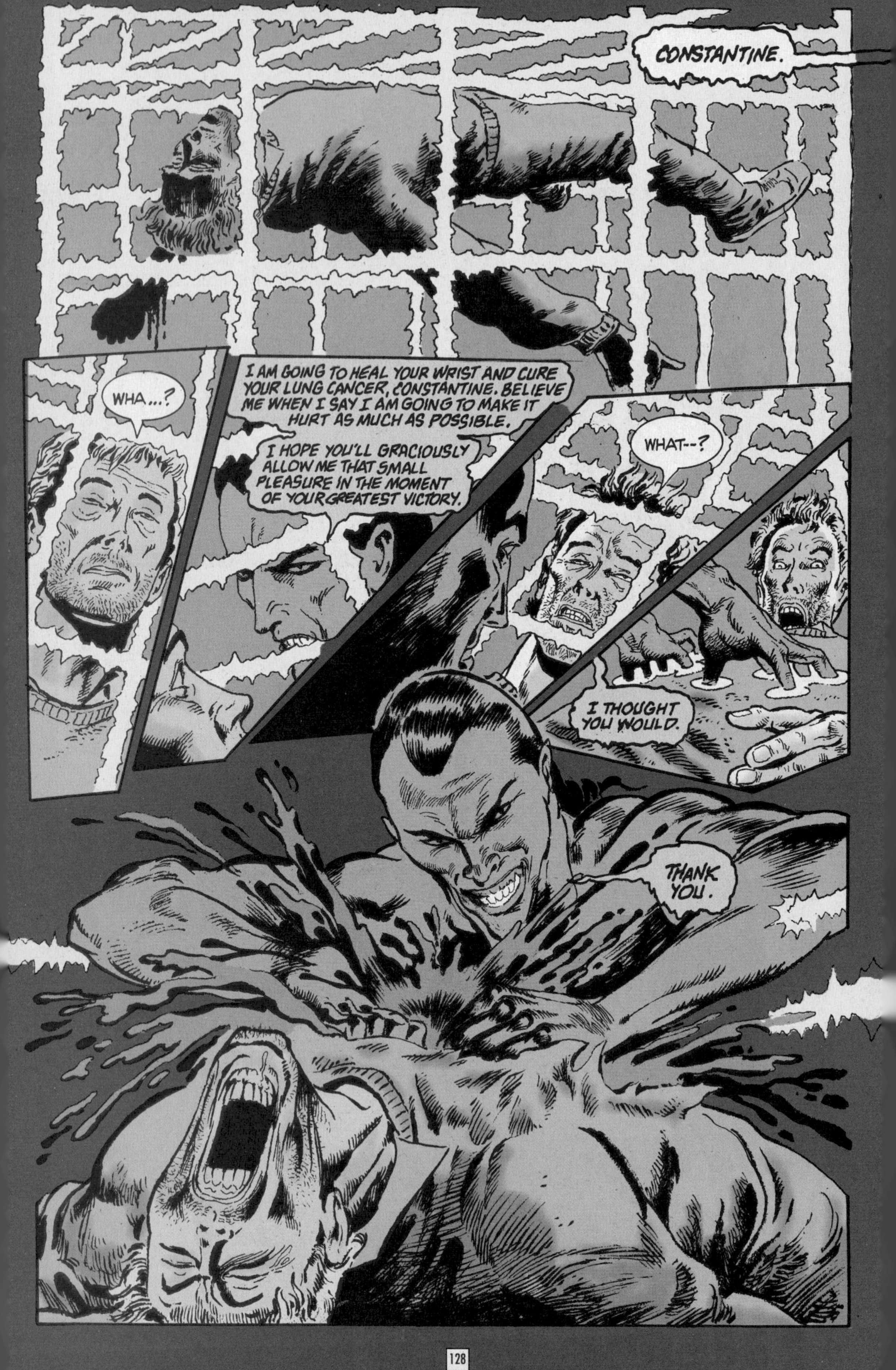
CONSTANTINE.
WHA...?
I AM GOING TO HEAL YOUR WRIST AND CURE YOUR LUNG CANCER, CONSTANTINE. BELIEVE ME WHEN I SAY I AM GOING TO MAKE IT HURT AS MUCH AS POSSIBLE.
I HOPE YOU'LL GRACIOUSLY ALLOW ME THAT SMALL PLEASURE IN THE MOMENT OF YOUR GREATEST VICTORY.
WHAT--?
I THOUGHT YOU WOULD.
THANK YOU.

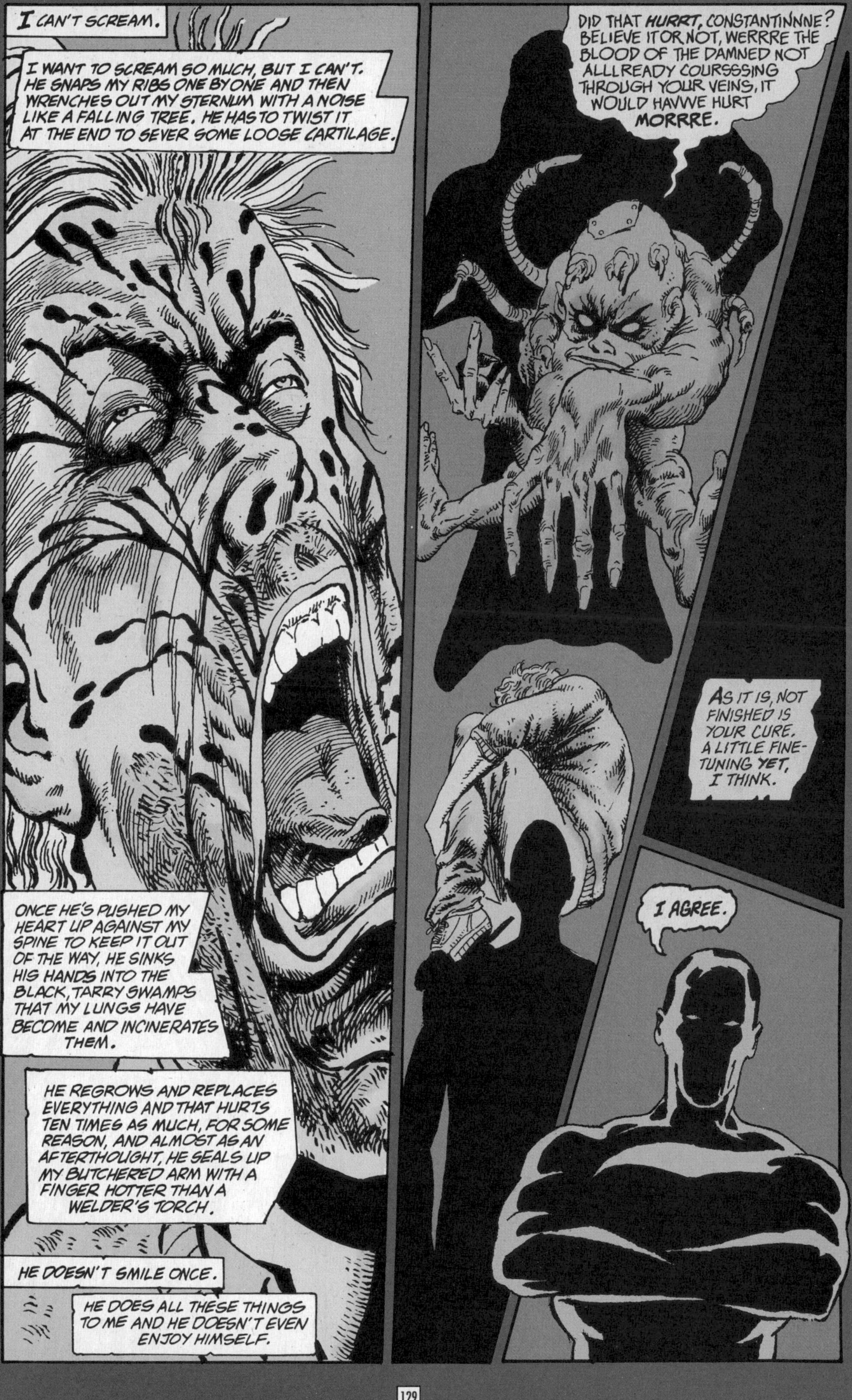
I CAN'T SCREAM.
I WANT TO SCREAM SO MUCH, BUT I CAN'T. HE SNAPS MY RIBS ONE BY ONE AND THEN WRENCHES OUT MY STERNUM WITH A NOISE LIKE A FALLING TREE. HE HAS TO TWIST IT AT THE END TO SEVER SOME LOOSE CARTILAGE.
ONCE HE'S PUSHED MY HEART UP AGAINST MY SPINE TO KEEP IT OUT OF THE WAY, HE SINKS HIS HANDS INTO THE BLACK, TARRY SWAMPS THAT MY LUNGS HAVE BECOME AND INCINERATES THEM.
HE REGROWS AND REPLACES EVERYTHING AND THAT HURTS TEN TIMES AS MUCH, FOR SOME REASON, AND ALMOST AS AN AFTERTHOUGHT, HE SEALS UP MY BUTCHERED ARM WITH A FINGER HOTTER THAN A WELDER'S TORCH.
HE DOESN'T SMILE ONCE.
HE DOES ALL THESE THINGS TO ME AND HE DOESN'T EVEN ENJOY HIMSELF.
DID THAT HURRT, CONSTANTINNNE? BELIEVE IT OR NOT, WERRRE THE BLOOD OF THE DAMNED NOT ALLLREADY COURSSSING THROUGH YOUR VEINS, IT WOULD HAVVVE HURT MORRRE.
AS IT IS, NOT FINISHED IS YOUR CURE. A LITTLE FINE-TUNING YET, I THINK.
I AGREE.

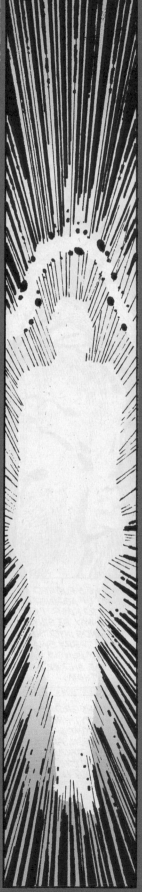

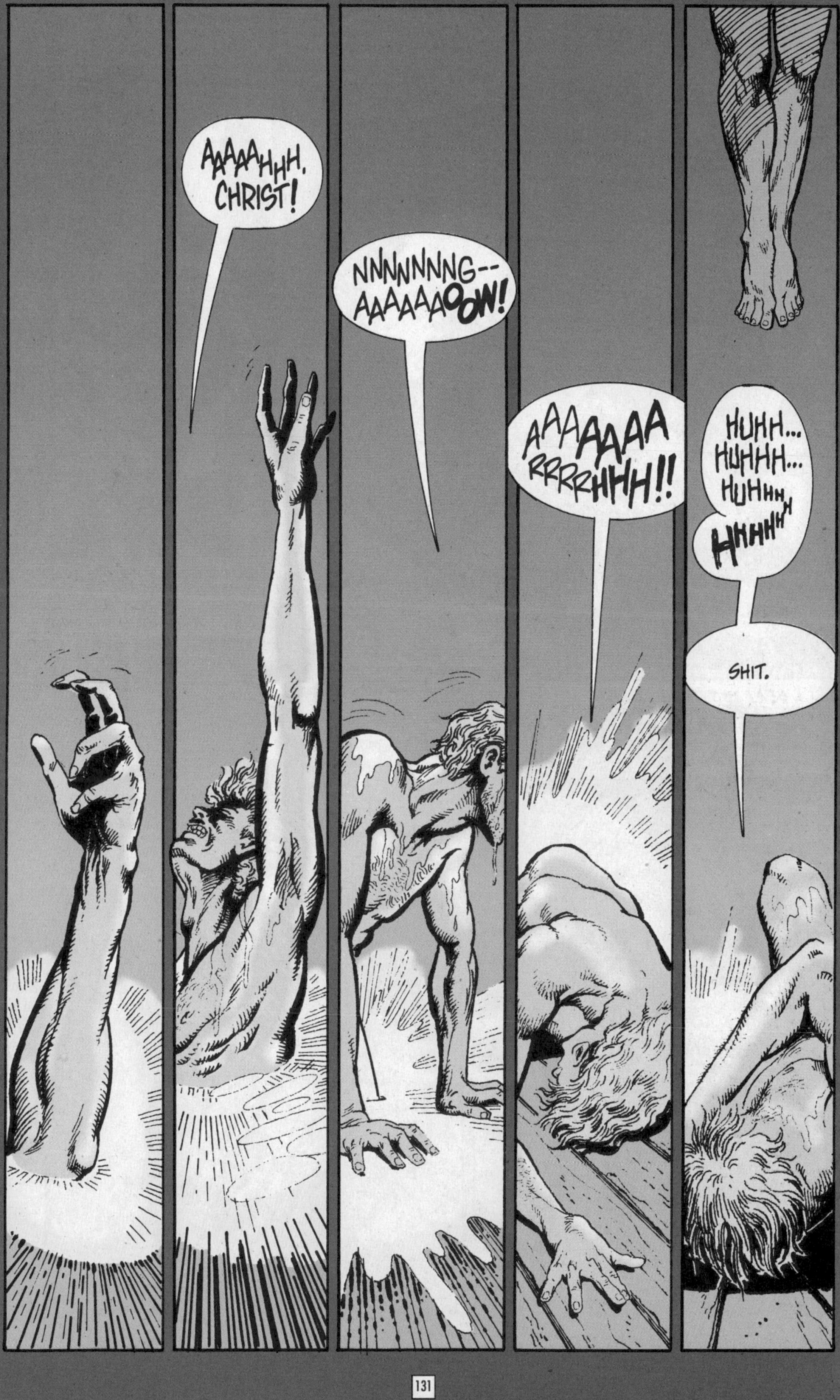
AAAAAHHH, CHRIST!
NNNNNNNG--AAAAAAOOW!
AAAAAAA RRRRHHH!!
HUHH... HUHHH... HUHHHH HHHHH
SHIT.

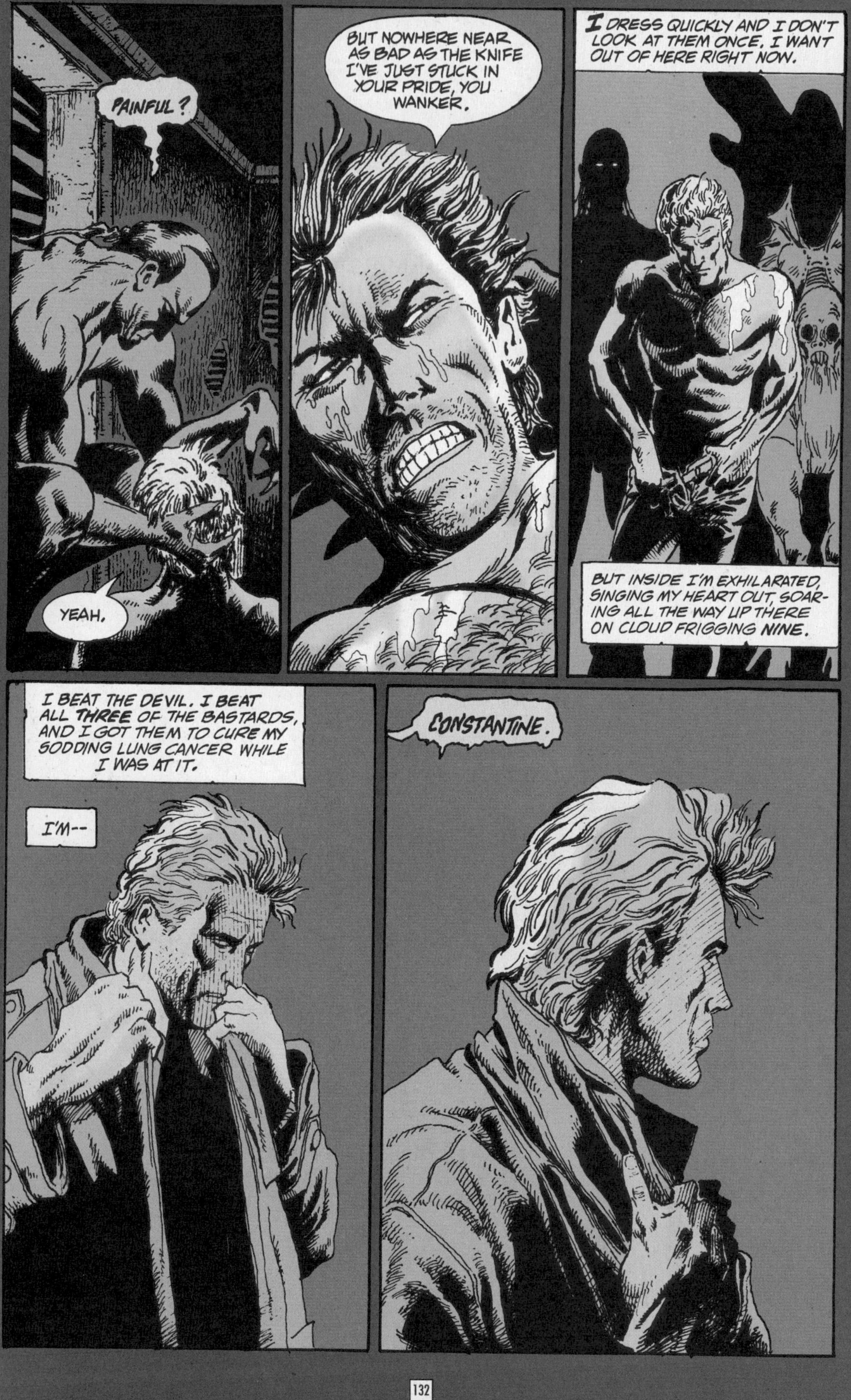
PAINFUL?
YEAH.
BUT NOWHERE NEAR AS BAD AS THE KNIFE I'VE JUST STUCK IN YOUR PRIDE, YOU WANKER.
I DRESS QUICKLY AND I DON'T LOOK AT THEM ONCE. I WANT OUT OF HERE RIGHT NOW.
BUT INSIDE I'M EXHILARATED, SINGING MY HEART OUT, SOARING ALL THE WAY UP THERE ON CLOUD FRIGGING NINE.
I BEAT THE DEVIL. I BEAT ALL THREE OF THE BASTARDS, AND I GOT THEM TO CURE MY SODDING LUNG CANCER WHILE I WAS AT IT.
I'M--
CONSTANTINE.

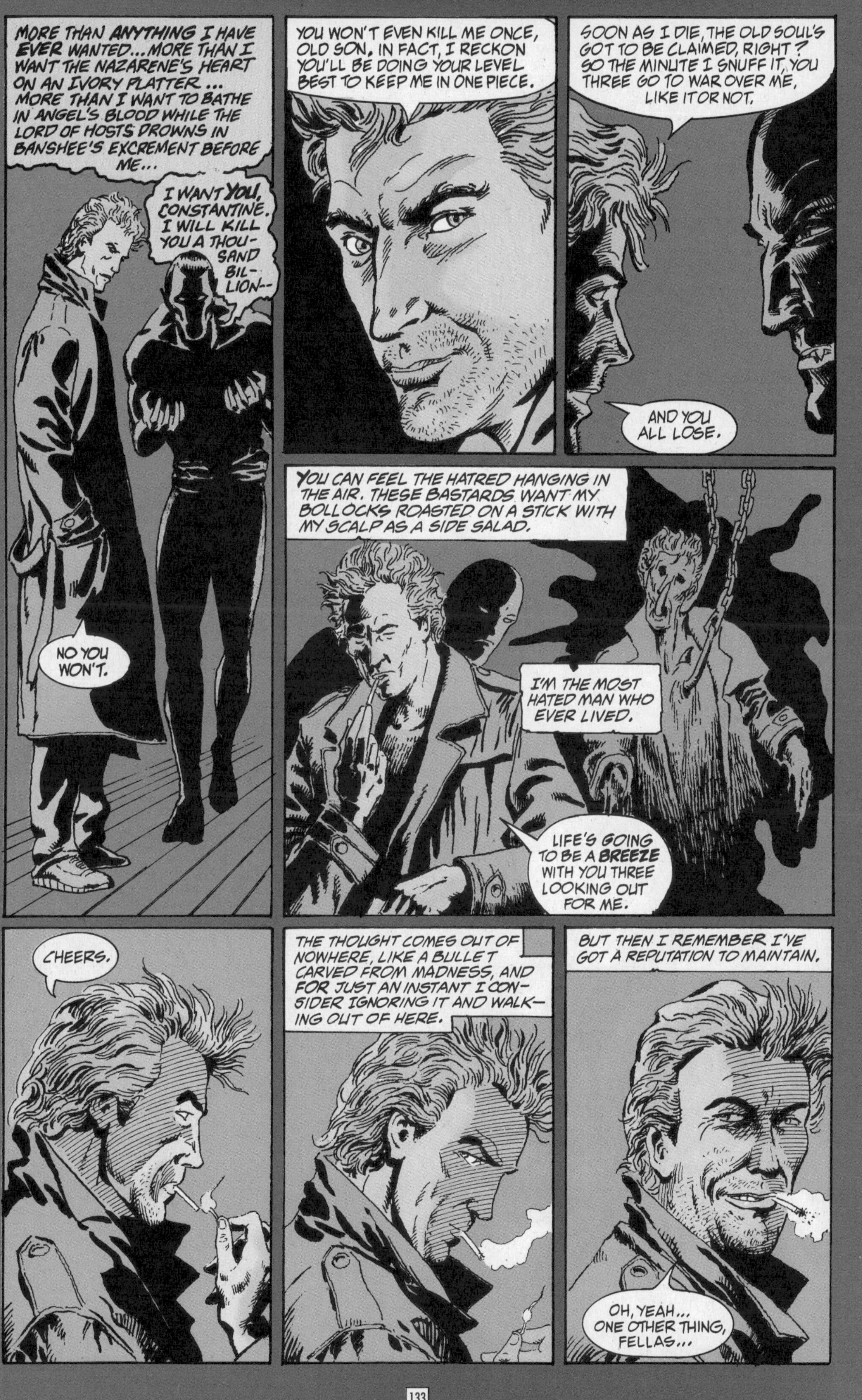

MORE THAN ANYTHING I HAVE EVER WANTED... MORE THAN I WANT THE NAZARENE'S HEART ON AN IVORY PLATTER... MORE THAN I WANT TO BATHE IN ANGEL'S BLOOD WHILE THE LORD OF HOSTS DROWNS IN BANSHEE'S EXCREMENT BEFORE ME...
I WANT YOU, CONSTANTINE. I WILL KILL YOU A THOU-SAND BIL-LION--
NO YOU WON'T.
YOU WON'T EVEN KILL ME ONCE, OLD SON. IN FACT, I RECKON YOU'LL BE DOING YOUR LEVEL BEST TO KEEP ME IN ONE PIECE.
SOON AS I DIE, THE OLD SOUL'S GOT TO BE CLAIMED, RIGHT? SO THE MINUTE I SNUFF IT, YOU THREE GO TO WAR OVER ME, LIKE IT OR NOT.
AND YOU ALL LOSE.
YOU CAN FEEL THE HATRED HANGING IN THE AIR. THESE BASTARDS WANT MY BOLLOCKS ROASTED ON A STICK WITH MY SCALP AS A SIDE SALAD.
I'M THE MOST HATED MAN WHO EVER LIVED.
LIFE'S GOING TO BE A BREEZE WITH YOU THREE LOOKING OUT FOR ME.
CHEERS.
THE THOUGHT COMES OUT OF NOWHERE, LIKE A BULLET CARVED FROM MADNESS, AND FOR JUST AN INSTANT I CON-SIDER IGNORING IT AND WALK-ING OUT OF HERE.
BUT THEN I REMEMBER I'VE GOT A REPUTATION TO MAINTAIN.
OH, YEAH... ONE OTHER THING, FELLAS...

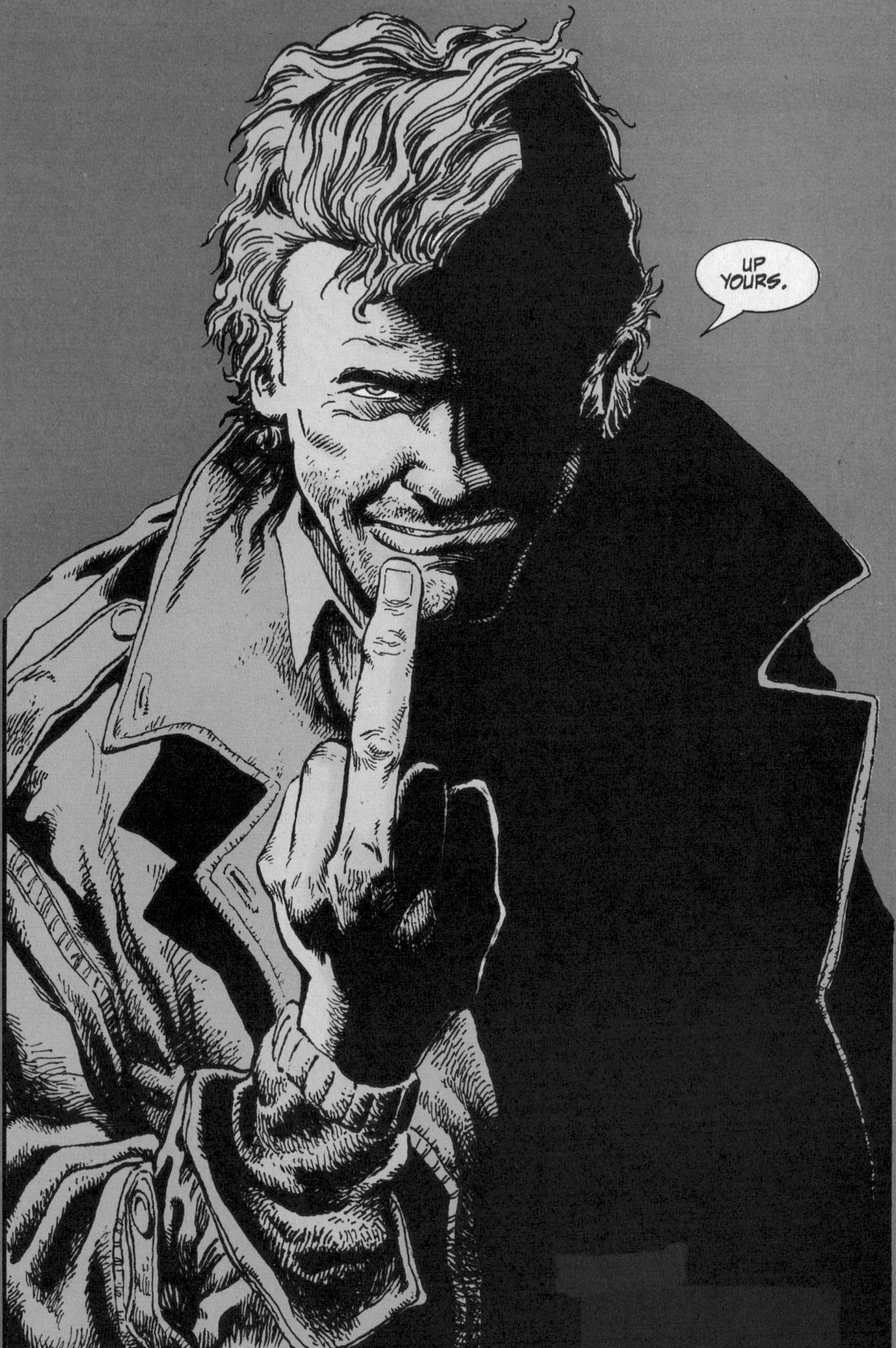
UP YOURS.

falling

into

hell

VI

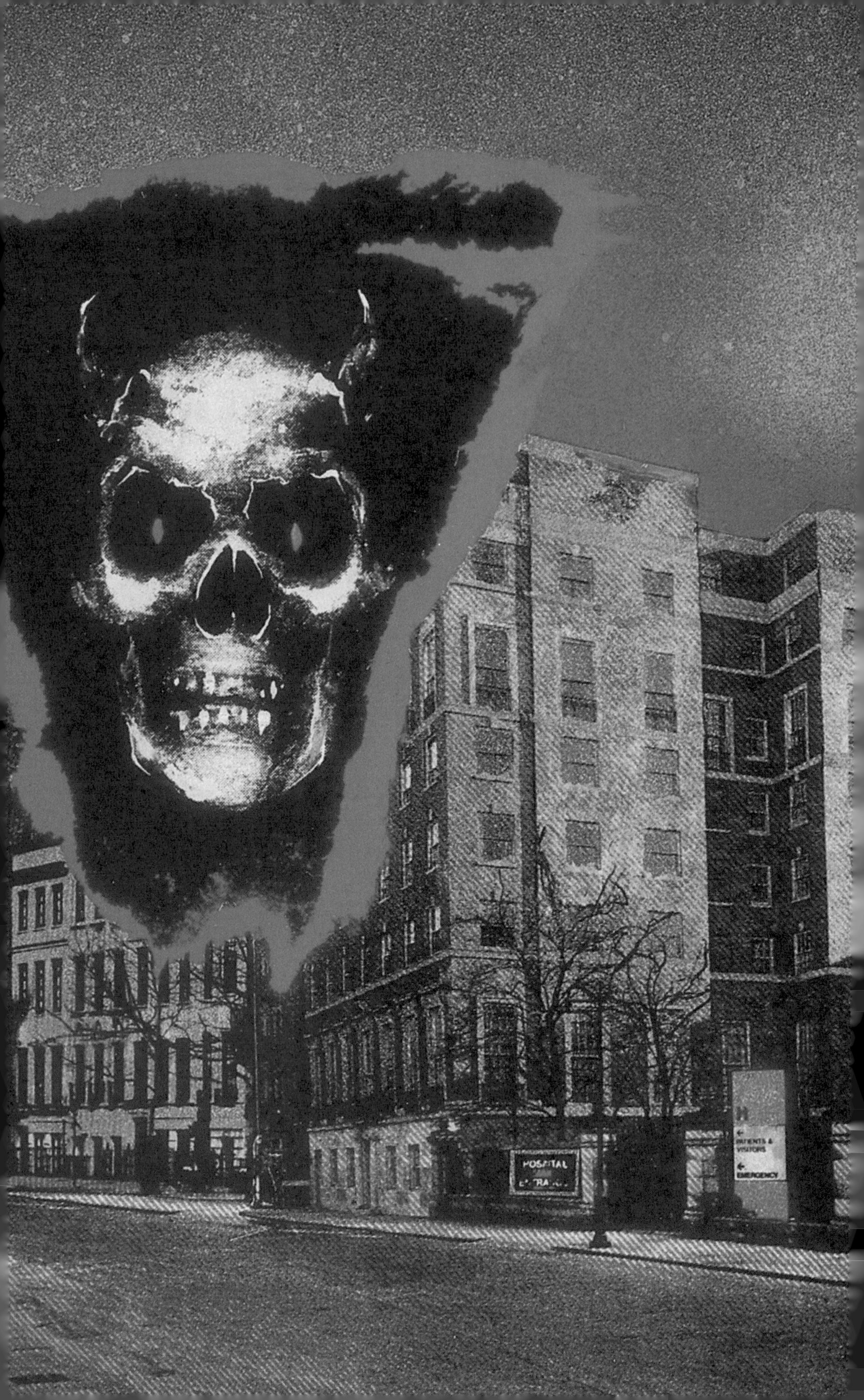
HOSPITAL
EMERGENCY

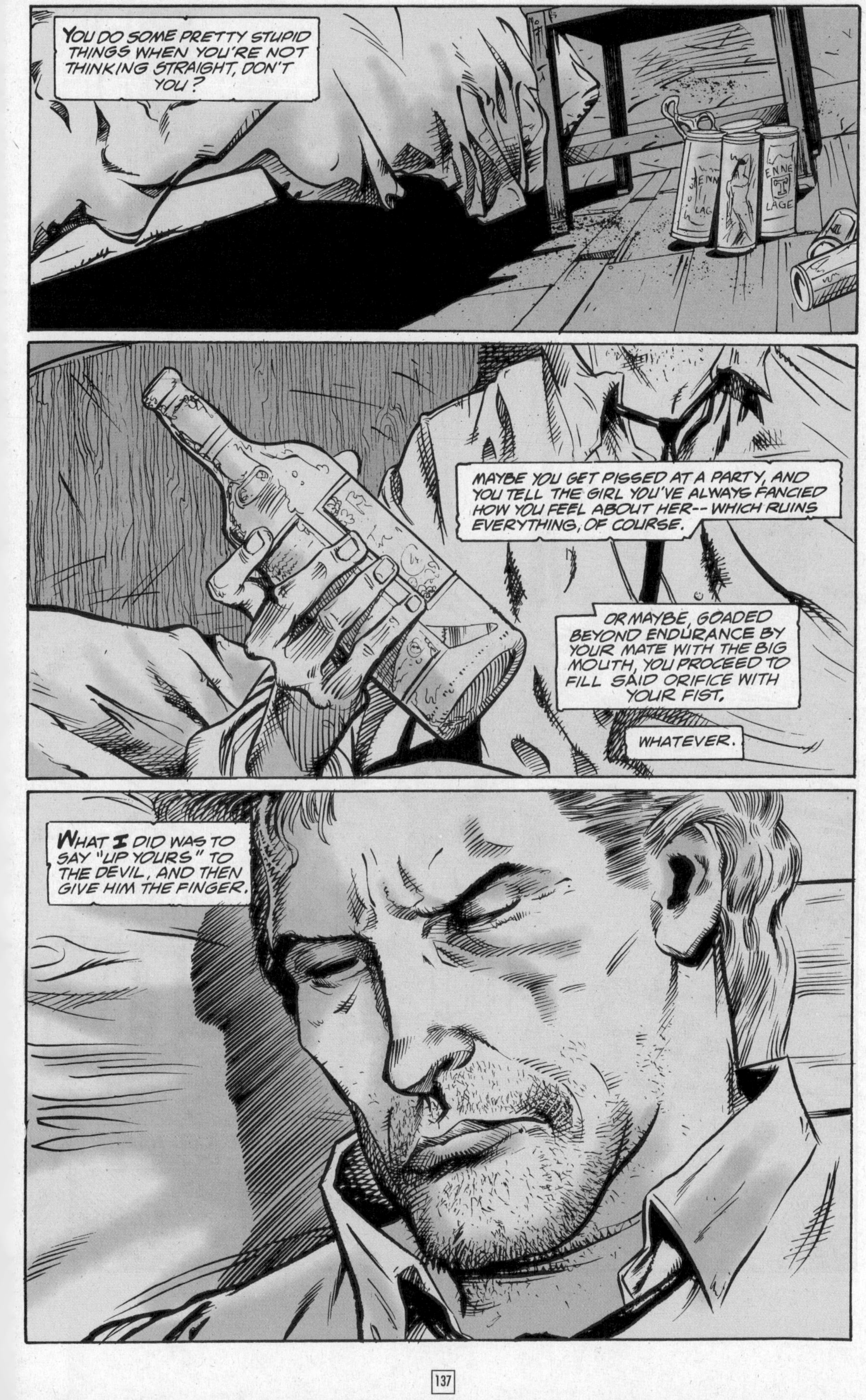
YOU DO SOME PRETTY STUPID THINGS WHEN YOU'RE NOT THINKING STRAIGHT, DON'T YOU?
MAYBE YOU GET PISSED AT A PARTY, AND YOU TELL THE GIRL YOU'VE ALWAYS FANCIED HOW YOU FEEL ABOUT HER-- WHICH RUINS EVERYTHING, OF COURSE.
OR MAYBE, GOADED BEYOND ENDURANCE BY YOUR MATE WITH THE BIG MOUTH, YOU PROCEED TO FILL SAID ORIFICE WITH YOUR FIST.
WHATEVER.
WHAT I DID WAS TO SAY "UP YOURS" TO THE DEVIL, AND THEN GIVE HIM THE FINGER.

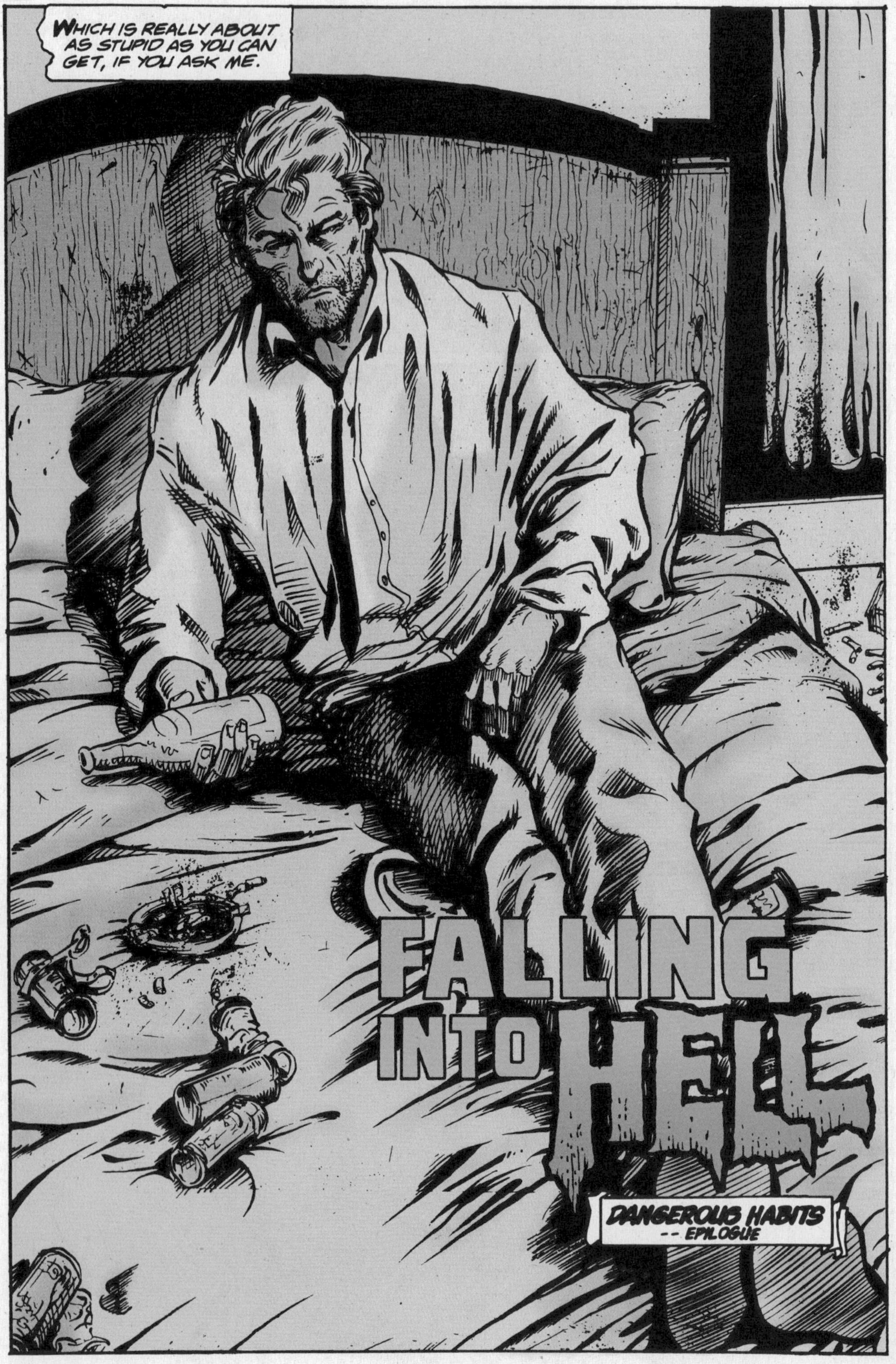
WHICH IS REALLY ABOUT AS STUPID AS YOU CAN GET, IF YOU ASK ME.
FALLING INTO HELL
DANGEROUS HABITS -- EPILOGUE

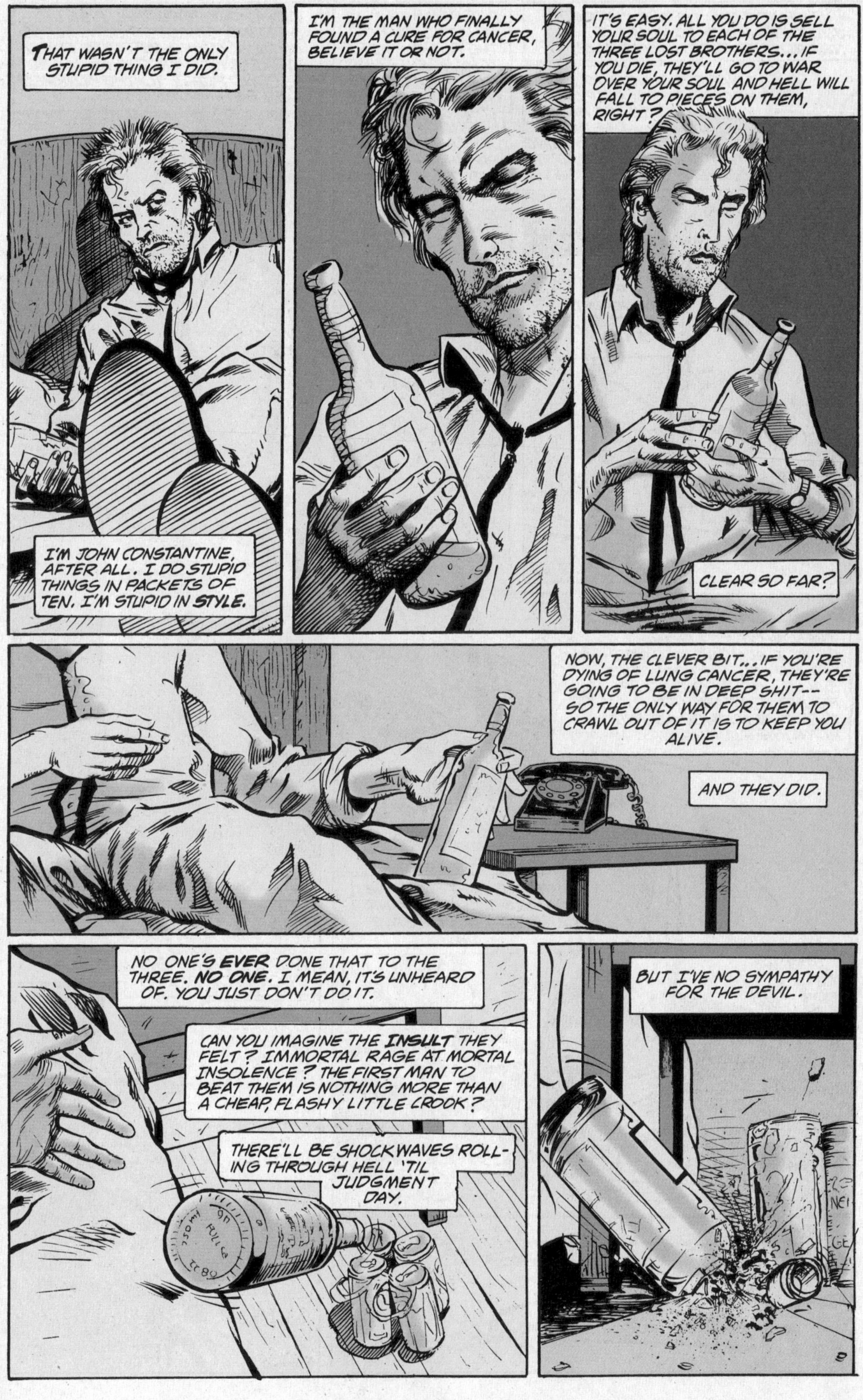
THAT WASN'T THE ONLY STUPID THING I DID.
I'M JOHN CONSTANTINE, AFTER ALL. I DO STUPID THINGS IN PACKETS OF TEN. I'M STUPID IN STYLE.
I'M THE MAN WHO FINALLY FOUND A CURE FOR CANCER, BELIEVE IT OR NOT.
IT'S EASY. ALL YOU DO IS SELL YOUR SOUL TO EACH OF THE THREE LOST BROTHERS... IF YOU DIE, THEY'LL GO TO WAR OVER YOUR SOUL AND HELL WILL FALL TO PIECES ON THEM, RIGHT?
CLEAR SO FAR?
NOW, THE CLEVER BIT... IF YOU'RE DYING OF LUNG CANCER, THEY'RE GOING TO BE IN DEEP SHIT-- SO THE ONLY WAY FOR THEM TO CRAWL OUT OF IT IS TO KEEP YOU ALIVE.
AND THEY DID.
NO ONE'S EVER DONE THAT TO THE THREE. NO ONE. I MEAN, IT'S UNHEARD OF. YOU JUST DON'T DO IT.
CAN YOU IMAGINE THE INSULT THEY FELT? IMMORTAL RAGE AT MORTAL INSOLENCE? THE FIRST MAN TO BEAT THEM IS NOTHING MORE THAN A CHEAP, FLASHY LITTLE CROOK?
THERE'LL BE SHOCKWAVES ROLLING THROUGH HELL 'TIL JUDGMENT DAY.
BUT I'VE NO SYMPATHY FOR THE DEVIL.

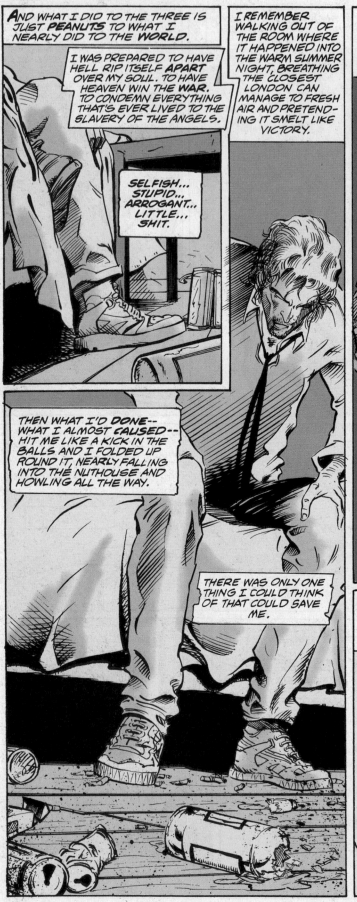

AND WHAT I DID TO THE THREE IS JUST **PEANUTS** TO WHAT I NEARLY DID TO THE **WORLD.**

I WAS PREPARED TO HAVE HELL RIP ITSELF **APART** OVER MY SOUL. TO HAVE HEAVEN WIN THE **WAR.** TO CONDEMN EVERYTHING THAT'S EVER LIVED TO THE SLAVERY OF THE ANGELS.

SELFISH... STUPID... ARROGANT... LITTLE... SHIT.

THEN WHAT I'D **DONE**-- WHAT I ALMOST **CAUSED**-- HIT ME LIKE A KICK IN THE **BALLS** AND I FOLDED UP ROUND IT, NEARLY FALLING INTO THE NUTHOUSE AND HOWLING ALL THE WAY.

THERE WAS ONLY ONE THING I COULD THINK OF THAT COULD SAVE ME.

I REMEMBER WALKING OUT OF THE ROOM WHERE IT HAPPENED INTO THE WARM SUMMER NIGHT, BREATHING THE CLOSEST LONDON CAN MANAGE TO FRESH AIR AND PRETEND-ING IT SMELT LIKE VICTORY.

A TWO-DAY PERSONAL PISS UP GETTING SMASHED SENSELESS UNTIL NOTHING MATTERED ANY-MORE AND EVERYTHING TOOK SECOND PLACE TO THE BLURRED PAIN BEHIND MY EYES.

OH, JESUS...

WELL, IT'S DONE ITS JOB. I FEEL LIKE SHIT, LIKE SOME GIT'S LINED MY GUTS WITH CONCRETE AND STUCK MY BRAINS IN A BUCKET OF SPEW.

BUT I'M THINKING STRAIGHT AGAIN.

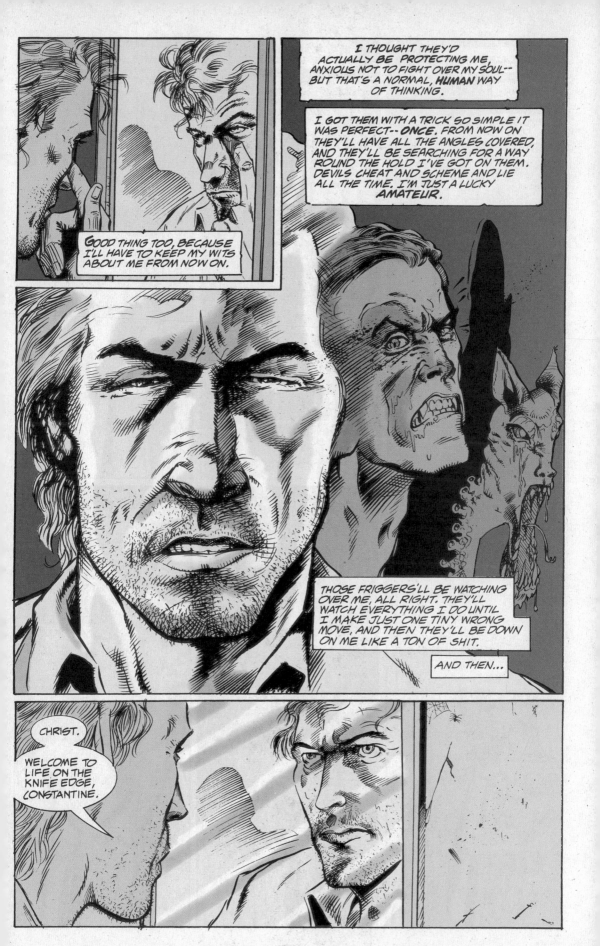

I THOUGHT THEY'D ACTUALLY BE PROTECTING ME, ANXIOUS NOT TO FIGHT OVER MY SOUL-- BUT THAT'S A NORMAL, *HUMAN* WAY OF THINKING.

I GOT THEM WITH A TRICK SO SIMPLE IT WAS PERFECT-- *ONCE.* FROM NOW ON THEY'LL HAVE ALL THE ANGLES COVERED, AND THEY'LL BE SEARCHING FOR A WAY 'ROUND THE HOLD I'VE GOT ON THEM. DEVILS CHEAT AND SCHEME AND LIE ALL THE TIME. I'M JUST A LUCKY *AMATEUR.*

GOOD THING TOO, BECAUSE I'LL HAVE TO KEEP MY WITS ABOUT ME FROM NOW ON.

THOSE FRIGGERS'LL BE WATCHING OVER ME, ALL RIGHT. THEY'LL WATCH EVERYTHING I DO UNTIL I MAKE JUST ONE TINY WRONG MOVE, AND THEN THEY'LL BE DOWN ON ME LIKE A TON OF SHIT.

AND THEN...

CHRIST.

WELCOME TO LIFE ON THE KNIFE EDGE, CONSTANTINE.

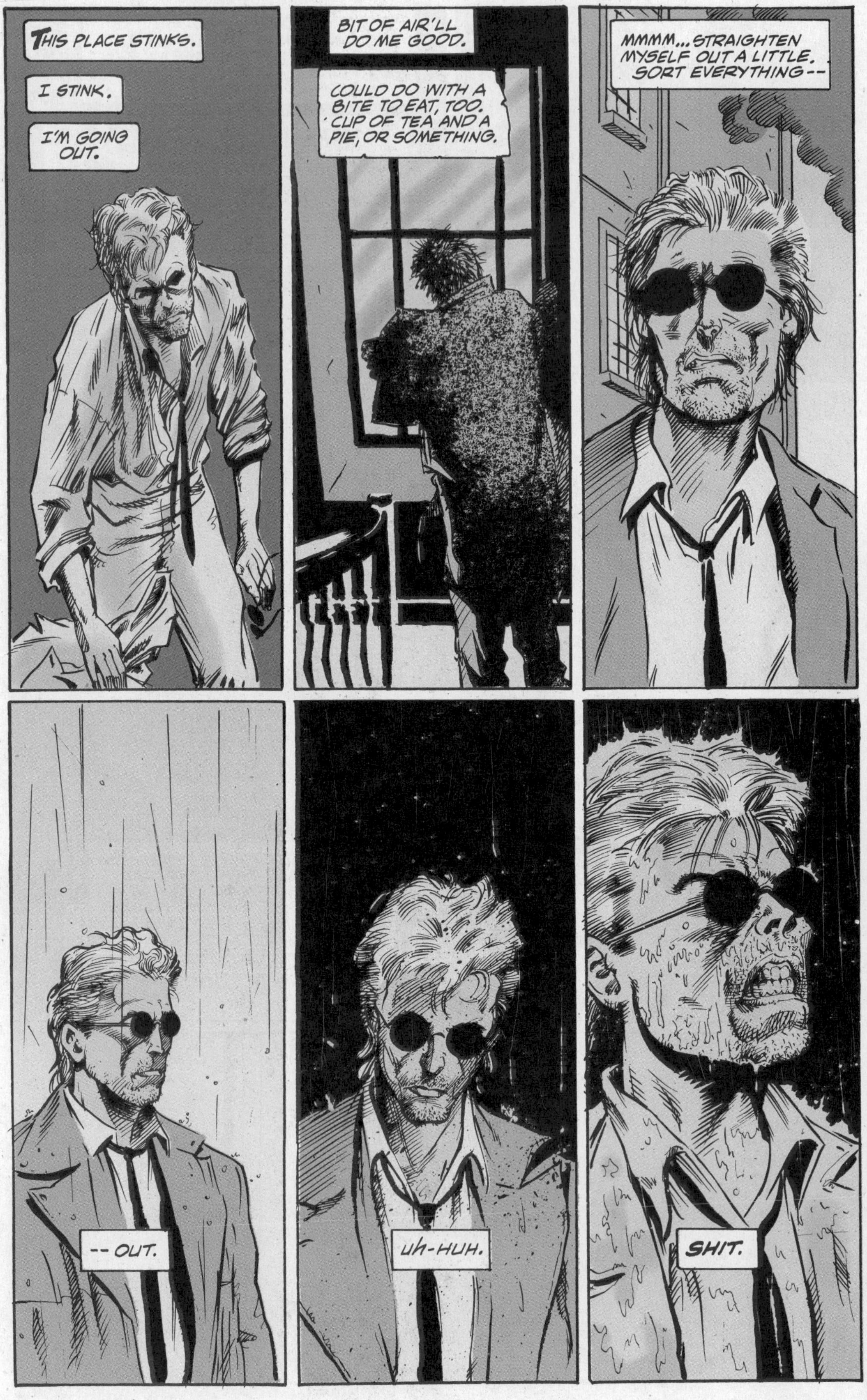
THIS PLACE STINKS.
I STINK.
I'M GOING OUT.
BIT OF AIR'LL DO ME GOOD.
COULD DO WITH A BITE TO EAT, TOO. CUP OF TEA AND A PIE, OR SOMETHING.
MMMM... STRAIGHTEN MYSELF OUT A LITTLE. SORT EVERYTHING--
--OUT.
UH-HUH.
SHIT.

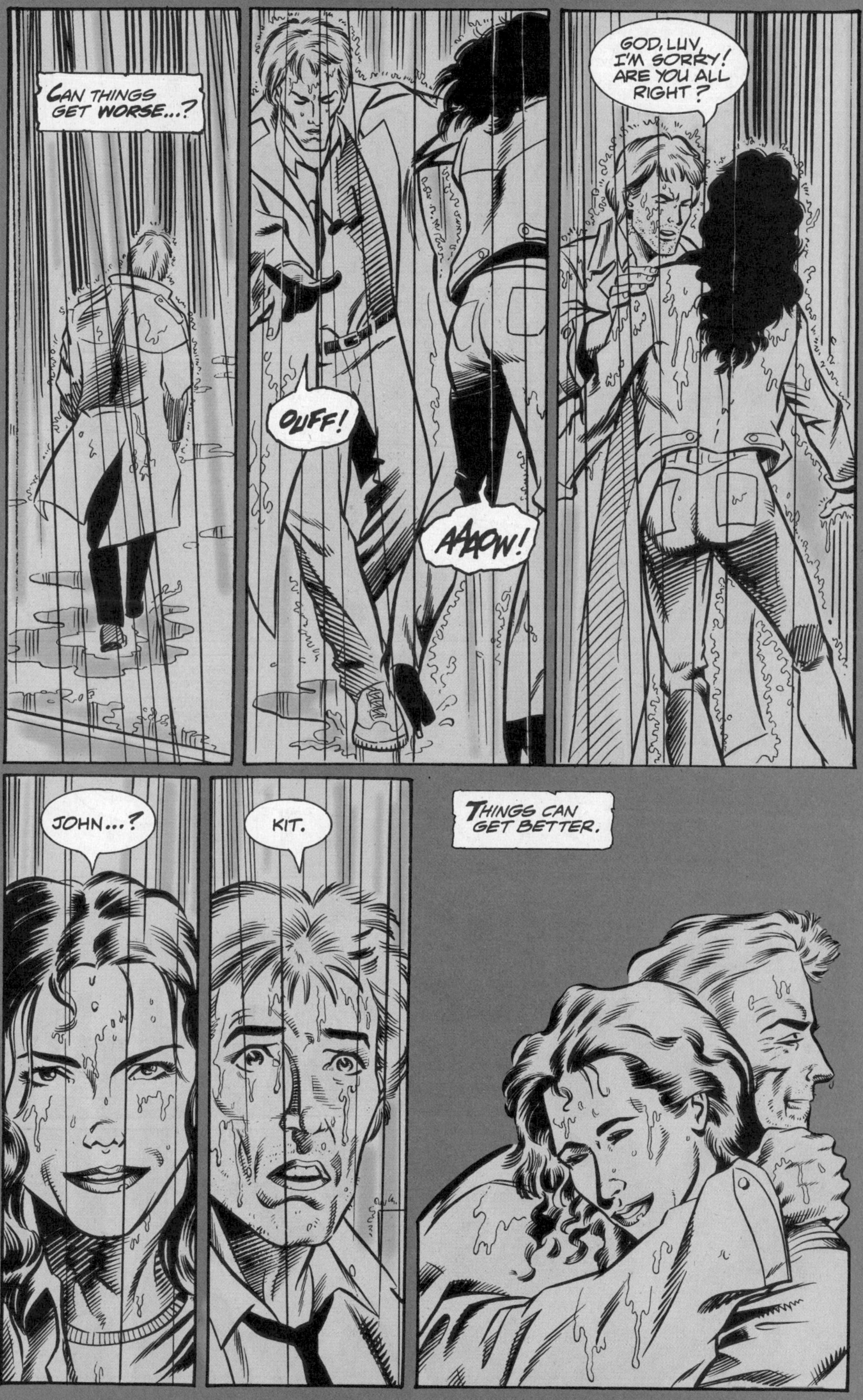
CAN THINGS GET WORSE...?
OUFF!
AAAOW!
GOD, LUV, I'M SORRY! ARE YOU ALL RIGHT?
JOHN...?
KIT.
THINGS CAN GET BETTER.

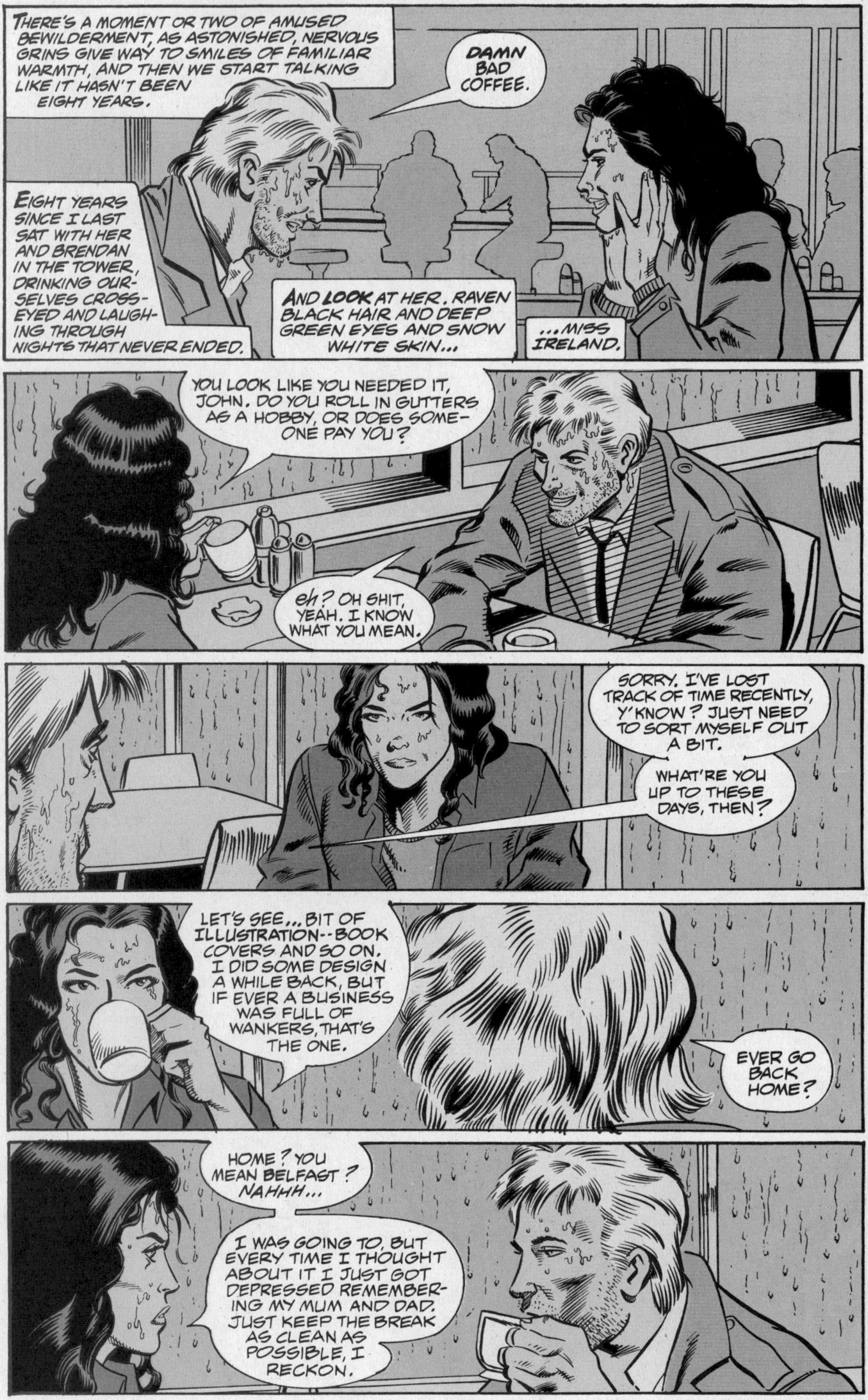
THERE'S A MOMENT OR TWO OF AMUSED BEWILDERMENT, AS ASTONISHED, NERVOUS GRINS GIVE WAY TO SMILES OF FAMILIAR WARMTH, AND THEN WE START TALKING LIKE IT HASN'T BEEN EIGHT YEARS.
DAMN BAD COFFEE.
EIGHT YEARS SINCE I LAST SAT WITH HER AND BRENDAN IN THE TOWER, DRINKING OURSELVES CROSS-EYED AND LAUGHING THROUGH NIGHTS THAT NEVER ENDED.
AND LOOK AT HER. RAVEN BLACK HAIR AND DEEP GREEN EYES AND SNOW WHITE SKIN...
...MISS IRELAND.
YOU LOOK LIKE YOU NEEDED IT, JOHN. DO YOU ROLL IN GUTTERS AS A HOBBY, OR DOES SOMEONE PAY YOU?
eh? OH SHIT, YEAH. I KNOW WHAT YOU MEAN.
SORRY. I'VE LOST TRACK OF TIME RECENTLY, Y'KNOW? JUST NEED TO SORT MYSELF OUT A BIT.
WHAT'RE YOU UP TO THESE DAYS, THEN?
LET'S SEE... BIT OF ILLUSTRATION--BOOK COVERS AND SO ON. I DID SOME DESIGN A WHILE BACK, BUT IF EVER A BUSINESS WAS FULL OF WANKERS, THAT'S THE ONE.
EVER GO BACK HOME?
HOME? YOU MEAN BELFAST? NAHHH...
I WAS GOING TO, BUT EVERY TIME I THOUGHT ABOUT IT I JUST GOT DEPRESSED REMEMBERING MY MUM AND DAD. JUST KEEP THE BREAK AS CLEAN AS POSSIBLE, I RECKON.

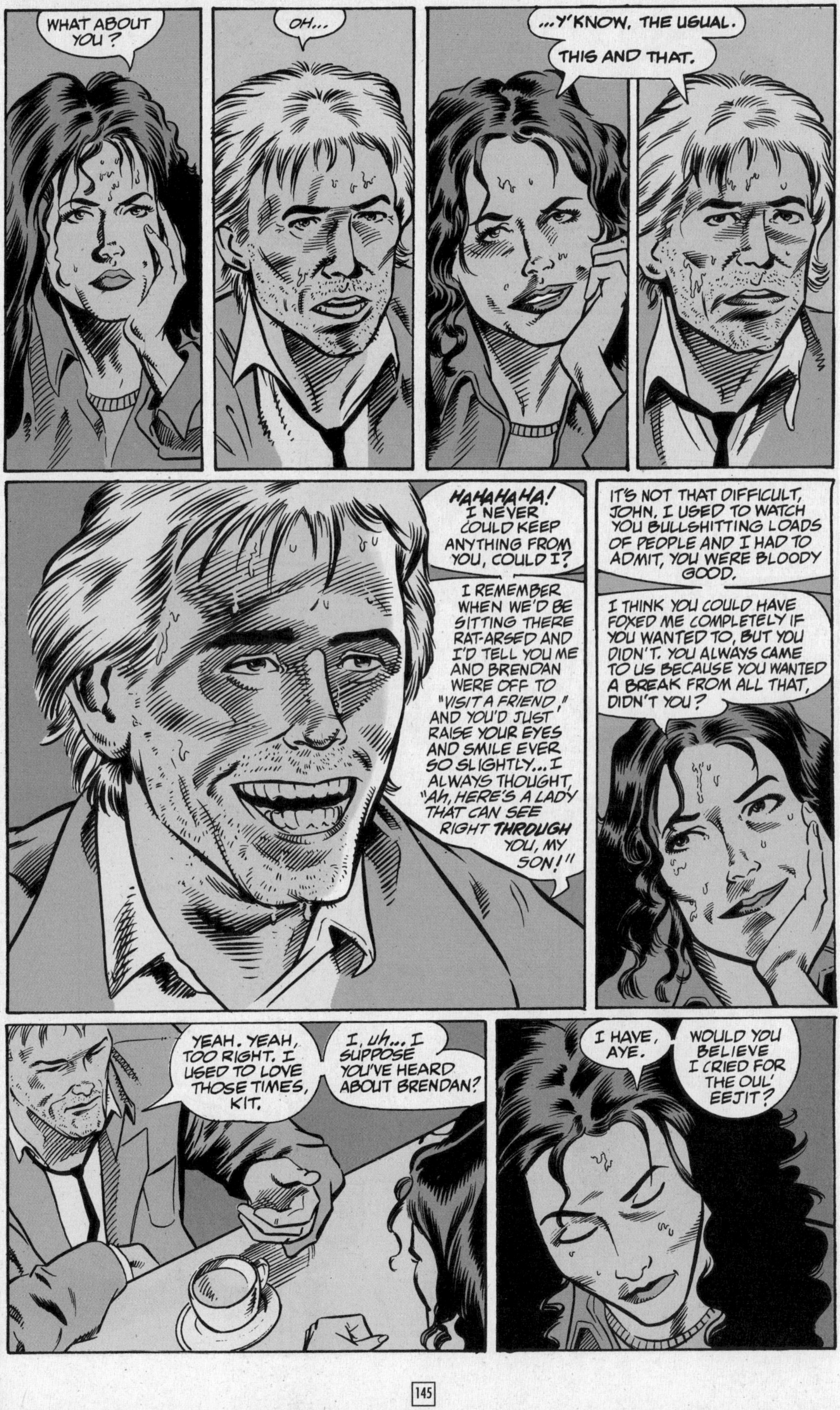
WHAT ABOUT YOU?
OH...
...Y'KNOW. THE USUAL.
THIS AND THAT.
HAHAHAHA! I NEVER COULD KEEP ANYTHING FROM YOU, COULD I?
I REMEMBER WHEN WE'D BE SITTING THERE RAT-ARSED AND I'D TELL YOU ME AND BRENDAN WERE OFF TO "VISIT A FRIEND," AND YOU'D JUST RAISE YOUR EYES AND SMILE EVER SO SLIGHTLY... I ALWAYS THOUGHT, "AH, HERE'S A LADY THAT CAN SEE RIGHT THROUGH YOU, MY SON!"
IT'S NOT THAT DIFFICULT, JOHN. I USED TO WATCH YOU BULLSHITTING LOADS OF PEOPLE AND I HAD TO ADMIT, YOU WERE BLOODY GOOD.
I THINK YOU COULD HAVE FOXED ME COMPLETELY IF YOU WANTED TO, BUT YOU DIDN'T. YOU ALWAYS CAME TO US BECAUSE YOU WANTED A BREAK FROM ALL THAT, DIDN'T YOU?
YEAH. YEAH, TOO RIGHT. I USED TO LOVE THOSE TIMES, KIT.
I, UH... I SUPPOSE YOU'VE HEARD ABOUT BRENDAN?
I HAVE, AYE.
WOULD YOU BELIEVE I CRIED FOR THE OUL' EEJIT?

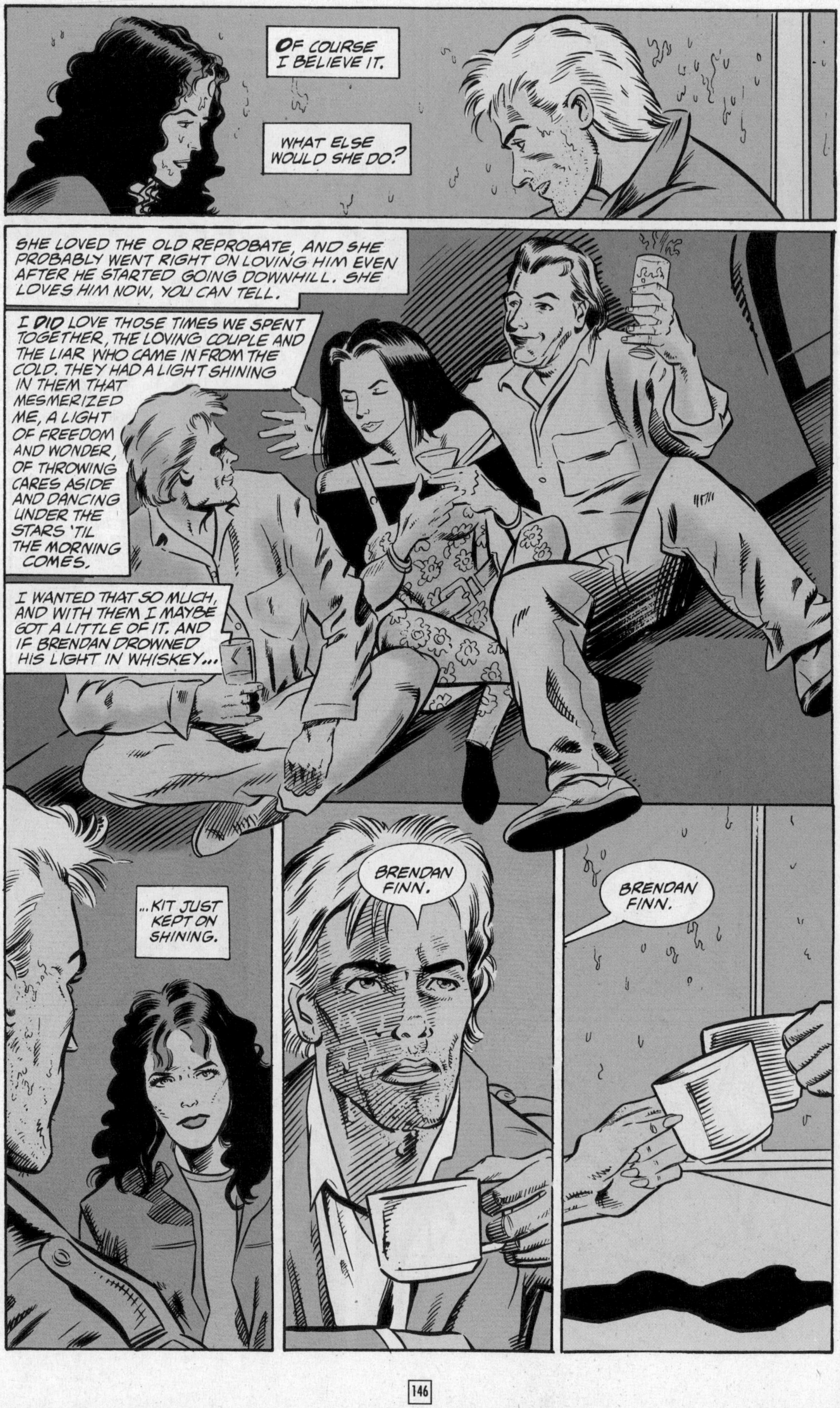
OF COURSE I BELIEVE IT.
WHAT ELSE WOULD SHE DO?
SHE LOVED THE OLD REPROBATE, AND SHE PROBABLY WENT RIGHT ON LOVING HIM EVEN AFTER HE STARTED GOING DOWNHILL. SHE LOVES HIM NOW, YOU CAN TELL.
I DID LOVE THOSE TIMES WE SPENT TOGETHER, THE LOVING COUPLE AND THE LIAR WHO CAME IN FROM THE COLD. THEY HAD A LIGHT SHINING IN THEM THAT MESMERIZED ME, A LIGHT OF FREEDOM AND WONDER, OF THROWING CARES ASIDE AND DANCING UNDER THE STARS 'TIL THE MORNING COMES.
I WANTED THAT SO MUCH, AND WITH THEM I MAYBE GOT A LITTLE OF IT. AND IF BRENDAN DROWNED HIS LIGHT IN WHISKEY...
...KIT JUST KEPT ON SHINING.
BRENDAN FINN.
BRENDAN FINN.

SEEMS A BIT ODD TOASTING THE OLD BUGGER WITH COFFEE, ALL THE SAME-- FANCY A DRINK?

UMMM... AYE, ALL RIGHT.

THE RED ROVER'S JUST NEAR--

HOLY SHIT!!

EH?

CHAS! JESUS, I FORGOT ALL ABOUT YOU!

YOU-- I THOUGHT-- YOUR LETTER SAID--

YOU BLOODY SAID YOU WERE FRIGGIN' SNUFFIN' IT!

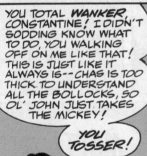

YOU TOTAL WANKER, CONSTANTINE! I DIDN'T SODDING KNOW WHAT TO DO, YOU WALKING OFF ON ME LIKE THAT! THIS IS JUST LIKE IT ALWAYS IS-- CHAS IS TOO THICK TO UNDERSTAND ALL THE BOLLOCKS, SO OL' JOHN JUST TAKES THE MICKEY!

YOU TOSSER!

HHHHH... SO, YOU'RE NOT DYING, THEN?

EH? CHRIST, NO. DO I LOOK DEAD?

RIGHT, RIGHT, MINE NOT TO REASON WHY AS BLOODY USUAL...SEE YOU DOWN THE NORTHHAMPTON FOR A PINT, OKAY?

OI! YOU CAN'T COME IN HERE AND SWEAR AND SHOUT! WHO D'YOU THINK YOU ARE?

SHUT YOUR MOUTH AND PISS OFF AND MAKE ME A CUP OF TEA, YOU LITTLE ARSEHOLE.

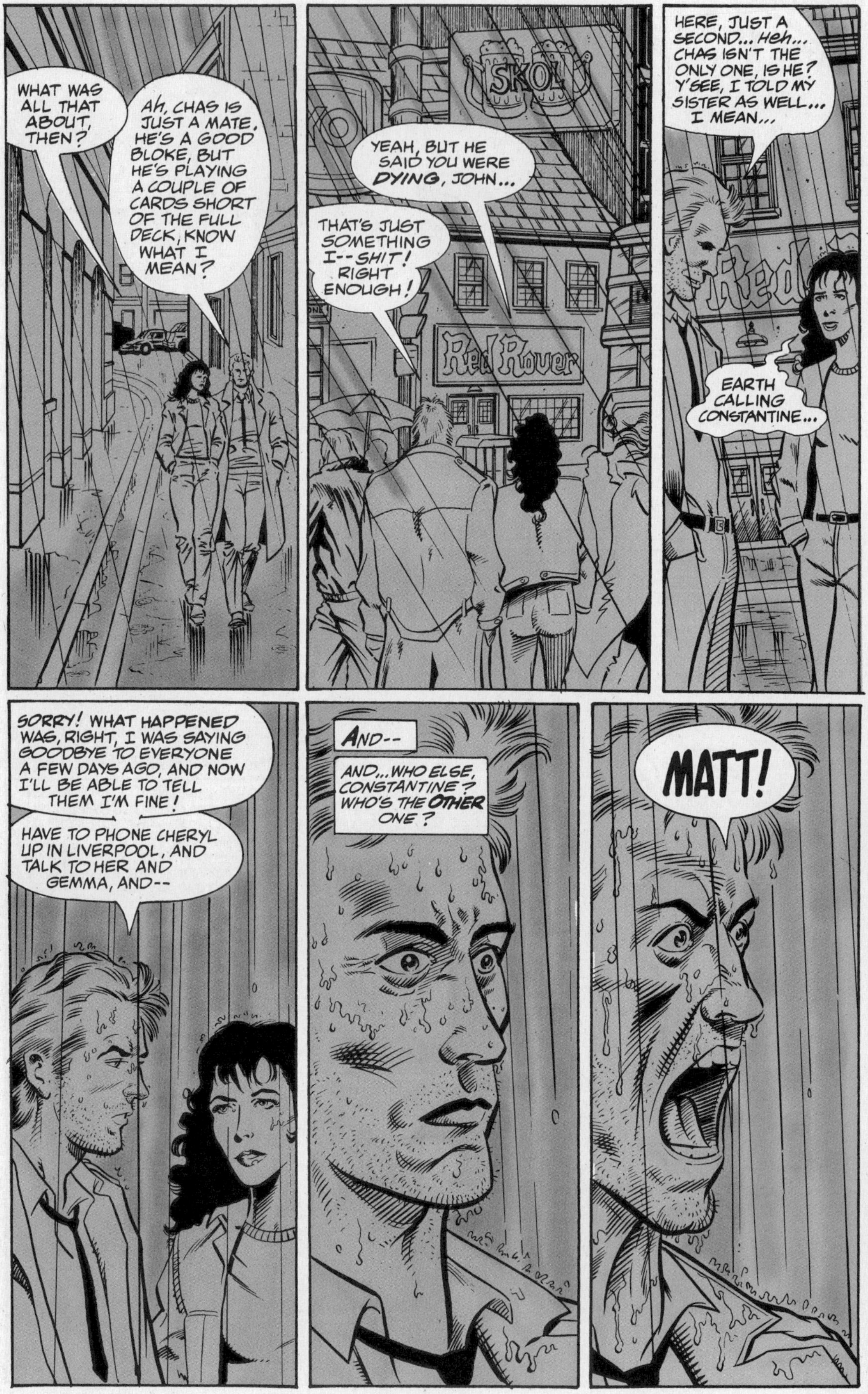
WHAT WAS ALL THAT ABOUT, THEN?
AH, CHAS IS JUST A MATE. HE'S A GOOD BLOKE, BUT HE'S PLAYING A COUPLE OF CARDS SHORT OF THE FULL DECK, KNOW WHAT I MEAN?
SKOL
YEAH, BUT HE SAID YOU WERE *DYING*, JOHN...
THAT'S JUST SOMETHING I-- *SHIT!* RIGHT ENOUGH!
Red Rover
HERE, JUST A SECOND... *Heh...* CHAS ISN'T THE ONLY ONE, IS HE? Y'SEE, I TOLD MY SISTER AS WELL... I MEAN...
EARTH CALLING CONSTANTINE...
SORRY! WHAT HAPPENED WAS, RIGHT, I WAS SAYING GOODBYE TO EVERYONE A FEW DAYS AGO, AND NOW I'LL BE ABLE TO TELL THEM I'M FINE!
HAVE TO PHONE CHERYL UP IN LIVERPOOL, AND TALK TO HER AND GEMMA, AND--
AND--
AND... WHO ELSE, CONSTANTINE? WHO'S THE *OTHER* ONE?
MATT!

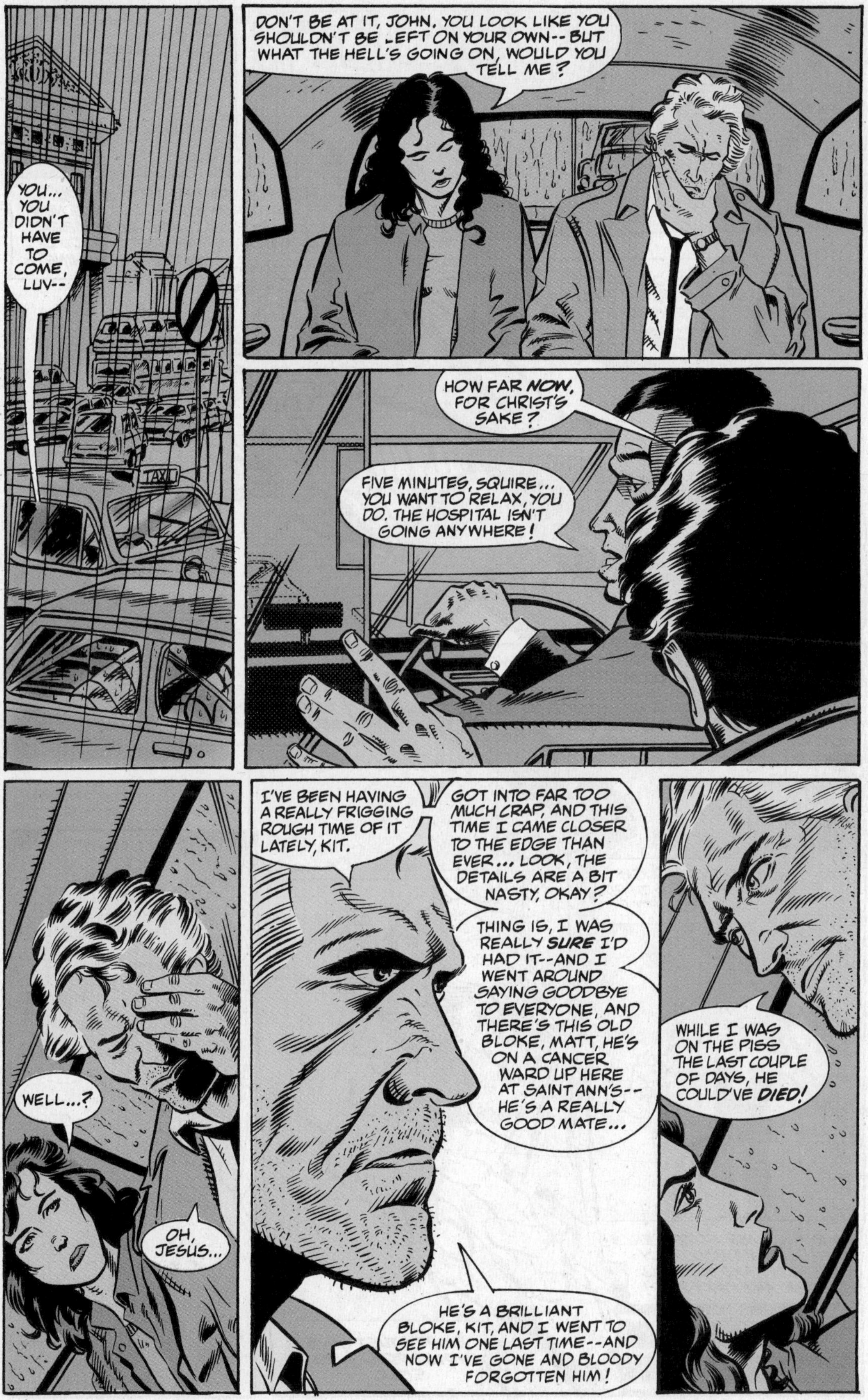

DON'T BE AT IT, JOHN. YOU LOOK LIKE YOU SHOULDN'T BE LEFT ON YOUR OWN-- BUT WHAT THE HELL'S GOING ON, WOULD YOU TELL ME?
YOU... YOU DIDN'T HAVE TO COME, LUV--
HOW FAR NOW, FOR CHRIST'S SAKE?
FIVE MINUTES, SQUIRE... YOU WANT TO RELAX, YOU DO. THE HOSPITAL ISN'T GOING ANYWHERE!
TAXI
WELL...?
OH, JESUS...
I'VE BEEN HAVING A REALLY FRIGGING ROUGH TIME OF IT LATELY, KIT.
GOT INTO FAR TOO MUCH CRAP, AND THIS TIME I CAME CLOSER TO THE EDGE THAN EVER... LOOK, THE DETAILS ARE A BIT NASTY, OKAY?
THING IS, I WAS REALLY SURE I'D HAD IT--AND I WENT AROUND SAYING GOODBYE TO EVERYONE, AND THERE'S THIS OLD BLOKE, MATT, HE'S ON A CANCER WARD UP HERE AT SAINT ANN'S--HE'S A REALLY GOOD MATE...
HE'S A BRILLIANT BLOKE, KIT, AND I WENT TO SEE HIM ONE LAST TIME--AND NOW I'VE GONE AND BLOODY FORGOTTEN HIM!
WHILE I WAS ON THE PISS THE LAST COUPLE OF DAYS, HE COULD'VE DIED!

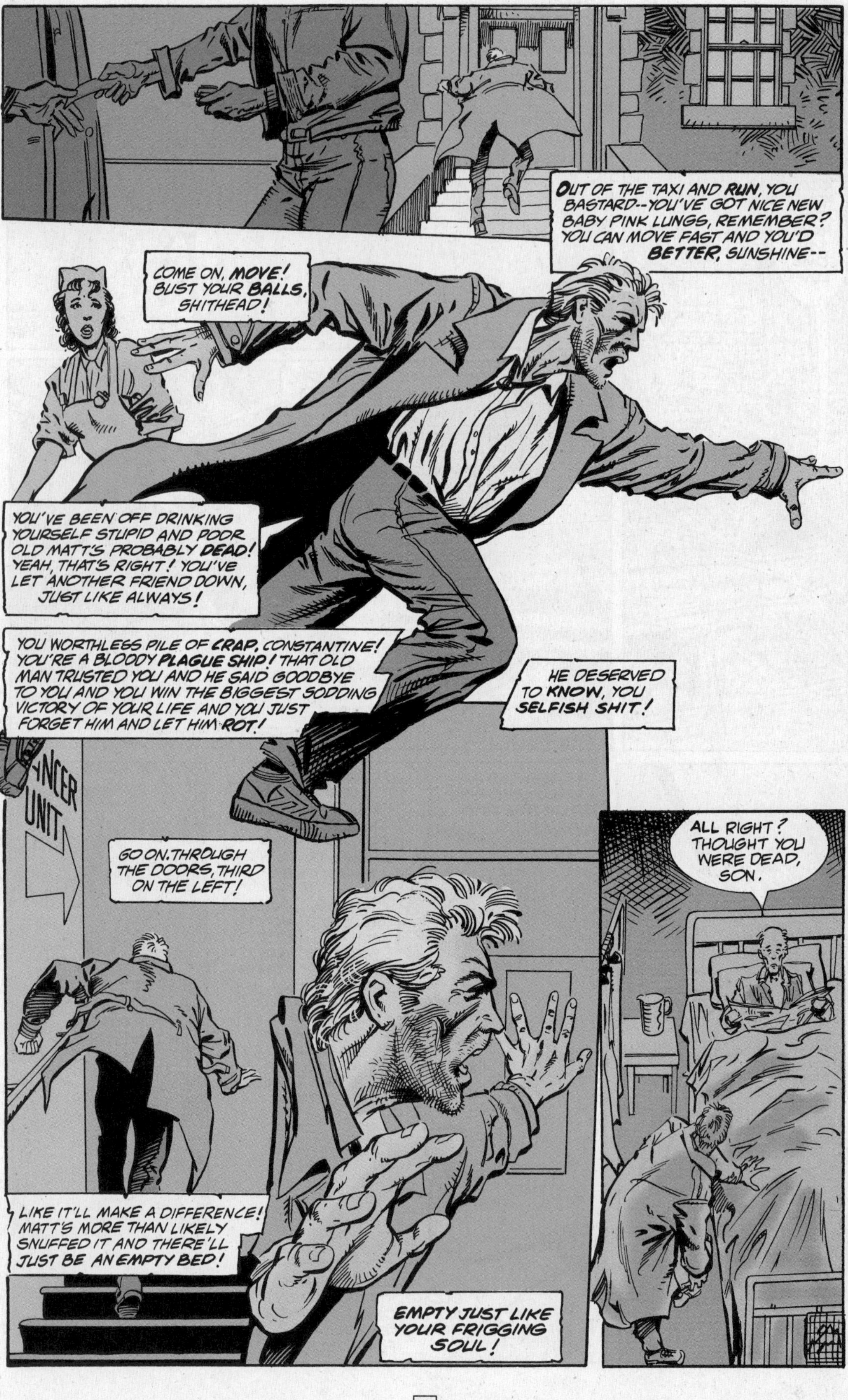
OUT OF THE TAXI AND RUN, YOU BASTARD--YOU'VE GOT NICE NEW BABY PINK LUNGS, REMEMBER? YOU CAN MOVE FAST AND YOU'D BETTER, SUNSHINE--
COME ON, MOVE! BUST YOUR BALLS, SHITHEAD!
YOU'VE BEEN OFF DRINKING YOURSELF STUPID AND POOR OLD MATT'S PROBABLY DEAD! YEAH, THAT'S RIGHT! YOU'VE LET ANOTHER FRIEND DOWN, JUST LIKE ALWAYS!
YOU WORTHLESS PILE OF CRAP, CONSTANTINE! YOU'RE A BLOODY PLAGUE SHIP! THAT OLD MAN TRUSTED YOU AND HE SAID GOODBYE TO YOU AND YOU WIN THE BIGGEST SODDING VICTORY OF YOUR LIFE AND YOU JUST FORGET HIM AND LET HIM ROT!
HE DESERVED TO KNOW, YOU SELFISH SHIT!
NCER UNIT
GO ON. THROUGH THE DOORS, THIRD ON THE LEFT!
LIKE IT'LL MAKE A DIFFERENCE! MATT'S MORE THAN LIKELY SNUFFED IT AND THERE'LL JUST BE AN EMPTY BED!
EMPTY JUST LIKE YOUR FRIGGING SOUL!
ALL RIGHT? THOUGHT YOU WERE DEAD, SON.

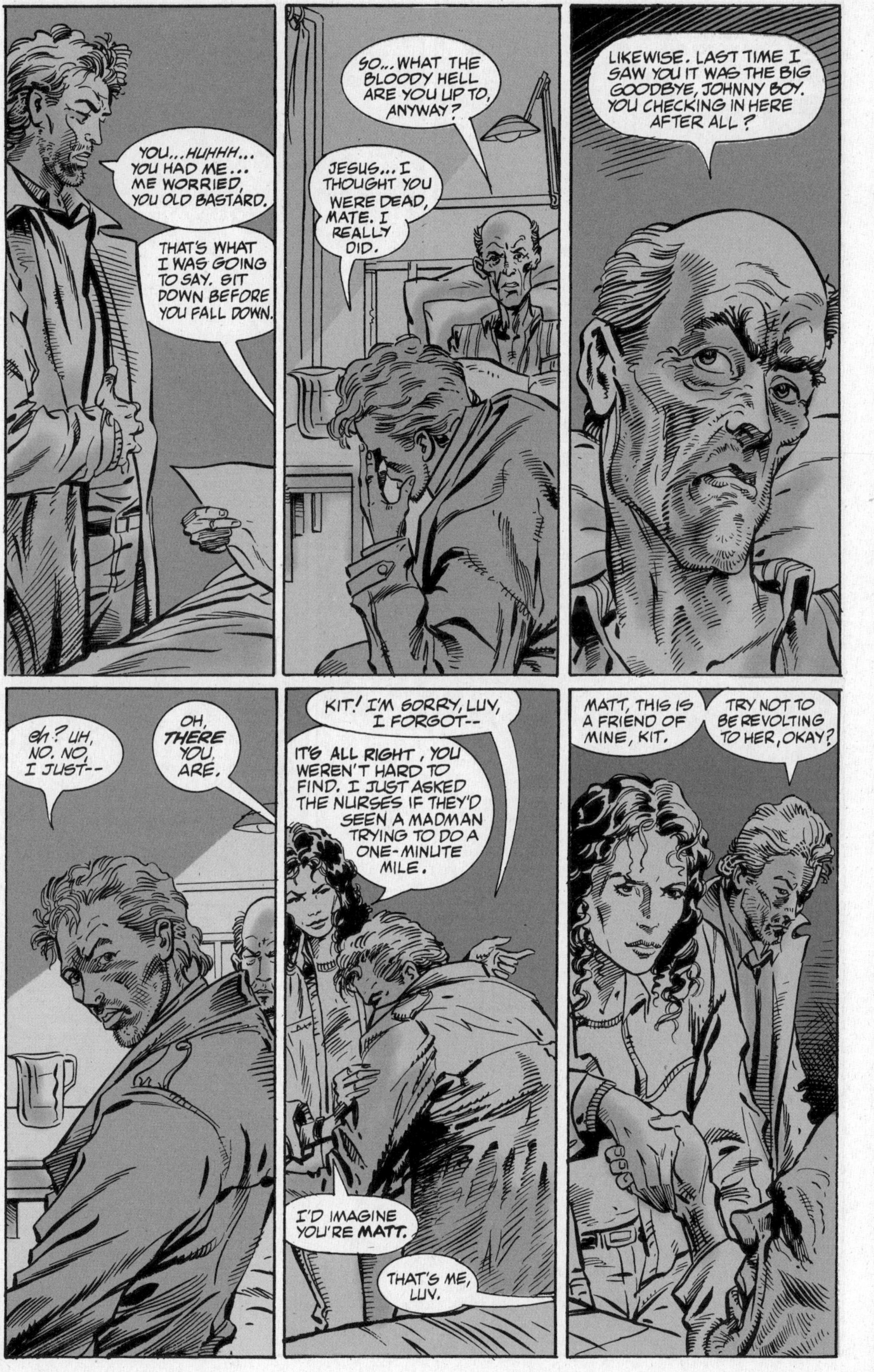
YOU... HUHHH... YOU HAD ME... ME WORRIED, YOU OLD BASTARD.
THAT'S WHAT I WAS GOING TO SAY. SIT DOWN BEFORE YOU FALL DOWN.
SO... WHAT THE BLOODY HELL ARE YOU UP TO, ANYWAY?
JESUS... I THOUGHT YOU WERE DEAD, MATE. I REALLY DID.
LIKEWISE. LAST TIME I SAW YOU IT WAS THE BIG GOODBYE, JOHNNY BOY. YOU CHECKING IN HERE AFTER ALL?
OH, THERE YOU ARE.
eh? UH, NO. NO, I JUST--
KIT! I'M SORRY, LUV, I FORGOT--
IT'S ALL RIGHT, YOU WEREN'T HARD TO FIND. I JUST ASKED THE NURSES IF THEY'D SEEN A MADMAN TRYING TO DO A ONE-MINUTE MILE.
I'D IMAGINE YOU'RE MATT.
THAT'S ME, LUV.
MATT, THIS IS A FRIEND OF MINE, KIT.
TRY NOT TO BE REVOLTING TO HER, OKAY?

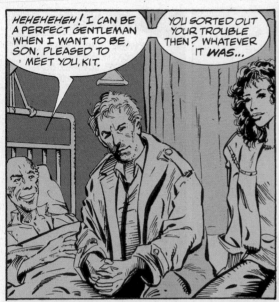

HEHEHEHEH! I CAN BE A PERFECT GENTLEMAN WHEN I WANT TO BE, SON, PLEASED TO MEET YOU, KIT.

YOU SORTED OUT YOUR TROUBLE THEN? WHATEVER IT *WAS*...

UH... MORE OR LESS, MATE. GOT A BIT BLOODY, BUT...

IT'S OKAY NOW.

I CAN SEE YOU BOYS HAVE QUITE A BIT TO TALK ABOUT, SO I'LL GET OUT OF YOUR WAY FOR A TICK... COFFEE?

TEA, PLEASE, LUV. THERE'S A MACHINE DOWNSTAIRS.

OHHHH... WHAT A *CORKER*, WELL DONE, MY SON...

HMMM? AH, NO. JUST FRIENDS. HAVEN'T SEEN HER IN QUITE A WHILE.

PRETTY GOOD FRIENDS, I'D SAY.

OH, I DON'T MEAN *THAT*-- I MEAN YOU MUST BE PRETTY CLOSE, THAT'S ALL. I WAS WATCHING HER LOOK AT YOU THERE. SHE *KNOWS* YOU, DOESN'T SHE?

WE GO BACK A BIT...

YEAH. SHE'S A LOVELY GIRL, JOHN. YOU WANT TO LOOK AFTER HER. AND I'LL TELL YOU WHY...

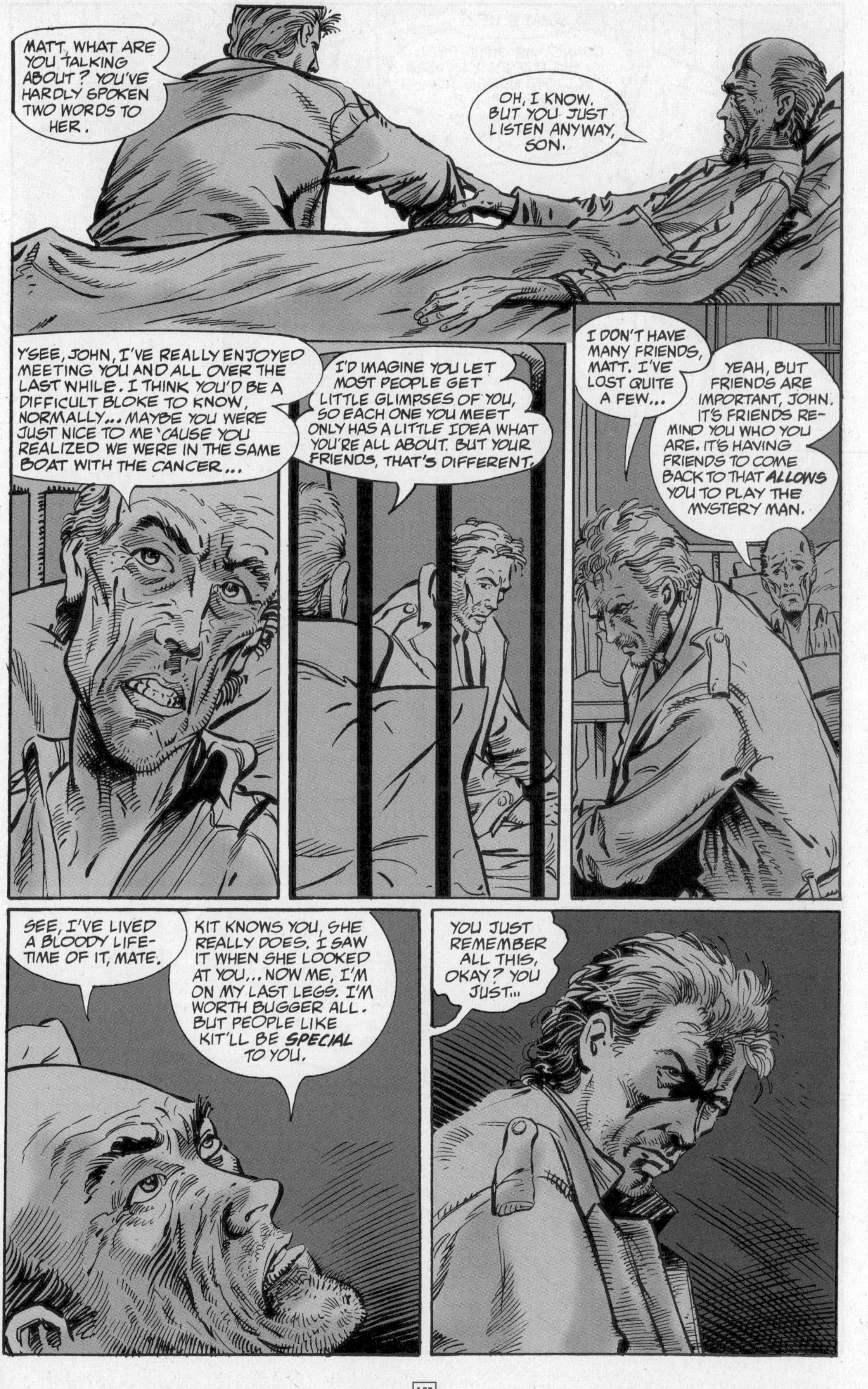
MATT, WHAT ARE YOU TALKING ABOUT? YOU'VE HARDLY SPOKEN TWO WORDS TO HER.
OH, I KNOW. BUT YOU JUST LISTEN ANYWAY, SON.
Y'SEE, JOHN, I'VE REALLY ENJOYED MEETING YOU AND ALL OVER THE LAST WHILE. I THINK YOU'D BE A DIFFICULT BLOKE TO KNOW, NORMALLY... MAYBE YOU WERE JUST NICE TO ME 'CAUSE YOU REALIZED WE WERE IN THE SAME BOAT WITH THE CANCER...
I'D IMAGINE YOU LET MOST PEOPLE GET LITTLE GLIMPSES OF YOU, SO EACH ONE YOU MEET ONLY HAS A LITTLE IDEA WHAT YOU'RE ALL ABOUT. BUT YOUR FRIENDS, THAT'S DIFFERENT.
I DON'T HAVE MANY FRIENDS, MATT. I'VE LOST QUITE A FEW...
YEAH, BUT FRIENDS ARE IMPORTANT, JOHN. IT'S FRIENDS RE-MIND YOU WHO YOU ARE. IT'S HAVING FRIENDS TO COME BACK TO THAT ALLOWS YOU TO PLAY THE MYSTERY MAN.
SEE, I'VE LIVED A BLOODY LIFE-TIME OF IT, MATE.
KIT KNOWS YOU, SHE REALLY DOES. I SAW IT WHEN SHE LOOKED AT YOU... NOW ME, I'M ON MY LAST LEGS. I'M WORTH BUGGER ALL. BUT PEOPLE LIKE KIT'LL BE SPECIAL TO YOU.
YOU JUST REMEMBER ALL THIS, OKAY? YOU JUST...

WHAT'S UP?

DUNNO. ME GUTS FEEL A BIT ROPEY. CAN YOU TELL THE NURSE TO GET US A PILL?

'SCUSE ME, LUV. GOT A PATIENT IN HERE COULD DO WITH A LOOK.

OH? WHO IS IT?

IT'S MATT-- MISTER HIGGINS. SAYS HE NEEDS A PILL.

OH YEAH... VERY DELICATE LIVER, THERE.

SHIT!

eh?

WHAT'S THE M......

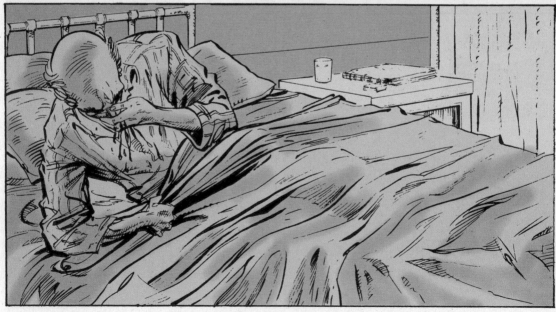

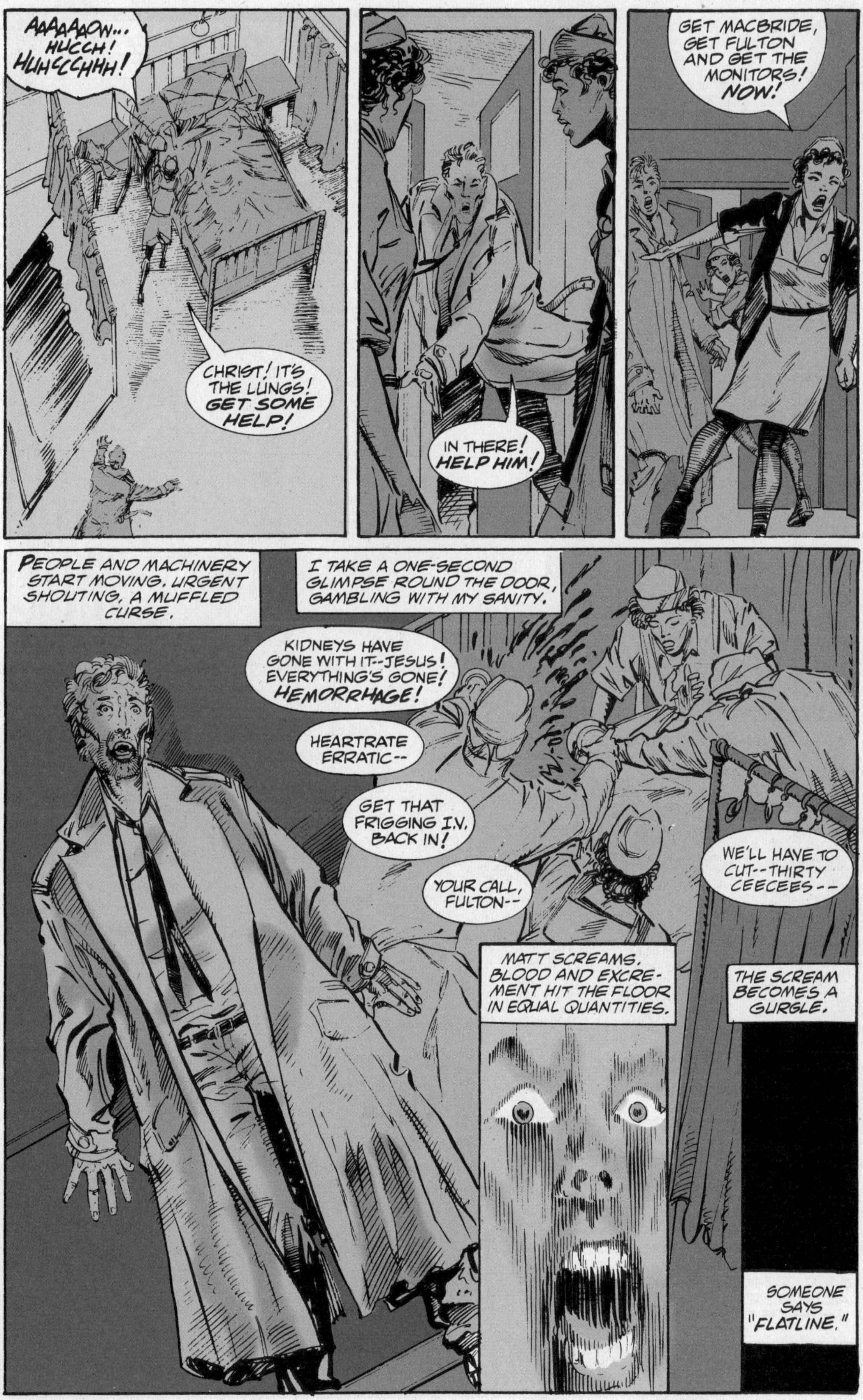
AAAAAAOW... HUCCH! HUHCCHHH!
CHRIST! IT'S THE LUNGS! GET SOME HELP!
IN THERE! HELP HIM!
GET MACBRIDE, GET FULTON AND GET THE MONITORS! NOW!
PEOPLE AND MACHINERY START MOVING. URGENT SHOUTING. A MUFFLED CURSE.
I TAKE A ONE-SECOND GLIMPSE ROUND THE DOOR, GAMBLING WITH MY SANITY.
KIDNEYS HAVE GONE WITH IT--JESUS! EVERYTHING'S GONE! HEMORRHAGE!
HEARTRATE ERRATIC--
GET THAT FRIGGING I.V. BACK IN!
YOUR CALL, FULTON--
WE'LL HAVE TO CUT--THIRTY CEECEES--
MATT SCREAMS. BLOOD AND EXCREMENT HIT THE FLOOR IN EQUAL QUANTITIES.
THE SCREAM BECOMES A GURGLE.
SOMEONE SAYS "FLATLINE."

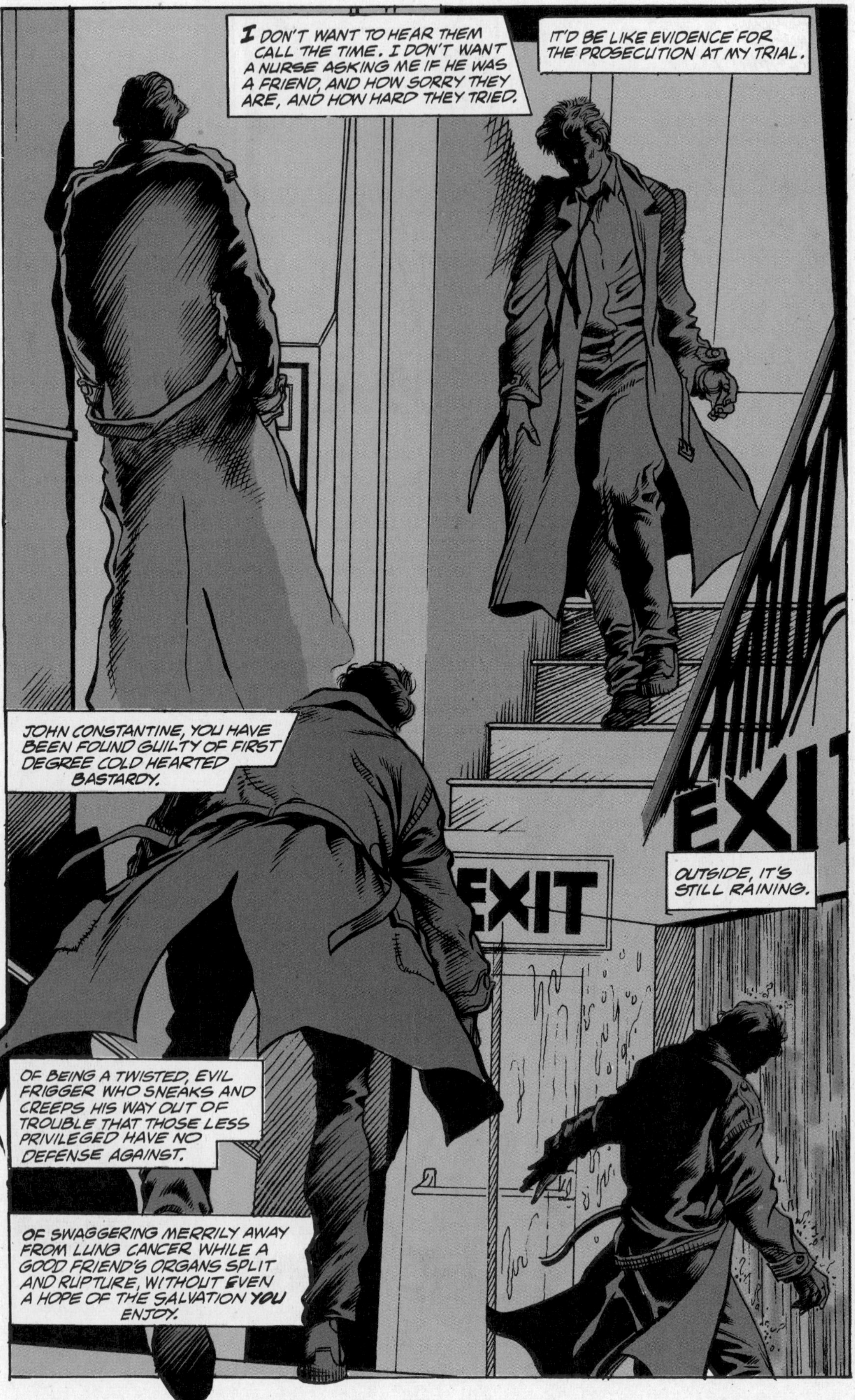
I DON'T WANT TO HEAR THEM CALL THE TIME. I DON'T WANT A NURSE ASKING ME IF HE WAS A FRIEND, AND HOW SORRY THEY ARE, AND HOW HARD THEY TRIED.
IT'D BE LIKE EVIDENCE FOR THE PROSECUTION AT MY TRIAL.
JOHN CONSTANTINE, YOU HAVE BEEN FOUND GUILTY OF FIRST DEGREE COLD HEARTED BASTARDY.
EXIT
EXIT
OUTSIDE, IT'S STILL RAINING.
OF BEING A TWISTED, EVIL FRIGGER WHO SNEAKS AND CREEPS HIS WAY OUT OF TROUBLE THAT THOSE LESS PRIVILEGED HAVE NO DEFENSE AGAINST.
OF SWAGGERING MERRILY AWAY FROM LUNG CANCER WHILE A GOOD FRIEND'S ORGANS SPLIT AND RUPTURE, WITHOUT EVEN A HOPE OF THE SALVATION YOU ENJOY.

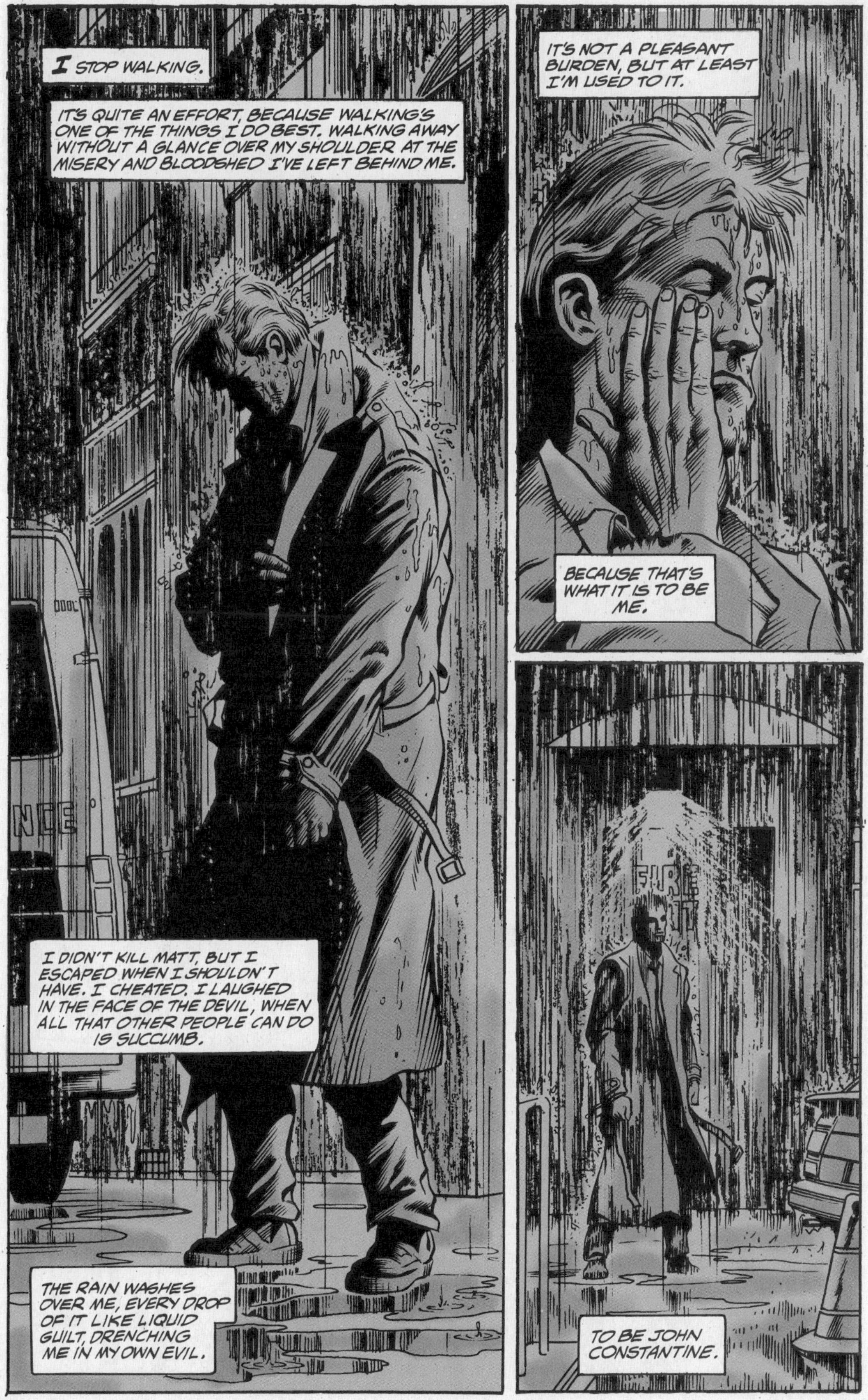
I STOP WALKING.
IT'S QUITE AN EFFORT, BECAUSE WALKING'S ONE OF THE THINGS I DO BEST. WALKING AWAY WITHOUT A GLANCE OVER MY SHOULDER AT THE MISERY AND BLOODSHED I'VE LEFT BEHIND ME.
I DIDN'T KILL MATT, BUT I ESCAPED WHEN I SHOULDN'T HAVE. I CHEATED. I LAUGHED IN THE FACE OF THE DEVIL, WHEN ALL THAT OTHER PEOPLE CAN DO IS SUCCUMB.
THE RAIN WASHES OVER ME, EVERY DROP OF IT LIKE LIQUID GUILT, DRENCHING ME IN MY OWN EVIL.
IT'S NOT A PLEASANT BURDEN, BUT AT LEAST I'M USED TO IT.
BECAUSE THAT'S WHAT IT IS TO BE ME.
TO BE JOHN CONSTANTINE.

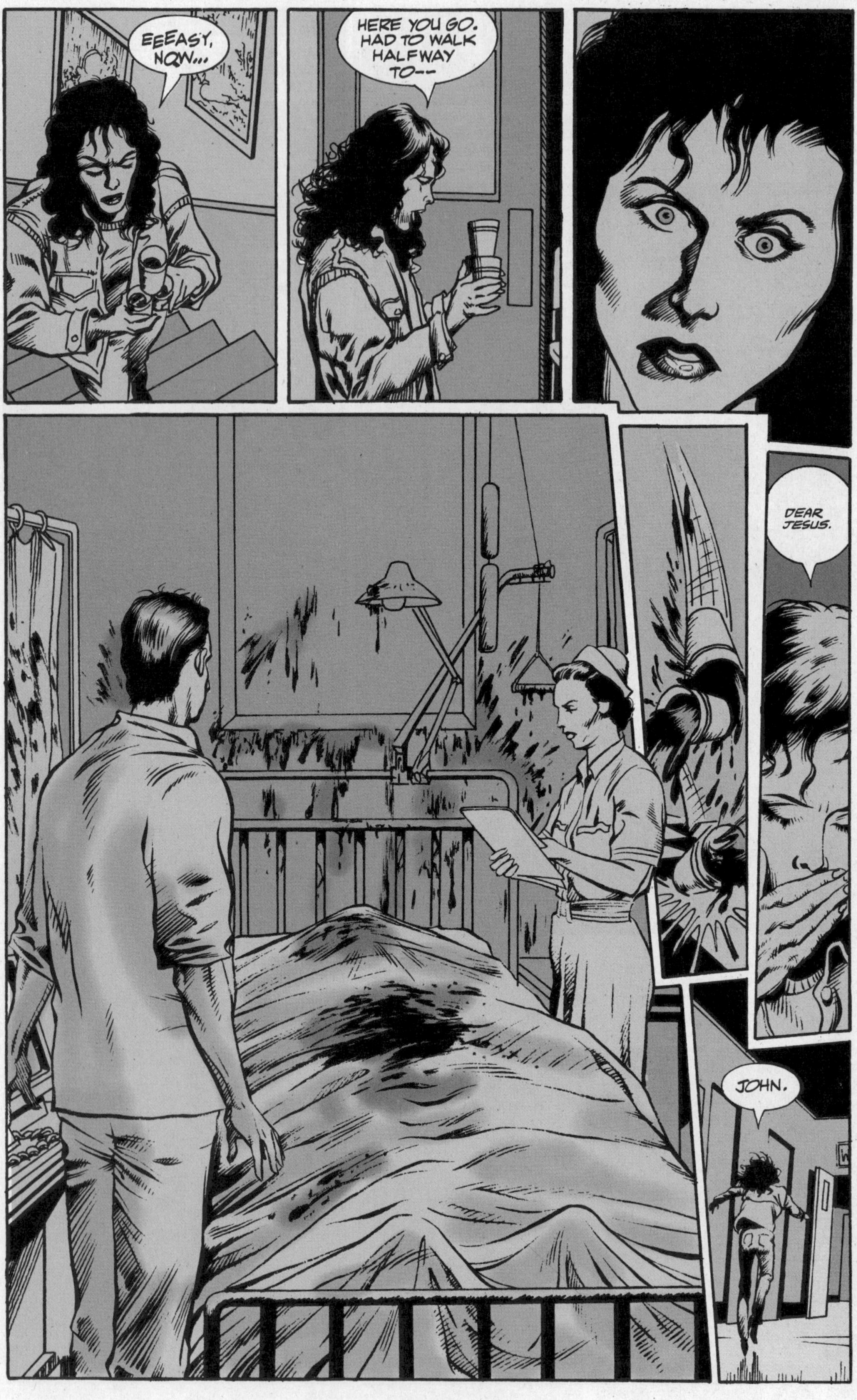
EEEASY, NOW...
HERE YOU GO. HAD TO WALK HALFWAY TO--
DEAR JESUS.
JOHN.

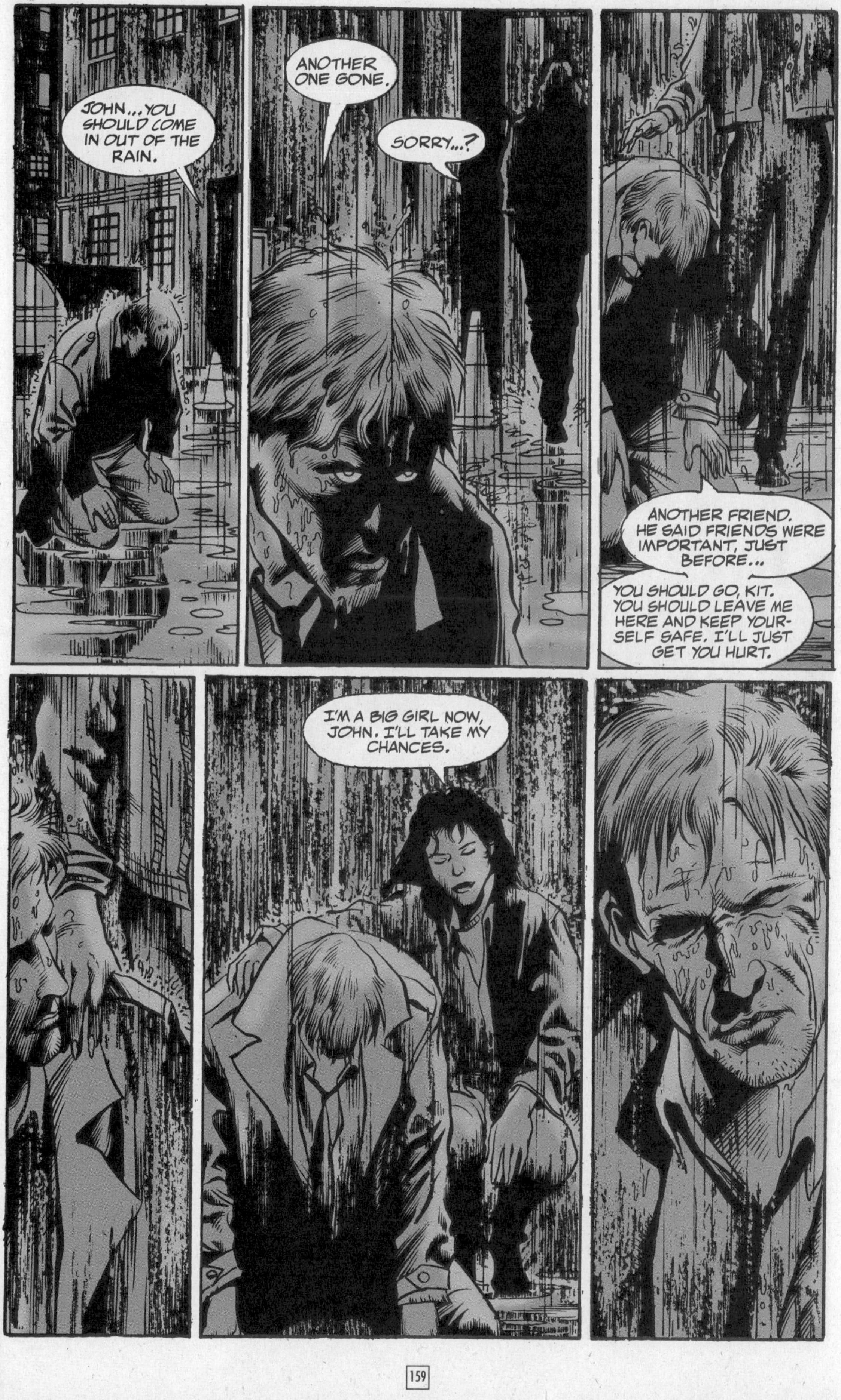
JOHN...YOU SHOULD COME IN OUT OF THE RAIN.
ANOTHER ONE GONE.
SORRY...?
ANOTHER FRIEND. HE SAID FRIENDS WERE IMPORTANT, JUST BEFORE...
YOU SHOULD GO, KIT. YOU SHOULD LEAVE ME HERE AND KEEP YOURSELF SAFE. I'LL JUST GET YOU HURT.
I'M A BIG GIRL NOW, JOHN. I'LL TAKE MY CHANCES.

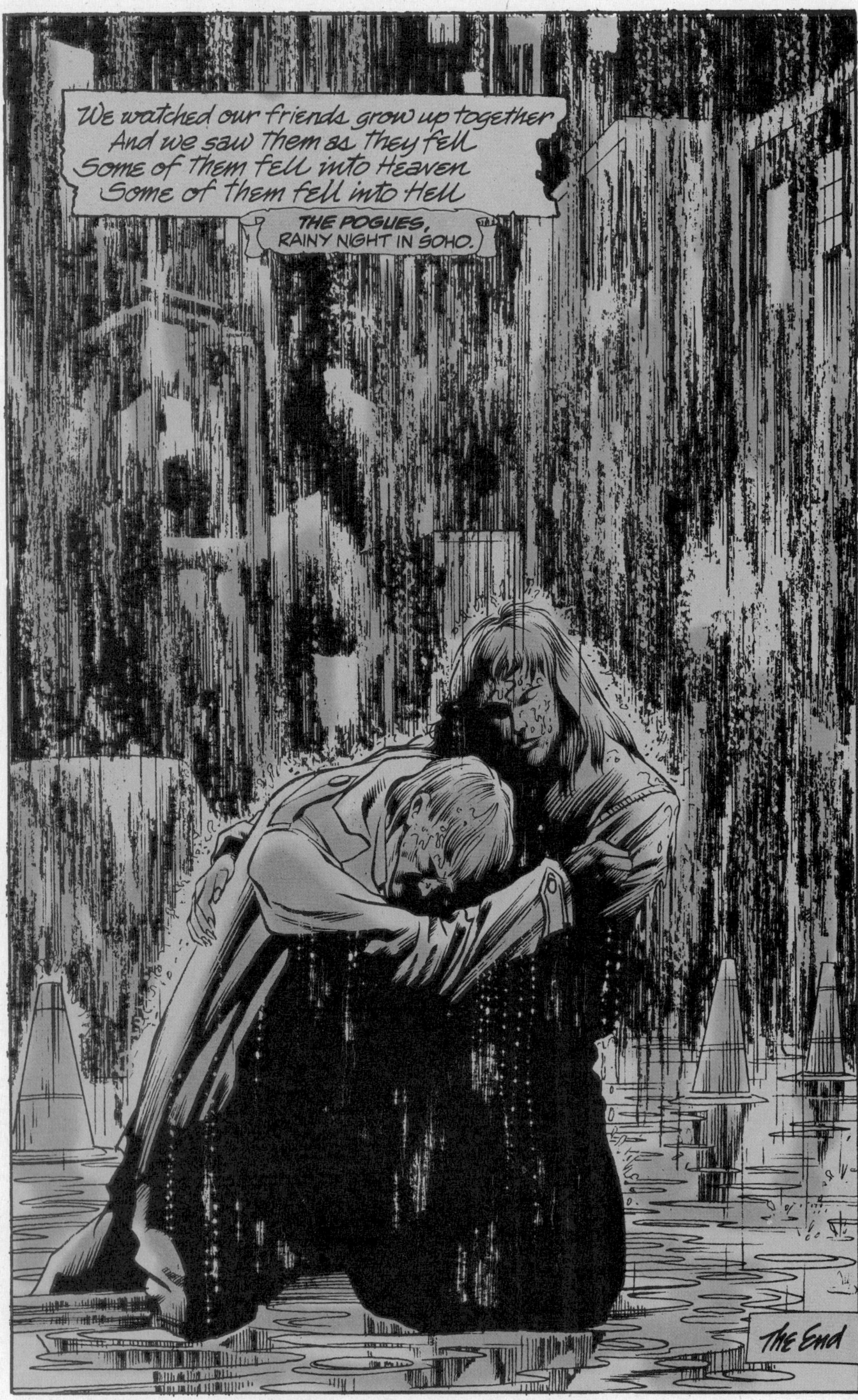
We watched our friends grow up together
And we saw them as they fell
Some of them fell into Heaven
Some of them fell into Hell
THE POGUES,
RAINY NIGHT IN SOHO.
THE End